THE ENVIRONMENT

A REVOLUTION
IN ATTITUDES

ISSN 1532-207X

THE ENVIRONMENT
A REVOLUTION IN ATTITUDES

Kim Masters Evans

INFORMATION PLUS® REFERENCE SERIES
Formerly published by Information Plus, Wylie, Texas

GALE
CENGAGE Learning™

Detroit • New York • San Francisco • New Haven, Conn • Waterville, Maine • London

The Environment: A Revolution in Attitudes

Kim Masters Evans
Paula Kepos, Series Editor

Project Editors: Kathleen J. Edgar, Elizabeth
  Manar

Permissions: Barb McNeil, Katherine Alverson

Composition and Electronic Capture: Evi Abou-El-
  Seoud

Manufacturing: Cynde Bishop

Gale
27500 Drake Rd.
Farmington Hills, MI 48331-3535

ISBN-13: 978-0-7876-5103-9 (set)   ISBN-10: 0-7876-5103-6 (set)
ISBN-13: 978-1-4144-0752-4   ISBN-10: 1-4144-0752-1

ISSN 1532-207X

This title is also available as an e-book.
ISBN-13: 978-1-4144-3828-3 (set)
ISBN-10: 1-4144-3828-1 (set)
Contact your Gale sales representative for ordering information.

Printed in the United States of America
1 2 3 4 5 6 7 12 11 10 09 08

TABLE OF CONTENTS

coastal water, and drinking water. How effective such laws have been is a matter of debate.

Many of the substances naturally found in the environment or released by modern, industrialized society are poisonous at certain dosages. They may be found in the home, workplace, or backyard, in the food and water people eat and drink, and in medications and consumer products. Common toxins include metals, pesticides, and other chemicals; radiation, particularly from radon exposure; indoor air pollutants, such as asbestos and mold; and food-borne contaminants, including pathogens. These toxins can have damaging effects on the environment and human health.

Forests, wetlands, soils, minerals, and oil, as well as entire ecosystems are endangered by the activities of humans. The diversity of life on Earth (biodiversity) is also at risk, with many species facing extinction. Local, national, and international efforts must be linked to deal with pressures on the environment.

PREFACE

The Environment: A Revolution in Attitudes is part of the *Information Plus Reference Series*. The purpose of each volume of the series is to present the latest facts on a topic of pressing concern in modern American life. These topics include today's most controversial and most studied social issues: abortion, capital punishment, care for the elderly, crime, the environment, health care, immigration, minorities, national security, social welfare, women, youth, and many more. Although written especially for the high school and undergraduate student, this series is an excellent resource for anyone in need of factual information on current affairs.

By presenting the facts, it is the intention of Gale, a part of Cengage Learning, to provide its readers with everything they need to reach an informed opinion on current issues. To that end, there is a particular emphasis in this series on the presentation of scientific studies, surveys, and statistics. These data are generally presented in the form of tables, charts, and other graphics placed within the text of each book. Every graphic is directly referred to and carefully explained in the text. The source of each graphic is presented within the graphic itself. The data used in these graphics are drawn from the most reputable and reliable sources, in particular from the various branches of the U.S. government and from major independent polling organizations. Every effort has been made to secure the most recent information available. The reader should bear in mind that many major studies take years to conduct, and that additional years often pass before the data from these studies are made available to the public. Therefore, in many cases the most recent information available in 2008 dated from 2005 or 2006. Older statistics are sometimes presented as well if they are of particular interest and no more-recent information exists.

Although statistics are a major focus of the *Information Plus Reference Series*, they are by no means its only content. Each book also presents the widely held positions and important ideas that shape how the book's subject is discussed in the United States. These positions are explained in detail and, where possible, in the words of their proponents. Some of the other material to be found in these books includes: historical background; descriptions of major events related to the subject; relevant laws and court cases; and examples of how these issues play out in American life. Some books also feature primary documents or have pro and con debate sections giving the words and opinions of prominent Americans on both sides of a controversial topic. All material is presented in an even-handed and unbiased manner; the reader will never be encouraged to accept one view of an issue over another.

HOW TO USE THIS BOOK

The condition of the world's environment is an issue of great concern to both Americans and people worldwide. Since the late nineteenth century, humankind's ability to alter the natural world, both deliberately and unintentionally, has increased. Many people fear that without proper restraint, humankind's actions could forever alter, or even eliminate, life on Earth. There are those, however, who feel that these fears are exaggerated, and that the substantial cost to business and industry for environmental protection should be minimized. The conflict between these two positions has serious environmental, political, and economic ramifications, both within the United States and worldwide. This book examines the steps that have been taken to protect Earth's natural environment and the controversies that surround them.

The Environment: A Revolution in Attitudes consists of eleven chapters and three appendixes. Each of the chapters is devoted to a particular aspect of the environment. For a summary of the information covered in each chapter, please see the synopses provided in the Table of

Contents at the front of the book. Chapters generally begin with an overview of the basic facts and background information on the chapter's topic, then proceed to examine subtopics of particular interest. For example, Chapter 8: Hazardous and Radioactive Waste begins by defining hazardous waste and describing the laws and agencies that regulate it. It then describes the major sources of hazardous waste—namely, industrial sites—as well as the sources of household hazardous waste. The chapter then moves on to a detailed discussion of how hazardous waste is dealt with, such as source reduction, recycling, and treatment. Discussion of hazardous waste includes a section on the Superfund program and how contaminated sites are handled. It ends with a section on electronic waste, such as cell phones and computers. The second half of the chapter covers radioactive waste, starting with the nature and sources of such waste, such as nuclear power plants. The difficulties of dealing with the most dangerous types of radioactive waste—including the public fear of these wastes—are discussed. The chapter ends with an examination of proposed long-term repositories for radioactive waste and the controversies surrounding them. Throughout the chapter special consideration is given to the problem of hazardous waste and the various methods used to clean up contaminated areas. Readers can find their way through a chapter by looking for the section and subsection headings, which are clearly set off from the text. Or, they can refer to the book's extensive Index if they already know what they are looking for.

Statistical Information

The tables and figures featured throughout *The Environment: A Revolution in Attitudes* will be of particular use to the reader in learning about this issue. The tables and figures represent an extensive collection of the most recent and important statistics on the environment, as well as related issues—for example, graphics in the book cover the amounts of different kinds of pollutants found in air across the United States; the major sources of groundwater pollution; the amount of wetland that is destroyed each year; and public opinion on whether the state of the environment has become better or worse in the last five years. Gale believes that making this information available to the reader is the most important way in which we fulfill the goal of this book: to help readers understand the issues and controversies surrounding the environment and reach their own conclusions about them.

Each table or figure has a unique identifier appearing above it, for ease of identification and reference. Titles for the tables and figures explain their purpose. At the end of each table or figure, the original source of the data is provided.

In order to help readers understand these often complicated statistics, all tables and figures are explained in the text. References in the text direct the reader to the relevant statistics. Furthermore, the contents of all tables and figures are fully indexed. Please see the opening section of the Index at the back of this volume for a description of how to find tables and figures within it.

Appendixes

In addition to the main body text and images, *The Environment: A Revolution in Attitudes* has three appendixes. The first is the Important Names and Addresses directory. Here the reader will find contact information for a number of government and private organizations that can provide further information on aspects of the environment. The second appendix is the Resources section, which can also assist the reader in conducting his or her own research. In this section, the author and editors of *The Environment: A Revolution in Attitudes* describe some of the sources that were most useful during the compilation of this book. The final appendix is the Index, making it even easier to find specific topics in this book.

ADVISORY BOARD CONTRIBUTIONS

The staff of Information Plus would like to extend their heartfelt appreciation to the Information Plus Advisory Board. This dedicated group of media professionals provides feedback on the series on an ongoing basis. Their comments allow the editorial staff who work on the project to continually make the series better and more user-friendly. Our top priorities are to produce the highest-quality and most useful books possible, and the Advisory Board's contributions to this process are invaluable.

The members of the Information Plus Advisory Board are:

- Kathleen R. Bonn, Librarian, Newbury Park High School, Newbury Park, California

- Madelyn Garner, Librarian, San Jacinto College–North Campus, Houston, Texas

- Anne Oxenrider, Media Specialist, Dundee High School, Dundee, Michigan

- Charles R. Rodgers, Director of Libraries, Pasco-Hernando Community College, Dade City, Florida

- James N. Zitzelsberger, Library Media Department Chairman, Oshkosh West High School, Oshkosh, Wisconsin

COMMENTS AND SUGGESTIONS

The editors of the *Information Plus Reference Series* welcome your feedback on *The Environment: A Revolution in Attitudes*. Please direct all correspondence to:

Editors
Information Plus Reference Series
27500 Drake Rd.
Farmington Hills, MI 48331-3535

CHAPTER 1
THE STATE OF THE ENVIRONMENT—AN OVERVIEW

We have not inherited the Earth from our fathers. We are borrowing it from our children.

—Native American saying

Photographs from outer space impress on the world that humankind shares one planet, and a small one at that. (See Figure 1.1.) Earth is one ecosystem. There may be differences in race, nationality, religion, and language, but everyone resides on the same orbiting planet.

General concern about the environment is a relatively recent phenomenon. It began in the United States during the turbulent 1960s and early 1970s, when social activism was a major force for change. Environmentalism was truly a grassroots movement in which public outcry spurred politicians to act. The result was a flurry of government regulations aimed at cleaning up the worst excesses of industrialism. Over the following decades the environmental movement continued to wield social and political influence, but the initial zeal for aggressive action faded as Americans turned their attention to other challenges. The economy, energy, and terrorism took precedence in the public consciousness. Around the turn of the millennium, environmental activism experienced a rebirth driven by concern about a "new" threat facing the world: global warming. This latest revolution in attitudes has unleashed a fresh passion about environmental issues and promises to provide a topic of lively debate for many years to come.

HISTORICAL ATTITUDES TOWARD THE ENVIRONMENT

The Industrial Revolution

Humankind has always altered the environment around itself. For much of human history, however, these changes were fairly limited. The world was too vast and people too few to have more than a minor effect on the environment, especially as they had only primitive tools and technology to aid them. All this began to change in the 1800s. First in Europe and then in the United States, powerful new machines, such as steam engines, were developed and put into use. These new technologies led to great increases in the amount and quality of goods that could be manufactured and the amount of food that could be harvested. As a result, the quality of life rose substantially and the population began to boom. The so-called Industrial Revolution was under way.

Even though the Industrial Revolution enabled people to live better in many ways, it also increased pollution. For many years pollution was thought to be an insignificant side effect of growth and progress. In fact, at one time people looked on the smokestacks belching black soot as a healthy sign of economic growth. The reality was that pollution, along with the increased demands for natural resources and living space that resulted from the Industrial Revolution, was beginning to have a significant effect on the environment.

The Environmental Revolution

For much of the early twentieth century Americans accepted pollution as an inevitable cost of economic progress. After World War II (1939–1945), however, more and more incidents involving pollution made people aware of the environmental problems caused by human activities. Los Angeles's "smog," a smoky haze of pollution that formed like a fog in the city, contributed a new word to the English language. Swimming holes became so polluted they were poisonous. Still, little action was taken.

In the 1960s environmental awareness began to increase, partly in response to the 1962 publication of a book by Rachel Carson (1907–1964), *Silent Spring*, which exposed the toll of the chemical pesticide dichloro-diphenyl-trichloroethane (DDT) on bird populations. Other signs of the drastic effects of pollution on the environment became more difficult to ignore. For example, in 1969 the Cuyahoga River near Cleveland, Ohio, burst into flames because of pollutants in the water.

FIGURE 1.1

The Earth, as seen from a U.S. satellite. *(U.S. National Aeronautics and Space Administration.)*

Environmental protection rapidly became popular with the public, particularly with the younger generation. In "Environment May Eclipse Vietnam as College Issue" (*New York Times*, November 29, 1969), Gladwin Hill reported on the astonishing increase in environmental interest. Concern about the environmental crisis was especially strong on college campuses, where it was threatening to become even more of an issue than the Vietnam War (1954–1975).

FACTORS CONTRIBUTING TO ENVIRONMENTAL ACTIVISM. What motivated Americans to this new awareness? The following are among the likely factors:

- An affluent economy and increased leisure time

- The emergence of an "activist" upper middle class that was college educated, affluent, concerned, and youthful

- The rise of television, an increasingly aggressive press, and advocacy journalism (supporting specific causes)

- An advanced scientific community with increasing funding, new technology, and vast communication capabilities

EARTH DAY AND THE BIRTH OF ENVIRONMENTAL PROTECTION. The idea for Earth Day began to evolve in the early 1960s. Nationwide "teach-ins" were being held on campuses across the country to protest the Vietnam War. The Democratic senator Gaylord Nelson (1916–2005) of Wisconsin, troubled by the apathy of U.S. leaders toward the environment, announced that a grassroots demonstration on behalf of the environment would be held in the spring of 1970, and he invited everyone to participate. On April 22, 1970, twenty million people participated in massive rallies on U.S. campuses and in large cities. Earth Day went on to become an annual event.

With public opinion plainly obvious, in 1970 Congress and President Richard M. Nixon (1913–1994) passed a series of unprecedented laws to protect the environment and created the U.S. Environmental Protection Agency (EPA), an organization devoted to setting limits on water and air pollutants and to investigating the environmental impact of proposed, federally funded projects. In the years that followed many more environmental laws were passed, setting basic rules for interaction with the environment. Most notable among these laws were the Clean Air Act of 1970, the Clean Water Act of 1972, the Endangered Species Act of 1973, the Safe Drinking Water Act of 1974, and the Resource Conservation and Recovery Act of 1976. Table 1.1 lists these and other major environmental actions by the federal government during the 1970s and 1980s.

Many activist organizations, such as Greenpeace and the Natural Resources Defense Council, were created to watch over and protect the environment. Virtually every state established one or more agencies charged with protecting the environment. Many universities and colleges began offering programs in environmental education. Billions of dollars were spent every year by state and federal governments for environmental protection and enhancement.

The Environmental Zeal Fades

Aggressive action led to major improvements in the state of the environment. Many of the most dangerous chemicals that once polluted the air and water were banned or their emissions into the environment greatly reduced. As the highly visible dangers—belching smokestacks and burning rivers—were improved, the initial zeal for environmental activism began to fade. Emerging environmental issues, such as ozone depletion in the atmosphere, were less obvious, more difficult to comprehend, and aroused less passion.

Another factor was money. The U.S. economy was booming during the 1960s and early 1970s, when environmental activism began. By the end of the 1970s the economy was burdened with high unemployment and high inflation rates, problems that lasted well into the 1980s. Americans fearing for their jobs rallied against environmental restrictions, believing that the restrictions threatened their livelihoods. This war of attitudes came to a head in 1990, when northern spotted owls were declared a threatened species in the Pacific Northwest. Millions of acres of forestland were set aside as habitat for the species, and logging was banned on federal lands within the area. Loggers protested bitterly about the loss of jobs, an argument that won sympathy from the American public. Conservative Republicans wielded power in the federal government beginning in the 1980s

TABLE 1.1

Federal environmental initiatives of the 1970s and 1980s

1970	President Richard Nixon creates EPA with a mission to protect the environment and public health.
	Congress amends the Clean Air Act to set national air quality, auto emission, and anti-pollution standards.
1971	Congress restricts use of lead-based paint in residences and on cribs and toys.
1972	EPA bans Dichlorodiphenyltrichloroethane (DDT), a cancer-causing pesticide, and requires extensive review of all pesticides.
	Congress passes the Clean Water Act, limiting raw sewage and other pollutants flowing into rivers, lakes, and streams.
1973	EPA begins phasing out leaded gasoline.
	EPA issues its first permit limiting a factory's polluted discharges into waterways.
	Congress passes the Endangered Species Act.
1974	Congress passes the Safe Drinking Water Act, allowing EPA to regulate the quality of public drinking water.
1975	Congress establishes fuel economy standards and sets tail-pipe emission standards for cars, resulting in the introduction of catalytic converters.
1976	Congress passes the Resource Conservation and Recovery Act, regulating hazardous waste from its production to its disposal.
	President Gerald Ford signs the Toxic Substances Control Act to reduce environmental and human health risks.
	EPA begins phase-out of cancer-causing Polychlorinated Biphenyl (PCB) production and use.
1977	President Jimmy Carter signs the Clean Air Act Amendments to strengthen air quality standards and protect human health.
1978	The federal government bans chlorofluorocarbons (CFCs) as propellants in aerosol cans because CFCs destroy the ozone layer, which protects the earth from harmful ultraviolet radiation.
1979	EPA demonstrates scrubber technology for removing air pollution from coal-fired power plants. This technology is widely adopted in the 1980s.
1980	Congress creates Superfund to clean up hazardous waste sites. Polluters are made responsible for cleaning up the most hazardous sites.
1986	Congress declares the public has a right to know when toxic chemicals are released into air, land, and water.
1987	The United States signs the Montreal Protocol, pledging to phase-out production of CFCs.
1988	Congress bans ocean dumping of sewage sludge and industrial waste.

SOURCE: Adapted from "In the 1970s," and "In the 1980s," in *Earth Day: Environmental Progress*, U.S. Environmental Protection Agency, April 5, 2007, http://www.epa.gov/earthday/history.htm (accessed June 19, 2007)

with policies that favored industry growth and less government regulation of business. A political backlash developed against environmentalists, who were derisively labeled as "tree huggers" and impractical zealots.

Even though the national economy improved tremendously in the 1990s, it did not eliminate people's concerns about the potential negative effects of environmental regulations on the economy. In 1994 the newly elected Republican-controlled Congress attempted to strike down a wide variety of federal regulations, including environmental regulations that they considered overly burdensome. Bills were introduced to relax regulations established under the Clean Water Act, the Endangered Species Act, the Superfund toxic-waste cleanup program, the Safe Drinking Water Act, and other environmental statutes. Much of that legislation ultimately failed to pass. However, congressional budget cuts for the agencies responsible for carrying out these acts meant that many of the laws were not strongly enforced.

The impact of environmental regulations on private property use has also played an important role in the change in attitudes. The Endangered Species Act and the wetlands provisions of the Clean Water Act spurred a grassroots private property rights movement. Many people became concerned that these acts, as well as other legislation, would allow the government to take or devalue properties without compensation. For example, if federal regulations prohibited construction on a plot of land that was protected by law, then the owner of that land often felt that the government was unfairly limiting the use of his or her property. At the very least, the owner wanted government compensation for decreasing the monetary value of the land.

Finally, there were those who felt that environmental regulation by the government, while not necessarily bad, had gone too far. Some believed that the federal government had overstepped its authority and should allow state and local governments to make their own rules on environmental issues. Similarly, some people felt that existing regulations were too strict and should be relaxed to generate economic growth.

By the 1990s many of the cheapest and easiest environmental problems to fix had already been resolved. Most of the remaining problems were so large or complicated that it was believed that tremendous amounts of money would have to be spent before even modest improvements would be seen. Despite the support of those who wanted to see further environmental improvements, such issues were competing for funds with other pressing issues such as acquired immune deficiency syndrome (AIDS), homelessness, and starvation in many parts of the world. In addition, since the terrorist attacks of September 11, 2001, environmental issues have been overshadowed by the threat of terrorism. Homeland security and military operations in Afghanistan and Iraq have become funding priorities.

Global Warming—A New Call for Action

During the 1990s new waves of social activism began to emerge around the world. The so-called anti-globalism or anticapitalism movement captured headlines with demonstrations, and sometimes violent riots, during meetings of the world's industrialized nations, including a summit of the World Trade Organization in Seattle, Washington, in 1999. The movement presented a variety of grievances involving social, labor, and environmental issues. At the same time, public awareness was growing about an emerging environmental problem called global warming. A scientific consensus slowly developed that human-related carbon emissions (primarily from the burning of fossil fuels) were overheating the world's climate and could cause irreparable harm.

In 1997 many countries joined an international agreement brokered by the United Nations (UN) in which carbon emission limits were placed on some nations. The U.S. government refused to embrace the agreement (the Kyoto Protocol to the UN Framework on Climate Change), because it did not limit emissions from China and India—two of the United States' biggest economic competitors. U.S. politicians feared that the agreement would place an undue economic burden on the United States.

In 2004 the movie *The Day after Tomorrow* dramatized the disastrous consequences of unchecked global warming. Two years later the former vice president Al Gore Jr. (1948–) released the book *An Inconvenient Truth: The Planetary Emergency of Global Warming and What We Can Do about It*, which reached number one on the *New York Times* best-seller list. A companion documentary film was also highly successful and significantly raised public awareness about the issue. Global warming became the pet environmental cause of celebrities, and new buzzwords were created:

- Carbon footprint—the amount of carbon emitted into the environment by a particular activity

- Carbon offsetting—reducing one's carbon footprint by taking action to reduce carbon emissions, such as planting trees (growing, healthy trees biologically soak up carbon dioxide)

- Carbon neutral—a condition in which an activity's carbon footprint is completely offset.

OFFSETTING CONTROVERSY. In 2002 the English rock band Coldplay made headlines by promising to offset the carbon footprint associated with the production of its album *A Rush of Blood to the Head* by paying for the planting of ten thousand mango trees in southern India. The planting was touted both as an environmental boon and a development opportunity for impoverished natives in the area to grow and sell mangoes. Carbon offsetting became the new form of environmental activism, first among the well-to-do, and then in the mainstream public. Companies and nonprofit organizations seized the opportunity to capitalize on "carbon consciousness." Travel booking companies and airlines began offering passengers the opportunity to buy offsets when they purchase their tickets. The proceeds go to offsetters, for-profit businesses or nonprofit organizations that promise to channel the money to planting trees or renewable energy projects. Major companies in this field include

the CarbonNeutral Company (formerly Future Forests), Trees for the Future, Climate Care, Native Energy, and TerraPass. The nonprofit organization Conservation Fund is also involved in offsetting through its Go Zero Program.

The practice of offsetting, however, has come under intense media scrutiny. Amrit Dhillon and Toby Harnden report in "How Coldplay's Green Hopes Died in the Arid Soil of India" (*Telegraph*, April 29, 2006) that few of the thousands of trees planted in India by Coldplay in 2002 survived because of lack of water, fertilizer, and pesticide application. An ongoing drought further aggravated the situation. Local residents who had planned to sell the mangoes from the free trees were sorely disappointed and complained they did not receive promised money for maintenance and watering expenses. A spokesman for the rock band declined to comment on the report.

In "Can You Be Traveling Green by Buying Offsets?" (*USA Today*, March 2, 2007), Barbara De Lollis notes that $110 million worth of voluntary offsets were purchased in 2006, up from only $6 million in 2004. Analysts note that offsetting has become a large and unregulated industry in the United States. Poor accountability and lack of performance standards and verifiability are common complaints among critics. Other articles focus on the scientific viability of offsetting carbon emissions. The article "Do Trees Make It OK to Drive an SUV?" (Associated Press, May 28, 2007) quotes one climate researcher who complains that planting trees "makes you feel warm and fuzzy ... but the reality is it's not going to have a significant effect."

Some organizations devoted to social and environmental improvement are skeptical of offsetting. The columnist Adam Ma'anit, in "If You Go down to the Woods Today ... " (*New Internationalist*, no. 391, July 2006), calls offsetting "the carbon con." He complains that "offsetting doesn't pressure companies to switch from fossil fuels to renewables or encourage governments to regulate polluting companies. It doesn't stop airport runways being built, planes being flown, cars being driven or even coal-fired power plants being brought online. In fact, it encourages them to continue and expand. It feeds on the good intentions of consumers and ethical business so that the fossil-fuel industry can thrive."

Advocates of offsetting contest the argument that the practice is simply a guilt alleviator for consumers reluctant to give up their energy-guzzling ways. The article "Do Trees Make It OK to Drive an SUV?" quotes a spokesperson for the nonprofit offsetting organization Carbonfund.org, who states that "the worst thing is to do nothing."

Buying Green

Offsetting is part of a broader environmental trend called buying green, with "green" meaning environmentally friendly. This movement encompasses recycled-content and energy-saving goods, natural (as opposed to synthetic) products, organically grown foods and clothing fibers, and ecotourism—vacations designed to minimize negative impact on ecologically sensitive areas. Green consumerism has both champions and critics. Advocates believe it helps to raise public awareness about environmental issues and is a good first step toward achieving social and political change. Detractors claim that consumerism in itself is bad for the environment. Alex Williams, in "Buying into the Green Movement" (*New York Times*, July 1, 2007), quotes environmental activists who complain that buying green has become chic and "eco-sexy" and gives the public a false sense that their purchasing decisions can solve complex environmental problems. These critics tout the traditional environmentalist viewpoint that consumption of all goods and resources should be reduced.

THE IMPACT OF ENVIRONMENTAL PROTECTION ON THE U.S. ECONOMY
How Government Regulations Work

Since federal and state governments began actively protecting the environment in the 1970s, they have acted primarily by creating rules—called regulations—that say how Americans can affect the environment around them. To get people and organizations to comply with these regulations, the government fines, imprisons, or otherwise punishes those who violate them.

Most federal regulations are aimed at controlling the environmental practices of businesses and industries, as their behavior is much easier to monitor and control than that of individual citizens. For example, to reduce air pollution the government might regulate the lawn mower industry by not allowing it to make lawn mowers that release more than a certain amount of pollutants. This is much easier for the government than the alternative: checking how much pollution is released when an individual mows his or her lawn and punishing that person if it is too much.

Attitudes of Business toward Environmental Regulation

Environmental regulations can interfere with the way a business would otherwise operate. Regulations may force businesses to design their products differently, install special machinery in their factories, or even stop certain activities entirely. In the most extreme cases entire industries might be shut down, such as when the government determined that the chemical DDT, once widely used as a pesticide, was too hazardous to human health to be used at all.

The changes required to comply with environmental regulations almost always result in smaller profits for those companies affected by such restrictions. This is especially true for industries that extract natural resources, such as mining and logging; industries that produce a great deal of pollution, such as electrical power generation; and industries whose products are potentially hazardous, such as the chemical industry. Compliance with governmental regulations is a significant cost item for some industries.

In 2002 the U.S. Census Bureau published the results from its latest survey of manufacturing, mining, and electric utility companies on their expenses for environmental compliance. In *Pollution Abatement Costs and Expenditures: 1999* (also known as PACE; November 2002, http://www.census.gov/prod/2002pubs/ma200-99.pdf), the bureau reports that in 1999 manufacturing industries spent $5.8 billion on pollution abatement capital expenditures (such as equipment) and $11.9 billion on pollution abatement operating costs. The EPA uses data from the PACE survey to estimate the costs to society of environmental regulations. The agency decided to revamp the survey after critics complained that it did not adequately reflect the true costs incurred by industry in meeting environmental requirements. In 2005 the EPA conducted a "pretest" of the new PACE survey on eighteen facilities within various industry sectors. The facilities were quizzed about their capital (building and installation) costs and operating costs for environmental compliance in 2004. As shown in Table 1.2, the facilities reported that the cost of treatment made up more than half (57%) of total operating costs in 2004. Disposal, recycling, and pollution prevention costs made up smaller percentages of total operating costs. Table 1.3 shows the distribution of operating costs by media (air, water, solids, or multimedia). Operating costs were slightly higher for controlling air emissions (37% of total) than for water discharges (31%), solids (29%), and multimedia pollutants (2%).

DOES ENVIRONMENTAL PROTECTION DESTROY JOBS?
By the end of the twentieth century the large-scale layoffs that some businesspeople predicted would result from environmental protection had not materialized. Michael Renner of the Worldwatch Institute, in *State of the World, 2000* (Lester Russell Brown, 2000), states that job loss as a result of environmental regulation has been relatively limited. According to Renner, at least as many people have gained jobs, because of the restrictions, as have lost them. He points out that environmental regulations have led to the creation of an entirely new industry that earns its profits by assisting other businesses with compliance, mostly by helping them to minimize pollution.

Even for those who accept this positive view of the overall effects of environmental regulation on business, it is unquestionable that some industries and their workers are badly hurt by environmental regulations. Renner contends that policy changes intended to protect the environment must have a clear and predetermined schedule. This

TABLE 1.2

Distribution of operating costs incurred by surveyed industries for pollution control, by activity, 2004

Sector	Treatment	Recycling	Disposal	Pollution prevention
Chemical	45%	17%	35%	3%
Computer and electrical equipment	40%	38%	15%	8%
Electric utility	44%	7%	48%	1%
Fab metal	84%	4%	12%	1%
Iron and steel	57%	6%	2%	35%
Paper	70%	5%	24%	1%
Other*	49%	12%	26%	13%
Average for all facilities	57%	11%	22%	10%

*Other includes furniture, petroleum, and plastics facilities.
Note: Sectors may not sum to 100 percent due to rounding.

SOURCE: "Table 3-5. Share of Operating Costs by Activity Category," in *Redesign of the Pollution Abatement Costs and Expenditures (PACE) Survey: Findings and Recommendations from the Pretest and Follow-up Visits: Final Report,* U.S. Environmental Protection Agency, December 2006, http://yosemite1.epa.gov/ee/epa/eermfile.nsf/vwAN/EE-0498-01.pdf/$File/EE-0498-01.pdf (accessed June 19, 2007)

TABLE 1.3

Distribution of operating costs incurred by surveyed industries for pollution control, by media, 2004

Sector	Air emissions	Water discharges	Solids	Multimedia pollutants
Chemical	15%	40%	43%	3%
Computer and electrical equipment	43%	44%	13%	2%
Electric utility	42%	3%	55%	0%
Fab metal	22%	55%	24%	0%
Iron and steel	41%	32%	25%	2%
Paper	42%	32%	25%	1%
Other*	44%	20%	29%	7%
Average for all facilities	37%	31%	29%	2%

*Other includes furniture, petroleum, and plastics facilities.
Note: Sectors may not sum to 100 percent due to rounding.

SOURCE: "Table 3-6. Distribution of Operating Costs by Media," in *Redesign of the Pollution Abatement Costs and Expenditures (PACE) Survey: Findings and Recommendations from the Pretest and Follow-up Visits: Final Report,* U.S. Environmental Protection Agency, December 2006, http://yosemite1.epa.gov/ee/epa/eermfile.nsf/vwAN/EE-0498-01.pdf/$File/EE-0498-01.pdf (accessed June 19, 2007)

way workers will know in advance what is expected of them, what jobs will be in demand, and what training is needed to get them into those positions. When environmental regulation results in shrinking profits and loss of jobs, however, attempts to expand such regulation will certainly be met with opposition from those whose livelihood would be affected.

The Business of Environmental Protection

For the United States and other nations to meet their environmental goals, an environmental protection industry has emerged. Its major activities include pollution control, waste management, cleanup of contaminated sites, pollution prevention, and recycling.

Environmental Business International (EBI) is a private organization that offers business and market information to the environmental industry. According to the EBI, the industry was driven by major legislation during the 1970s and 1980s. Over the following decades economic growth and adaptation of ISO standards were important factors driving the market; ISO standards are voluntary standards developed by the International Organization for Standardization (ISO). They were adopted by many industries during the 1990s as a means of showing compliance with certain levels of environmental conduct. The environmental industry is in a transition phase. In the past this industry focused on remedial cleanup; in the future it expects to focus more on prevention.

The EBI reports in "U.S. Environmental Industry Data 2006" (2007, http://environmental-industry.com/usandglobeni.html) that the U.S. environmental industry was a $264.6 billion business in 2005. Revenues were generated by both private and public entities. Solid waste management was the most expensive service ($47.8 billion), followed by wastewater treatment works ($35.6 billion) and water utilities ($35.1 billion).

LITIGATION AND ENVIRONMENTAL POLICY

The courts have been an important forum for developing environmental policy, because they allow citizens to challenge complex environmental laws and to affect the decision-making process. Both supporters and opponents of environmental protection have successfully used the courts to change environmental policy and law. Successful challenges can force the legislature to change laws or even have the law suspended as unconstitutional. A lawsuit can also be filed to seek compensation for harm to a person, property, or economic interest. Sometimes, lawsuits have prompted the creation of entirely new laws, such as the federal Superfund Law (1980) and the Toxic Substances Control Act (1976). Even the threat of a lawsuit, given the bad publicity it can bring, is sometimes enough to get a business or the government to change its behavior.

There are many different situations under which an individual or organization can go to court over environmental laws and regulations. One common occurrence is for an individual or group to sue the government to block a law or regulation from going into effect. For example, when the government halted logging in northwestern forests because of threats to endangered owls, logging companies fought to halt enforcement of those protections because that would decrease the industry's income and cause the loss of jobs.

Some lawsuits are filed not to block an environmental law or regulation from going into effect but because the claimants feel that the government owes them compensation for the negative effects of the law. In 1986 David Lucas bought two residential lots on a South Carolina barrier island. He planned to build houses on these lots, just as had been done on other nearby lots. At the time he bought the land this was entirely legal, but in 1988 South Carolina passed the Beachfront Management Act. Designed to protect the state's beaches from erosion, it prohibited new construction on land in danger of eroding, which included the land Lucas owned.

Lucas went to court claiming that the Beachfront Management Act had violated the Fifth Amendment of the U.S. Constitution by preventing him from building on his property. The Fifth Amendment states, among other things, that "private property shall not be taken for a public use, without just compensation." Lucas argued that preventing him from building on his property was equivalent to taking it, so the government of South Carolina had to compensate him for it. On June 29, 1992, the U.S. Supreme Court, in *Lucas v. South Carolina Coastal Council* (505 U.S. 1003), agreed with Lucas in a 7–2 decision, and South Carolina was ordered to compensate him.

Supporters of environmental protection have also filed lawsuits. These situations generally occur when people feel the government is not properly enforcing the law. Environmental groups such as the Sierra Club and Greenpeace have sued the government on many occasions to compel it to officially recognize certain species as endangered.

ENVIRONMENTAL JUSTICE— AN EVOLVING ISSUE

The so-called environmental justice issue stems from concerns that poor people and racial minorities are disproportionately subject to environmental hazards. The EPA defines environmental justice as "fair treatment for people of all races, cultures, and incomes, regarding the development of environmental laws, regulations, and policies" (August 1, 2007, http://www.epa.gov/oswer/ej/aboutej.htm).

Examples of environmental injustice include the following claims:

- Low-income Americans, especially minorities, may be more likely than other groups to live near landfills, incinerators, and hazardous waste facilities.

- Low-income and African-American children often have higher than normal levels of lead in their blood.

- Greater proportions of Hispanics and African-Americans than whites live in communities that fail to meet air quality standards.

- Higher percentages of hired farm workers in the United States are minorities that may experience pesticide-related illnesses as a result of their work.

- Low-income and minority fishermen who use fish as their sole source of protein are generally not well informed about the risk of eating contaminated fish from certain lakes, rivers, and streams.

The Impetus behind the Movement

The environmental justice movement gained national attention in 1982 with a demonstration against the construction of a hazardous waste landfill in Warren County, North Carolina, a county with a predominantly African-American population. A resulting 1983 congressional study—the *Siting of Hazardous Waste Landfills and Their Correlation with Racial and Economic Status of Surrounding Communities* (June 1, 1983, http://archive.gao.gov/d48t13/121648.pdf)—found that, for three out of four landfills surveyed, African-Americans made up most of the population living nearby and that at least 26% of the population in those communities was below the poverty level. In 1987 the United Church of Christ published the nationwide study *Toxic Waste and Race in the United States*, reporting that race was the most significant factor among the variables tested in determining locations of hazardous waste facilities.

In 1992 the EPA report *Environmental Equity: Reducing Risk for All Communities* (June 1992, http://www.epa.gov/history/topics/justice/01.htm) concluded that racial minorities and low-income people bore a disproportionate burden of environmental risk. These groups were exposed to lead, air pollutants, hazardous waste facilities, contaminated fish, and agricultural pesticides in far greater frequencies than the general population.

That same year the EPA established the Office of Environmental Justice to address environmental impacts affecting minority and low-income communities. In 1994 President Bill Clinton (1946–) issued Executive Order 12898, *Federal Actions to Address Environmental Justice in Minority Populations and Low-Income Populations* (February 11, 1994, http://www.epa.gov/history/topics/justice/02.htm), requiring federal agencies to develop a comprehensive strategy for including environmental justice in their decision making.

Recent Reports and Incidents

U.S. COMMISSION ON CIVIL RIGHTS. In 2003 the U.S. Commission on Civil Rights (USCCR) published the report *Not in My Backyard: Executive Order 12,898 and Title VI as Tools for Achieving Environmental Justice* (October 2003, http://www.law.umaryland.edu/marshall/usccr/documents/cr2003X100.pdf). The report examines the level to which various government agencies, including the EPA, have implemented Executive Order 12898 and Title VI (the Civil Rights Act of 1964).

Agency performance is based on four major criteria:

- Collecting data on the health and environmental impacts of agency activities on "communities of color and low-income populations"

- Incorporating the principles of environmental justice into agency policies, programs, and activities

- Allowing "affected communities" to participate in environmental decision-making processes

- Granting "affected communities" access to scientific data and information related to the enforcement of Title VI and Executive Order 12898

The report concludes that the EPA has experienced "limited success" in implementing the principles of environmental justice, but that "significant problems and shortcomings" still exist. A lack of commitment from agency leaders is cited as a major problem.

Only four of the USCCR's eight commissioners signed the report. The other four refused to sign, noting in an attached letter that they believed the report was "based upon a misguided application of federal antidiscrimination law to complex environmental and public health problems." The dissenting commissioners acknowledged that there are legitimate concerns about the health of people living near "environmental hazards." They prefer that these issues be addressed under environmental laws, rather than under civil rights laws. They complain that "environmental justice activists seek to create a federal civil rights claim every time an environmental or public health problem affects minorities."

CITIZENS AGAINST POLLUTION. In 2004 a federal lawsuit against the chemical company Monsanto was settled for $300 million. The suit was spearheaded by a grassroots environmental group out of Anniston, Alabama, called Citizens against Pollution. It was brought on behalf of 18,477 residents living in poor, mostly African-American neighborhoods in the city's west end. The suit alleged that since the 1960s a Monsanto plant had discharged large amounts of polychlorinated biphenyls (PCBs) into a creek running through the area. PCBs are mixtures of synthetic organic chemicals that are now known to be extremely persistent in the environment and toxic to life. Lawyers had evidence linking PCB exposure to a variety of serious illnesses and even deaths suffered by members of the community over decades.

Without admitting fault, Monsanto agreed to pay $300 million to settle the case. According to Ellen Barry, in "A Neighborhood of Poisoned Dreams" (*Los Angeles Times*, April 13, 2004), the plaintiffs, who were originally thrilled with the settlement, were shocked when they learned the lawyers would receive $120 million of the money. This left $180 million to be split among thousands of plaintiffs, resulting in an average payout of only $7,725 per person. A case brought by a different set of plaintiffs in state court resulted in a settlement of $300 million to be split among twenty-five hundred plaintiffs. An additional $75 million was earmarked toward cleanup efforts, and $25 million was set aside to build a neighborhood health clinic. In total the lawsuits resulted in a settlement of nearly $700 million, the largest payout ever in a tort case (a civil action resulting from a wrongful act) involving toxic chemicals.

THE CHEERS CONTROVERSY. In 2005 the EPA was forced to cancel a planned pesticide study after the media accused the agency of targeting low-income minority children as test subjects. The Children's Health Environmental Exposure Research Study (CHEERS) was supposed to collect data on children's exposure to household pesticides and chemicals. The study called for the monitoring of sixty young children (aged three and younger) in and around Jacksonville, Florida, with the help of the county health department. According to the EPA, volunteering families were to do the following things over a two-year period:

- Keep records of their normal pesticide usage

- Maintain an activity diary for their child and videotape some of the child's everyday activities with a supplied video recorder

- Collect food and urine samples

- Put a small sensor badge on their child for several weeks

- Allow periodic visits by EPA researchers to collect data

The EPA instructions for families noted that they were to follow their normal pesticide application routine

TABLE 1.4

Major federal environmental and wildlife protection acts

Environmental protection acts

Clean Air Act (CAA)—Prevent the deterioration of air quality
Clean Water Act (CWA)—Regulate sources of water pollution
Comprehensive Environmental Response, Compensation, and Liability (CERCLA or Superfund)—Address problems of abandoned hazardous waste sites
Emergency Planning & Community Right-To-Know Act (EPCRA)—Help local communities protect public health, safety, and the environment from chemical hazards
Federal Insecticide, Fungicide and Rodenticide Act (FIFRA)—Control pesticide distribution, sale, and use
National Environmental Policy Act (NEPA)—The basic national charter for protection of the environment. It establishes policy, sets goals, and provides means for carrying out the policy.
Oil Pollution Act of 1990 (OPA)—Prevent and respond to catastrophic oil spills
Pollution Prevention Act (PPA)—Reduce the amount of pollution produced via recycling, source reduction, and sustainable agriculture
Resource Conservation and Recovery Act (RCRA)—Protect human health and the environment from dangers associated with waste management
Safe Drinking Water Act (SDWA)—Protect the quality of drinking water
Toxic Substances Control Act (TSCA)—Test, regulate, and screen all chemicals produced in or imported into the U.S.

Wildlife protection acts

Bald and Gold Eagle Protection Act (BGEPA)—Provide a program for the conservation of bald and golden eagles
Endangered Species Act (ESA)—Conserve the various species of fish, wild life, and plants facing extinction
Lacey Act—Control the trade of exotic fish, wildlife, and plants
Migratory Bird Treaty Act (MBTA)—Protect migratory birds during their nesting season

SOURCE: Adapted from "Major Environmental Laws," in *Guide to Environmental Issues*, U.S. Environmental Protection Agency, Office of Enforcement and Compliance Assurance, June 26, 1998, http://www.epa.gov/epahome/laws.htm (accessed July 19, 2007)

and were not being asked to apply new or different pesticides in their homes. Besides the video camera, each family was to receive cash compensation for their time.

The EPA began publicizing the CHEERS study and asking for families to volunteer to participate in the fall of 2004. The issue became a public relations nightmare for the agency. Media stories pointed out that the study area contained many low-income minority neighborhoods. Critics accused the EPA of enticing poor families to expose their children to pesticides in return for cash and video cameras. Part of the funding for the study was to come from the American Chemistry Council, a trade group representing chemical manufacturers. This also aroused criticism about the intent of the study.

The issue became highly politicized in March 2005, when confirmation hearings began for Stephen L. Johnson (1951–), the Bush administration's choice to head the agency. Some Senate Democrats threatened to block Johnson's confirmation unless the study was canceled. The EPA insisted that the study objectives were being distorted by the media and for political reasons. However, in April 2005 the EPA canceled the CHEERS study.

TOXIC WASTE AND RACE AT TWENTY, 1987–2007. Robert D. Bullard et al.—in *Toxic Waste and Race at Twenty, 1987–2007: Grassroots Struggles to Dismantle Environmental Racism in the United States* (March 2007, http://www.ejnet.org/ej/twart.pdf), a report that was prepared for the United Church of Christ and that relies on population and demographic data from the 2000 census and a database of commercial hazardous waste facilities—find that:

- Racial minorities make up the majority (56%) of the population in neighborhoods within nearly two miles of U.S. hazardous waste facilities.

- The 5.1 million Americans of color who live in neighborhoods containing one or more commercial hazardous waste facilities include 2.5 million Hispanics, 1.8 million African-Americans, and 616,000 people of other races or ethnic backgrounds.

- The poverty rates in neighborhoods hosting commercial hazardous waste facilities are 1.5 times greater than the rates in non-host neighborhoods.

Bullard et al. conclude that the evidence supporting environmental racism is strong, noting that "race continues to be an independent predictor of where hazardous wastes are located, and it is a stronger predictor than income, education and other socioeconomic indicators."

"NEW" CRIME: ENVIRONMENTAL CRIME

Table 1.4 lists the major environmental and wildlife protection acts of the federal government. As recently as the 1980s few Americans understood that harming the environment could be considered a crime. Since that time, however, a substantial portion of the American public has begun to recognize the seriousness of environmental offenses, believing that damaging the environment is a serious crime and that corporate officials should be held responsible for offenses committed by their firms. Even though the immediate consequences of an offense may not be obvious or severe, environmental crime is a serious problem and does have victims; the cumulative costs in damage to the environment and the toll to humans in illness, injury, and death can be considerable.

Law enforcement agencies generally believe that successful criminal prosecution—even the threat of it—is the best deterrent to environmental crime. Under the dual sovereignty doctrine, both state and federal governments can independently prosecute environmental crimes without violating the double jeopardy or due process clauses of the U.S. Constitution.

As attitudes toward environmental crimes have changed, the penalties for such offenses have become harsher. Federal criminal enforcement has grown from a misdemeanor penalty for dumping contaminants into waterways without a permit to a felony for clandestine (secret) dumping. Several federal laws now include criminal penalties. Companies, their officials, and staff can be prosecuted for knowingly violating any one of a number of crimes. Such crimes include transporting hazardous waste to an unlicensed facility, storing and disposing of hazardous waste without a permit, failing to notify of a hazardous substance release, falsifying documents, dumping into a wetland, and violating air quality standards.

Figure 1.2 shows the numbers of criminal investigations conducted by the EPA Criminal Enforcement Program for the fiscal years 2002 to 2006 and the number of defendants charged with environmental crimes. In 2006, 305 investigations took place and 278 defendants were charged with crimes. Convicted defendants received 154 years of incarceration during 2006 and paid $43 million in fines and restitution. (See Figure 1.3.)

Since the 1970s environmental laws have become more complicated. The increasing strictness of these laws may have contributed to the growing incidence of environmental violations. First, many businesses have found compliance increasingly expensive, and many are simply avoiding the costs even if it means violating the law. These companies consider the penalties just another "cost of doing business." Second, businesses and their legal counsel are becoming increasingly savvy in avoiding prosecution through the use of dummy corporations, intermediaries, and procedural techniques.

Smuggling and black-market sales of banned hazardous substances also resulted from environmental legislation. In 1997 federal officials reported that the sale of contraband Freon (a refrigerant used in air conditioning systems) had become more profitable than the sale of cocaine at that time. Freon is one of the chlorofluorocarbons (CFCs), a class of chemicals known to cause ozone depletion in the atmosphere. In Mexico, which shares a two-thousand-mile border with the United States, Freon is still legal to manufacture and export, but these activities are banned in the United States. Freon, however, continues to exist in the cooling systems of many older model cars in the United States, which means a demand also exists.

Another type of environmental crime gaining attention, called ecoterrorism, occurs when radical environmental groups use economic sabotage to stop what they see as threats to the environment. According to James F. Jarboe of the Federal Bureau of Investigation (FBI), in "The Threat of Eco-Terrorism" (February 12, 2002, http://www.fbi.gov/congress/congress02/jarboe021202.htm), the Earth Liberation Front (and the related Animal Liberation Front) are

FIGURE 1.2

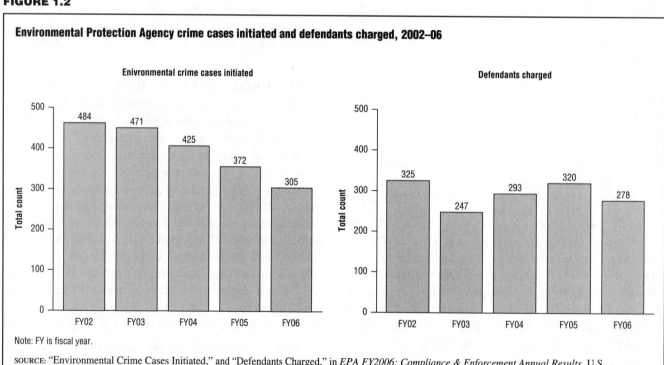

Environmental Protection Agency crime cases initiated and defendants charged, 2002–06

Enivronmental crime cases initiated

Defendants charged

Note: FY is fiscal year.

SOURCE: "Environmental Crime Cases Initiated," and "Defendants Charged," in *EPA FY2006: Compliance & Enforcement Annual Results*, U.S. Environmental Protection Agency, November 15, 2006, http://www.epa.gov/compliance/resources/reports/endofyear/eoy2006/fy2006results.pdf (accessed June 19, 2007)

FIGURE 1.3

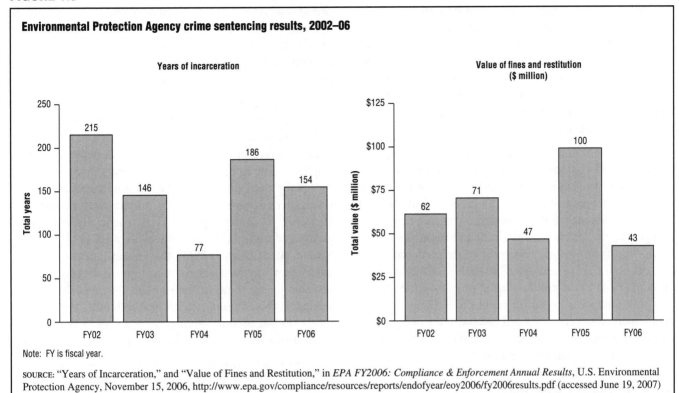

Environmental Protection Agency crime sentencing results, 2002–06

Years of incarceration

Value of fines and restitution
($ million)

Note: FY is fiscal year.

SOURCE: "Years of Incarceration," and "Value of Fines and Restitution," in *EPA FY2006: Compliance & Enforcement Annual Results*, U.S. Environmental Protection Agency, November 15, 2006, http://www.epa.gov/compliance/resources/reports/endofyear/eoy2006/fy2006results.pdf (accessed June 19, 2007)

blamed for more than six hundred attacks and nearly $43 million in property damage since the late 1990s. The group is accused of setting fire to a genetics laboratory, uprooting experimental crops, and damaging buildings. The FBI has named the Earth Liberation Front one of the most dangerous domestic terrorist groups in the United States.

THE INTERNATIONAL RESPONSE TO ENVIRONMENTAL PROBLEMS

Environmental issues have never been neatly bound by national borders. Activities taking place in one country often affect the environment of other countries, if not that of the entire planet. In fact, many of the most important aspects of environmental protection involve areas that are not located within any particular country, such as the oceans, or that belong to no one, such as the atmosphere. In an attempt to deal with these issues, the international community has held a number of conferences and developed many declarations, agreements, and treaties. The major ones are listed in Table 1.5.

A First Major Step: The Stockholm Conference

In 1972 the UN met in Stockholm, Sweden, for a conference on the environment. Delegates from 113 countries gathered, with each reporting the state of his or her nation's environment—forests, water, farmland, and other natural resources. The countries represented

TABLE 1.5

Major international conventions, treaties, and declarations related to the environment

International Convention for the Regulation of Whaling (1946)
The Antarctic Treaty (1959)
Convention on Wetlands of International Importance (Ramsar, Iran, 1971)
United Nations Conference on the Human Environment (Stockholm, 1972)
The Stockholm Declaration (1972)
London Convention on the Prevention of Marine Pollution by Dumping of Wastes and Other Matter (1972)
International Convention for the Prevention of Pollution from Ships (MARPOL, 1973/1978)
Convention on International Trade in Endangered Species of Wild Fauna and Flora (CITES, 1974)
Geneva Convention on Long-Range Transboundary Air Pollution (1979)
The Vienna Convention for the Protection of the Ozone Layer (1985)
The Montreal Protocol on Substances That Deplete the Ozone Layer (1987)
The Basel Convention on the Movement of Transboundary Hazardous Wastes and Their Disposal (1989)
Convention on Environmental Impact Assessment in a Transboundary Context (Espoo, Finland, 1991)
United Nations Conference on Environment and Development (Earth Summit, Rio de Janeiro, 1992)
The Framework Convention on Climate Change (1992)
The Kyoto Protocol (1997)
The Convention on Biological Diversity (1992)
Agenda 21 (1992)
The Rio Declaration (1992)
Statement on Forest Principles (1992)
The Rotterdam Convention on the Prior Informed Consent Procedures for Certain Hazardous Chemicals and Pesticides in International Trade (1998)
The Stockholm Convention on Priority Organic Pollutants (2001)

SOURCE: Created by Kim Masters Evans for Thomson Gale, 2007

essentially fell into two groups. The industrialized countries were primarily concerned about how to protect the environment by preventing pollution and overpopulation and conserving natural resources. The less developed nations were more concerned about problems of widespread hunger, disease, and poverty that they all faced. They did consider the environment important, however, and were willing to protect it as long as doing so did not have a major negative economic impact on their citizens.

By the end of the two-week meeting, the delegates had agreed that the human environment had to be protected, even as industrialization proceeded in the less developed countries. They established the UN Environment Program (UNEP), which included Earthwatch, a program to monitor changes in the physical and biological resources of the Earth. The most important outcome of the conference was awareness of Earth's ecology as a whole. For the first time in global history, the environmental problems of both rich and poor nations were put in perspective. General agreement emerged to protect natural resources, encourage family planning and population control, and protect against the negative effects of industrialization.

Some Difficulties Facing International Environmental Protection

Since the 1972 conference, hundreds of environmental treaties have been signed. From this, one might assume that great progress has been made, but this is not truly the case. Most experts believe that international cooperation is not keeping pace with the world's ever-growing interdependence and the rapidly deteriorating condition of much of the environment. Carbon dioxide levels are at record highs, water shortages exist around the world, fisheries are becoming depleted, and many scientists are warning that large numbers of species are becoming extinct. The reason for this is that, even though nations agree on the fact that the environment must be safeguarded, they disagree sharply on the issue of what role each nation should play in protecting it.

Less developed nations are generally unwilling to alter their laws and economy to end environmentally destructive ways, because a shift to environmentally friendly practices would be too expensive, they claim, for their economies to handle. Yet, the richer, industrialized nations generally refuse to alter their own behavior unless the less developed nations do so as well. Their reason is not so much the cost of change rather than believing it unfair that the less developed nations want them to carry most of the burden of environmental protection.

The less developed nations respond by pointing out that the industrialized nations became rich with the very same practices they now want the less developed nations to stop using. They claim it is unfair to be expected to limit their economic development in ways that the industrialized nations themselves never would have done.

This is a difficult disagreement but not an impossible one to resolve. When both sides are willing to compromise, agreements can be reached. These compromises usually require the industrialized nations to make bigger changes in their behavior and to help the less developed nations change without too negative an impact on their economies.

Even agreements such as these face many obstacles. Environmental agreements seldom include a means of enforcement but rely instead on each signing country to keep its word. Faced with the actual, immediate costs of implementing environmental agreements, many countries eventually back down from their commitments. U.S. representatives have signed many international agreements. However, U.S. participation is not officially authorized unless and until these agreements are ratified by the U.S. Senate. As a result, in 2007 the United States was a signatory party on many international agreements but was not yet abiding by some of them. Most international treaties related to the environment are set up so that the requirements do not become binding until a specified minimum number of parties (countries) have ratified the agreements.

1992 EARTH SUMMIT. The 1992 Earth Summit in Rio de Janeiro, Brazil, is an example of a conference where compromises were made and agreements reached but little change actually resulted. Mounting global concern for the environment prompted the UN to convene the summit meeting. Approximately 180 governments participated, making it one of the largest and most important environmental summits ever. As with prior environmental summits, the conference was split between industrialized and developing nations.

The main accomplishments of the Earth Summit were pacts on global warming and biodiversity. President George H. W. Bush (1924–) attended the summit and, while there, signed the global warming treaty for the United States. President Clinton signed the biodiversity treaty in 1993. These agreements came about largely because the industrialized nations also agreed to commit 0.7% of their gross national products (the total value of goods and services produced by a country over a particular period of time) by 2000 to assist developing countries with compliance.

Problems arose soon after the summit ended. Participating countries submitted annual reports to the fifty-three-nation UN Commission on Sustainable Development (CSD), a standing body that was set up to implement the Rio agreements. The CSD concluded in 1994 that most countries were failing to provide the money and expertise necessary to implement the plans set at Rio. According to Pamela Chasek and Langston James (Kimo) Goree VI, in "Commission on Sustainable Development: Year-End Update" (*Earth Negotiations Bulletin*, December 16, 1994), Klaus Toepfer of Germany, the chairman of the CSD, reported that the world's efforts to finance the goals had fallen "significantly short of expectations and requirements and could undermine the basis of the global partnership for sustainable development."

By 1996 a number of national governments, including the United States, had prepared plans for environmental protection and submitted them to the CSD. Hundreds of municipalities had also written plans of action. The CSD once again found, however, that other issues had crowded out environmental concerns. As developed and less developed nations alike worried about the potential effects of implementing the Rio agreements, they found reasons to delay implementation and reduce funding for those programs that had been implemented.

WORLD TRADE ORGANIZATION. The World Trade Organization (WTO) is an international organization whose purpose is to encourage free trade between its members. Most of the world's nations are members. Even though the WTO was officially founded in 1995, it is the result of decades of international cooperation under the General Agreement on Tariffs and Trade (GATT). The WTO continues to administer the free trade system established under GATT.

One of the primary missions of the WTO is to eliminate barriers to free trade. Doing so can have a negative effect on environmental protection, however, because laws designed to protect the environment often have the effect of restricting trade. If the WTO finds that a member nation is restricting trade in violation of GATT, other members are permitted to raise their tariffs (import taxes) on goods from that nation until the barriers to trade are eliminated. Most of the time nations quickly change their laws to eliminate barriers to trade, rather than suffer high taxes.

Because it has forced many environmental laws to be weakened over the years, the WTO is greatly disliked by many environmentalists in the United States. Also, there are groups that think the organization's power over internal U.S. affairs is too great. When the WTO met in Seattle, Washington, in 1999, tens of thousands of activists, including environmental activists, protested in the city. This massive protest succeeded in overshadowing the WTO meeting itself and drew public attention to the problems—environmental and otherwise—with free trade organizations. This was due in no small part to the violent rioting and property damage caused by some protesters.

Americans are not the only ones who take issue with some of the WTO's actions regarding the environment. For example, Europeans opposed to genetically modifying food, a procedure in widespread use in the United States by 2002, wanted restrictions placed on the sale of U.S. food in Europe, but such restrictions would violate GATT and invite retaliation by the United States.

NORTH AMERICAN FREE TRADE AGREEMENT. The North American Free Trade Agreement (NAFTA), which was signed in 1994, is another major free trade agreement

with the potential to negatively impact environmental protection in the United States. Members of NAFTA include the United States, Canada, and Mexico, and the purpose of the agreement is to eliminate trade barriers—such as most tariffs, investment restrictions, and import quotas—between these three countries. Even though its scope is much smaller than the WTO, NAFTA has an even greater impact on the three member countries than GATT.

A significant difference between NAFTA and GATT is that NAFTA is the first treaty of its kind ever to be accompanied by an environmental protection agreement. To discourage countries from weakening environmental standards in the name of increasing foreign trade, the United States, Canada, and Mexico signed the North American Agreement on Environmental Cooperation (NAAEC). Under the NAAEC (1993, http://www.cec.org/pubs_info _resources/law_treat_agree/naaec/index.cfm?varlan=english), a member country can be challenged if it or one of its states fails to enforce its environmental laws. A challenge can be brought by one of the member nations, or any interested party (such as an environmental protection group) can petition the NAAEC commission. If the commission finds a member country is showing a "persistent pattern of failure … to effectively enforce its environmental law," that country may be fined. If the fines are not paid, the other members are permitted to suspend NAFTA benefits in an amount not exceeding the amount of the assessed fine.

Even with the NAAEC, some U.S. environmentalists and state officials feared that NAFTA could result in the weakening of many humane laws and the reversal of thirty years of advances in animal protection and environmental cleanup. In response, Congress provided more protection for state laws and included more environmental language than in any previous trade agreement. The implementing legislation for NAFTA in the United States allows states much input and requires that they receive notification of actions that may affect them. In addition, during NAFTA discussions, the Border Environment Cooperation Commission and the North American Development Bank were created. Independent of NAFTA itself, these agencies are intended to ensure that policy discussions are open and fairly enforced, to consider allegations that a country is not enforcing environmental laws, to help communities finance environmental infrastructures, and to resolve disputes, particularly those that cross borders.

Despite all these measures designed to make sure that NAFTA does not trample on environmental protection, environmentalists still see the need for concern. They point out that U.S. laws designed to protect certain animals could be challenged as barriers to free trade under NAFTA. They also point to the increased pollution in Mexico and along its border with the United States that has resulted from the increase in trade between these two countries.

PUBLIC OPINION ON THE ENVIRONMENT

Quality of the Environment

In March 2007 the Gallup Organization conducted its annual poll regarding environmental issues. As shown in Figure 1.4, participants were asked to rate the overall quality of the U.S. environment as excellent, good, only fair, or poor. Only 5% of those asked gave the environment an excellent rating. Another 35% rated the environment in good condition, whereas 48% considered it in fair condition and 11% rated it in poor condition. This breakdown is similar to that obtained in polls dating back to 2001.

Another question from Gallup's 2007 *Environment* poll (http://www.galluppoll.com/content/?ci=1615&pg=1) asked if people believed the quality of the environment as a whole was getting better, getting worse, or staying the same. In 2007 a majority of respondents (67%) expressed the pessimistic view that the environment is getting worse. Another 25% believed that the environment is improving, and 7% thought it is about the same. This breakdown has remained relatively constant since the question was first asked in 2001.

Grading the Environmental Movement

As part of its 2007 poll, Gallup asked people to rate the overall performance of the environmental movement.

FIGURE 1.4

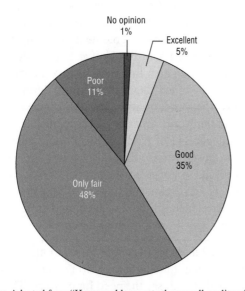

Public opinion on the quality of the environment, March 2007

HOW WOULD YOU RATE THE OVERALL QUALITY OF THE ENVIRONMENT IN THIS COUNTRY TODAY—AS EXCELLENT, GOOD, ONLY FAIR, OR POOR?

SOURCE: Adapted from "How would you rate the overall quality of the environment in this country today—as excellent, good, only fair, or poor?" in *Environment*, The Gallup Organization, 2007, http://www.galluppoll.com/content/?ci=1615&pg=1 (accessed June 19, 2007). Copyright © 2007 by The Gallup Organization. Reproduced by permission of The Gallup Organization.

FIGURE 1.5

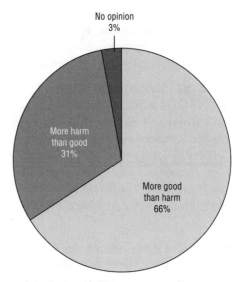

Public opinion on the success of the environmental movement, March 2007

ALL THINGS CONSIDERED, DO YOU THINK THE ENVIRONMENTAL MOVEMENT IN THIS NATION HAS DONE MORE GOOD THAN HARM, OR MORE HARM THAN GOOD? WOULD YOU SAY IT HAS DONE—DEFINITELY MORE GOOD THAN HARM, PROBABLY MORE GOOD THAN HARM, PROBABLY MORE HARM THAN GOOD, OR DEFINITELY MORE HARM THAN GOOD?

SOURCE: Adapted from "All things considered, do you think the environmental movement in this nation has done more good than harm, or more harm than good? Would you say it has done—definitely more good than harm, probably more good than harm, probably more harm than good, or definitely more harm than good?" in *Environment*, The Gallup Organization, 2007, http://www.galluppoll.com/content/?ci=1615&pg=1 (accessed June 19, 2007). Copyright © 2007 by The Gallup Organization. Reproduced by permission of The Gallup Organization.

As shown in Figure 1.5, a majority of those asked (66%) felt that the movement had done more good than harm, whereas 31% thought it had done more harm than good.

Environmental Protection Efforts

In *Environment*, Gallup reports that in 2005 it also asked poll participants to rate their level of trust in the ability of various entities to protect the quality of the nation's environment. These entities are listed below along with the percentage of respondents expressing a "great deal" of trust in them.

- Local environmental organizations (26%)
- National environmental organizations (25%)
- Federal environmental agencies, such as the EPA (22%)
- State environmental agencies (16%)
- Small businesses (15%)
- The Democratic Party (15%)
- Local government agencies (11%)

- The U.S. Congress (11%)
- The Republican Party (9%)
- Large corporations (7%)

Personal Participation

In its 2007 poll Gallup asked participants to rate their level of personal participation in the environmental movement. As shown in Figure 1.6, only 21% of those asked considered themselves active participants in the environmental movement. Far more (49%) were sympathetic to the movement but not active. Another 23% expressed neutral feelings about it, and 5% were unsympathetic. Overall, the percentage of people describing themselves as active participants was up slightly in 2007 from a range of 14% to 19% recorded in polls conducted between 2000 and 2006.

Americans were generally positive about their personal performance in protecting the environment. More than half (52%) said they were doing a "good" job at protecting the environment, whereas 7% rated their personal performance as "excellent." Slightly more than a third (34%) gave themselves an "only fair" rating, and 5% said their personal role was "poor."

Competing Interests: Environment, Energy, and Economy

For many years the Gallup Organization has polled people about which should take priority: the environment or economic growth. The vast majority of polls conducted between 1984 and 2000 showed strong support for the environment, even at the risk of curbing economic growth. In all these polls at least 58% of the people asked agreed with this view. The tide began to turn during the early 2000s as economic growth became a higher priority.

The March 2007 poll showed that 55% of those asked believed that environmental protection should be given priority, even if it risked curbing economic growth. More than one-third (37%) felt that economic growth should be given priority, even if it meant that the environment would suffer to some extent. According to Gallup, a small percentage (4%) advocated giving equal priority to environmental protection and economic growth.

The percentage breakdown was similar for a poll question regarding the development of U.S. energy supplies versus environmental protection. Gallup found in 2007 that 58% of respondents felt that protection of the environment should have priority, even if it might limit the amount of energy supplies, such as oil, coal, and gas, that the nation could produce. Another 34% of people thought that development of energy supplies should have priority over the environment. A small percentage (3%) indicated that the two should have equal priority. Likewise, a small percentage (2%) said that neither should be given priority.

FIGURE 1.6

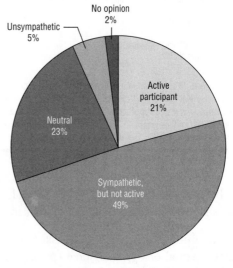

Americans rate their level of personal participation in the environmental movement, March 2007

THINKING SPECIFICALLY ABOUT THE ENVIRONMENTAL MOVEMENT, DO YOU THINK OF YOURSELF AS—AN ACTIVE PARTICIPANT IN THE ENVIRONMENAL MOVEMENT, SYMPATHETIC TOWARDS THE MOVEMENT, BUT NOT ACTIVE, NEUTRAL, OR UNSYMPATHETIC TOWARDS THE ENVIRONMENTAL MOVEMENT?

No opinion 2%
Unsympathetic 5%
Active participant 21%
Neutral 23%
Sympathetic, but not active 49%

SOURCE: Adapted from "Thinking specifically about the environmental movement, do you think of yourself as—an active participant in the environmental movement, sympathetic towards the movement, but not active, neutral, or unsympathetic towards the environmental movement?" in *Environment*, The Gallup Organization, 2007, http://www.galluppoll.com/content/?ci=1615&pg=1 (accessed June 19, 2007). Copyright © 2007 by The Gallup Organization. Reproduced by permission of The Gallup Organization.

Americans Rate Their Priorities and Concerns

In "Iraq Still Tops Policy Agenda, but Immigration, Gas Prices Gain" (June 1, 2007, http://www.galluppoll.com/content/?ci=27742&pg=1), Lydia Saad of the Gallup Organization reports on a May 2007 poll, in which participants were asked to name one or two issues they believed should be the top priorities for the president and Congress. The results revealed that the environment and pollution ranked seventh on the list and was cited by only 4% of respondents. This gave it lower priority than the war in Iraq (69%), immigration and illegal aliens (24%), energy sources and prices (17%), and the economy (16%); it was equal in priority to education (4%) and terrorism (4%).

In Gallup's 2007 environmental poll, participants were asked to rate various environmental issues in regard to the amount of concern they feel about them: a great deal, a fair amount, a little, or none. Pollsters found that the pollution of drinking water had the highest percentage of respondents expressing a great deal of concern. (See Table 1.6.) It topped the list with 58%, followed by pollution of rivers, lakes, and reservoirs with 53%, and contamination of soil

TABLE 1.6

Public opinion on environmental problems, March 2007

[Based on the percentage saying they worry a "great deal" about each problem]

	%
Pollution of drinking water	58
Pollution of rivers, lakes, and reservoirs	53
Contamination of soil and water by toxic waste	52
Maintenance of the nation's supply of fresh water for household needs	51
Air pollution	46
Damage to the earth's ozone layer	43
The loss of tropical rain forests	43
The "greenhouse effect" or global warming	41
Extinction of plant and animal species	39
Acid rain	25

SOURCE: Joseph Carroll, "Environmental Worries," in *Polluted Drinking Water Is Public's Top Environmental Concern*, The Gallup Organization, April 20, 2007, http://www.galluppoll.com/content/?ci=27274&pg=1 (accessed June 19, 2007). Copyright © 2007 by The Gallup Organization. Reproduced by permission of The Gallup Organization.

and water by toxic waste with 52%. In general, water-related issues garnered the most amount of concern.

In the same poll respondents were asked to indicate whether they favored or opposed some specific environmental and energy proposals. As shown in Table 1.7, Americans showed the highest level of support for spending government funds on the development of alternate fuel sources for automobiles. This proposal was favored by 86% of those asked. Higher emissions and pollution standards for business and industry were supported by 84% of respondents. Other proposals garnering greater than 80% approval were more strongly enforcing federal environmental regulations (82%) and spending more government money on the development of solar and wind power (81%).

How Reliable Are Polls on Environmental Issues?

Some experts suggest that opinion polls are an unreliable guide to how voters actually feel about environmental issues. Even though polls of Americans indicate that concern for environmental issues is substantial, this same level of concern does not manifest itself when it comes to actual voting and purchasing decisions. Some observers suggest that people often claim in polls that they are interested in environmental issues because they are trying to give the pollster the answer that he or she wants to hear. In other words, they are giving what they think is the "right" answer. In actuality, respondents may be more interested in other issues and, in the voting booth, may vote other than their poll answers would indicate.

ENVIRONMENTAL EDUCATION
Teaching about the Environment in Schools

Many states require schools to incorporate environmental concepts, such as ecology, conservation, and environmental law, into many subjects at all grade levels. Some even require special training in environmentalism for teachers. According to *Environmental Education Grants Program: Grants Awarded 1992–2006* (2007, http://www.epa.gov/enviroed/pdf/grantmaps2006r1.pdf), the EPA indicates that it has given grants to nearly thirty-two hundred such projects at a cost of more than $40 million. Figure 1.7 shows the breakdown of the type of organizations that received the grants. More than half (51.3%) of the grant recipients were nonprofit organizations. Figure 1.8 indicates the environmental issues addressed by the grants. The highest percentages were devoted to general environmental literacy (37.4%), water (32.4%), and issues of biodiversity, ecosystems, habitat, and species (26.8%).

Even though the mandating of environmental education pleases environmentalists, and studies show that most Americans support environmental education, some people still have concerns. Critics claim that most environmental education in the schools is based on flawed information, biased presentations, and questionable objectives. Critics also say it leads to brainwashing and

TABLE 1.7

Public opinion on specific environmental proposals, March 2007

NEXT I AM GOING TO READ SOME SPECIFIC ENVIRONMENTAL PROPOSALS. FOR EACH ONE, PLEASE SAY WHETHER YOU GENERALLY FAVOR OR OPPOSE IT. HOW ABOUT— ?

[In random order]

Percentage expressing opinion:	Favor	Oppose	No opinion
Spending government money to develop alternate sources of fuel for automobiles	86	12	1
Setting higher emissions and pollution standards for business and industry	84	15	1
More strongly enforcing federal environmental regulations	82	15	3
Spending more government money on developing solar and wind power	81	17	1
Setting higher auto emissions standards for automobiles	79	18	2
Imposing mandatory controls on carbon dioxide emissions and other greenhouse gases	79	19	2
Expanding the use of nuclear energy	50	46	4
Opening up the Arctic National Wildlife Refuge in Alaska for oil exploration	41	57	2

SOURCE: Adapted from "Next, here are some things that can be done to deal with the energy situation. For each one, please say whether you generally favor or oppose it. How about—," in *Environment*, The Gallup Organization, 2007, http://www.galluppoll.com/content/?ci=1615&pg=1 (accessed June 19, 2007). Copyright © 2007 by The Gallup Organization. Reproduced by permission of The Gallup Organization.

FIGURE 1.7

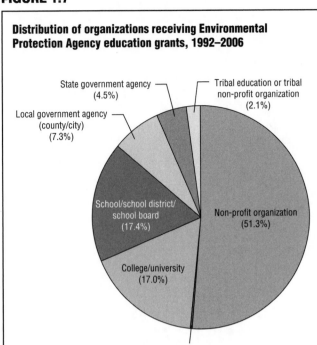

Distribution of organizations receiving Environmental Protection Agency education grants, 1992–2006

State government agency (4.5%)

Tribal education or tribal non-profit organization (2.1%)

Local government agency (county/city) (7.3%)

Non-profit organization (51.3%)

School/school district/ school board (17.4%)

College/university (17.0%)

Non-commercial broadcaster (0.3%)

SOURCE: "Types of Organizations," in *Environmental Education Grants Program: Grants Awarded 1992–2006*, U.S. Environmental Protection Agency, 2007, http://www.epa.gov/enviroed/pdf/grantmaps2006r1.pdf (accessed June 19, 2007)

FIGURE 1.8

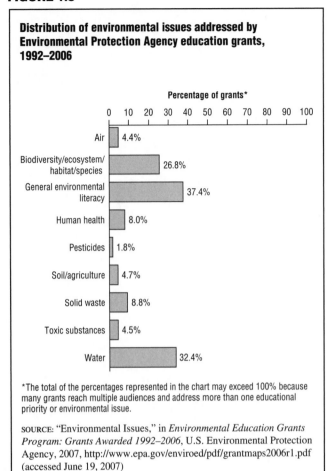

Distribution of environmental issues addressed by Environmental Protection Agency education grants, 1992–2006

Percentage of grants*

Air 4.4%
Biodiversity/ecosystem/ habitat/species 26.8%
General environmental literacy 37.4%
Human health 8.0%
Pesticides 1.8%
Soil/agriculture 4.7%
Solid waste 8.8%
Toxic substances 4.5%
Water 32.4%

*The total of the percentages represented in the chart may exceed 100% because many grants reach multiple audiences and address more than one educational priority or environmental issue.

SOURCE: "Environmental Issues," in *Environmental Education Grants Program: Grants Awarded 1992–2006*, U.S. Environmental Protection Agency, 2007, http://www.epa.gov/enviroed/pdf/grantmaps2006r1.pdf (accessed June 19, 2007)

pushing a regulatory mind-set on students. Some critics contend that, at worst, impressionable children are being trained to believe that the environment is in immediate danger of catastrophe because of consumption, economic growth, and free-market capitalism.

Lacking Basic Knowledge

In *Environmental Literacy in America* (September 2005, http://www.neefusa.org/pdf/ELR2005.pdf), Kevin Coyle of the National Environmental Education and Training Foundation (now the National Environmental Education Foundation) summarizes findings on the depth of knowledge of environmental issues by American students and adults based on polls and studies.

Coyle notes, "At a time when Americans are confronted with increasingly challenging environmental choices, we learn that our citizenry is by and large both uninformed and misinformed." Some common misconceptions mentioned by Coyle are:

- 45 million Americans believe that the oceans are a source of freshwater.

- 120 million Americans believe that spray cans contain CFCs, even though CFCs were banned in the 1970s.

- 120 million Americans believe that disposable diapers are the major problem at municipal solid waste landfills. In reality, they make up only approximately 1% of the problem.

Coyle finds that media sources, such as television and newspapers, are the primary source of environmental information for both children and adults. According to Coyle, the media's influence is powerful, even though most media outlets provide "superficial information." The public's reliance on the media for environmental education is blamed for the persistence of commonly held but mistaken beliefs that Coyle calls environmental myths.

Coyle estimates that 80% of Americans believe in incorrect and outdated environmental myths. Less that one-third (32%) demonstrated "basic awareness" of environmental topics as evidenced by their performance on basic quizzes. Even though Coyle notes that Americans' poor level of environmental literacy is "worrisome," he is heartened by survey data showing that more than three-quarters of Americans support greater governmental and business efforts to fund and present environmental education.

CHAPTER 2
AIR QUALITY

THE AIR PEOPLE BREATHE

According to the U.S. Environmental Protection Agency (EPA), in "Why Should You Be Concerned about Air Pollution?" (June 25, 2007, http://www.epa.gov/air/caa/peg/concern.html), the average person breathes in more than three thousand gallons of air each day. Because air is so essential to life, it is important that it be free of pollutants. Throughout the world poor air quality contributes to hundreds of thousands of deaths and diseases each year, as well as to dying forests and lakes and the corrosion of stone buildings and monuments. Air quality is also important to quality of life and recreation because air pollution causes haze that decreases visibility during outdoor activities.

Air pollutants are generated by natural and anthropogenic (human-related) sources. Fossil fuels and chemicals have played a major role in society's pursuit of economic growth and higher standards of living. However, burning fossil fuels and releasing toxic chemicals into the air alter Earth's chemistry and can threaten the very air on which life depends.

Air quality plays a major and complex role in public health. Among the factors that must be considered are the levels of pollutants in the air, the levels of individual exposure to these pollutants, individual susceptibility to toxic substances, and the time of exposure related to ill effects from certain substances. Blaming health effects on specific pollutants is also complicated by the health impact of nonenvironmental causes (such as heredity or poor diet).

Scientists do know that air pollution is related to a number of respiratory diseases, including bronchitis, pulmonary emphysema, lung cancer, bronchial asthma, eye irritation, weakened immune system, and premature lung tissue aging. In addition, lead contamination causes neurological and kidney disease and can be responsible for impaired fetal and mental development. The American Lung Association estimates in "Clean Air Is up to You!" (2007, http://www.alaw.org/air_quality/outdoor_air_qual ity/clean_air_is_up_to_you.html) that the annual health cost of exposure to the most serious air pollutants is at $40 billion to $50 billion.

THE HISTORY OF AIR POLLUTION LEGISLATION

Air pollution from the burning of fossil fuels was a problem in urban areas of England as early as the fourteenth century. In 1307 King Edward I (1239–1307) banned the burning of coal in London "to avoid the sulfurous smoke" and commanded Londoners to burn wood instead. The ban was short lived, however, as a wood shortage forced the city to switch back to coal. Historians record that future British monarchs also tried unsuccessfully to curtail the use of coal to reduce air pollution.

The onset of the Industrial Revolution in the late 1700s was accompanied by a tremendous increase in the use of fossil fuels and air pollution in England and the United States. Major U.S. cities began passing smoke ordinances during the late 1800s. Air pollution control remained a local issue for several more decades.

By the late 1940s smog had become a serious problem in many urban areas. Extensive industrial growth during World War II (1939–1945), a boom in car ownership, and unregulated outdoor burning were the primary culprits. Los Angeles and other large U.S. cities suffered from smog during hot summer months. In 1952 London experienced an episode of smog so severe that thousands of people prematurely died from respiratory illnesses aggravated by poor air quality. The incident was a wake-up call for many governments. Air pollution legislation was quickly passed in England and across Europe.

U.S. Air Pollution Legislation

In the United States concerns about smog led to the passage of the Air Pollution Control Act of 1955. It provided grants to public health agencies to research the threats posed to human health by air pollution. In 1963 the first Clean Air Act (CAA) was passed. It set aside even more grant money for research and data collection and encouraged the development of emissions standards for major sources of pollution. The act was amended several times through the remainder of the decade to expand research priorities and local air pollution control agencies and set national emission standards for some sources.

THE CAA OF 1970. In 1970 the CAA received a major overhaul. It required the newly established EPA to set the National Ambient Air Quality Standards (NAAQS) for major pollutants. These standards are divided into two classes:

- Primary standards are designed to protect public health, with special focus on so-called sensitive populations, including children, the elderly, and people with chronic respiratory problems, such as asthma.

- Secondary standards are designed to protect the overall welfare of the public by reducing air pollution that impairs visibility and damages resources, such as crops, forests, animals, monuments, and buildings.

State environmental agencies have to prepare state implementation plans to show how they plan to achieve compliance with the NAAQS. Counties that meet the NAAQS for a particular pollutant are called attainment areas for that pollutant; counties that do not meet the NAAQS are called nonattainment areas.

The revised CAA also required the setting of National Emissions Standards for Hazardous Air Pollutants and resulted in the New Source Performance Standards (NSPS). These are technology-based standards that apply when certain types of facilities are first constructed or undergo major modifications. Even though the NSPS are set by the EPA, state governments are responsible for enforcing them.

In 1977 the CAA was amended again. The major change was expansion of a program called the Prevention of Significant Deterioration (PSD). The PSD program is designed to ensure that new facilities built in attainment areas do not significantly degrade the air quality.

THE CLEAN AIR ACT AMENDMENTS OF 1990. In 1990 the CAA was substantially revised to better address three issues of growing concern: acid rain, urban air pollution (particularly smog), and emissions of toxic air pollutants. In addition, a national permits program was established, and enforcement and compliance procedures were strengthened. The Clean Air Act Amendments (CAAA) of 1990 included new and innovative approaches to air pollution legislation. Market-based programs allow businesses more choices in how they achieve pollution control goals. Economic incentives were also included to reduce the reliance on regulations to obtain certain goals. An outline of the major sections of the CAAA is:

- Title I—Air Pollution Prevention and Control

- Title II—Emission Standards for Moving Sources

- Title III—General

- Title IV—Acid Deposition Control

- Title V—Permits

- Title VI—Stratospheric Ozone Protection

WHAT ARE THE MAJOR AIR POLLUTANTS?

The CAAA of 1990 established the NAAQS for six major air pollutants:

- Carbon monoxide

- Lead

- Nitrogen oxides

- Ozone

- Particulate matter

- Sulfur oxides

These are called the priority or criteria pollutants and are identified as serious threats to human health. The CAAA required states to develop plans to implement and maintain the NAAQS. The states can have stricter rules than the federal program but not more lenient ones. In addition, regulations developed under the CAAA cover nearly two hundred chemical substances classified as hazardous air pollutants, which are also called air toxics.

The EPA has documented air pollution trends in the United States since 1970. Two kinds of trends are tracked for priority pollutants: emissions and air quality concentrations. Emissions are calculated estimates of the total tonnage of these pollutants released into the air annually. Air quality concentrations are based on data collected at thousands of monitoring sites around the country. The EPA maintains a database called the National Emission Inventory that characterizes the emissions of air pollutants in the United States based on data input from state and local agencies. The most recent comprehensive report on priority pollutant emission sources is the *National Air Quality and Emissions Trends Report, 2003* (September 2003, http://www.epa.gov/air/airtrends/aqtrnd03/), which is based on emissions data from 2001 and 2002.

Table 2.1 compares emissions of the principal air pollutants for various years between 1970 and 2006. The table shows that emissions have declined for each pollutant. This occurred even as the United States experienced massive increases in the gross domestic product (the total value of goods and services produced by a nation) and vehicle miles traveled and moderate increases in overall energy consumption and population. However, there is still much work to be done to clear the air. The EPA estimates that during 2006 nearly 137 million tons of air pollutants were emitted in the United States.

TABLE 2.1

Trends in national air pollutants, selected years 1970–2006

	Millions of tons per year								
	1970	1975	1980	1985	1990	1995	2000	2005	2006
Carbon monoxide (CO)	197	184	178	170	144	120	102	91	88
Nitrogen oxides (NO$_x$)	27	26	27	26	25	25	22	19	18
Particulate matter (PM)									
PM$_{10}$	12	7	6	4	3	3	2	2	2
PM$_{2.5}$	NA	NA	NA	NA	2	2	2	1	1
Sulfur dioxide (SO$_2$)	31	28	26	23	23	19	16	15	14
Volatile organic compounds (VOC)	34	30	30	27	23	22	17	15	15
Lead	0.221	0.16	0.074	0.023	0.005	0.004	0.002	0.003	0.002
Totals	**302**	**276**	**267**	**249**	**218**	**189**	**159**	**142**	**137**

Notes:
1. In 1985 and 1996 EPA refined its methods for estimating emissions. Between 1970 and 1975, EPA revised its methods for estimating PM emissions.
2. The estimates for 2002 are from 2002 National Emissions Inventory v2; the estimates for 2003 and beyond are preliminary and based on 2002 NEI v2.
3. For CO, NO$_x$, SO$_2$ and VOC emissions, fires are excluded because they are highly variable; for direct PM emissions both fires and dust are excluded.
4. PM estimates do not include condensable PM.
5. EPA has not estimated PM$_{2.5}$ emissions prior to 1990.
6. The 1999 estimate for lead is used for 2000, and the 2002 estimate for lead is used for 2005 and 2006.
7. PM$_{2.5}$ emissions are not added when calculating the total because they are included in the PM$_{10}$ estimate.
8. Fires and dust are excluded.

SOURCE: "National Air Pollutant Emissions Estimates (fires and dust excluded) For Major Pollutants," in *Air Quality and Emissions—Progress Continues in 2006*, U.S. Environmental Protection Agency, June 12, 2007, http://www.epa.gov/airtrends/econ-emissions.html (accessed July 19, 2007)

Carbon Monoxide

Carbon monoxide (CO) is a colorless, odorless gas created when the carbon in certain fuels is not burned completely. These fuels include coal, natural gas, oil, gasoline, and wood.

EMISSIONS AND SOURCES. The EPA reports in *Air Quality and Emissions—Progress Continues in 2006* (June 12, 2007, http://www.epa.gov/airtrends/econ-emissions.html) that in 2006 approximately eighty-eight million tons of CO were emitted into the air. As shown in Table 2.2, CO emissions have decreased by 74% since 1980. Transportation has historically been the largest source of CO emissions. Figure 2.1 shows the primary sources of CO emissions in 2002. Transportation accounted for the vast majority (77%) of CO emissions that year. Miscellaneous processes accounted for 15% of CO emissions. Stationary source fuel combustion (for example, in power plants), industrial processes, and waste disposal and recycling each contributed 4% or less to the total.

AIR QUALITY. Air quality concentrations of CO from 1990 to 2006 are shown in Figure 2.2 based on monitoring data from 243 sites around the country. Over this time period, CO concentrations decreased by 62%. In 2006 the average measured CO concentration at the monitoring sites was just under three parts per million (three parts CO per million parts of air).

Despite these improvements, there are still areas of the country with air quality concentrations of CO that are consistently above the NAAQS. These nonattainment areas are designated as having "serious" or "moderate" CO pollution, depending on the air quality concentrations. In August

TABLE 2.2

Percent change in air quality concentrations, 1980 vs. 2006 and 1990 vs. 2006

	1980 vs 2006	1990 vs 2006
NO$_2$	−41	−30
O$_3$ (1-hr)	−29	−14
(8-hr)	−21	−9
SO$_2$	−66	−53
PM$_{10}$ (24-hr)	—	−30
PM$_{2.5}$ (annual)	—	−15
PM$_{2.5}$ (24-hr)	—	−17
CO	−74	−62
Pb	−95	−54

Notes: In the table above for PM (particulate matter) these are percent changes between 1999 vs, 2006.
NO$_2$=Nitrogen dioxide. O$_3$=Ozone. SO$_2$=Sulfur dioxide. PM$_{10}$=Particulate matter less than 10 microns. PM$_{2.5}$=Particulate matter less than 2.5 microns. CO=Carbon monoxide. Pb=Lead.

SOURCE: "Percent Change in Air Quality," in *Air Quality and Emissions—Progress Continues in 2006*, U.S. Environmental Protection Agency, June 12, 2007, http://www.epa.gov/airtrends/econ-emissions.html (accessed July 19, 2007)

2007 the EPA (http://www.epa.gov/oar/oaqps/greenbk/cnc.html) classified Las Vegas, Nevada, as a serious CO nonattainment area, and El Paso, Texas, Missoula, Montana, and Reno, Nevada, were moderate CO nonattainment areas.

ADVERSE HEALTH EFFECTS. CO is a dangerous gas that enters a person's bloodstream through the lungs. It reduces the ability of blood to carry oxygen to the body's cells, organs, and tissues. The health danger is highest for people suffering from cardiovascular diseases.

FIGURE 2.1

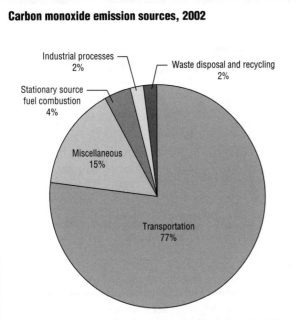

Carbon monoxide emission sources, 2002

Industrial processes
2%

Waste disposal and recycling
2%

Stationary source
fuel combustion
4%

Miscellaneous
15%

Transportation
77%

SOURCE: Adapted from Stacy C. Davis and Susan W. Diegel, "Table 12.1. Total National Emissions of the Criteria Air Pollutants by Sector, 2002," in *Transportation Energy Data Book: Edition 26*, U.S. Department of Energy, Oak Ridge National Laboratory, May 2007, http://cta.ornl.gov/data/tedb26/Edition26_Full_Doc.pdf (accessed June 5, 2007)

Lead

Lead (Pb) is a metal that can enter the atmosphere via combustion or industrial processing of lead-containing materials.

EMISSIONS AND SOURCES. The EPA reports that lead emissions declined from 740,000 tons in 1980 to 2,000 tons in 2006, a decrease of 95%. (See Table 2.1 and Table 2.2.) Before 1985 the major source of lead emissions in the United States was the leaded gasoline used in automobiles. Conversion to unleaded gasoline produced a dramatic reduction in lead emissions. As a result, ground transportation has virtually been eliminated as a source of lead emissions. As shown in Figure 2.3, industrial processes (chiefly metals smelting and battery manufacturing) are responsible for 78% of lead emissions. The contribution by the transportation sector (12%) is largely because of airplane traffic.

AIR QUALITY. Air quality concentrations of lead based on monitoring data from forty-two sites from 1980 to 2006 are shown in Figure 2.4. Over this time period, lead concentrations decreased by 54%. Despite great progress in lead reduction, the EPA (http://www.epa.gov/oar/oaqps/greenbk/lnc.html) noted in August 2007 that there were still two lead nonattainment areas in the country: East Helena, Montana, and Jefferson County, Missouri.

FIGURE 2.2

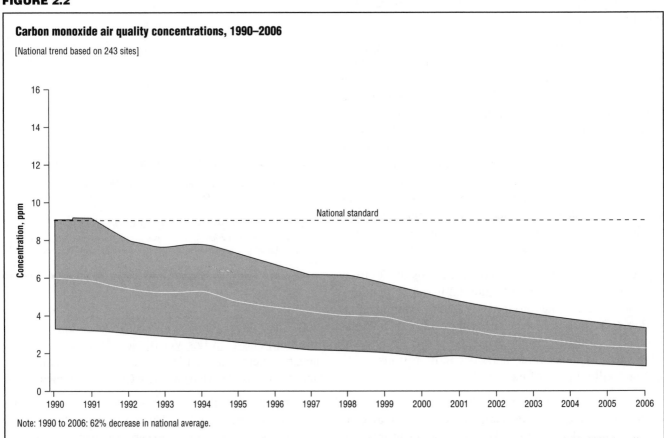

Carbon monoxide air quality concentrations, 1990–2006

[National trend based on 243 sites]

National standard

Concentration, ppm

Note: 1990 to 2006: 62% decrease in national average.

SOURCE: "CO Air Quality, 1990–2006," in *National Trends in Carbon Monoxide Levels*, U.S. Environmental Protection Agency, April 30, 2007, http://www.epa.gov/air/airtrends/carbon.html (accessed June 5, 2007)

FIGURE 2.3

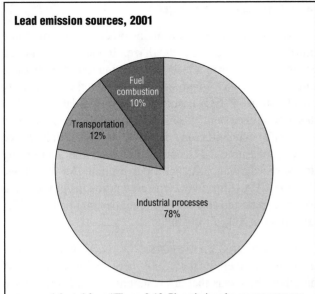

Lead emission sources, 2001

SOURCE: Adapted from "Figure 2-12. Pb emissions by source category, 2001," in *National Air Quality and Emissions Trends Report, 2003*, U.S. Environmental Protection Agency, September 2003, http://www.epa.gov/air/airtrends/aqtrnd03/pdfs/chapter2crit.pdf (accessed June 5, 2007)

ADVERSE HEALTH EFFECTS. Lead is a particularly dangerous pollutant because it accumulates in the blood, bones, and soft tissues of the body. It can adversely affect the nervous system, kidneys, liver, and other organs. Excessive concentrations are associated with neurological impairments, mental retardation, and behavioral disorders. Even low doses of lead can damage the brain and nervous system of fetuses and young children. Atmospheric lead that falls onto vegetation poses an ingestion hazard to humans and animals.

Nitrogen Dioxide

Nitrogen dioxide (NO_2) is a reddish-brown gas that forms in the atmosphere when nitrogen oxide (NO) is oxidized. Inhalation of even low concentrations of NO_2 for short time periods can be harmful to the human body's breathing functions. Longer exposures are considered damaging to the lungs and may cause people to be more susceptible to certain respiratory problems, such as infections.

The chemical formula NO_x is used collectively to describe NO, NO_2, and other nitrogen oxides.

EMISSIONS AND SOURCES. As shown in Table 2.1, there were eighteen million tons of NO_x emitted during 2006. Emissions have decreased by 41% since 1980. (See Table 2.2.) Most of this improvement occurred during the late 1990s and early 2000s.

NO_2 primarily comes from burning fuels such as gasoline, natural gas, coal, and oil. The exhaust from transportation vehicles is the major source of NO_x, accounting for 54% of emissions during 2002. (See Figure 2.5.) Fuel combustion in power plants, homes, and businesses accounted for 39% of NO_x emissions. Minor contributors

FIGURE 2.4

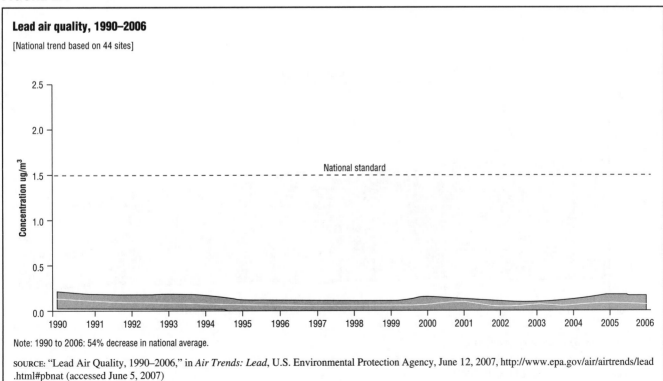

Lead air quality, 1990–2006

[National trend based on 44 sites]

Note: 1990 to 2006: 54% decrease in national average.

SOURCE: "Lead Air Quality, 1990–2006," in *Air Trends: Lead*, U.S. Environmental Protection Agency, June 12, 2007, http://www.epa.gov/air/airtrends/lead.html#pbnat (accessed June 5, 2007)

FIGURE 2.5

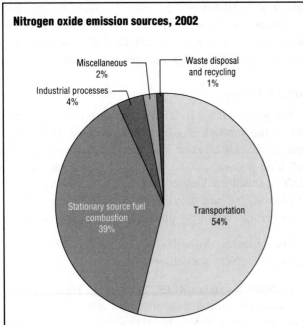

Nitrogen oxide emission sources, 2002

SOURCE: Adapted from Stacy C. Davis and Susan W. Diegel, "Table 12.1. Total National Emissions of the Criteria Air Pollutants by Sector, 2002," in *Transportation Energy Data Book: Edition 26*, U.S. Department of Energy, Oak Ridge National Laboratory, May 2007, http://cta.ornl.gov/data/tedb26/Edition26_Full_Doc.pdf (accessed June 5, 2007)

include industrial processes, miscellaneous sources, and waste disposal and recycling.

AIR QUALITY. NO_2 is a major precursor of smog and contributes to acid rain and haze. It can also undergo reactions in the air that lead to the formation of particulate matter and ozone. Figure 2.6 illustrates the air quality concentrations of NO_2 based on monitoring data from 170 sites around the country from 1990 to 2006. Over this time period NO_2 concentrations decreased by 30%. In 2006 the average measured NO_2 concentration at the monitoring sites was less than 0.02 parts per million. As of August 2007 the EPA (http://www.epa.gov/oar/oaqps/greenbk/nin dex.html) reported that all U.S. counties attained the EPA standards for NO_2 air quality.

ADVERSE HEALTH EFFECTS. NO_x reacts with ammonia and water droplets in the atmosphere to form nitric acid and other chemicals that are potentially harmful to human health. Inhalation of these particles can interfere with respiratory processes and damage lung tissue. Particles inhaled deeply into the lungs can cause or aggravate respiratory conditions such as bronchitis and emphysema.

Ozone

Ozone is a gas naturally present in Earth's upper atmosphere. The National Safety Council's Environmental Health Center indicates in *Reporting and Climate Change: Understanding the Science* (June 2000, http://www.nsc.org/EHC/

FIGURE 2.6

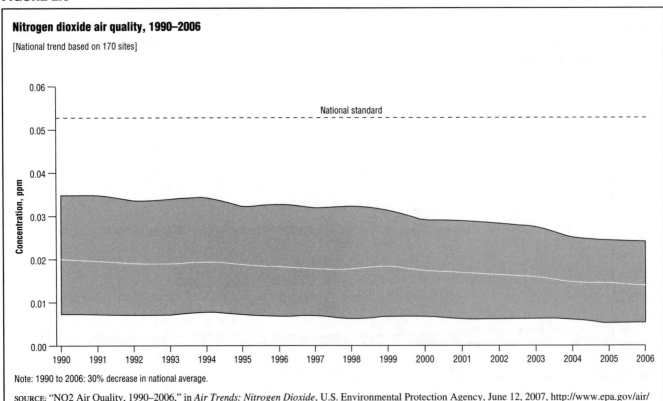

Nitrogen dioxide air quality, 1990–2006

[National trend based on 170 sites]

Note: 1990 to 2006: 30% decrease in national average.

SOURCE: "NO2 Air Quality, 1990–2006," in *Air Trends: Nitrogen Dioxide*, U.S. Environmental Protection Agency, June 12, 2007, http://www.epa.gov/air/airtrends/nitrogen.html (accessed June 19, 2007)

guidebks/climtoc.htm) that approximately 90% of Earth's ozone lies in the stratosphere at altitudes greater than about twenty miles. Ozone molecules at this level absorb ultraviolet radiation from the sun and prevent it from reaching the ground. Thus, stratospheric ozone (the ozone layer) is good for the environment. By contrast, tropospheric (ground-level) ozone is a potent air pollutant with serious health consequences. It is the most complex, pervasive, and difficult to control of the six priority pollutants.

EMISSIONS AND SOURCES. Unlike other air pollutants, ground-level ozone is not emitted directly into the air. It forms mostly on sunny, hot days because of complex chemical reactions that take place when the atmosphere contains other pollutants, primarily volatile organic compounds (VOCs) and NO_x. Such pollutants are called ozone precursors because their presence in the atmosphere leads to ozone creation.

VOCs are carbon-containing chemicals that easily become vapors or gases. Paint thinners, degreasers, and other solvents contain a great number of VOCs, which are also released from burning fuels such as coal, natural gas, gasoline, and wood.

As shown in Table 2.1, VOC emissions dropped from thirty-four million tons per year in 1970 to fifteen million tons per year in 2006. Figure 2.7 provides a breakdown of sources for VOC emissions in 2002. Transportation accounted for nearly half of the emissions (44%), followed closely by industrial processes (42%). Minor contributors included stationary source fuel combustion, miscellaneous sources, and waste disposal and recycling.

AIR QUALITY. Ozone has different health and environmental effects, depending on the time of exposure. The EPA monitors average eight-hour and one-hour ozone levels and sets different standards for each. Ozone concentrations can vary greatly from year to year, depending on the emissions of ozone precursors and weather conditions.

As shown in Figure 2.8, the average national ozone concentration, based on an eight-hour average, decreased by 9% between 1990 and 2006. Between 1980 and 2006 the average one-hour concentration decreased by 29%. (See Figure 2.9.)

In August 2007 the EPA (http://www.epa.gov/oar/oaqps/greenbk/gnc.html) reported that there were dozens of locations around the country classified as nonattainment for ozone air quality. One area was classified as "severe" nonattainment for the eight-hour ozone standard: the Los Angeles basin in California. Locations classified as "serious" nonattainment for the eight-hour standard included three other California areas: Riverside County, Sacramento, and the San Joaquin Valley. Many

FIGURE 2.7

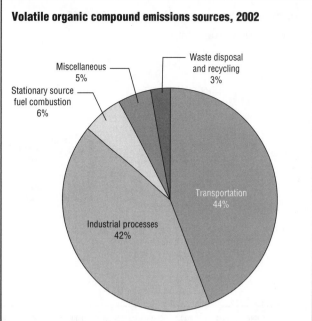

Volatile organic compound emissions sources, 2002

SOURCE: Adapted from Stacy C. Davis and Susan W. Diegel, "Table 12.1. Total National Emissions of the Criteria Air Pollutants by Sector, 2002," in *Transportation Energy Data Book: Edition 26*, U.S. Department of Energy, Oak Ridge National Laboratory, May 2007, http://cta.ornl.gov/data/tedb26/Edition26_Full_Doc.pdf (accessed June 19, 2007)

other areas in and around major cities were deemed "moderate" or "marginal" nonattainment.

OZONE CONTRIBUTES TO SMOG. Ground-level ozone is the primary component in smog. Smog, a word made up by combining the words smoke and fog, is probably the most well-known form of air pollution. It retards crop and tree growth, impairs health, and limits visibility. When temperature inversions occur (the warm air stays near the ground instead of rising) and winds are calm, such as during the summer, smog may hang over a huge area for days at a time. As traffic and other pollution sources add more pollutants to the air, the smog gets worse. Wind often blows smog-forming pollutants away from their sources; this is why smog frequently can be miles away from where the pollutants were created.

Most people associate dirty air with cities and the areas around them. There is good reason for this, because some of the worst smog in the country occurs in urban areas such as Los Angeles—a city known for its air quality problems. In a major industrial nation such as the United States, however, smog is not limited just to cities. The Great Smoky Mountains, located in western North Carolina and eastern Tennessee, are seeing more air pollution. Harmful emissions from various coal-burning facilities located outside the mountain range, as well as pollution from motor vehicles, are damaging the mountains' environment.

FIGURE 2.8

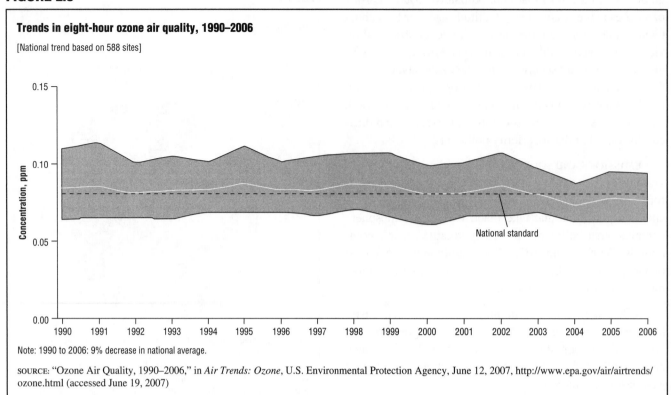

Trends in eight-hour ozone air quality, 1990–2006

[National trend based on 588 sites]

Note: 1990 to 2006: 9% decrease in national average.

SOURCE: "Ozone Air Quality, 1990–2006," in *Air Trends: Ozone*, U.S. Environmental Protection Agency, June 12, 2007, http://www.epa.gov/air/airtrends/ozone.html (accessed June 19, 2007)

FIGURE 2.9

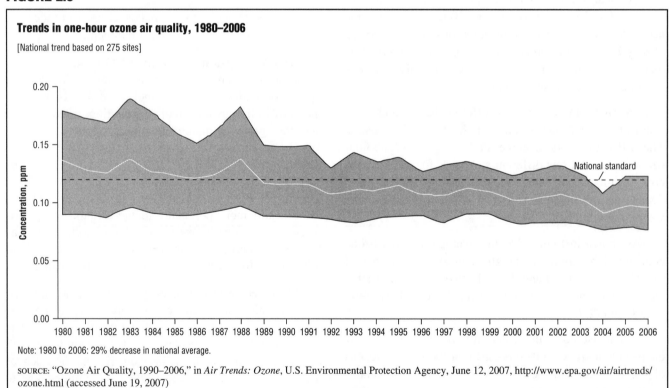

Trends in one-hour ozone air quality, 1980–2006

[National trend based on 275 sites]

Note: 1980 to 2006: 29% decrease in national average.

SOURCE: "Ozone Air Quality, 1990–2006," in *Air Trends: Ozone*, U.S. Environmental Protection Agency, June 12, 2007, http://www.epa.gov/air/airtrends/ozone.html (accessed June 19, 2007)

Ground-level ozone is harmful to ecosystems, particularly vegetation. Ozone exposure reduces forest yields by stunting the growth of seedlings and increasing stresses on trees. Such damage can take years to become evident. In *Latest Finds on National Air Quality: 2002 Status and Trends* (August 2003, http://epa.gov/air/airtrends/aqtrnd

02/2002_airtrends_final.pdf), the EPA notes that between 1993 and 2002 it monitored ozone levels based on eight-hour average concentrations at twenty-eight national parks around the country. The results indicate that ozone levels increased at eighteen of the parks, remained unchanged at four other parks, and decreased at six parks.

ADVERSE HEALTH EFFECTS. Even the smallest amounts of ozone can cause breathing difficulties. Ozone exposure can cause serious problems with lung functions, leading to infections, chest pain, and coughing. According to the EPA, ozone exposure is linked with increased emergency room visits and hospital admissions because of respiratory problems such as lung inflammation and asthma. Ozone causes or aggravates these problems, particularly in people working outdoors, the elderly, and children. Children are especially susceptible to the harmful effects of ozone because they spend a great deal of time outside and because their lungs are still developing.

According to Lara J. Akinbami of the Centers for Disease Control and Prevention, in "The State of Childhood Asthma, United States, 1980–2005" (*Advance Data from Vital and Health Statistics*, no. 381, December 12, 2006), the percentage of American children with asthma more than doubled between 1980 and 2005. In 1980, 3.6% of all children aged seventeen and younger suffered from asthma. By 2005 this figure had climbed to 8.9%. In general, asthma levels are greater among children who live in inner cities, areas that are also prone to higher concentrations of ozone, smog, and other air pollutants. Long-term exposure of any age group to moderate levels of ozone is thought to cause irreversible lung damage because of premature aging of the tissues.

The EPA maintains the Air Quality Index (AQI) as a means for warning the public when air pollutants exceed unhealthy levels. The AQI values range from zero to five hundred. Higher values correspond to greater levels of air pollution and increased risk to human health. An AQI value of one hundred is assigned to the concentration of an air pollutant equal to its NAAQS. For example, the average eight-hour ozone level considered unhealthy is 0.08 parts per million (ppm). Table 2.3 shows the ozone AQI. Index values are commonly reported during summertime radio and television newscasts to warn people about the dangers of ozone exposure.

In *State of the Air: 2007* (May 1, 2007, http://lungaction.org/reports/stateoftheair2007.html), the American Lung Association assesses the quality of air in U.S. communities. The organization ranks metropolitan areas and counties in terms of their air pollutant levels. The ten metropolitan areas with the worst ozone pollution in 2007 were:

- Los Angeles, Long Beach, and Riverside, California
- Bakersfield, California

TABLE 2.3

Air Quality Index (AQI): Ozone

Index values	Level of health concern	Cautionary statements
0–50	Good	None
51–100*	Moderate	Unusually sensitive people should consider limiting prolonged outdoor exertion.
101–150	Unhealthy for sensitive groups	Active children and adults, and people with respiratory disease, such as asthma, should limit prolonged outdoor exertion.
151–200	Unhealthy	Active children and adults, and people with respiratory disease, such as asthma, should avoid prolonged outdoor exertion; everyone else, especially children, should limit outdoor exertion.
201–300	Very unhealthy	Active children and adults, and people with respiratory disease, such as asthma, should avoid all outdoor exertion; everyone else, especially children, should limit outdoor exertion.
301–500	Hazardous	Everyone should avoid all outdoor exertion.

*Generally, an AQI of 100 for ozone corresponds to an ozone level of 0.08 parts per million (averaged over 8 hours).

SOURCE: "Air Quality Index (AQI): Ozone," in *Air Quality Index—A Guide to Air Quality and Your Health*, U.S. Environmental Protection Agency, Office of Air and Radiation, June 2000, http://www.airinfonow.org/pdf/aqi_cl.pdf (accessed July 27, 2007)

- Visala and Porterville, California
- Fresno and Madera, California
- Houston, Baytown, and Huntsville, Texas
- Merced, California
- Dallas and Fort Worth, Texas
- Sacramento and Arden-Arcade, California; and Truckee, Nevada
- Baton Rouge and Pierre Part, Louisiana
- New York City; Newark, New Jersey; and Bridgeport, Connecticut

Particulate Matter

Particulate matter (PM) is the general term for the mixture of solid particles and/or liquid droplets found in the air. The primary particles are those emitted directly to the atmosphere—for example, dust, dirt, and soot (black carbon). Secondary particles form in the atmosphere because of complex chemical reactions among gaseous emissions and include sulfates, nitrates, ammoniums, and organic carbon compounds. For example, sulfate particulates can form when sulfur dioxide emissions from industrial facilities and power plants undergo chemical reactions in the atmosphere.

The EPA tracks two sizes of PM: PM_{10} and $PM_{2.5}$. PM_{10} particles are those less than or equal to ten micrometers in diameter. This is roughly one-seventh the diameter of a human hair and small enough to be breathed into the lungs. $PM_{2.5}$ are the smallest of these particles (less than or equal to 2.5 micrometers in diameter). $PM_{2.5}$ is also called fine PM. The particles ranging in size between 2.5 and 10 micrometers in diameter are known as coarse PM. Most coarse PM is primary particles, whereas most fine PM is secondary particles.

EMISSIONS AND SOURCES. The EPA tracks trends in direct PM emissions from certain anthropogenic sources, mainly fuel combustion at power plants and in homes and businesses, industrial processes, and transportation exhaust. These are called traditionally inventoried sources. As shown in Table 2.1 and Table 2.2, direct PM emissions of both sizes declined dramatically between 1990 and 2006.

The EPA believes that the bulk of PM_{10} in the atmosphere comes from fugitive dust and agricultural and forestry practices that stir up soil. Fugitive dust is dust thrown up into the air when vehicles travel over unpaved roads and during land-disturbing construction activities such as bulldozing. In 2002 these sources were estimated to account for 85% of all PM_{10} emissions as shown in Figure 2.10. However, these sources are not as great a concern to air quality as the traditionally inventoried sources. This is because soil, dust, and dirt thrown up into the air does not typically travel far from its original location or climb far into the atmosphere.

Most $PM_{2.5}$ is not comprised of primary particles from direct emissions but of secondary particles that form in the atmosphere. The EPA tracks secondary $PM_{2.5}$ particle types at monitoring sites around the country. Data collected in 2001 and 2002 indicate that sulfates, ammonium, and carbon are the principal secondary particles found in the eastern part of the nation. These pollutants are largely associated with coal-fired power plants. In western states (particularly California), carbon and nitrates make up most of the secondary particles. On a national level secondary $PM_{2.5}$ concentrations are generally higher in urban areas than in rural areas.

AIR QUALITY. When PM hangs in the air, it creates a haze, limiting visibility. PM is one of the major components of smog and can have adverse effects on vegetation and sensitive ecosystems. Long-term exposure to PM can damage painted surfaces, buildings, and monuments.

Figure 2.11 shows the historical trend in PM_{10} air quality based on data collected by the EPA from 381 monitoring sites. Between 1990 and 2006 PM_{10} concentrations decreased by 30%. The EPA (http://www.epa .gov/oar/oaqps/greenbk/pnc.html) reported in August 2007 that dozens of areas around the country were non-attainment for PM_{10} concentrations. Areas classified "serious" nonattainment were in Southern California and parts of Nevada and Arizona.

In 1999 the EPA began nationwide tracking of $PM_{2.5}$ air quality concentrations. Between 1999 and 2006 these

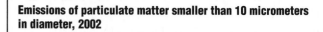

FIGURE 2.10

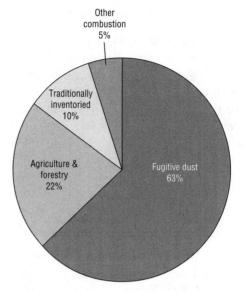

Emissions of particulate matter smaller than 10 micrometers in diameter, 2002

Other combustion 5%

Traditionally inventoried 10%

Agriculture & forestry 22%

Fugitive dust 63%

SOURCE: Adapted from "Figure 2-43. National Direct PM_{10} Emissions by Source Category, 2002," in *Air Trends: More Details on Lead*, U.S. Environmental Protection Agency, Office of Air Quality Planning and Standards, December 3, 2003

concentrations decreased by 15% based on data collected from 750 monitoring sites. (See Figure 2.12.) In August 2007 the EPA (http://www.epa.gov/oar/oaqps/greenbk/ qnc.html) noted that there were thirty-nine locations around the country deemed nonattainment for $PM_{2.5}$, mostly major- and medium-sized metropolitan areas. Under the CAA, states with nonattainment areas must submit to the EPA by 2008 a plan for reducing air pollutant emissions that lead to the formation of $PM_{2.5}$ particles in the atmosphere. The plan must list the enforceable measures to be taken and provide a schedule to become attainment as quickly as possible.

ADVERSE HEALTH EFFECTS. PM can irritate the nostrils, throat, and lungs and aggravate respiratory conditions such as bronchitis and asthma. PM exposure can also endanger the circulatory system and is linked with cardiac arrhythmias (episodes of irregular heartbeats) and heart attacks. $PM_{2.5}$ particles are the most damaging, because their small size allows them access to deeper regions of the lungs. These small particles have been linked with the most serious health effects in humans. Particulates pose the greatest health risk to those with heart or lung problems, the elderly, and especially children, who are particularly susceptible because of the greater amount of time they spend outside and the fact that their lungs are not fully developed.

FIGURE 2.11

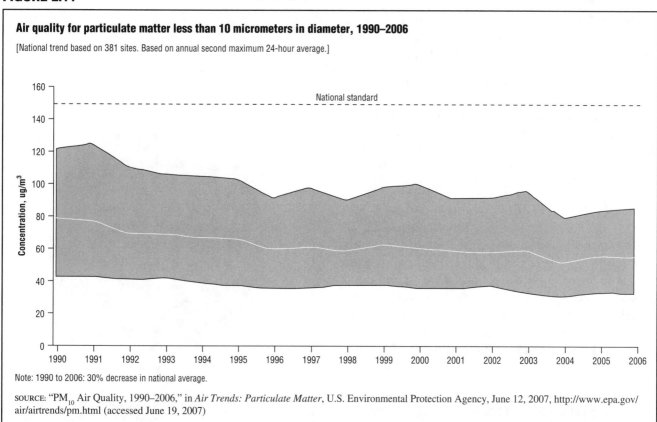

Air quality for particulate matter less than 10 micrometers in diameter, 1990–2006

[National trend based on 381 sites. Based on annual second maximum 24-hour average.]

Note: 1990 to 2006: 30% decrease in national average.

SOURCE: "PM₁₀ Air Quality, 1990–2006," in *Air Trends: Particulate Matter*, U.S. Environmental Protection Agency, June 12, 2007, http://www.epa.gov/air/airtrends/pm.html (accessed June 19, 2007)

FIGURE 2.12

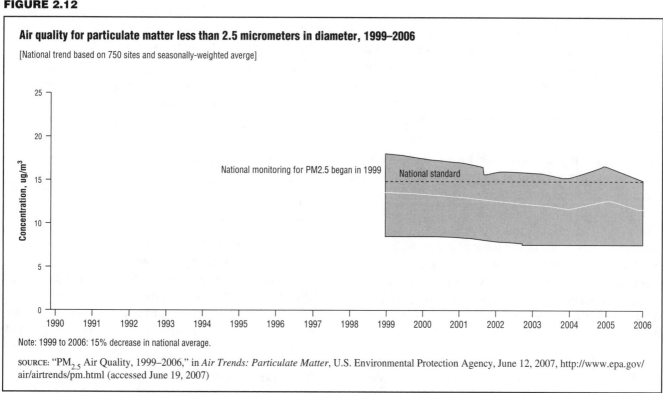

Air quality for particulate matter less than 2.5 micrometers in diameter, 1999–2006

[National trend based on 750 sites and seasonally-weighted averge]

Note: 1999 to 2006: 15% decrease in national average.

SOURCE: "PM₂.₅ Air Quality, 1999–2006," in *Air Trends: Particulate Matter*, U.S. Environmental Protection Agency, June 12, 2007, http://www.epa.gov/air/airtrends/pm.html (accessed June 19, 2007)

Sulfur Dioxide

Sulfur dioxide (SO_2) is a gas composed of sulfur and oxygen. The chemical formula SO_x is used collectively to describe sulfur oxide, SO_2, and other sulfur oxides.

EMISSIONS AND SOURCES. One of the primary sources of SO_2 is the combustion of fossil fuels containing sulfur. Coal (particularly high-sulfur coal common to the eastern United States) and oil are the major fuel sources associated with SO_2. Power plants have historically been the main source of SO_2 emissions. Some industrial processes and metal smelting also cause SO_2 to form.

From 1940 to 1970 SO_2 emissions increased as a result of the growing use of fossil fuels, especially coal, in industry and power plants. Since 1970 total SO_2 emissions have dropped because of greater reliance on cleaner fuels with lower sulfur content and the increased use of pollution control devices, such as scrubbers, to clean emissions. Between 1970 and 2006 SO_2 emissions declined by more than half as shown in Table 2.1. A 66% decrease was obtained between 1980 and 2006. (See Table 2.2.)

Fuel combustion in stationary sources (for example, in power plants) has traditionally produced most SO_2 emissions. In 2002 this source accounted for 85% of SO_2 emissions. (See Figure 2.13.) Industrial processes contributed another 9%. Transportation, miscellaneous sources, and waste disposal and recycling were minor contributors.

AIR QUALITY. Trends in air quality concentrations of SO_2 are shown in Figure 2.14. The average concentration fell by 53% between 1990 and 2006. The EPA (http://www.epa.gov/oar/oaqps/greenbk/snc.html) reported in August 2007 that there were ten nonattainment areas around the country for SO_2. These included locations in Montana, Utah, New Jersey, Pennsylvania, Arizona, and Guam.

SO_2 is a major contributor to acid rain, haze, and particulate matter. Acid rain is of particular concern because acid deposition harms aquatic life by lowering the pH (which stands for potential hydrogen and means the level of acidity; a lower value indicates more acid) of surface waters; impairs the growth of forests; causes the depletion of natural soil nutrients; and corrodes buildings, cars, and monuments. Acid rain is largely associated with the eastern United States because eastern coal tends to be higher in sulfur content than coal mined in the western United States.

In 1990 Congress established the Acid Rain Program under Title IV of the 1990 CAAA. The program called for major reductions in SO_2 and NO_x emissions from certain coal-fired power plants and other combustion units gener-

FIGURE 2.13

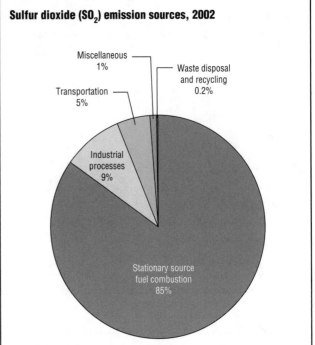

Sulfur dioxide (SO_2) emission sources, 2002

Miscellaneous 1%
Waste disposal and recycling 0.2%
Transportation 5%
Industrial processes 9%
Stationary source fuel combustion 85%

SOURCE: Adapted from Stacy C. Davis and Susan W. Diegel, "Table 12.1. Total National Emissions of the Criteria Air Pollutants by Sector, 2002," in *Transportation Energy Data Book: Edition 26*, U.S. Department of Energy, Oak Ridge National Laboratory, May 2007, http://cta.ornl.gov/data/tedb26/Edition26_Full_Doc.pdf (accessed June 19, 2007)

ating electricity around the country. The EPA notes in *Acid Rain Program: 2005 Progress Report* (October 2006, http://epa.gov/airmarkets/progress/docs/2005report.pdf) that the program set two emissions goals:

- Reduce SO_2 emissions by half (in other words, by ten million tons) by 2010 compared with the emissions released in 1980 and maintain a cap after 2010.

- Achieve a two-million-ton reduction in NO_x emissions compared with the NO_x emissions projected for 2000 if the program had not been implemented.

The program expects to meet its goals by tightening annual emission limits on thousands of power plants around the country.

ADVERSE HEALTH EFFECTS. Inhaling SO_2 in polluted air can impair breathing in those with asthma or even in healthy adults who are active outdoors. As with other air pollutants, children, the elderly, and those with preexisting respiratory and cardiovascular diseases and conditions are the most susceptible to adverse effects from breathing this gas.

The Clear Skies Controversy

In 2002 President George W. Bush (1946–) proposed his Clear Skies initiative to set nationwide caps on emis-

FIGURE 2.14

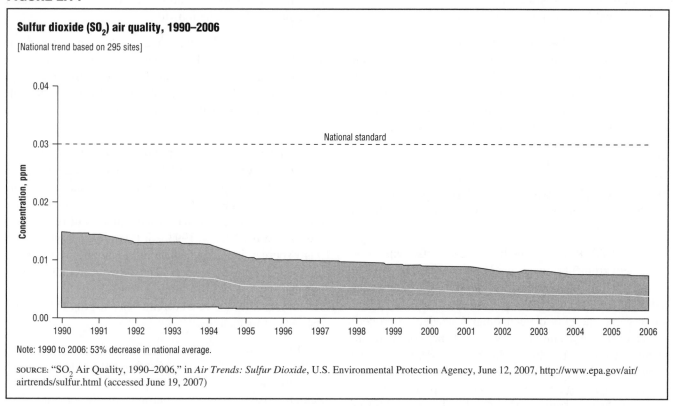

Sulfur dioxide (SO₂) air quality, 1990–2006

[National trend based on 295 sites]

Note: 1990 to 2006: 53% decrease in national average.

SOURCE: "SO₂ Air Quality, 1990–2006," in *Air Trends: Sulfur Dioxide*, U.S. Environmental Protection Agency, June 12, 2007, http://www.epa.gov/air/airtrends/sulfur.html (accessed June 19, 2007)

sions of sulfur dioxide, nitrogen oxides, and mercury from power plants. Even though Clear Skies legislation has been introduced in Congress several times, as of September 2007 it had not been passed. According to the EPA, in "Clear Skies: Basic Information" (March 2, 2006, http://www.epa.gov/clearskies/basic.html), the program would reduce sulfur dioxide emissions by 73%, mercury emissions by 69%, and nitrogen dioxide emissions by 67% from 2000 levels when fully implemented by 2018.

However, environmental groups are opposed to the proposed Clear Skies Act because it would institute a cap-and-trade system. This would set overall caps on emissions but allow utility companies operating below emission limits to sell credits to other companies having trouble meeting the limits. Even though a similar system is used to control emissions that cause acid rain, critics believe this approach is not appropriate for more potent air pollutants, such as mercury. They fear that the cap-and-trade system would allow utility plants in some areas to release unacceptably high levels of these pollutants.

Nevertheless, some of the objectives of the Clear Skies Act have been implemented by the EPA through other programs, including the Clean Air Interstate Rule and the Clean Air Mercury Rule.

CLEAN AIR INTERSTATE RULE. In 2005 the EPA issued the Clean Air Interstate Rule (CAIR; April 5,

2007, http://www.epa.gov/cair/) to tackle problems in the eastern United States with air pollutants that move across state boundaries. CAIR puts permanent caps on emissions of NOₓ and SO₂ in twenty-eight eastern states and the District of Columbia. The rule is projected to reduce SO₂ emissions by more than 70% and reduce NOₓ emissions by more than 60% compared with 2003 levels. Control of these pollutants is expected to reduce the formation of fine particulate matter, acid rain, and ground-level ozone across the country.

The program is to be carried out using the cap-and-trade system. The EPA predicts that full implementation of CAIR in 2015 will provide between $85 billion and $100 billion in annual health benefits and substantially reduce premature deaths in the eastern United States. Improvements are expected in visibility within southeastern national parks, which have been plagued by smog in recent years.

CLEAN AIR MERCURY RULE. Mercury is a hazardous air pollutant that can fall out of the atmosphere into water supplies, where it is absorbed by fish and shellfish. The consumption of contaminated fish and shellfish is the primary source of mercury exposure to humans. Sources of mercury emissions to the air include gold mines, institutional boilers, chlorine production, waste incinerators, and coal-fired power plant boilers. The EPA (April 5, 2007, http://www.epa.gov/camr/pdfs/slide1.pdf) indicates that approximately forty-eight tons of mercury were emitted to the air by power plants in 1999, accounting for 43% of total U.S. mercury emissions.

In 2005 the EPA issued the Clean Air Mercury Rule (CAMR) to limit and reduce mercury emissions nationwide from coal-fired power plants. The EPA reports in "Clear Skies: Basic Information" that the CAMR two-phase program sets up an optional cap-and-trade system that will be fully implemented by 2018 and should reduce mercury emissions by nearly 70% from 1999 levels. The first-phase cap under the program takes effect in 2010 and is expected to reduce mercury emissions to around twenty-six tons per year. The last-phase cap implemented by 2018 will reduce mercury emissions to around fifteen tons per year.

The CAMR was immediately unpopular with some state governments, particularly those in the eastern United States, where many coal-fired power plants operate. The EPA chose 2018 for the final cap, because it claims that the control technologies needed to properly restrict mercury emissions will not be commercially available until after 2010. However, in *Mercury Emissions from Electric Power Plants: States Are Setting Stricter Limits* (February 22, 2007, http://ndep.nv.gov/mercury/docs/crs_report_022207.pdf), James E. McCarthy of the Congressional Research Service notes that eighteen states have established more stringent emissions limits for mercury that go into effect sooner than those set in the CAMR program. Even though the state programs rely on different mechanisms for achieving reductions, McCarthy indicates that many of them prohibit interstate and in-state trading of mercury credits, because they fear the creation of mercury "hot spots" in their jurisdictions. The high incidence of states opting out of the federal CAMR program casts doubts on its reliance on national emission trading as an effective means to reduce U.S. mercury emissions.

Air Toxics

Hazardous air pollutants (HAPs), also referred to as air toxics, are pollutants that can cause severe health effects and/or ecosystem damage. Serious health risks linked to HAPs include cancer, immune system disorders, neurological problems, reproductive effects, and birth defects. The CAA lists 188 substances as HAPs and targets them for regulation in Section 112 (b) (1). The air toxics program complements the NAAQS program. Examples of HAPs are benzene, dioxins, arsenic, beryllium, mercury, and vinyl chloride.

The major sources of HAP emissions include transportation vehicles, construction equipment, power plants, factories, and refineries. Some air toxics come from common sources. For example, benzene emissions are associated with gasoline. Air toxics are not subject to intensive national monitoring; the EPA and state environmental agencies monitor air toxic levels at approximately three hundred sites nationwide.

In 2003 the EPA launched the National Air Toxic Trend Site network. It is designed to follow trends in high-risk air toxics such as benzene, chromium, and formaldehyde. The EPA has also awarded grants to state and local environmental agencies to conduct short-term monitoring of air toxics.

NATIONAL-SCALE AIR TOXICS ASSESSMENTS. In May 2002 the EPA released the 1996 National-Scale Air Toxics Assessment (http://www.epa.gov/ttn/atw/nata/). During 1996 approximately 4.6 million tons of air toxics were released into the air, down from a baseline value of 6 million tons between 1990 and 1993. Air toxics were emitted from many sources, including industrial and mobile (vehicles and nonroad equipment) sources. The known carcinogens posing the greatest risks to human health were benzene and chromium. The suspected carcinogen showing the greatest risk was formaldehyde.

In February 2006 the EPA released the 1999 National-Scale Air Toxics Assessment (http://www.epa.gov/ttn/atw/nata1999/). It evaluates 177 HAPs plus particulate matter from the burning of diesel fuel. The assessment inventoried air toxics emissions, estimated ambient concentrations and population exposures, and characterized the potential public health risks, including cancer and noncancer effects. Table 2.4 shows that toluene, xylenes, hydrochloric acid, benzene, and formaldehyde were the five most commonly emitted air toxics in 2002. Overall, the EPA finds that most Americans face a lifetime cancer risk because of exposure to outdoor air toxics of between one and twenty-five in a million. In other words, out of one million people, between one and twenty-five of them face an increased chance of developing cancer because of breathing outdoor air toxics. The upper range applies to people in urban areas. The risk is even greater (more than fifty in a million) for people living in certain high-risk areas, such as transportation corridors (areas where major roads and/or other modes of transport are clustered).

THE TOXICS RELEASE INVENTORY. The Toxics Release Inventory (TRI) was established under the Emergency Planning and Community Right-to-Know Act of 1986. The TRI program requires annual reports on the waste management activities and toxic chemical releases of certain industrial facilities using specific toxic chemicals. The TRI list includes more than 650 toxic chemicals.

According to the EPA, in the *2005 Toxics Release Inventory (TRI) Public Data Release eReport* (March 2007, http://www.epa.gov/tri/tridata/tri05/pdfs/eReport.pdf), in 2005 there were nearly 4.3 billion pounds of chemical releases reported by covered facilities. The vast majority (88%) of the releases were on-site releases to air, land,

TABLE 2.4

The five most commonly emitted air toxics, 2002

Pollutant	Percentage of total air toxics emissions	Primary sources of emissions	Health effects
Toluene	18	Mobile sources	Impairment of the nervous system with symptoms including tiredness, dizziness, sleepiness, confusion, weakness, memory loss, nausea, loss of appetite, and hearing and color vision loss; kidney problems; unconsciousness; and death.
Xylenes	13	Mobile sources, asphalt paving	Irritation of the skin, eyes, nose, and throat; headaches, dizziness, memory loss, and changes in sense of balance; lung problems; stomach discomfort; possible effects on the liver and kidneys; unconsciousness; and death.
Hydrochloric acid	12	Coal-fired utility and industrial boilers	Eye, nose, and respiratory tract irritation; corrosion of the skin, eyes, mucous membranes, esophagus, and stomach; severe burns; ulceration; scarring; inflammation of the stomach lining; chronic bronchitis; and inflammation of the skin.
Benzene	9	Mobile sources, open burning, pesticide application	Drowsiness, dizziness, vomiting, irritation of the stomach, sleepiness, convulsions, rapid heart rate, headaches, tremors, confusion, unconsciousness, anemia, excessive bleeding, weakened immune system, increased incidence of cancer (leukemia), and death.
Formaldehyde	7	Mobile sources, open burning	Irritation of the eyes, nose, throat, and skin; severe pain; vomiting; coma; limited evidence of cancer; and death.

Note: Health effects are dependent upon the concentration of the air toxic and the length of exposure.

SOURCE: "Table 1. The Five Most Commonly Emitted Air Toxics, 2002," in *Clean Air Act: EPA Should Improve the Management of Its Air Toxics Program*, U.S. Government Accountability Office, June 2006, http://www.gao.gov/new.items/d06669.pdf (accessed June 19, 2007)

and water. The remainder were off-site releases (when a facility sends toxic chemicals to another facility where they are then released). On-site air emissions amounted to 1.5 billion pounds and accounted for 35% of the total.

EPA'S AIR TOXICS PROGRAM UNDER FIRE. Since the passage of the original CAA in 1970, the EPA has concentrated on reducing emissions of the priority pollutants described earlier. Critics complain that the nation's air toxics program has been slow to be implemented effectively. This controversy is described by the U.S. Governmental Accountability Office (GAO), in *Clean Air Act: EPA Should Improve the Management of Its Air Toxics Program* (June 2006, http://www.gao.gov/new.items/d06669.pdf). The GAO states that the 1970 CAA required EPA to list HAPs and develop regulations for their control. The agency moved slowly in this area, developing regulations for only seven HAPs over the following two decades. As a result, Congress made dramatic changes to the air toxics program in the 1990 CAA.

The amended law listed a number of air toxics and directed the EPA to develop technology-based emissions limits for them applicable to eighty-four thousand "major stationary sources," such as chemical plants and incinerators that emit at least ten tons per year of a single HAP or at least twenty-five tons per year of combined HAPs. These standards are called maximum achievable control technology (MACT) limits. The EPA was supposed to follow up eight years after issuing the MACT limits to ensure that the limits were still effectively protecting human health and environmental quality from residual risks posed by the emissions. In addition, the EPA was to regulate HAP emissions from small stationary sources,

such as dry cleaners and small manufacturers, and evaluate the feasibility of regulating mobile sources, such as automobiles. The GAO finds that the EPA has met less than half of the CAA requirements and has been late meeting the vast majority of those it has completed.

THE AUTOMOBILE'S CONTRIBUTION TO AIR POLLUTION

For several decades following the passage of the original CAA in 1970, air pollution from industrial sources was the primary focus of lawmakers and the public. As dramatic achievements in air quality were obtained in this sector, more attention was focused on air pollutants associated with transportation. Table 2.5 shows that in 2002 highway vehicles were major sources of U.S. emissions of CO (55.5%), NO_x (34.9%), and VOCs (27.5%), and minor sources of other criteria air pollutants.

Exhaust Emission Limits

The 1990 CAAA included a program to control air pollution from new motor vehicles. The so-called EPA Tier 1 emission standards were issued in 1991 and took effect in the mid-1990s. They applied to all new light-duty vehicles weighing less than eighty-five hundred pounds. This included cars, pick-up trucks, and sports utility vehicles (SUVs). There were different emissions standards by weight class within Tier 1. In 1997 the EPA issued regulations for the National Low Emission Vehicle (NLEV) program, a voluntary program modeled after California standards for emission reductions from motor vehicles.

Because of California's extreme air pollution problems, the CAAA allowed states to set stricter emission

TABLE 2.5

Total national emissions of the criteria air pollutants by sector, 2002

[Millions of short tons/percentage]

Sector	CO	NO$_x$	VOC	PM-10	PM-2.5	SO$_2$	NH$_3$
Highway vehicles	55.5%	34.9%	27.5%	0.9%	2.2%	1.8%	8.0%
Aircraft	0.2%	0.4%	0.1%	0.0%	0.0%	0.1%	0.0%
Railroads	0.1%	4.2%	0.2%	0.1%	0.3%	0.3%	0.0%
Vessels	0.1%	4.8%	0.2%	0.2%	0.6%	1.0%	0.0%
Other off-highway	21.4%	10.0%	15.8%	1.1%	3.3%	1.3%	0.8%
Transportation total	**86.61**	**11.45**	**7.23**	**0.52**	**0.43**	**0.70**	**0.29**

Note: CO=Carbon monoxide. NO$_x$=Nitrogen oxides. PM-10=Particulate matter less than 10 microns. PM-2.5=Particulate matter less than 2.5 microns. SO$_2$=Sulfur dioxide. VOC=Volatile organic compounds. NH$_3$=Ammonia.

SOURCE: Adapted from Stacy C. Davis and Susan W. Diegel, "Table 12.1. Total National Emissions of the Criteria Air Pollutants by Sector, 2002," in *Transportation Energy Data Book: Edition 26*, U.S. Department of Energy, Oak Ridge National Laboratory, May 2007, http://cta.ornl.gov/data/tedb26/ Edition26_Full_Doc.pdf (accessed June 29, 2007)

standards than those required by the amendments, which California did. These included strict new laws on automobile pollution. The California low-emission vehicle (LEV) regulations were originally adopted in 1991 and became applicable in 1994. LEV II regulations were passed in 1998 and became applicable with 2004 model year vehicles. The LEV I and II programs classify vehicles into the following emissions categories:

- TLEV—transitional low-emission vehicle (this category was phased out in 2004)

- LEV—low-emission vehicle

- ULEV—ultra low-emission vehicle

- SULEV—super ultra low-emission vehicle

- ZEV—zero-emission vehicle

- PZEV—partial zero-emission vehicle (meets SULEV limits, has zero evaporative emissions, and a 15-year/ 150,000-mile warranty on emissions equipment)

- AT PZEV—advanced technology partial zero-emission vehicle (meets PZEV limits and uses additional clean technology such as alternative fuel, electric drive, or other advanced technology system)

The remaining forty-nine states have the option of choosing either the standards of California or the federal CAAA. Some states have tougher tests for auto emissions than others. In most major metropolitan areas owners of cars and light trucks are required to pay for exhaust emission tests. For those that do not pass, repairs must be made to bring them into compliance.

EPA TIER 2 LIMITS. In 1999 the EPA introduced its Tier 2 federal emission limits for new vehicles. They took effect in 2004 and include a five-year schedule for complete implementation. Emission limits apply to CO, NO$_x$, PM, formaldehyde (HCHO), and nonmethane organic gases (NMOG). The latter are carbon-containing compounds that combine with NO$_x$ in sunlight to produce smog. Table 2.6 lists the emissions standards that will be in effect in 2009 when the Tier 2 standards are fully implemented. Manufacturers are allowed the flexibility to certify new vehicles to different sets of exhaust emissions standards called "bins." The manufacturers must choose bins for their vehicles that ensure that their corporate sales fleet emits an average of no more than 0.07 grams of NO$_x$ per mile. Table 2.6 also shows California LEV II standards for comparison with EPA's Tier 2 standards.

Gasoline Formulations

During the 1980s lead was phased out of gasoline to provide substantial improvements in air quality. A variety of other federal and state standards have gone into effect that dictate particular properties of gasoline, such as volatility (tendency to evaporate) and levels of NO$_x$, heavy metals, toxic compounds, sulfur, and oxygen. The CAA requires the use of specially blended gasoline in areas of the country deemed nonattainment for ozone or CO levels. Attainment areas can choose to opt-in to these requirements. All the varying standards have resulted in the creation of many so-called boutique gasolines that greatly complicate the distribution dynamics for gasoline in the country. Critics complain that a gasoline shortage in one area can often not be relieved by shipping in gasoline from another part of the country because of the highly varying standards. The Energy Policy Act of 2005 limits the number of boutique fuels that can be designated by the states and requires a study of possible methods for harmonizing the nation's fuel system requirements. In 2006 the EPA formed a task group to examine issues associated with boutique fuels and published the findings in *Report to the President: Task Force on Boutique Fuels* (June 2006, http://epa.gov/otaq/boutique/resources/bftf6 2306finalreport.pdf).

TABLE 2.6

Light vehicle exhaust emission standards proposed to go into effect in 2009

[Grams/mile. Gasoline and diesel unless noted otherwise. Vehicle size up to 8,500 pounds. Gross vehicle weight (GVW) unless otherwise noted.]

		12,000 miles				
Useful life:	Bins, category, size	NMOG	CO	NO_x	PM	HCHO
U.S emission standards	Bins					
	8	0.125	4.2	0.20	0.02	0.018
	7	0.090	4.2	0.15	0.02	0.018
	6	0.090	4.2	0.10	0.01	0.018
	5	0.090	4.2	0.07	0.01	0.018
	4	0.070	2.1	0.04	0.01	0.011
	3	0.055	2.1	0.03	0.01	0.011
	2	0.010	2.1	0.02	0.01	0.004
	1	0.000	0.0	0.00	0.00	0.000
	Average[a]	—	—	0.07	—	—
	Category					
California LEV II emission standards				(Diesel only)		
	LEV[b]	0.090	4.2	0.07	0.01	0.018
	ULEV	0.055	2.1	0.07	0.01	0.011
	SULEV	0.010	1.0	0.02	0.01	0.004
	ZEV[c]	0.000	0.0	0.00	0.00	0.000

[a]Includes medium-duty passenger vehicles which are also required to meet bin standards.
[b]A LEV option 1 with higher NO_x levels also exists for up to 4% of LDTs above 3,750 lbs.
[c]Only apply to cars and LDTs 0-3750 lbs LVW.
Notes:
NMOG=Non-methane organic gases.
CO=Carbon monoxide.
NO_x=Nitrogen oxides.
PM=Particulate matter.
HCHO=Formaldehyde.
LEV=Low emission vehicle.
ULEV=Ultra low emission vehicle.
SULEV=Super ultra low emission vehicle.
ZEV=Zero emission vehicle.
LDT=Light duty truck.

SOURCE: Stacy C. Davis and Susan W. Diegel, "Table 12.13. Light Vehicle Exhaust Emission Standards in Effect in 2009 when U.S. Tier 2 Standards are Final (grams/mile)," in *Transportation Energy Data Book: Edition 26*, U.S. Department of Energy, Oak Ridge National Laboratory, May 2007, http://cta.ornl.gov/data/tedb26/Edition26_Full_Doc.pdf (accessed June 29, 2007)

REFORMULATED GASOLINE. Reformulated gasoline (RFG) is a boutique fuel specially blended to diminish ground-level ozone formation through limits on volatility and on benzene, NO_x, and toxic emissions. These limits vary by season, with stricter limits imposed during the summer months, when ozone formation is more common. Historically, RFG has required the addition of oxygen. This process produces a lower-octane fuel and usually an increase in price. Low-octane fuels can cause more engine knocking and pinging, making the fuels less desirable to consumers. Oxygenation of fuel makes combustion more complete. Incomplete fuel combustion is a major cause of CO emissions. Even though RFG combustion results in lower CO emissions, higher carbon dioxide emissions result because of the presence of additional oxygen.

The most frequently used oxygenates in RFG have been ethanol and methyl tertiary-butyl ether (MTBE). Fuel ethanol is derived from fermented agricultural products such as corn. MTBE is a chemical compound made from methanol and isobutylene and is soluble in water.

The CAA standards that went into effect in 1995 required those areas with the worst polluted air to sell RFG. By the early 2000s RFG accounted for more than one-third of all gasoline sold. However, increasing problems with MTBE found in water bodies led to state bans against the chemical. The passage of the 2005 Energy Policy Act provided for the removal of the RFG oxygen requirement and effectively eliminated the use of MTBE in RFG.

Corporate Average Fuel Economy Standards

In 1973 the Organization of Petroleum Exporting Countries (OPEC) imposed an oil embargo that provided a painful reminder to Americans of how dependent the country had become on foreign sources of fuel. Congress passed the 1975 Automobile Fuel Efficiency Act, which set the initial Corporate Average Fuel Economy (CAFE) standards.

CAFE standards required each domestic automaker to increase the average mileage of the new cars sold to 27.5 miles per gallon (mpg) by 1985. Under CAFE rules automakers could still sell the big, less efficient cars with powerful eight-cylinder engines, but to meet average fuel efficiency rates they also had to sell smaller, more efficient cars. Automakers that failed to meet each year's CAFE standards were required to pay fines. Those who managed to surpass the rates earned credits that they could use in years when they fell below CAFE requirements.

In *Light-Duty Automotive Technology and Fuel Economy Trends: 1975 through 2005* (July 2005, http://www.epa.gov/otaq/cert/mpg/fetrends/420r05001.pdf), Robert M. Heavenrich of the EPA states that the CAFE standard was lowered during the mid to late 1980s and then raised back to 27.5 mpg for 1990 model automobiles. In 1996 a standard of 20.7 mpg was established for light trucks. This category includes pickup trucks, minivans, and SUVs. In 2003 the National Highway Traffic Safety Administration issued a rule setting new CAFE standards for light trucks produced in model years 2005 to 2007. The standard increased to 21 mpg for 2005, to 21.7 mpg for 2006, and to 22.2 mpg for 2007. The CAFE standard for passenger cars for these model years remained 27.5 mpg. In June 2007 the U.S. Senate passed an energy bill increasing CAFE standards to 35 mpg for cars and light trucks by 2020. As of October 2007, these new standards had not received passage by the U.S. House of Representatives.

CAFE standards are important to air quality, because higher standards have emissions benefits. Better fuel efficiency lowers tailpipe exhaust emissions of greenhouse gases (for example, carbon dioxide). Also, decreased demand for fuel reduces air pollutant emissions from the gasoline production and distribution industries.

Alternative Fuels

Early pollution-reducing efforts by vehicle manufacturers focused on reducing tailpipe emissions instead of eliminating their formation in the first place. Automakers introduced lighter engines, fuel injection systems, catalytic converters, and other technological improvements. In recent decades concerns about U.S. dependence on foreign oil supplies and environmental issues have focused attention on the development of alternative fuels for transportation vehicles. The Energy Policy Act of 1992 defines alternative fuels as those that are "substantially non-petroleum and yield energy security and environmental benefits." Under the act the following are designated as alternative fuels:

- Coal-derived liquid fuels

- Liquefied petroleum gas (propane)

- Natural gas and liquid fuels domestically produced from natural gas

- Methanol, ethanol, and other alcohols

- Blends of 85% or more of alcohol with gasoline

- Biodiesel and other fuels derived from biological materials

- Electricity

- Hydrogen

- P-series fuels (blends of natural gas liquids, ethanol, and the biomass-derived co-solvent methyltetrahydrofuran)

Table 2.7 summarizes information for some of the major alternative fuels related to their physical state, sources, and environmental impacts. Even though these fuels offer advantages, their use may substitute one problem for another. For example, the alcohol fuel methanol reduces ozone formation but increases formaldehyde, a human carcinogen, and is twice as toxic as gasoline if it comes in contact with the skin. Engines require twice as much methanol as gasoline to travel a similar distance. Natural gas reduces hydrocarbons and CO but increases NO_x.

In the *Transportation Energy Data Book: Edition 26* (May 2007, http://cta.ornl.gov/data/tedb26/Edition26_Full_Doc.pdf), Stacy C. Davis and Susan W. Diegel of the Oak Ridge National Laboratory report that in 2004 nearly 548,000 alternative fuel vehicles (AFVs) were in use in the United States. Over 194,000 relied on liquefied petroleum gas, another 146,000 depended on alcohol fuel containing at least 85% ethanol, nearly 144,000 used compressed natural gas, and close to 56,000 used electricity.

ALTERNATIVE FUELS AND THE MARKETPLACE. AFVs cannot become a viable transportation option unless a fuel supply is readily available. Ideally, the infrastructure for supplying alternative fuels will be developed simultaneously with the vehicles. According to the Alternative Fuels Data Center of the U.S. Department of Energy (DOE; October 10, 2006, http://www.eere.energy.gov/afdc/infrastructure/station_counts.html), which tabulates the number of alternative fuel stations by state and fuel type, in 2006 there were 5,627 of these stations around the country. Nearly half (2,423 stations) provide liquefied petroleum gas. Together, California (880 stations) and Texas (658 stations) accounted for 27% of all the stations.

Market success of alternative fuels and AFVs depends on public acceptance. People are accustomed to using gasoline as their main transportation fuel, and it is readily available. As federal and state requirements for alternative fuels increase, so should the availability of such fuels as well as their acceptance by the general public. In the long run, electricity and hydrogen seem the most promising of the alternative fuels for vehicles.

ELECTRIC VEHICLES: PROMISE AND REALITY. The electric vehicle (EV) is not a new invention. Popular during the 1890s, the quiet, clean, and simple vehicle was expected to dominate the automotive market of the twentieth century. Instead, it quietly disappeared as automakers chose to

TABLE 2.7

Characteristics of major alternative fuels

	Gasoline	No. 2 diesel	Biodiesel	Compressed natural gas (CNG)	Electricity	Ethanol (E85)	Hydrogen	Liquified natural gas (LNG)	Liquefied petroleum gas (LPG)	Methanol (M85)
Main fuel source	Crude oil	Crude oil	Soy bean oil, waste cooking oil, animal fats, and rapeseed oil	Underground reserves	Coal; however, nuclear, natural gas, hydroelectric, and renewable resources can also be used	Corn, grains, or agricultural waste	Natural gas, methanol, and other energy sources	Underground reserves	A by-product of petroleum refining or natural gas processing	Natural gas, coal, or, woody biomass
Physical state	Liquid	Liquid	Liquid	Compressed gas	N/A	Liquid	Compressed gas or liquid	Liquid	Liquid	Liquid
Types of vehicles available today	All types of vehicle classes	Many types of vehicle classes	Any vehicle that runs on diesel today—no modifications are needed for up to 5% blends. Many engines also compatible with up to 20% blends	Many types of vehicle classes	Neighborhood electric vehicles, bicycles, light-duty vehicles, medium and heavy duty trucks and buses	Light-duty vehicles, medium and heavy-duty trucks and buses—these vehicles are flexible fuel vehicles that can be fueled with E85 (ethanol), gasoline, or any combination of the two fuels	No vehicles are available for commercial sale yet, but some vehicles are being leased for demonstration purposes	Medium and heavy-duty trucks and buses	Light-duty vehicles, which can be fueled with propane or gasoline, medium and heavy-duty trucks and buses that run on propane	Mostly heavy-duty buses are available
Environmental impacts of burning the fuel	Produces harmful emissions; however, gasoline and gasoline vehicles are rapidly improving and emissions are being reduced	Produces harmful emissions; however, diesel and diesel vehicles are rapidly improving and emissions are being reduced especially with after-treatment devices	Reduces particulate matter and global warming gas emissions compared to conventional diesel; however, NOₓ emissions may be increased	CNG vehicles can demonstrate a reduction in ozone forming emissions compared to some conventional fuels, however, HC emissions may be increased	EVs have zero tailpipe emissions; however, some amount of emissions can be contributed to power generation	E-85 vehicles can demonstrate a 25% reduction in ozone-forming emissions compared to reformulated gasoline	Zero regulated emissions for fuel cell-powered vehicles, and only NOₓ emissions possible for internal combustion engines operating on hydrogen	LNG vehicles can demonstrate a reduction in ozone forming emissions compared to some conventional fuels, however, HC emissions may be increased	LPG vehicles can demonstrate a 60% reduction in ozone-forming emissions compared to reformulated gasoline	M-85 vehicles can demonstrate a 40% reduction in ozone-forming emissions compared to reformulated gasoline
Fuel availability	Available at all fueling stations	Available at select fueling stations	Available in bulk from an increasing number of suppliers. There are 22 states that have some biodiesel stations available to the public	More than 1,100 CNG stations can be found across the country California has the highest concentration of CNG stations. Home fueling will be available in the fall of 2005.	Most homes, government facilities, fleet garages, and businesses have adequate electrical capacity for charging, but, special hookup or upgrades may be required. More than 600 electric charging stations are available in California and Arizona.	Most of the E-85 fueling stations are located in the Midwest, but in all, approximately 150 stations are available in 23 states	There are only a small number of hydrogen stations across the country. Most are available for private use only	Public LNG stations are limited (only 35 nationally). LNG is available through several suppliers of cryogenic liquids	LPG is the most accessible alternative fuel in the U.S. There are more than 3,300 stations nation wide	Methanol remains a qualified alternative fuel as defined by EPAct, but it is not commonly used

SOURCE: Adapted from *Alternative Fuels Comparison Chart*, U.S. Department of Energy, National Renewable Energy Laboratory, Alternative Fuels Data Center, 2007, http://www.eere.energy.gov/afdc/pdfs/afv_info.pdf (accessed June 4, 2007)

invest billions of dollars in the internal combustion engine. It has taken a century, but the EV has returned.

The primary difficulty with EVs lies in inadequate battery power. The cars have a range of seventy to one hundred miles on a single charge and must be recharged often. In addition, EVs are expensive. Despite their high price, EVs have many advantages, including low noise, simple design and operation, and low service and maintenance costs. Over time the cost gap between cars that pollute and EVs that do not will narrow. With advances in battery development, the gap could close entirely.

HYDROGEN-FUELED VEHICLES ON THE HORIZON. Hydrogen is the simplest naturally occurring element and can be found in materials such as water, natural gas, and coal. For decades advocates of hydrogen have promoted it as the fuel of the future because it is abundant, clean, and cheap. Hydrogen researchers from universities, laboratories, and private companies claim that their industry has already produced vehicles that could be ready for consumers if problems of fuel supply and distribution could be solved. Other experts contend that economics and safety concerns will limit hydrogen's wider use for decades.

In 2002 the DOE formed a government-industry partnership called Freedom Cooperative Automotive Research (FreedomCAR). The goal of FreedomCAR is to develop highly fuel-efficient vehicles that operate using hydrogen produced from renewable energy sources. Industrial partners in the venture include Ford, General Motors, and Chrysler. FreedomCAR research takes place at facilities operated by the DOE's National Renewable Energy Laboratory in Golden, Colorado.

In his 2003 State of the Union Address (January 28, 2003, http://www.whitehouse.gov/news/releases/2003/01/20030128-19.html), President Bush announced the creation of the Hydrogen Fuel Initiative (HFI). This $1.2 billion program is designed to develop the technology needed for commercially viable hydrogen-powered fuel cells by 2020. Fuel cells designed for transportation vehicles and home/business use are to be developed. The HFI has three primary missions as part of its goals:

- Lower the cost of hydrogen production to make it cost effective with gasoline production by 2010

- Develop hydrogen fuel cells that provide the same vehicle range (at least three hundred miles of travel) as conventional gasoline fuel tanks

- Lower the cost of hydrogen fuel cells to be comparable in cost with internal combustion engines

The DOE predicts that hydrogen fuel cell vehicles will reach the mass consumer market by 2020.

ADVANCED TECHNOLOGY VEHICLES (HYBRIDS). Many experts believe that the most feasible solution in the near future is to produce vehicles that use a combination of gasoline and one of the alternative fuel sources. These are called advanced technology vehicles or hybrid vehicles. Figure 2.15 depicts a hybrid automobile that relies on a small internal combustion engine and electricity (from batteries).

Table 2.8 provides information about 2007 model year hybrid vehicles for sale in the United States as of June 2007. Manufacturers continue research on hybrid cars, which they hope will eventually satisfy American tastes and pocketbooks and provide even greater fuel efficiency.

The EPA's "Green Vehicle Guide"

The EPA, in the "Green Vehicle Guide" (May 24, 2007, http://www.epa.gov/greenvehicles/index.htm), provides a database of emission information about thousands of vehicles (cars, light trucks, SUVs, and minivans) from domestic and foreign manufacturers for model years dating back to 2000. For each model users can obtain two scores compiled by the EPA: an air pollution score and a greenhouse gas score. The air pollution score reflects the presence in exhaust emissions of pollutants that cause health problems and smog formation. Scores range from zero to ten, where ten is the best score, having zero emissions. The air pollution scores are tied to the EPA Tier II and California LEV II emissions standards. The greenhouse gas score provides a relative rating of the exhaust emissions of carbon dioxide, a primary contributor to the enhanced greenhouse effect associated with global warming. The score ranges from zero to ten, where ten is the best score. The score is calculated based on a vehicle's fuel economy (miles per gallon of fuel) and fuel type (gasoline, diesel, ethanol blend, etc.). Models that

FIGURE 2.15

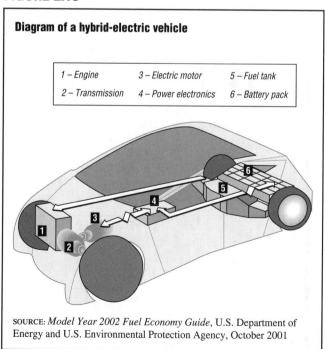

Diagram of a hybrid-electric vehicle

| 1 – Engine | 3 – Electric motor | 5 – Fuel tank |
| 2 – Transmission | 4 – Power electronics | 6 – Battery pack |

SOURCE: *Model Year 2002 Fuel Economy Guide*, U.S. Department of Energy and U.S. Environmental Protection Agency, October 2001

TABLE 2.8

Hybrid electric vehicles available for sale to the public, model year 2007

Manufacturer	Model	Vehicle body	Emission certification standard	Fuel economy (city)	Fuel economy (highway)
Toyota	Prius	Sedan	SULEV and AT PZEV and Tier 2, Bin 3	60 mpg	51 mpg
Honda	Civic	Sedan	SULEV and AT PZEV	49 mpg	51 mpg
Toyota	Camry	Sedan	AT PZEV	40 mpg	38 mpg
Ford Motor Company	Escape Hybrid	SUV	SULEV and AT PZEV	36 mpg	31 mpg
Ford Motor Company	Mercury Mariner	SUV	SULEV and ATPZEV	33 mpg	29 mpg
Toyota	Highlander	SUV	SULEV and AT PZEV	31 mpg	27 mpg
Toyota	Lexus RX 400h	SUV	SULEV	31 mpg	27 mpg
Honda	Accord	Sedan	SULEV and AT PZEV	28 mpg	35 mpg
General Motors-Saturn	VUE Green Line	SUV	ULEV and Tier 2, Bin 5	27 mpg	32 mpg
Toyota	Lexus GS 450h	Sedan	SULEV	25 mpg	28 mpg
Nissan	Altima	Sedan	AT PZEV	N/A	N/A

Notes: SULEV=Super ultra low emission vehicle. ULEV=Ultra low emission vehicle. ZEV=Zero emission vehicle. PZEV=Partial zero emission vechicle. AT PZEV=Advanced technology partial zero emission vechicle.

SOURCE: Adapted from "Model Year 2007: Alternative Fuel Vehicles and Advanced Technology Vehicles," in *Current Model Listing*, U.S. Department of Energy, Alternative Fuels Data Center, August 24, 2006, http://www.eere.energy.gov/afdc/pdfs/my2007_afv_atv.pdf (accessed June 19, 2007)

achieve scores of at least six in both tests receive the EPA's Smartway rating. Those that score nine or above in both tests are deemed Smartway Elite vehicles. According to the EPA (May 18, 2007, http://epa.gov/greenvehicles/all-rank-07.htm), only six 2007 models achieved Smartway Elite status: Toyota Prius Hybrid, Honda Civic Hybrid, Nissan Altima Hybrid, Toyota Camry Hybrid, Ford Escape Hybrid, and Honda Civic (compressed natural gas fuel).

THE CAA—A HUGE SUCCESS

In 1970 Congress passed the landmark CAA, proclaiming that it would restore urban air quality. It was no coincidence that the law was passed during a fourteen-day Washington, D.C., smog alert. The act was amended several times over the following decades, including a massive overhaul in 1990 resulting in the CAAA. Even though the act has had mixed results, and many goals remain to be met, most experts credit it with making great strides toward cleaning up the air.

In *The Benefits and Costs of the Clean Air Act, 1970 to 1990* (October 1997, http://www.epa.gov/oar/sect812/copy .html), the first report mandated by the CAA on the monetary costs and benefits of controlling pollution, the EPA concludes that the economic value of clean air programs is forty-two times greater than the total costs of air pollution control during the twenty-year period. The study finds that many positive consequences occurred in the U.S. economy because of CAA programs and regulations. The CAA affected industrial production, investment, productivity, consumption, employment, and economic growth. In fact, the study estimates that total agricultural benefits from the CAA were almost $10 billion. The EPA compares benefits with direct costs or expenditures. The total costs of the CAA

were $523 billion for the twenty-year period; total benefits equaled $22.2 trillion—a net benefit of approximately $21.7 trillion.

According to *The Benefits and Costs of the Clean Air Act Amendments of 1990* (November 1999, http://www .epa.gov/oar/sect812/1990-2010/fullrept.pdf), the second mandated review of the CAA and the most comprehensive and thorough review ever conducted, the act produced major reductions in pollution that causes illness and disease, smog, acid rain, haze, and damage to the environment. Using a sophisticated array of computer models and the latest cost data, the EPA finds that by 2010 the act will have prevented twenty-three thousand Americans from dying prematurely and averted more than 1.7 million asthma attacks. The CAA will prevent forty-seven thousand episodes of acute bronchitis, ninety-one thousand occurrences of shortness of breath, 4.1 million lost work days, and thirty-one million days in which Americans would have had to restrict activity because of illness. Another twenty-two thousand respiratory-related hospital admissions will be averted, as well as forty-two thousand admissions for heart disease and forty-eight hundred emergency room visits for asthma.

The EPA estimates that the benefits of CAA programs in the reduction of illness and premature death alone will total about $110 billion. By contrast, the study finds that the cost of achieving these benefits is only about $27 billion, which is a fraction of the value of the benefits. In addition, the study reports that there are other benefits that scientists and economists cannot quantify and express in monetary terms, such as controlling cancer-causing air toxins and bringing benefits to crops and ecosystems by reducing pollutants.

At the same time, many cities are still not in compliance with the law. One reason efforts to clean the air have been only partly successful is that they have focused on specific measures to combat individual pollutants rather than addressing the underlying social and economic structures that create the problem—for example, the distance between many Americans' residences and their places of work.

PUBLIC OPINION ABOUT AIR POLLUTION

Every year the Gallup Organization conducts a poll on the environment around the time of the nation's celebration of Earth Day. In *Environment* (2007, http://www.gallup poll.com/content/?ci=1615&pg=1), poll participants were asked about their level of concern related to particular environmental problems. (See Table 2.9.) The results show that in March 2004, 46% of those asked expressed a great deal of concern about air pollution, compared with 33% who expressed a fair amount of concern. Another 15% indicated a little concern, and 5% expressed no concern.

The percentage of poll respondents indicating a great deal of concern about air pollution has dropped dramatically in recent years from a high of 63% in 1989. During the 2007 poll Gallup also asked people their opinion about some specific environmental proposals. The results indicated that 86% of those asked favored government spending to develop alternative fuel sources for automo-

biles and 79% favored setting higher emissions standards for automobiles.

TABLE 2.9

Public concern about air pollution, 1989–2007

	Great deal	Fair amount	Only a little	Not at all	No opinion
	%	%	%	%	%
2007 Mar 11–14	46	33	15	5	*
2006 Mar 13–16	44	34	15	7	*
2004 Mar 8–11	39	30	23	8	*
2003 Mar 3–5	42	32	20	6	*
2002 Mar 4–7	45	33	18	4	*
2001 Mar 5–7	48	34	14	4	*
2000 Apr 3–9	59	29	9	3	*
1999 Apr 13–14	52	35	10	3	*
1999 Mar 12–14	47	33	16	4	*
1997 Oct 27–28	42	34	18	5	1
1991 Apr 11–14	59	28	10	4	*
1990 Apr 5–8	58	29	9	4	*
1989 May 4–7	63	24	8	4	*

*Less than 0.5%.

SOURCE: "I'm going to read you a list of environmental problems. As I read each one, please tell me if you personally worry about this problem a great deal, a fair amount, only a little, or not at all. First, how much do you personally worry about—Air Pollution," in *Environment*, The Gallup Organization, 2007, http://www.galluppoll.com/content/?ci=1615&pg=1 (accessed June 19, 2007). Copyright © 2007 by The Gallup Organization. Reproduced by permission of The Gallup Organization.

CHAPTER 3
THE ENHANCED GREENHOUSE EFFECT AND GLOBAL WARMING

WHAT IS CLIMATE?

Climate and weather are not the same thing. Both describe conditions in the lower atmosphere—for example, wet or dry, cold or warm, stormy or fair, and cloudy or clear. Weather is the short-term local state of the atmosphere. Weather conditions can change from moment to moment and can differ in two places that are relatively close together. Climate describes the average pattern of weather conditions experienced by a region over a long period. For example, Florida has a warm climate but can experience days and even weeks of cold weather.

Earth's climate as a whole has not changed much for a few thousand years. In general, most of the planet has been warm enough for humans, animals, and plants to thrive. This was not so in the distant past, when the climate fluctuated between long periods of cold and warmth, each lasting for many thousands of years. Scientists are not sure what triggered these major climate changes. A variety of factors are believed to be involved, including movement of the tectonic plates, changes in Earth's orbit around the sun, and variations in atmospheric gases.

Scientists believe that the last ice age occurred about eighteen thousand years ago. During this period ice sheets and glaciers spread to cover vast regions of the Earth, including most of North America and Europe.

Earth's temperature depends on a delicate balance of energy inputs and outputs, chemical processes, and physical phenomena. As shown in Figure 3.1, solar radiation passes through Earth's atmosphere and warms the Earth. The Earth emits infrared radiation. Some outgoing infrared radiation is not allowed to escape into outer space but is trapped beneath the atmosphere. The amount of energy that is trapped depends on many variables. One major factor is atmospheric composition. Some gases, such as water vapor, carbon dioxide, and methane, act to trap heat beneath the atmosphere in the same way that glass panels trap heat in a greenhouse. The panels allow sunlight into the greenhouse, but prevent heat from escaping.

Earth's surface temperature is about sixty degrees Fahrenheit warmer than it would be if natural greenhouse gases were not present. Without this natural warming process, Earth would be much colder and could not sustain life as it now exists.

It is necessary, however, to distinguish between the "natural" and an "enhanced" greenhouse effect. The natural greenhouse effect provides a warm atmosphere for Earth that is necessary for life. The theory behind the enhanced greenhouse effect is that human activities can load the atmosphere with too much carbon dioxide and other heat-trapping gases. This could increase Earth's temperature above that expected from the natural greenhouse effect, an effect known as global warming. Such a temperature increase would be accompanied by major climatic changes.

The primary human activities linked to the enhanced greenhouse effect are the burning of fossil fuels (mainly coal and oil) and their derivatives (such as gasoline), and destruction of large amounts of vegetation that normally absorb carbon dioxide. (See Figure 3.2.)

GREENHOUSE GASES

Greenhouse gases are gases in the atmosphere that allow shortwave radiation (sunlight) from the sun to pass through to the Earth but absorb and reradiate long wave infrared radiation (heat) coming from the Earth's surface. This process serves to warm the lower atmosphere (the troposphere). The troposphere extends from the Earth's surface to approximately eight miles above the surface, as shown in Figure 3.3.

FIGURE 3.1

Role of radiation in greenhouse effect

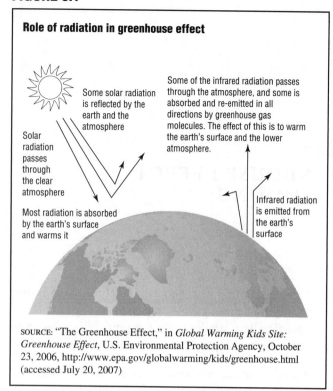

SOURCE: "The Greenhouse Effect," in *Global Warming Kids Site: Greenhouse Effect*, U.S. Environmental Protection Agency, October 23, 2006, http://www.epa.gov/globalwarming/kids/greenhouse.html (accessed July 20, 2007)

Water Vapor

Scientists know that water vapor is the most prevalent greenhouse gas in the atmosphere. According to the National Safety Council's Environmental Health Center, in "A 'Wet Blanket' Greenhouse Gas" (January 24, 2000, http://www.nsc.org/EHC/climate/ccucla6.htm), water vapor makes up as much as 2% of the atmosphere and is responsible for approximately two-thirds of the natural greenhouse effect. Scientists believe, however, that humans have little to no influence on the amount of water vapor in the atmosphere. Water vapor is part of the natural water cycle that takes place on and around the Earth. Water evaporates from the surface, condenses into clouds, and then returns to the surface as precipitation. The water cycle is also a heat cycle, transferring heat around the Earth and back and forth between the surface and the atmosphere. Water vapor cycles quickly through the atmosphere, lingering for a few days at most.

Carbon Dioxide

Carbon dioxide (CO_2) is a heavy colorless gas that, according to the Environmental Health Center, makes up approximately 0.037% of the atmosphere. CO_2 is a respiration product from all living things (plants, animals, and humans). It is also released during the decay or combustion of organic materials. Huge amounts of CO_2 are cycled back and forth between the oceans and the atmosphere. Likewise, vegetation absorbs CO_2 from the air. The result of all these processes is a global carbon cycle that maintains CO_2 at suitable levels in the atmosphere to sustain a natural greenhouse effect.

Before the 1800s humans had little impact on atmospheric CO_2 levels. The Industrial Revolution ushered in widespread use of fossil fuels, primarily coal, oil, and natural gas. Combustion of these carbon-loaded fuels releases large amounts of CO_2. The burning of fossil

FIGURE 3.2

Greenhouse effect

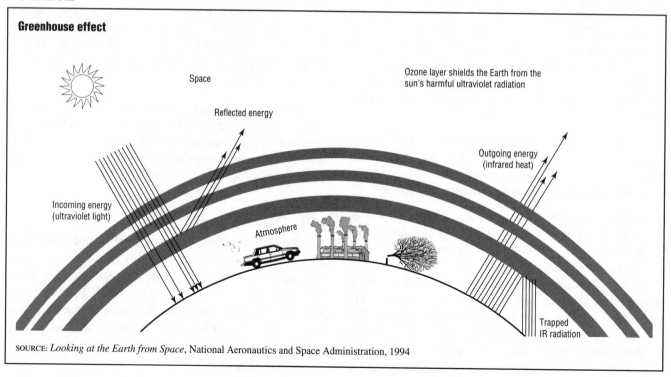

SOURCE: *Looking at the Earth from Space*, National Aeronautics and Space Administration, 1994

FIGURE 3.3

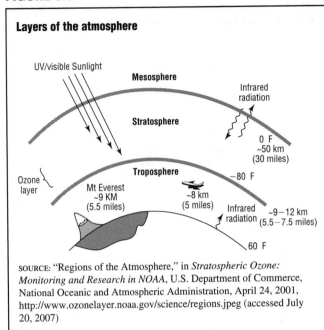

Layers of the atmosphere

UV/visible Sunlight

Mesosphere

Infrared radiation

Stratosphere

0 F ~50 km (30 miles)

Troposphere

−80 F

Ozone layer

Mt Everest ~9 KM (5.5 miles)

~8 km (5 miles)

Infrared radiation

~9−12 km (5.5−7.5 miles)

60 F

SOURCE: "Regions of the Atmosphere," in *Stratospheric Ozone: Monitoring and Research in NOAA*, U.S. Department of Commerce, National Oceanic and Atmospheric Administration, April 24, 2001, http://www.ozonelayer.noaa.gov/science/regions.jpeg (accessed July 20, 2007)

kets for beef and milk products are driving a booming livestock business.

Humans contribute to atmospheric methane levels through activities that concentrate and magnify biological decomposition. This includes landfilling organic materials, raising livestock, cultivating rice in paddies, collecting sewage for treatment, and constructing artificial wetlands. In addition, methane is a by-product of the combustion of biomass and is vented (intentionally and unintentionally) during the extraction and processing of fossil fuels. It also results from incomplete combustion of fossil fuels. Methane is believed to break down in the atmosphere after approximately nine to fifteen years.

Ozone

Ozone (O_3) is a blue-tinted gas naturally found in Earth's atmosphere. In *Reporting and Climate Change: Understanding the Science* (June 2000, http://www.nsc.org/ EHC/guidebks/climtoc.htm), the National Safety Council's Environmental Health Center notes that approximately 90% of the ozone is in the stratosphere, the atmospheric layer lying above the troposphere. The so-called ozone layer absorbs harmful ultraviolet radiation from the sun to prevent it from reaching the ground. Scientists believe that stratospheric ozone is being depleted by the introduction of certain industrial chemicals, primarily chlorine and bromine. This depletion has serious consequences in terms of ultraviolet radiation effects and probably lessens the warmth-trapping capability of ozone at this level.

Tropospheric ozone is the primary component in smog, a potent air pollutant. It is not emitted directly into the air but forms because of complex reactions that occur when other air pollutants, primarily volatile organic compounds and nitrogen oxides, are present. The primary sources of these ozone precursors include industrial chemical processes and fossil fuel combustion. The atmospheric lifetime of ozone ranges from weeks to months.

Nitrous Oxide

Nitrous oxide (N_2O) is a colorless gas found in trace amounts in the atmosphere. Soils naturally release the gas as a result of bacterial processes called nitrification and denitrification. Soils found in tropical areas and moist forests are believed to be the largest contributors. Oxygen-poor waters and sediments in oceans and estuaries are also natural sources. Even though nitrous oxide makes up a much smaller portion of greenhouse gases than CO_2, it is much more (perhaps 310 times more) powerful than CO_2 at trapping heat. Agriculture is and has been the major source of nitrous oxide emissions in the United States, followed by energy and industrial sources. As shown in Table 3.1, agricultural soil management accounted for 365.1 teragrams (or 78%) of total nitrous oxide emissions during 2005.

fuels by industry and motor vehicles is, by far, the leading source of CO_2 emissions in the United States, accounting for 5,751.2 teragrams (or 94%) of the nation's emission of greenhouse gases in 2005. (See Table 3.1.) Other anthropogenic (human-caused) sources include deforestation, burning of biomass (combustible organic materials, such as wood scraps and crop residues), and certain industrial processes. The atmospheric lifetime (how long a gas stays in the atmosphere) of CO_2 is estimated to be fifty to two hundred years.

Methane

Methane (CH_4) is a colorless gas found in trace (extremely small) amounts in the atmosphere. It is the primary component of natural gas—the gas trapped beneath the Earth's crust that is mined and burned for energy. Methane is an important component of greenhouse emissions, second only to CO_2. (See Figure 3.4.) Even though there is less methane in the atmosphere, scientists believe that it may be much more effective at trapping heat in the atmosphere than CO_2. During the 1900s methane's concentration in the atmosphere more than doubled. Scientists generally attribute these increases to human sources, such as landfills, natural gas systems, agricultural activities, coal mining, and wastewater treatment.

As shown in Table 3.1, methane emissions from landfills, enteric fermentation, and natural gas systems accounted for 356.2 teragrams (or 66%) of total U.S. emissions in 2005. Enteric fermentation is a natural digestive process that occurs in domestic animals, such as cattle and sheep, and releases methane. Growing mar-

TABLE 3.1

Trends in U.S. greenhouse gas emissions and sinks, in teragrams of carbon dioxide equivalents, selected years 1990–2005

[Teragrams CO_2 equivalent]

Gas/source	1990	1995	2000	2001	2002	2003	2004	2005
CO_2	**5,061.6**	**5,384.6**	**5,940.0**	**5,843.0**	**5,892.7**	**5,952.5**	**6,064.3**	**6,089.5**
Fossil fuel combustion	4,724.1	5,030.0	5,584.9	5,511.7	5,557.2	5,624.5	5,713.0	5,751.2
Non-energy use of fuels	117.3	133.2	141.0	131.4	135.3	131.3	150.2	142.4
Cement manufacture	33.3	36.8	41.2	41.4	42.9	43.1	45.6	45.9
Iron and steel production	84.9	73.3	65.1	57.9	54.6	53.4	51.3	45.2
Natural gas systems	33.7	33.8	29.4	28.8	29.6	28.4	28.2	28.2
Municipal solid waste combustion	10.9	15.7	17.9	18.3	18.5	19.5	20.1	20.9
Ammonia production and urea application	19.3	20.5	19.6	16.7	17.8	16.2	16.9	16.3
Lime manufacture	11.3	12.8	13.3	12.9	12.3	13.0	13.7	13.7
Limestone and dolomite use	5.5	7.4	6.0	5.7	5.9	4.7	6.7	7.4
Soda ash manufacture and consumption	4.1	4.3	4.2	4.1	4.1	4.1	4.2	4.2
Aluminum production	6.8	5.7	6.1	4.4	4.5	4.5	4.2	4.2
Petrochemical production	2.2	2.8	3.0	2.8	2.9	2.8	2.9	2.9
Titanium dioxide production	1.3	1.7	1.9	1.9	2.0	2.0	2.3	1.9
Ferroalloy production	2.2	2.0	1.9	1.5	1.3	1.3	1.4	1.4
Phosphoric acid production	1.5	1.5	1.4	1.3	1.3	1.3	1.4	1.4
CO_2 consumption	1.4	1.4	1.4	0.8	1.0	1.3	1.2	1.3
Zinc production	0.9	1.0	1.1	1.0	0.9	0.5	0.5	0.5
Lead production	0.3	0.3	0.3	0.3	0.3	0.3	0.3	0.3
Silicon carbide production and consumption	0.4	0.3	0.2	0.2	0.2	0.2	0.2	0.2
Land-use change and forestry (sink)[a]	*(712.8)*	*(828.8)*	*(756.7)*	*(767.5)*	*(811.9)*	*(811.9)*	*(824.8)*	*(828.5)*
International bunker fuels[b]	*113.7*	*100.6*	*101.1*	*97.6*	*89.1*	*83.7*	*97.2*	*97.2*
Wood biomass and ethanol consumption[b]	*219.3*	*236.8*	*228.3*	*203.2*	*204.4*	*209.6*	*224.8*	*206.5*
CH_4	**609.1**	**598.7**	**563.7**	**547.7**	**549.7**	**549.2**	**540.3**	**539.3**
Landfills	161.0	157.1	131.9	127.6	130.4	134.9	132.1	132.0
Enteric fermentation	115.7	120.6	113.5	112.5	112.6	113.0	110.5	112.1
Natural gas systems	124.5	128.1	126.6	125.4	125.0	123.7	119.0	111.1
Coal mining	81.9	66.5	55.9	55.5	52.0	52.1	54.5	52.4
Manure management	30.9	35.1	38.7	40.1	41.1	40.5	39.7	41.3
Petroleum systems	34.4	31.1	27.8	27.4	26.8	25.8	25.4	28.5
Wastewater treatment	24.8	25.1	26.4	25.9	25.8	25.6	25.7	25.4
Forest land remaining forest land	7.1	4.0	14.0	6.0	10.4	8.1	6.9	11.6
Stationary combustion	8.0	7.8	7.4	6.8	6.8	7.0	7.1	6.9
Rice cultivation	7.1	7.6	7.5	7.6	6.8	6.9	7.6	6.9
Abandoned coal mines	6.0	8.2	7.3	6.7	6.1	5.9	5.8	5.5
Mobile combustion	4.7	4.3	3.5	3.2	3.1	2.9	2.8	2.6
Petrochemical production	0.9	1.1	1.2	1.1	1.1	1.1	1.2	1.1
Iron and steel production	1.3	1.3	1.2	1.1	1.0	1.0	1.0	1.0
Field burning of agricultural residues	0.7	0.7	0.8	0.8	0.7	0.8	0.9	0.9
Ferroalloy production	+	+	+	+	+	+	+	+
Silicon carbide production and consumption	+	+	+	+	+	+	+	+
International bunker fuels[b]	*0.2*	*0.1*	*0.1*	*0.1*	*0.1*	*0.1*	*0.1*	*0.1*
N_2O	**482.0**	**484.2**	**499.8**	**502.5**	**479.2**	**459.8**	**445.2**	**468.6**
Agricultural soil management	366.9	353.4	376.8	389.0	366.1	350.2	338.8	365.1
Mobile combustion	43.7	53.7	53.2	49.7	47.1	43.8	41.2	38.0
Nitric acid production	17.8	19.9	19.6	15.9	17.2	16.7	16.0	15.7
Stationary combustion	12.3	12.8	14.0	13.5	13.4	13.7	13.9	13.8
Manure management	8.6	9.0	9.6	9.8	9.7	9.3	9.4	9.5
Wastewater treatment	6.4	6.9	7.6	7.6	7.7	7.8	7.9	8.0
Adipic acid production	15.2	17.2	6.0	4.9	5.9	6.2	5.7	6.0
Settlements remaining settlements	5.1	5.5	5.6	5.5	5.6	5.8	6.0	5.8

Humans have significantly increased the release of nitrous oxide from soils through use of nitrogen-rich fertilizers. Other anthropogenic sources include combustion of fossil fuels and biomass, wastewater treatment, and certain manufacturing processes, particularly the production of nylon and nitric acid. Nitrous oxide has an atmospheric lifetime of approximately 120 years.

Engineered Gases

Engineered gases are synthetic gases specially designed for modern industrial and commercial purposes.

TABLE 3.1

Trends in U.S. greenhouse gas emissions and sinks, in teragrams of carbon dioxide equivalents, selected years 1990–2005 [CONTINUED]

N₂O product usage	4.3	4.5	4.8	4.8	4.3	4.3	4.3	4.3
Forest land remaining forest land	0.8	0.6	1.7	1.0	1.4	1.2	1.1	1.5
Field burning of agricultural residues	0.4	0.4	0.5	0.5	0.4	0.4	0.5	0.5
Municipal solid waste combustion	0.5	0.5	0.4	0.4	0.4	0.4	0.4	0.4
International bunker fuels[b]	*1.0*	*0.9*	*0.9*	*0.9*	*0.8*	*0.8*	*0.9*	*0.9*
HFCs, PFCs, and SF₆	**89.3**	**103.5**	**143.8**	**133.8**	**143.0**	**142.7**	**153.9**	**163.0**
Substitution of ozone-depleting substances	0.3	32.2	80.9	88.6	96.9	105.5	114.5	123.3
HCFC-22 production	35.0	27.0	29.8	19.8	19.8	12.3	15.6	16.5
Electrical transmission and distribution	27.1	21.8	15.2	15.1	14.3	13.8	13.6	13.2
Semiconductor manufacture	2.9	5.0	6.3	4.5	4.4	4.3	4.7	4.3
Aluminum production	18.5	11.8	8.6	3.5	5.2	3.8	2.8	3.0
Magnesium production and processing	5.4	5.6	2.4	2.4	2.9	2.6	2.7	
		3.0						
Total	**6,242.0**	**6,571.0**	**7,147.2**	**7,027.0**	**7,064.6**	**7,104.2**	**7,203.7**	**7,260.4**
Net emissions (sources and sinks)	**5,529.2**	**5,742.2**	**6,390.5**	**6,259.5**	**6,252.7**	**6,292.3**	**6,378.9**	**6,431.9**

+Does not exceed 0.05 Tg CO₂ Eq.
[a]Parentheses indicate negative values or sequestration. The net CO₂ flux total includes both emissions and sequestration, and constitutes a sink in the United States. Sinks are only included in net emissions total.
[b]Emissions from International bunker fuels and biomass combustion are not included in totals.
Notes:
Totals may not sum due to independent rounding
CO₂=Carbon dioxide
CH₄=Methane
N₂O=Nitrogen oxides
HFCs=Hydrofluorocarbons
PFCs=perfluorocarbons
SF₆=Sulfur hexafluoride

SOURCE: "Table ES-2. Recent Trends in U.S. Greenhouse Gas Emissions and Sinks," in *Inventory of U.S. Greenhouse Gas Emissions and Sinks: 1990–2005*, U.S. Environmental Protection Agency, April 2007, http://www.epa.gov/climatechange/emissions/downloads06/07ES.pdf (accessed June 19, 2007)

FIGURE 3.4

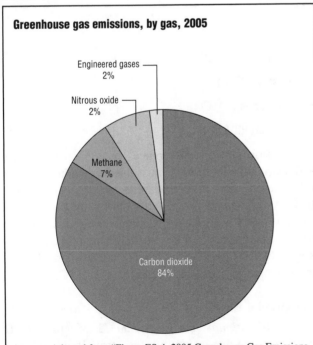

Greenhouse gas emissions, by gas, 2005

Engineered gases 2%
Nitrous oxide 2%
Methane 7%
Carbon dioxide 84%

SOURCE: Adapted from "Figure ES-4. 2005 Greenhouse Gas Emissions by Gas," in *Inventory of U.S. Greenhouse Gas Emissions and Sinks: 1990–2005*, U.S. Environmental Protection Agency, April 2007, http://www.epa.gov/climatechange/emissions/downloads06/07ES.pdf (accessed June 19, 2007)

They are also known as "high GWP gases," because they have a high global warming potential when compared with CO₂. They include hydrofluorocarbons (HFCs), perfluorocarbons (PFCs), and sulfur hexafluoride (SF₆).

HFCs are chemicals that contain hydrogen, fluorine, and carbon. They are popular substitutes in industrial applications for chlorofluorocarbons (CFCs). CFCs are commonly used in cooling equipment, fire extinguishers, as propellants, and for other uses. They are one of the culprits blamed for the depletion of stratospheric ozone.

PFCs are a class of chemicals containing fluorine and carbon. They are also increasingly used by industry as substitutes for ozone-depleting CFCs. SF₆ is a colorless, odorless gas commonly used as an insulating medium in electrical equipment and as an etchant (an etching agent) in the semiconductor industry.

Even though emissions of these chemicals are small in comparison with other greenhouse gases, they are of particular concern because of their long life in the atmosphere. PFCs and SF₆ have atmospheric lifetimes of thousands of years and are actually far more potent greenhouse gases than CO₂ per unit of molecular weight.

FIGURE 3.5

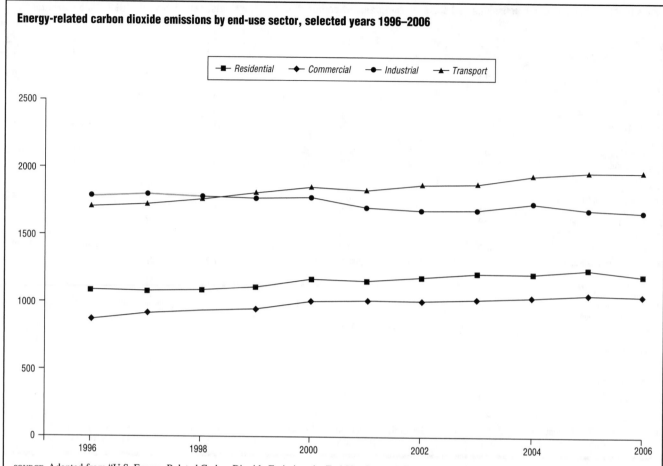

Energy-related carbon dioxide emissions by end-use sector, selected years 1996–2006

SOURCE: Adapted from "U.S. Energy-Related Carbon Dioxide Emissions by End-Use Sector (Million Metric Tons Carbon Dioxide)," in *U.S. Carbon Dioxide Emissions from Energy Sources: 2006 Flash Estimate*, U.S. Department of Energy, Energy Information Administration, May 2007, http://www.eia.doe.gov/oiaf/1605/flash/pdf/flash.pdf (accessed July 19, 2007)

Indirect Greenhouse Gases

There are several gases considered indirect greenhouse gases because of their effects on the chemical environment of the atmosphere. These gases include reactive nitrogen oxides, carbon monoxide, and volatile organic compounds. Most of their emissions are from anthropogenic sources, primarily combustion and industrial processes.

U.S. Greenhouse Gases and Sources

The U.S. Environmental Protection Agency (EPA) reports that CO_2 accounted for 84% of greenhouse gas emissions in the United States in 2005. (See Figure 3.4.) Methane was second with 7% of the total, followed by nitrous oxide with 7% and other greenhouse gases, such as HFCs, PFCs, and SF_6, with 2%.

Figure 3.5 shows the major U.S. sectors that have produced energy-related emissions of CO_2 since 1996. In *Inventory of U.S. Greenhouse Gas Emissions and Sinks: 1990–2005* (April 2007, http://www.epa.gov/climatechange/emissions/downloads06/07CR.pdf), the EPA reports that the contributions of these major sectors in 2005 were:

- Transportation (33%)
- Industry (27%)
- Residences (21%)
- Commercial (18%)

Emissions from most sources have increased since 1996. During the late 1990s emissions from industry began to decline and continued that trend into the early 2000s. The EPA attributes the decline to a shift in the overall U.S. economy from a focus on manufacturing industries to service-based businesses. Residential emissions are mainly because of CO_2 generated from the combustion of fossil fuels (such as oil) for heating purposes.

International Emissions of Greenhouse Gases

In *International Energy Annual 2004* (July 2006, http://www.eia.doe.gov/pub/international/iealf/tableh1co2.xls), the Energy Information Administration presents data collected on CO_2 emissions related to fossil fuel use around the world. As shown in Figure 3.6, the United States was responsible for the largest portion (23%) of

FIGURE 3.6

World carbon dioxide emissions from the consumption and flaring of fossil fuels, 2004

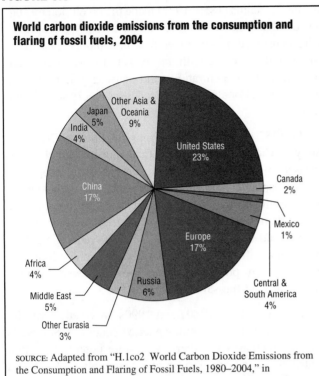

SOURCE: Adapted from "H.1co2 World Carbon Dioxide Emissions from the Consumption and Flaring of Fossil Fuels, 1980–2004," in *International Energy Annual 2004*, U.S. Department of Energy, Energy Information Administration, July 2006, http://www.eia.doe.gov/pub/international/iealf/tableh1co2.xls (accessed July 20, 2007)

FIGURE 3.7

Average annual growth predicted for energy-related carbon dioxide emissions in Organization for Economic Cooperation and Development economies, 2004–30

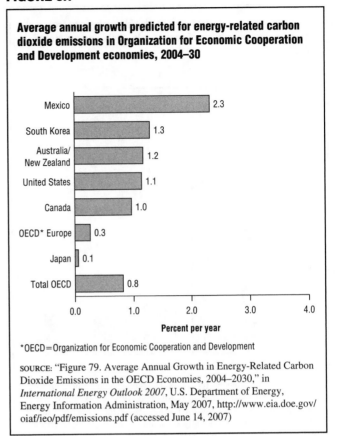

*OECD=Organization for Economic Cooperation and Development

SOURCE: "Figure 79. Average Annual Growth in Energy-Related Carbon Dioxide Emissions in the OECD Economies, 2004–2030," in *International Energy Outlook 2007*, U.S. Department of Energy, Energy Information Administration, May 2007, http://www.eia.doe.gov/oiaf/ieo/pdf/emissions.pdf (accessed June 14, 2007)

such emissions in 2004, followed by Europe (17%) and China (17%). The five countries with the largest CO_2 emissions in 2004 in units of million metric tons were:

- United States, 5,912
- China, 4,707
- Russia, 1,684
- Japan, 1,262
- India, 1,112

In its energy and emissions analyses the U.S. Department of Energy (DOE) assesses countries based on whether or not they are members of the Organization for Economic Cooperation and Development (OECD). The OECD was founded in 1961 and is an international organization of democratic countries with free market economies (such as the United States). OECD countries are developed nations characterized by mature economies and industries and relatively slow rates of growth in population and fuel usage. Non-OECD countries include developing nations in which population, industrial base, and fuel usage are growing quickly. Examples include China, India, Russia, and most other areas of Central and South America, Asia, the Middle East, and Africa.

As shown in Figure 3.7 and Figure 3.8, non-OECD economies are expected to experience the highest average annual growth in energy-related CO_2 emissions between

FIGURE 3.8

Average annual growth predicted for energy-related carbon dioxide emissions in non–Organization for Economic Cooperation and Development economies, 2004–30

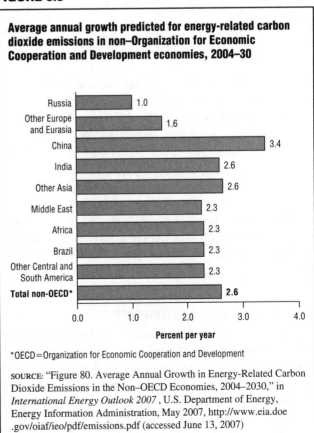

*OECD=Organization for Economic Cooperation and Development

SOURCE: "Figure 80. Average Annual Growth in Energy-Related Carbon Dioxide Emissions in the Non–OECD Economies, 2004–2030," in *International Energy Outlook 2007*, U.S. Department of Energy, Energy Information Administration, May 2007, http://www.eia.doe.gov/oiaf/ieo/pdf/emissions.pdf (accessed June 13, 2007)

FIGURE 3.9

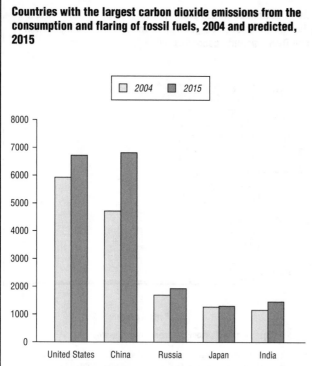

Countries with the largest carbon dioxide emissions from the consumption and flaring of fossil fuels, 2004 and predicted, 2015

☐ 2004   ■ 2015

SOURCE: Adapted from "H.1co2 World Carbon Dioxide Emissions from the Consumption and Flaring of Fossil Fuels, 1980–2004," in *International Energy Annual 2004*, U.S. Department of Energy, Energy Information Administration, July 2006, http://www.eia.doe.gov/pub/international/iealf/tableh1co2.xls (accessed June 19, 2007) and "Figure 80. Average Annual Growth in Energy-Related Carbon Dioxide Emissions in the Non-OECD Economies, 2004–2030," in *International Energy Outlook 2007*, U.S. Department of Energy, Energy Information Administration, May 2007, http://www.eia.doe.gov/oiaf/ieo/pdf/emissions.pdf (accessed July 19, 2007)

2004 and 2030. U.S. CO_2 emissions are expected to grow at a relatively low rate of 1.1% per year over this period. By comparison, China's average CO_2 emissions are predicted to increase by 3.4% annually and India's by 2.6% annually. At these rates China's CO_2 emissions will surpass those of the United States by 2015. (See Figure 3.9.) China and other developing nations are heavily reliant on coal to fuel their industrial development and electricity production, whereas developed nations, such as the United States, rely more on cleaner burning fuels such as natural gas. Environmentalism as a social and political force is also much more mature in developed nations.

CHANGES IN THE ATMOSPHERE

Earth's atmosphere was first compared to a glass vessel in 1827 by the French mathematician Jean-Baptiste Fourier (1768–1830). In the 1850s the British physicist John Tyndall (1820–1893) tried to measure the heat-trapping properties of various components of the atmosphere. By the 1890s scientists had concluded that the great increase in combustion in the Industrial Revolution had the potential to change

the atmosphere's load of CO_2. In 1896 the Swedish chemist Svante Arrhenius (1859–1927) made the revolutionary suggestion that human activities could actually disrupt this delicate balance. He theorized that the rapid increase in the use of coal that came with the Industrial Revolution could increase CO_2 concentrations and cause a gradual rise in temperatures. For almost six decades his theory stirred little interest.

In 1957 studies at the Scripps Institute of Oceanography in California suggested that, indeed, half the CO_2 released by industry was being permanently trapped in the atmosphere. The studies showed that atmospheric concentrations of CO_2 in the previous thirty years were greater than in the previous two centuries and that the gas had reached its highest level in 160,000 years. Scientists can estimate the makeup of Earth's atmosphere long ago by testing air pockets in ice sheets believed to have formed around the same time.

Findings in the 1980s and 1990s provided more disturbing evidence of atmospheric changes. Scientists detected increases in other, even more potent gases that contribute to the greenhouse effect, notably CFC-11 and CFC-12, methane, nitrous oxide, and halocarbons (CFCs, methyl chloroform, and hydrochlorofluorocarbons).

T. J. Blasing and Karmen Smith of the Carbon Dioxide Information Analysis Center estimate in "Recent Greenhouse Gas Concentrations" (July 2006, http://cdiac.ornl.gov/pns/current_ghg.html) that the average "natural" background atmospheric concentration of CO_2 before 1750 was 280 parts per million. Likewise, the average methane level before 1750 was around 730 parts per billion. Increases in these gases in recent years are shown in Figure 3.10 for CO_2 and in Figure 3.11 for methane. These data were collected by the National Oceanic and Atmospheric Administration (NOAA) from its Earth System Research Laboratory (ESRL). The ESRL is headquartered in Boulder, Colorado, and operates observatories in Point Barrow, Alaska; Trinidad Head, California; Mauna Loa, Hawaii; American Samoa; and the South Pole. The agency compiles long-term records on air quality and solar radiation data. In 2006 the average global CO_2 concentration exceeded 380 parts per million. The average global methane concentration was around 1,775 parts per billion.

Scientists agree that atmospheric concentrations of gases known to play a role in the natural greenhouse effect are increasing. There is scientific consensus that this increase is driving up Earth's temperature.

A RECENT WARMING TREND

Scientists do not know how much the global temperature has varied on its own in the last one thousand years. Temperature records based on thermometers go back only about 150 years. Therefore, investigators have turned to

FIGURE 3.10

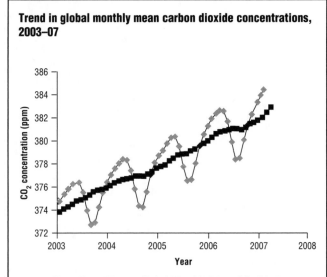

Trend in global monthly mean carbon dioxide concentrations, 2003–07

SOURCE: Pieter Tans, "Recent Global Monthly Mean CO₂," in *Recent Global Monthly Mean CO₂*, U.S. Department of Commerce, National Oceanic & Atmospheric Administration, Earth System Research Laboratory, May 2007, http://www.esrl.noaa.gov/gmd/ccgg/trends/ (accessed June 12, 2007)

proxy (indirect) means of measuring past temperatures. These methods include chemical evidence of climatic change contained in fossils, corals, ancient ice, and growth rings in trees.

In 1998 Michael E. Mann, Raymond S. Bradley, and Malcolm K. Hughes surveyed proxy evidence of temperatures in the Northern Hemisphere since 1400 and reported their findings in "Northern Hemisphere Temperatures during the Past Millennium: Inferences, Uncertainties, and Limitations" (*Geophysical Research Letters*, vol. 26, no. 6, 1999). They note that the twentieth century was the warmest century of the past six hundred years. Mann, Bradley, and Hughes conclude that the warming trend seems to be closely connected to the emission of greenhouse gases by humans. Some experts, however, question whether studies of proxy evidence will ever be reliable enough to yield valuable information on global warming.

Three international agencies have compiled long-term data on surface temperatures: the British Meteorological Office in Bracknell, United Kingdom, the National Climatic Data Center in Asheville, North Carolina, and the National Aeronautics and Space Administration (NASA) Goddard Institute for Space Studies in New York. Temperature measurements from these organizations report that the 1990s were the warmest decade of the twentieth century and the warmest decade since humans began measuring temperatures in the mid-nineteenth century. The average global surface temperature was approximately one degree Fahrenheit warmer

than at the turn of the twentieth century, and this rise increased more rapidly since 1980.

NASA reports in "2006 Was Earth's Fifth Warmest Year" (February 8, 2007, http://www.nasa.gov/centers/goddard/news/topstory/2006/2006_warm.html) that the five warmest meteorological years recorded since the 1890s are:

- 2005
- 1998
- 2002
- 2003
- 2006

A meteorological year runs from the beginning of winter to the end of autumn. Figure 3.12 shows the anomaly (deviation from the normal) for global mean (average) surface temperatures from 1880 through 2006, compared with the mean from 1951 to 1980. There has been a strong warming trend over the past three decades with the Earth warming by approximately 0.6 degrees Celsius (or nearly 1.1 degrees Fahrenheit). Examination of the worldwide anomalies for 2006 indicate that a few parts of the Earth have cooled, whereas most others have warmed. The most dramatic warming trend is seen over the Arctic (North Pole), Alaska, Siberia, and Antarctica (South Pole) regions.

THE INTERNATIONAL COMMUNITY TAKES ACTION
The World Meteorology Organization Speaks Up

At the 1972 Stockholm Conference, the world's first ecological summit, climate change was not even listed among the threats to the environment. Many Earth scientists and meteorologists, however, were becoming alarmed about the growing evidence supporting the notion of an enhanced greenhouse effect. In 1979 the World Meteorological Organization (WMO) established its World Climate Program to collect data and research the complex components of the Earth's climate system. The WMO is a nongovernmental agency under the United Nations Environment Program (UNEP).

According to the Intergovernmental Panel on Climate Change, in *16 Years of Scientific Assessment in Support of the Climate Convention* (December 2004, http://www.ipcc.ch/about/anniversarybrochure.pdf), at its 1979 conference the WMO acknowledged that "man's activities on Earth may cause significant extended regional and even global changes of climate." This was the first major step in the response of the international community to the threat of global warming.

In 1985 representatives of the WMO, the UNEP, and the International Council for Science met in Austria to

FIGURE 3.11

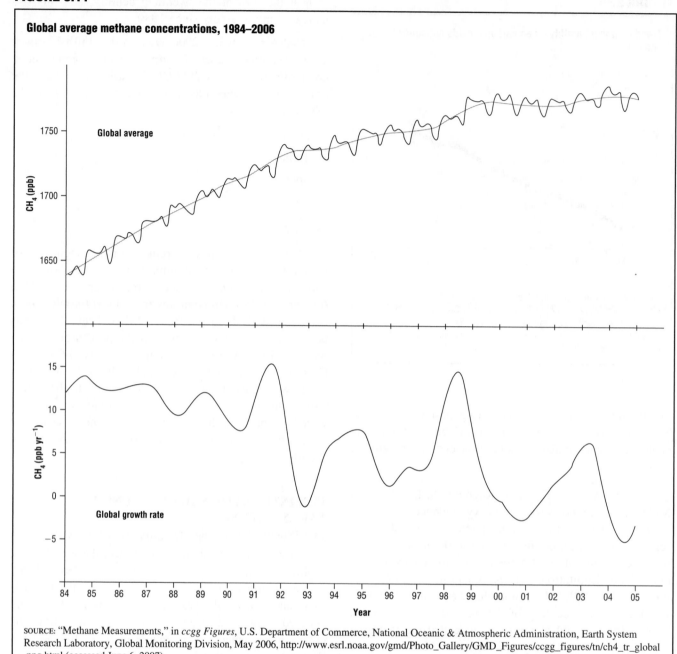

Global average methane concentrations, 1984–2006

SOURCE: "Methane Measurements," in *ccgg Figures*, U.S. Department of Commerce, National Oceanic & Atmospheric Administration, Earth System Research Laboratory, Global Monitoring Division, May 2006, http://www.esrl.noaa.gov/gmd/Photo_Gallery/GMD_Figures/ccgg_figures/tn/ch4_tr_global .png.html (accessed June 6, 2007)

discuss the role of CO_2 and other greenhouse gases in climate change. They predicted that rising levels of these gases would cause an increase in the global temperature during the first half of the twenty-first century.

The Intergovernmental Panel on Climate Change

In 1988 the WMO and the UNEP established the Intergovernmental Panel on Climate Change (IPCC). The IPCC set up three working groups to assess available scientific information on climate change, estimate the expected impacts of climate change, and formulate strategies for responding to the problem. The first IPCC assessment report was issued in 1990.

Several signs of climate change were noted by the IPCC in its report:

- The average warm-season temperature in Alaska had risen nearly three degrees Fahrenheit in the previous fifty years.

- Glaciers had generally receded and become thinner on average by about thirty feet in the previous forty years.

FIGURE 3.12

Trend in annual global mean temperatures, 1880–2006

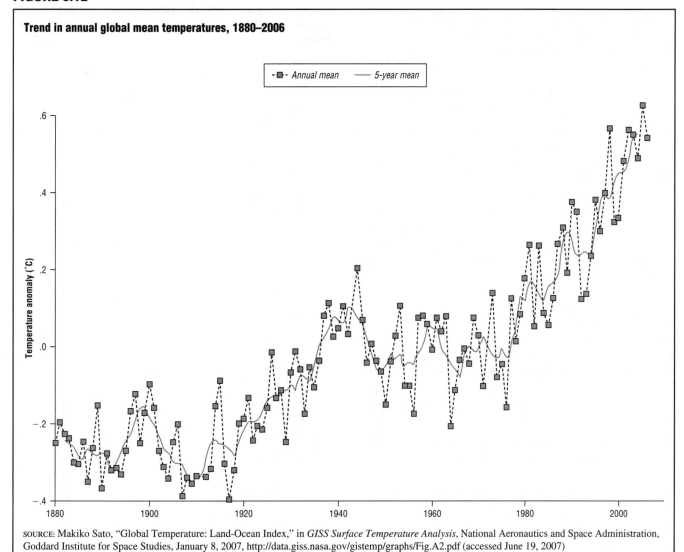

SOURCE: Makiko Sato, "Global Temperature: Land-Ocean Index," in *GISS Surface Temperature Analysis*, National Aeronautics and Space Administration, Goddard Institute for Space Studies, January 8, 2007, http://data.giss.nasa.gov/gistemp/graphs/Fig.A2.pdf (accessed June 19, 2007)

- There was about 5% less sea ice in the Bering Sea than in the 1950s.

- Permafrost was thawing, causing the ground to subside, opening holes in roads, producing landslides and erosion, threatening roads and bridges, and causing local floods.

- Ice cellars in northern villages had thawed and become useless.

- More precipitation was falling as rain than snow in northern areas, and the snow was melting faster, causing more running and standing water.

The IPCC report was the most comprehensive summary of climate-change science to date. It represented the input of approximately four hundred international scientists and acknowledged that global warming was a real threat to the Earth's climate.

Using computer models, IPCC researchers predicted that the global mean temperature would increase by 0.5 degrees Fahrenheit each decade during the twenty-first century. They also predicted that the global mean sea level would rise by 2.4 inches per decade. However, the scientists noted that there were a number of uncertainties in their assumptions based on lack of data.

The United Nations Framework Convention on Climate Change

In 1992 the United Nations (UN) adopted the UN Framework Convention on Climate Change (UNFCCC). The UNFCCC was an international agreement presented for signatures at the 1992 Earth Summit in Rio de Janeiro, Brazil. The stated objective of the agreement was: "Stabilization of greenhouse gas concentrations in the atmosphere at a level that would prevent dangerous anthropogenic interference with the climate system. Such a level should be achieved within a timeframe sufficient to allow ecosystems to adapt naturally to climate change, to ensure that food production is not threatened and to enable economic development to proceed in a sustainable manner."

The agreement set specific goals for developed countries to track and publish detailed inventories of their greenhouse gas emissions. However, it did not include specific emissions targets that countries had to meet. The UNFCCC was signed by more than one hundred countries, including the United States. Many environmentalists criticized the treaty as too weak because it did not establish specific targets that governments must meet. The treaty did not include specific targets mainly because the United States refused to accept them. The U.S. Senate ratified (formally approved into law) the UNFCCC. The treaty went into effect in 1994.

In 1995, 120 parties to the global warming treaty met in Berlin, Germany, in what is known as the Berlin Mandate to determine the success of existing treaties and to embark on discussions of emissions after 2000. Differences persisted along North-South lines, with developing countries making essentially a moral argument for requiring more of the richer nations. They pointed out that the richer nations are responsible for most of the pollution. The Berlin talks essentially failed to endorse binding timetables for reductions in greenhouse gases.

A Landmark Judgment—The 1995 IPCC Report

In 1995 the IPCC reassessed the state of knowledge about climate change and published its findings in its second assessment report, *Climate Change 1995* (http://www.ipcc.ch/pub/reports.htm). The panel reaffirmed its earlier conclusions and updated its forecasts, predicting that, if no further action is taken to curb emissions of greenhouse gases, temperatures will increase 1.4 degrees to 6.3 degrees Fahrenheit by 2100. The panel concluded that the evidence suggests a human influence on global climate. The cautiously worded statement was a compromise following intense discussions. Nonetheless, it was a landmark conclusion because the panel, until then, had maintained that global warming and climate changes could have been the result of natural variability.

The Kyoto Protocol

In 1997 delegates from 166 countries met in Kyoto, Japan, at the UN Climate Change Conference to negotiate actions to reduce global warming. Some developed nations, including the United States, wanted to require all countries to reduce their emissions. Developing countries, however, felt the industrialized nations had caused, and were still causing, most global warming and therefore should bear the brunt of economic sacrifices to clean up the environment. The conference developed an agreement known as the

TABLE 3.2

Greenhouse gas emission reduction targets under the Kyoto Protocol

Country	Reduction target (percent)
Australia	+8.0
Austria (R)	−13.0
Belgium (R)	−7.5
Bulgaria (R)	−8.0
Canada (R)	−6.0
Croatia	−5.0
Czech Republic (R)	−8.0
Denmark (R)	−21.0
Estonia (R)	−8.0
European Community (R)*	−8.0
Finland (R)	0.0
France (R)	0.0
Germany (R)	−21.0
Greece (R)	+25.0
Hungary (R)	−6.0
Iceland (R)	+10.0
Ireland (R)	+13.0
Italy (R)	−6.5
Japan (R)	−6.0
Latvia (R)	−8.0
Liechtenstein	−8.0
Lithuania (R)	−8.0
Luxembourg (R)	−28.0
Monaco	−8.0
Netherlands (R)	−6.0
New Zealand (R)	0.0
Norway (R)	+1.0
Poland (R)	−6.0
Portugal (R)	+27.0
Romania (R)	−8.0
Russia	0.0
Slovakia (R)	−8.0
Slovenia (R)	−8.0
Spain (R)	+15.0
Sweden (R)	+4.0
Switzerland (R)	−8.0
Ukraine	0.0
United Kingdom (R)	−12.5
United States	−7.0

Notes:
(R)=Country has ratified, accepted, approved, or acceded to the Kyoto Protocol.
*European Union member countries renegotiated their individual targets under the EU Shared Burden Agreement, which was agreed to in 1998 and reaffirmed in the ratification of the Kyoto Protocol in 2002.

SOURCE: "Table 17. Quantified Emissions Reduction Targets Under the Kyoto Protocol by Country," in *International Energy Outlook: 2004*, U.S. Department of Energy, Energy Information Administration, Office of Integrated Analysis and Forecasting, April 2004, http://www.eia.doe.gov/oiaf/archive/ieo04/environmental_tables. html (accessed July 20, 2007)

Kyoto Protocol to the UNFCCC. Different targets were set for different countries to meet specific economic and social circumstances. (See Table 3.2.) Even though China and India were not required to commit to specific limits, they did have to pledge to develop national programs for dealing with climate change. Overall, the Kyoto Protocol is expected to effect a total reduction in greenhouse gas emissions of at least 5% by 2012, compared with 1990 levels.

The treaty also set up an emission trading system that allowed countries exceeding their pollution limits to purchase on an open market credits from countries that pollute less. This provision was viewed as necessary to U.S. congressional approval. The developing nations feared that such a trading system would allow rich countries to buy their way into compliance rather than make unpopular emissions cuts. Enforcement mechanisms were not agreed to, nor did developing nations commit to binding participation. Regardless, Vice President Al Gore Jr. (1948–) signed the Kyoto Protocol on behalf of the United States. However, President Bill Clinton (1946–) never submitted it to the Senate for ratification. The political climate at the time was unfavorable for a treaty that bound the United States to specific emissions limits but did not set limits on developing nations, such as China and India.

The Kyoto Protocol was set up to take effect when two conditions were met:

- It was ratified by at least fifty-five countries.

- The ratifying countries accounted for at least 55% of CO_2 emissions based on 1990 levels.

In March 2001 President George W. Bush (1946–) indicated that the United States would not ratify the treaty because it would cost an estimated $400 billion and 4.9 million jobs to comply. In 2002 the treaty was ratified by major entities including the European Union, Japan, China, Canada, and India. It came into effect in February 2005 following ratification by Russia in late 2004. The UNFCCC (http://unfccc.int/kyoto_protocol/background/status_of_ratification/items/2613.php) noted in June 2007 that the Kyoto Protocol had been ratified by more than 174 nations. The notable exceptions were the United States and Australia.

The IPCC's 2001 Assessment Report

In 2001 the IPCC released its third assessment report: *Climate Change 2001* (http://www.ipcc.ch/pub/reports.htm). It actually consisted of four reports: *Climate Change 2001: The Scientific Basis, Climate Change 2001: Impacts, Adaptation, and Vulnerability, Climate Change 2001: Mitigation,* and *Climate Change 2001: The Synthesis Report.* The IPCC's assessment covered the adaptability and vulnerability of North America to climate change impacts likely to occur from global warming. Among the suggested possible effects of global warming were:

- Expansion of some diseases in North America

- Increased erosion, flooding, and loss of wetlands in coastal areas

- Risk to "unique natural ecosystems"

- Changes in seasonal snowmelts, which would have effects on water users and aquatic ecosystems

- Some initial benefits for agriculture, but those benefits would decline over time and possibly "become a net loss"

The IPCC's 2007 Assessment Report

In 2007 the three working groups of the IPCC had each released their version of the assessment report. These reports were:

- Working Group I—*Climate Change 2007: The Physical Science Basis* (http://ipcc-wg1.ucar.edu/wg1/wg1-report.html)

- Working Group II—*Climate Change 2007: Impacts, Adaptation, and Vulnerability* (http://www.ipcc-wg2.org/)

- Working Group III—*Climate Change 2007: Mitigation* (http://arch.rivm.nl/env/int/ipcc/pages_media/AR4-chapters.html)

The IPCC's so-called Synthesis Report (http://www.ipcc.ch/activity/ar4outline.htm), which integrates information from all three working group reports, was expected to be released in November 2007.

The report from Working Group I concludes that there is "very high confidence that the global average net effect of human activities since 1750 has been one of warming." The report defines "very high confidence" as meaning that there is over a nine out of ten chance that a hypothesis is correct. This is the strongest wording yet from the IPCC indicting human activities for global warming. The report estimates that humans have driven a warming effect (technically known as radiative forcing) of +1.6 watts per square meter since 1750. Various emission modeling scenarios predict that the Earth will continue to warm by approximately 0.2 degrees Celsius (0.36 degrees Fahrenheit) per decade over the next twenty years.

Working Group II notes that "observational evidence from all continents and most oceans shows that many natural systems are being affected by regional climate changes, particularly temperature increases." These effects include an earlier occurrence of springtime events and a poleward movement in the ranges of plant and animal species. In addition, many changes are reported in ice and snow ecosystems near the Earth's poles. Warming water body temperatures are linked to range changes for algae, plankton, and fish species.

Estimated future impacts of global warming include the loss of freshwater store because of melting glaciers, greater extent of drought areas coupled with more frequent "heavy precipitation" events that tend to cause flooding, and acidification of the Earth's oceans because of greater carbon take-up. The latter effect is particularly troubling for ocean coral, which is sensitive to pH (potential hydrogen; the level of acidity; a lower value indicates more acid) changes. Approximately 20% to 30% of plant and animals species are deemed to be at increased risk of extinction if the global average temperature increases by more than 1.5 to 2.5 degrees Celsius (2.7 to 4.5 degrees Fahrenheit).

Sea level rises are expected to expose millions of people to increased risk of flooding, exacerbate coastal erosion, and endanger coastal ecosystems. Even though increasing temperatures should help lower the number of deaths caused by cold exposure in far northern and southern regions, this benefit is expected to be more than offset by higher death rates in the temperate regions of the Earth, particularly in developing countries.

Working Group III focuses on the mitigative (corrective) measures that have been and can be taken by governments to reduce greenhouse gas emissions in seven sectors: energy supply, transport, buildings (e.g., lighting and insulation decisions), industry, agriculture, forestry, and waste handling and treatment. The report describes technologies and practices that are currently commercially available and those that are projected to be commercialized before 2030. The report admits that most computer models predict losses in the gross domestic product (GDP; the total value of goods and services produced by a nation) associated with emission abatement measures; however, some models predict GDP gains because they assume that the creation of revenue-earning technological advancements will be spurred by mitigation policies. In addition, it is expected that overall improvements in air pollution will bring health benefits that may offset some mitigation costs.

For the energy sector, Working Group III recommends that industrialized countries upgrade their energy infrastructure, developing countries invest in new energy infrastructure, and both types of countries promote renewable energy resources and measures for energy efficiency improvement. Specific recommendations include eliminating fossil fuel subsidies and imposing carbon taxes on fossil fuels. The report notes that nations must balance the short-term economic costs of quickly achieving dramatic emission reductions against the medium- and long-term costs that will arise because of continued global warming if mitigation is delayed.

In October 2007 the IPCC and Gore were jointly awarded the 2007 Nobel Peace Prize for their work "to build up and disseminate greater knowledge about man-made climate change, and to lay the foundations for the measures that are needed to counteract such change." The prize committee noted that thousands of scientists from more than one hundred countries had collaborated through the IPCC to investigate the causes and effects of climate warming.

THE UNITED STATES GOES ITS OWN WAY

The U.S. Constitution grants the president the power to make treaties with foreign powers but only with the consent of two-thirds of the Senate. In other words, the president or a designee (such as the vice president) can sign treaties, but they do not become binding under U.S. law until they are approved by the Senate. The administration of President George H. W. Bush (1924–) supported and signed the UNFCCC, which was ratified by the Senate, but opposed precise deadlines for CO_2 limits, arguing that the extent of the problem was too uncertain to justify painful economic measures. In 1989 President Bush established the U.S. Global Change Research Program (USGCRP), which was authorized by Congress in the Global Change Research Act of 1990.

In 1993 President Clinton took office. Later that year the United States released, in accordance with the UNFCCC, *The Climate Change Action Plan* (http://www.gcrio.org/USCCAP/toc.html), which detailed the nation's response to climate change. The plan included a set of measures by both government and the private sector to lay a foundation for the nation's participation in world response to the climate challenge.

The plan called for measures to reduce emissions for all greenhouse gases to 1990 levels by 2000. However, the U.S. economy grew at a more robust rate than anticipated, which led to increased emissions. Furthermore, Congress did not provide full funding for the actions contained in the plan.

Even though the United States had a comprehensive global warming program in place, Congress was reluctant to take steps to reduce emissions. However, the Clinton administration implemented some policies that did not require congressional approval. These included tax incentives and investments focusing on improving energy efficiency and renewable energy technologies, coordinating federal efforts to develop renewable fuels technology, and requiring all federal government agencies to reduce greenhouse gas emissions below 1990 levels by 2010. President Clinton also established the U.S. Climate Change Research Initiative to study areas of uncertainty about global climate change science and identify priorities for public investments.

The United States and the Kyoto Protocol

As noted earlier, the United States is a party to the UNFCCC but has never ratified the Kyoto Protocol to the UNFCCC. Vice President Gore signed the Kyoto Protocol in 1998 on behalf of the Clinton administration, but this was largely a symbolic gesture. At the time Gore noted, "We will not submit the Protocol for ratification without the meaningful participation of key developing countries in efforts to address climate change." The Senate had already made clear through a nonbinding, but unanimous, resolution passed in 1997 that it would not ratify the Kyoto Protocol as written because some nations were excluded from emissions limits and the treaty was deemed damaging to U.S. economic interests. The resolution was sponsored by Senators Robert Byrd (D-WV; 1917–) and Chuck Hagel (R-N; 1946–) and is often referred to as the Byrd-Hagel Resolution.

When President George W. Bush took office in 2001, he affirmed his administration's steadfast opposition to the Kyoto Protocol. He established a new cabinet-level management structure to oversee government investments in climate change science and technology. Both the U.S. Climate Change Research Initiative and the USGCRP were placed under the oversight (supervision) of the interagency Climate Change Science Program (CCSP), which reports integrated research that is sponsored by thirteen federal agencies. The CCSP is overseen by the Office of Science and Technology Policy, the Council on Environmental Quality, and the Office of Management and Budget.

According to the article "California Greenhouse Gas Bill Approved by State Senate" (FOXNews.com, August 31, 2006), more than one hundred bills dealing with greenhouse gases and climate change have been introduced in Congress but have failed to move forward because of lack of consensus among legislators about how to deal with the issue. The exclusion of China from the Kyoto Protocol's emission limits is a major sticking point for many U.S. politicians, who fear that the United States would be put at an economic disadvantage if it had to meet specific limits. The United States' continued refusal to ratify the Kyoto Protocol or develop a similar control plan at the national level has elicited strong criticism from foreign and domestic sources. The editorial "Warming and Global Security" (*New York Times*, April 20, 2007) complains that "in an alliance of denial, China and the United States are using each other's inaction as an excuse to do nothing."

Greenhouse Gas Intensity

In 2002 Bush advocated his own plan for the U.S. response to the greenhouse gas problem. Rather than specific emission limits, he called for a reduction in greenhouse gas intensity (GGI), that is, greenhouse gas emissions per unit of economic growth. GGI has come to be defined primarily as metric tons of greenhouse gases emitted per million dollars of the GDP (assuming each dollar has the same purchasing value as it did in 2000). In this way, greenhouse gas emissions are tied to an economic indicator.

Critics complain that the GGI can be reduced without necessarily decreasing greenhouse gas emissions. This can occur if the U.S. economy (as measured by the GDP) continues to grow robustly as it has in recent years. If the GDP increases at a faster rate than emissions, the calculated intensity value will decrease; however, actual emissions will still be increasing. In fact, the DOE

FIGURE 3.13

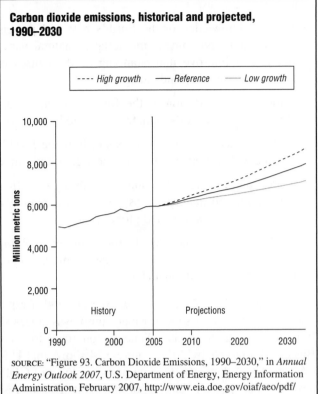

Carbon dioxide emissions, historical and projected, 1990–2030

SOURCE: "Figure 93. Carbon Dioxide Emissions, 1990–2030," in *Annual Energy Outlook 2007*, U.S. Department of Energy, Energy Information Administration, February 2007, http://www.eia.doe.gov/oiaf/aeo/pdf/trend_6.pdf (accessed June 14, 2007)

expects U.S. emissions to increase. Figure 3.13 shows historical emissions and projects future emissions for three economic scenarios: low, reference (medium), and high growth rates over the coming decades.

Recent Reports and Updates

In May 2002 the U.S. Global Change Research Information Office released the *U.S. Climate Action Report—2002* (http://www.gcrio.org/CAR2002/). The report acknowledges that greenhouse gases resulting from human activities are accumulating in the atmosphere and that they are causing air and ocean temperatures to increase. It does not rule out, however, the still-unknown role of natural variability in global warming. In addition, the report reiterates that the Bush administration plans to reduce the nation's GGI by 18% over the following decade through a combination of existing regulations and voluntary, incentive-based measures.

In July 2003 the CCSP published two major reports: *Strategic Plan for the U.S. Climate Change Science Program* (http://www.climatescience.gov/Library/stratplan2003/final/ccspstratplan2003-all.pdf) and *The U.S. Climate Change Science Program: Vision for the Program and Highlights of the Scientific Strategic Plan* (http://www.climatescience.gov/Library/stratplan2003/vision/ccsp-vision.pdf). Together, these documents outline the approach the CCSP plans to take to achieve its five main scientific goals:

- Improve knowledge of the Earth's past and present climate and environment, including its natural variability, and improve understanding of the causes of observed variability and change

- Improve quantification of the forces bringing about changes in the Earth's climate and related systems

- Reduce uncertainty in projections of how the Earth's climate and related systems may change in the future

- Understand the sensitivity and adaptability of different natural and managed ecosystems and human systems to climate and related global changes

- Explore the uses and identify the limits of evolving knowledge to manage risks and opportunities related to climate variability and change

In May 2007 the *Climate Action Report—2006* (http://www.state.gov/g/oes/rls/rpts/car/index.htm) was released. It indicates that the United States is on track to meet Bush's GGI targets by 2012. Figure 3.14 shows that U.S. GGI and CO_2 intensity (CO_2 emissions per dollar of GDP) have declined steadily since 1990. In a White House press statement (May 23, 2007, http://www.whitehouse.gov/news/releases/2007/05/20070523-8.html), Bush noted that from 2005 to 2006 U.S. CO_2 emissions declined by seventy-eight million metric tons (a 1.3% decrease), whereas the U.S. economy grew by 3.3%. This resulted in a reduction in CO_2 intensity of 4.5%, the largest annual improvement achieved since 1990 and a significant step toward the president's goal of reducing GGI by 18% by 2012.

California Goes Its Own Way

As described in Chapter 2, the Clean Air Act allows states to set stricter air pollution standards than those imposed by the federal government if the EPA grants permission to do so. During the early 1990s California used this process to establish emission standards for vehicles more stringent than those set by the EPA for priority pollutants and air toxics. CO_2 was not included. Growing concern about global warming and the federal government's lack of enthusiasm for the Kyoto Protocol has spurred the state to launch its own campaign against greenhouse gases.

In 2005 Governor Arnold Schwarzenegger (1947–) issued an executive order establishing emissions targets for greenhouse gas emissions. He also created a Climate Action Team under the direction of the California Environmental Protection Agency to coordinate the state's climate policy. In August 2006 the California legislature passed AB 32, which adopted Schwarzenegger's plans into law. It calls for the state to reduce its greenhouse gas emissions by 2020 to 1990 levels. This represents an

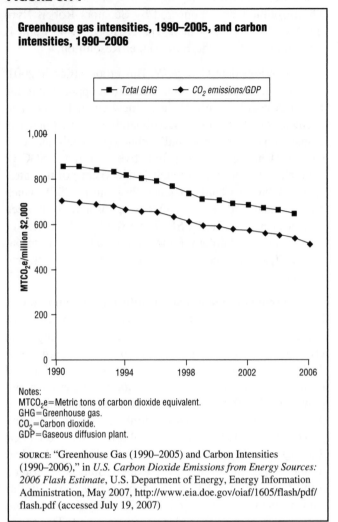

FIGURE 3.14

Greenhouse gas intensities, 1990–2005, and carbon intensities, 1990–2006

Legend: ■ Total GHG   ◆ CO_2 emissions/GDP

Y-axis: $MTCO_2e$/million $2,000

Notes:
$MTCO_2e$=Metric tons of carbon dioxide equivalent.
GHG=Greenhouse gas.
CO_2=Carbon dioxide.
GDP=Gaseous diffusion plant.

SOURCE: "Greenhouse Gas (1990–2005) and Carbon Intensities (1990–2006)," in *U.S. Carbon Dioxide Emissions from Energy Sources: 2006 Flash Estimate*, U.S. Department of Energy, Energy Information Administration, May 2007, http://www.eia.doe.gov/oiaf/1605/flash/pdf/flash.pdf (accessed July 19, 2007)

approximate 25% reduction, compared with what emissions would be without the program. (See Figure 3.15.) The plan includes a market-based trading program in which industries emitting greenhouse gases can buy or sell credits among themselves to meet the limits.

Opponents to the plan worry about its economic consequences, fearing that it will drive businesses from California and raise consumer prices, particularly for gasoline. Advocates counter that California companies will create profitable technological innovations for the world marketplace that will ultimately offset and even surpass the short-term costs of tighter emission limits.

The Fight over Vehicle Emission Limits

Because transportation is the state's largest single source of greenhouse gas emissions, California proposes to achieve the reductions, in part, through strict new standards on the emissions of CO_2 from vehicles. This plan has encountered stiff resistance from the federal government, because CO_2 is neither a priority or toxic pollutant under federal standards. Eleven other states, all

FIGURE 3.15

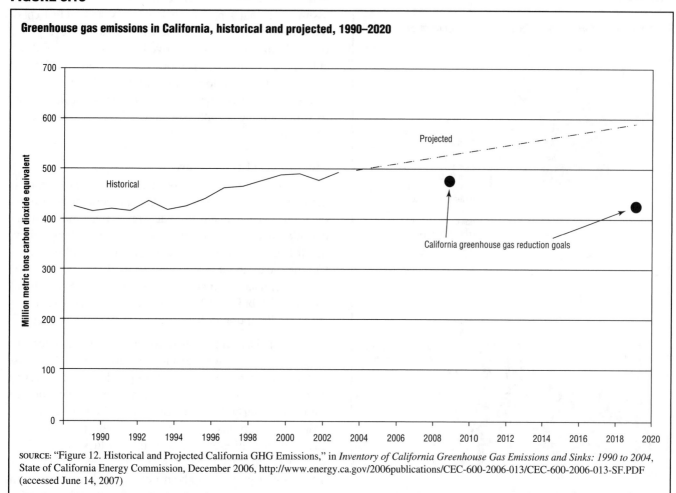

Greenhouse gas emissions in California, historical and projected, 1990–2020

SOURCE: "Figure 12. Historical and Projected California GHG Emissions," in *Inventory of California Greenhouse Gas Emissions and Sinks: 1990 to 2004*, State of California Energy Commission, December 2006, http://www.energy.ca.gov/2006publications/CEC-600-2006-013/CEC-600-2006-013-SF.PDF (accessed June 14, 2007)

clustered in the northeastern United States, have also asked the EPA for permission to establish their own vehicle emission limits on CO_2. At first, the EPA argued that it did not have the authority to act, because greenhouse gas emissions do not fall under the Clean Air Act. In April 2007 this argument was ruled invalid by the U.S. Supreme Court in *Commonwealth of Massachusetts v. U.S. Environmental Protection Agency* (415 F. 3d 50).

As of September 2007 the EPA was still considering the states' requests; however, political analysts believe the agency will delay making a decision until after the 2008 national elections. Automakers are staunchly opposed to the prospect of differing vehicle emission standards from state to state. They have lobbied the EPA to deny the states' petitions.

In early 2007 Schwarzenegger also proposed a new standard for low-carbon fuels in California. If adopted, this would force petroleum refiners to reduce the carbon content of fuels by 10% by 2020. It would also encourage development and investment in alternative fuels other than gasoline.

Major U.S. Cities Embrace the Kyoto Protocol

In February 2002 Seattle Mayor Greg Nickels (1955–) launched the U.S. Mayors Climate Protection Agreement (2007, http://www.seattle.gov/mayor/climate/default.htm# what), in which the mayors of U.S. cities agree to abide by the provisions of the Kyoto Protocol in an attempt to lower greenhouse gas emissions in their cities by 2012. As of 2007, more than six hundred mayors representing sixty-seven million people had joined this initiative.

INFLUENCES ON EARTH'S CLIMATE

Besides the greenhouse effect, there are many other natural and anthropogenic factors believed to affect Earth's climate. The following sections describe some of these factors and the scientific knowledge and uncertainties about them.

The Effects of the Forests

Forests act as sinks, or repositories, absorbing and storing carbon. This is an example of carbon sequestration (long-term storage of carbon that keeps it out of the atmosphere). Living trees naturally absorb and neutralize

FIGURE 3.16

The effect of forests on carbon dioxide concentrations

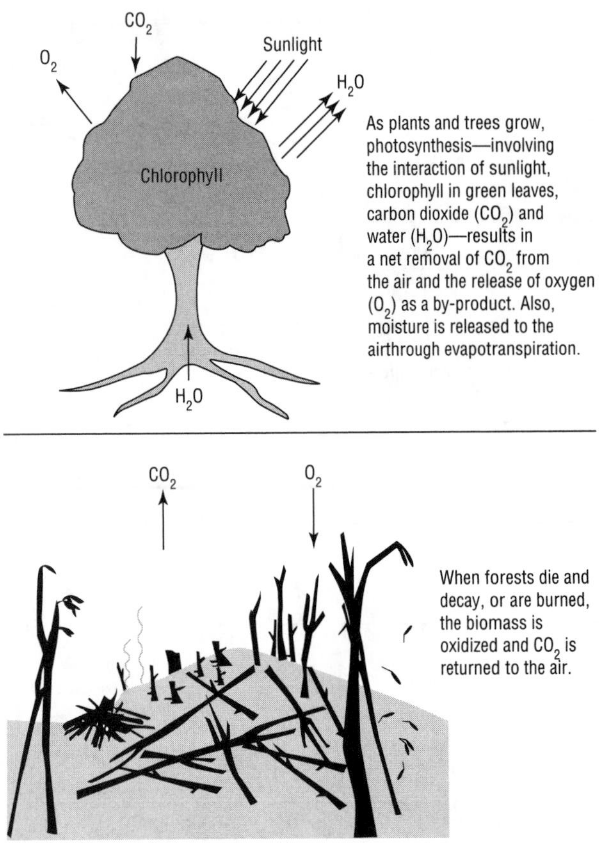

As plants and trees grow, photosynthesis—involving the interaction of sunlight, chlorophyll in green leaves, carbon dioxide (CO_2) and water (H_2O)—results in a net removal of CO_2 from the air and the release of oxygen (O_2) as a by-product. Also, moisture is released to the air through evapotranspiration.

When forests die and decay, or are burned, the biomass is oxidized and CO_2 is returned to the air.

SOURCE: "Figure 2a," and "Figure 2b," in *Biosphere, NASA Facts*, National Aeronautics and Space Administration, Goddard Space Flight Center, April 1998

CO_2, although scientists do not agree on the extent to which forests can soak up excess amounts. The increasing levels of CO_2 in the atmosphere might conceivably be tolerated in Earth's normal CO_2 cycle if not for the additional complicating factor of deforestation. The burning of the Amazon rain forest and other forests has had a twofold effect: the immediate release of large amounts of CO_2 into the atmosphere from the fires and the loss of trees to neutralize the CO_2 in the atmosphere. (See Figure 3.16.)

In 2006 the scientific community was stunned when Frank Keppler et al. showed in "Methane Emissions from Terrestrial Plants under Aerobic Conditions" (*Nature*, no. 439, January 12, 2006) that live vegetation releases methane—a potent greenhouse gas. Keppler and his colleagues estimated that on a global scale live plants (such as trees) could be emitting up to 236 million metric tons of methane per year. Some observers used the revelation to cast doubt on the conventional wisdom that forests clean the air of greenhouse gases. Other researchers questioned the methods used by Keppler and his col-

leagues to arrive at their conclusions, particularly the assumption that small-scale laboratory and field experiment results can be extrapolated (scaled up) to a global basis. Some scientists believed that Keppler and his cohorts' experimental methods were flawed and that living plants produce no or virtually no methane emissions. The so-called methane mystery has spurred a fierce controversy among scientists that is likely to continue for some time.

The Effects of the Oceans

The oceans are, by far, the largest reservoir of carbon in the carbon cycle. Oceanographers and ecologists disagree over the carbon cycle–climate connection and over the ocean's capacity to absorb CO_2. Some scientists believe that the oceans can absorb one billion to two billion tons of CO_2 per year, about the amount the world emitted in 1950. Until scientists can more accurately determine how much CO_2 can be buffered by ocean processes, the extent and speed of disruption in the carbon supply remains unclear.

Oceans have a profound effect on global temperature because of their huge capacity to store heat and because they can moderate levels of atmospheric gases. Covering more than 70% of Earth and holding 97% of the water on the planet's surface, oceans function as huge reservoirs of heat. Ocean currents transport this stored heat and dissolved gases so that different areas of the world serve as either sources or sinks for these components. Even though scientists know a great deal about oceanic and air circulation, they are less certain about the ocean's ability to store additional CO_2 or about how much heat it will absorb.

The Effects of Clouds

Surprisingly little is known about clouds—where they occur, their role in energy and water transfer, and their ability to reflect solar heat. Earth's climate maintains a balance between the energy that reaches Earth from the sun and the energy that radiates back from Earth into space. Scientists refer to this as Earth's radiation budget. The components of Earth's system are the planet's surface, atmosphere, and clouds.

Different parts of Earth have different capacities to reflect solar energy. These are known as albedo effects. *Albedo* comes from the Latin word for "whiteness." Oceans and forests have relatively low albedo values, because they reflect only a small portion of the sun's energy. By contrast, deserts and snow reflect a large portion of solar energy.

NASA's Earth Science Enterprise is a satellite-based program that includes many scientific studies of clouds. These studies reveal that:

- The effect of clouds on climate depends on the balance between the incoming solar radiation and the absorption of Earth's outgoing radiation.

- Low clouds have a cooling effect because they are optically thicker and reflect much of the incoming solar radiation out to space.

- High, thin cirrus clouds have a warming effect because they transmit most of the incoming solar radiation while also trapping some of Earth's radiation and radiating it back to the surface.

- Deep convective clouds have neither a warming nor a cooling effect because their reflective and absorptive abilities cancel one another.

The Effects of Solar Cycles

Scientists have known for centuries that the sun goes through cycles; it has seasons, storms, and rhythms of activity with sunspots and flares appearing in cycles of roughly eleven years. Some scientists contend that these factors play a role in climate change on Earth. Some research, though sketchy and controversial, suggests that the sun's variability could account for some, if not all, of global warming to date. The biggest correlation occurred centuries ago—between 1640 and 1720—when sunspot activity fell sharply and Earth cooled about two degrees Fahrenheit. (The sun is brighter when sunspots appear and dimmer when they disappear.) Other scientists believe that sun variability could indeed be a component of recent global warming, but only in combination with anthropogenic factors.

The Effects of El Niño and La Niña

For centuries fishermen in the Pacific Ocean off the coast of South America have known about the phenomenon called El Niño. At irregular yearly intervals, during December and January, fish in those waters virtually vanish, bringing fishing to a standstill. Fishermen called this occurrence El Niño, which means "the Child," because it occurs around the celebration of the birth of Jesus. Even though it originates in the Pacific, El Niño's effects are felt around the world. Computers, satellites, and improved data gathering find that the El Niño phenomenon is responsible for drastic climate change.

An El Niño occurs because of interactions between atmospheric winds and sea surfaces. In normal years trade winds blow from east to west across the eastern Pacific. They drag the surface waters westward across the ocean, causing deeper, cold waters to rise to the surface. This upwelling of deep ocean waters carries nutrients from the bottom of the ocean that feed fish populations in the upper waters.

In an El Niño the westward movement of waters weakens, causing the upwelling of deep waters to cease. The resulting warming of the ocean waters further weakens the trade winds and strengthens El Niño. Without upwelling, the nutrient content of deep waters is diminished, which in turn causes the depletion of fish popula-

tions. The warm waters that normally lie in the western part of the Pacific shift eastward. This turbulence creates eastward weather conditions, in which towering cumulus clouds reach high into the atmosphere with strong vertical forces and the weakening of normal east-to-west trade winds. An El Niño is the warm phase of a phenomenon known as El Niño/Southern Oscillation, which can also include a cold phase known as a La Niña.

According to NOAA (August 7, 2007, http://www.cpc.ncep.noaa.gov/products/analysis_monitoring/enso stuff/ensoyears.shtml), El Niños occurred off and on between 1991 and 1995 and then during 1997–98, 2002–03, 2004–05, and 2006–07. These events disrupted the ocean-atmosphere system in the Pacific Ocean with subsequent effects on weather around the planet. Some scientists believe that the sudden and unexpected El Niño that formed during the summer of 2006 lessened hurricane formation during a season that had been predicted to be active. The El Niño caused increased wind shear over the Caribbean region, which tended to suppress hurricane formation. As an additional advantage, a strong low pressure system that dominated over the eastern United States pushed hurricanes away from the mainland and out into sea. The occurrence of more frequent and stronger hurricanes is a prediction widely associated by the public with global warming, because hurricanes thrive in warm waters. However, as this example shows, climate events are difficult to predict because of a number of variables.

The Effects of Aerosols

Aerosols are extremely tiny particles and/or liquid droplets that disperse in the atmosphere. Primary natural sources include volcanoes, forest fires, soil, sand, dust, sea salt, and scores of biological organisms and refuse particles (bacteria, pollen, dead skin cells, dander, spores, fungi, marine plankton, etc.). Aerosols are also produced by many fuel combustion and industrial processes and are a component of soot and smoke.

Aerosols in the atmosphere have direct and indirect effects on climate. A direct effect is that they scatter and absorb radiation. Indirectly they also modify the formation and water content of clouds. Aerosols can linger for several years in the troposphere and are returned to Earth in precipitation. Even though their exact effects on climate are not well understood, it is believed that they have a temporary cooling effect on the atmosphere.

VOLCANIC ACTIVITY. Volcanic activity, such as the 1991 eruption of the Mount Pinatubo volcano in the Philippines, can temporarily reduce the amount of solar radiation reaching the Earth. Volcanoes spew vast quantities of particles and gases into the atmosphere, including sulfur dioxide, which combines with water to form tiny supercooled droplets. The droplets create a long-lasting global haze that reflects and scatters sunlight, reducing energy from the sun and preventing its rays from heating the Earth, thereby causing the planet to cool. Scientists report that the Pinatubo eruption reduced solar radiation by more than 3%, compared with the baseline amount occurring in 1958.

This effect was previously seen in 1982, when the eruption of the El Chichon volcano in Mexico depressed global temperatures for about four years. In 1815 a major eruption of the Tambora volcano in Indonesia produced serious weather-related disruptions, such as crop-killing summer frosts in the United States and Canada. It became known as the "year without a summer." Furthermore, for several years following the Tambora eruption, people around the world commented on the beautiful sunsets, which were caused by the suspension of volcano-related particulate matter in the atmosphere.

The IPCC Rates Scientific Understanding about Climate Factors

In each of its assessments the IPCC rates the level of scientific understanding about climate factors that affect radiative forcing—the heating and cooling of Earth. The fourth assessment report rates as "high" the level of scientific understanding about the heating effect of long-lived greenhouse gases, such as CO_2. Less is known about the heating effect of tropospheric ozone and the believed cooling effect of stratospheric ozone. Likewise, there is still much to learn about surface albedo and its contribution to cooling and heating. The IPCC rates as "low" the level of scientific understanding about some forcing components, including solar irradiance, airplane vapor contrails, and aerosols in the atmosphere.

SOME RESEARCHERS QUESTION THE CAUSES OF GLOBAL WARMING

Even though there is widespread agreement among scientists that Earth's temperature has warmed in recent years, there is lingering debate over the causes of this warming. Some scientists believe that major climate events should be viewed in terms of thousands of years, not just a century. A record of only the past century may indicate, but not prove, that a major change has occurred. Is it caused by anthropogenic greenhouse gases, or is it natural variability?

Among the claims of critics of global climate warming are:

- Climate has been known to change dramatically within a relatively short period without any human influence.

- Temperature readings already showed increased temperatures before CO_2 levels rose significantly (before 1940).

- Natural variations in climate may exceed any human-caused climate change.

- Some of the increase in temperatures can be attributed to sunspot activity.

- If warming should occur, it will not stress Earth; it may even have benefits, such as for agriculture, and may delay the next ice age.

- Reducing emissions will raise energy prices, reduce the GDP, and produce job losses in the United States.

- Even though clouds are crucial to climate predictions, so little is known about them that computer models cannot produce accurate predictions.

There are a handful of scientists notably known for their criticism of the IPCC and its conclusions about anthropogenic causes of global warming. They believe that modeling results exaggerate the role of CO_2 emissions on climate and attack what they see as environmental hysteria on a subject about which much is still unknown by the scientific community. In the op-ed "Climate of Fear: Global-Warming Alarmists Intimidate Dissenting Scientists into Silence" (*Wall Street Journal*, April 12, 2006), Richard Lindzen of the Massachusetts Institute of Technology complains that "scientists who dissent from the alarmism have seen their grant funds disappear, their work derided, and themselves libeled as industry stooges, scientific hacks or worse."

PUBLIC OPINION ABOUT GLOBAL WARMING

In March 2007 the Gallup Organization conducted its annual poll on topics related to the environment. Participants were asked several questions about the greenhouse effect and global warming.

As shown in Figure 3.17, only 22% of those asked thought they understood very well the "greenhouse effect" issue. Nearly one out of five admitted either that they did not understand it very well (19%) or not at all (4%). Just over half (55%) said they understood the issue fairly well. When asked about the causes of global warming, a majority (60%) said that the temperature increase was due to the effects of pollution from human activities. (See Figure 3.18.) More than a third (35%) blamed natural causes.

Opinion was evenly split on whether the seriousness of global warming has been exaggerated or not. (See Figure 3.19.) Gallup found that 34% of those responding felt that the seriousness had been generally underestimated. Another 29% thought it was generally correct, and 33% felt that the seriousness was generally exaggerated. As shown in Figure 3.20, nearly two-thirds (63%) of those asked stated that global warming will not pose a "serious threat" to their way of life during their lifetime. Thirty five percent of respondents believed that it will pose a "serious threat."

FIGURE 3.17

FIGURE 3.18

Public understanding about the issue of global warming, March 2007

NEXT, THINKING ABOUT THE ISSUE OF GLOBAL WARMING, SOMETIMES CALLED THE "GREENHOUSE EFFECT," HOW WELL DO YOU FEEL YOU UNDERSTAND THIS ISSUE—WOULD YOU SAY VERY WELL, FAIRLY WELL, NOT VERY WELL, OR NOT AT ALL?

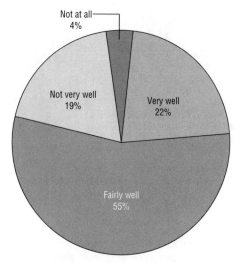

SOURCE: Adapted from "Next, thinking about the issue of global warming, sometimes called the 'greenhouse effect,' how well do you feel you understand this issue—would you say very well, fairly well, not very well, or not at all?" in *Environment*, The Gallup Organization, 2007, http://www.galluppoll.com/content/?ci=1615&pg=1 (accessed June 19, 2007). Copyright © 2007 by The Gallup Organization. Reproduced by permission of The Gallup Organization.

Public opinion on the causes of global warming, March 2007

AND FROM WHAT YOU HAVE HEARD OR READ, DO YOU BELIEVE INCREASES IN THE EARTH'S TEMPERATURE OVER THE LAST CENTURY ARE DUE MORE TO— THE EFFECTS OF POLLUTION FROM HUMAN ACTIVITIES (OR) NATURAL CHANGES IN THE ENVIRONMENT THAT ARE NOT DUE TO HUMAN ACTIVITIES?

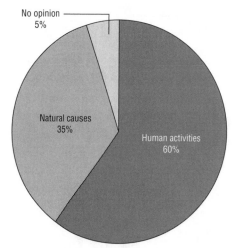

SOURCE: Adapted from "And from what you have heard or read, do you believe increases in the Earth's temperature over the last century are due more to—[ROTATED: the effects of pollution from human activities (or) natural changes in the environment that are not due to human activities]?" in *Environment*, The Gallup Organization, 2007, http://www.galluppoll.com/content/?ci=1615&pg=1 (accessed June 19, 2007). Copyright © 2007 by The Gallup Organization. Reproduced by permission of The Gallup Organization.

Gallup also asked people about specific measures that individuals and the U.S. government could take to reduce global warming. The results indicate that large majorities of people support steps such as using fluorescent lightbulbs and solar panels to make their homes more energy efficient and riding mass transit whenever possible. There was also widespread support for government research and usage of renewable energy sources, even if it means increasing taxes.

Even though Gallup's 2007 poll did not specifically ask poll participants about the Kyoto Protocol, this topic has been addressed in previous Gallup polls. In 2005 pollsters found that more people support the treaty than oppose it. Figure 3.21 illustrates that 42% of poll respondents indicated that the United States should agree to abide by the provisions of the treaty, compared with 23% who disagreed. A sizable percentage (35%) of those asked had no opinion on the matter.

FIGURE 3.19

**Public opinion on whether the media exaggerates the
seriousness of global warming, March 2007**

THINKING ABOUT WHAT IS SAID IN THE NEWS, IN YOUR VIEW IS THE
SERIOUSNESS OF GLOBAL WARMING—GENERALLY EXAGGERATED,
GENERALLY CORRECT, OR IS IT GENERALLY UNDERESTIMATED?

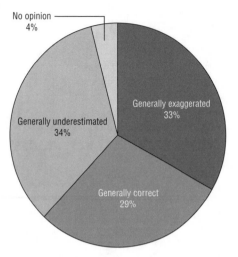

SOURCE: Adapted from "Thinking about what is said in the news, in your
view is the seriousness of global warming—[ROTATED: generally
exaggerated, generally correct, or is it generally underestimated]?" in
Environment, The Gallup Organization, 2007, http://www.galluppoll
.com/content/?ci=1615&pg=1 (accessed June 19, 2007). Copyright ©
2007 by The Gallup Organization. Reproduced by permission of The
Gallup Organization.

FIGURE 3.20

**Public opinion on the seriousness of the threat posed by
global warming, March 2007**

DO YOU THINK THAT GLOBAL WARMING WILL POSE A SERIOUS THREAT TO YOU
OR YOUR WAY OF LIFE IN YOUR LIFETIME?

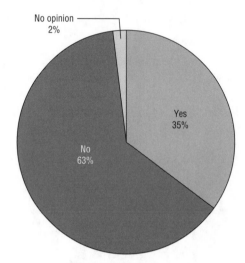

SOURCE: Adapted from "Do you think that global warming will pose a
serious threat to you or your way of life in your lifetime?" in
Environment, The Gallup Organization, 2007, http://www.galluppoll
.com/content/?ci=1615&pg=1 (accessed June 19, 2007). Copyright ©
2007 by The Gallup Organization. Reproduced by permission of The
Gallup Organization.

FIGURE 3.21

Public opinion on whether the U.S. should abide by the Kyoto agreement on global warming, April 2005

"BASED ON WHAT YOU HAVE HEARD OR READ, DO YOU THINK THE UNITED STATES SHOULD, OR SHOULD NOT, AGREE TO ABIDE BY THE PROVISIONS OF THE KYOTO AGREEMENT ON GLOBAL WARMING?"

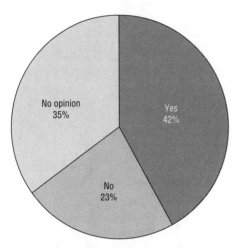

No opinion
35%

Yes
42%

No
23%

SOURCE: Adapted from "Based on what you have heard or read, do you think the United States should, or should not, agree to abide by the provisions of the Kyoto agreement on global warming?" in *Environment*, The Gallup Organization, April 2005, http://www.gallup.com/poll/content/default.aspx?ci=1615 (accessed August 4, 2005). Copyright © 2005 by The Gallup Organization. Reproduced by permission of The Gallup Organization.

CHAPTER 4
A HOLE IN THE SKY: OZONE DEPLETION

EARTH'S PROTECTIVE OZONE LAYER

Ozone is a gas naturally present in Earth's atmosphere. Unlike regular oxygen, which contains two oxygen atoms (O_2), ozone contains three oxygen atoms (O_3). A molecule of regular oxygen can be converted to ozone by ultraviolet (UV) radiation, electrical discharge (such as from lightning), or complex chemical reactions. These processes split apart the two oxygen atoms, which are then free to bind with other loose oxygen atoms to form ozone.

Ozone exists in Earth's atmosphere at two levels: the troposphere and the stratosphere. (See Figure 4.1.) Tropospheric (ground-level) ozone accounts for only a small portion of Earth's total ozone, but it is a potent air pollutant with serious health consequences. Ground-level ozone is the primary component in smog and is formed via complex chemical reactions involving emissions of industrial chemicals and through fossil fuel combustion. Ozone formation is intensified during hot weather, when more radiation reaches the ground. Smog retards crop and tree growth, impairs health, and limits visibility.

Approximately 90% of the Earth's ozone lies in the stratosphere at altitudes greater than about twenty miles. (See Figure 4.2.) Ozone molecules at this level protect life on Earth by absorbing UV radiation from the sun and preventing it from reaching the ground. The so-called ozone layer is actually a scattering of molecules constantly undergoing change from oxygen to ozone and back. Even though most of the ozone changes back to oxygen, a small amount of ozone persists. As long as this natural process stays in balance, the overall ozone layer remains thick enough to protect the Earth from harmful UV radiation from the sun. The amount of ozone in the stratosphere varies greatly, depending on location, altitude, and temperature.

EVIDENCE OF OZONE DEPLETION

Many scientists believe that the introduction of certain chemicals into the stratosphere alters the natural ozone balance by depleting ozone molecules. Chlorine and bromine atoms are particularly destructive. They can bind to loose oxygen atoms and prevent them from reforming either oxygen or ozone. Chlorine and bromine are found in the sea salt from ocean spray. Chlorine is also present in the form of hydrochloric acid, which is emitted with volcanic gases. These are natural sources of ozone-depleting chemicals.

In the mid-1970s scientists began to speculate that the ozone layer was rapidly being destroyed by reactions involving industrial chemicals that contained chlorine and bromine. Two chemists, F. Sherwood Rowland (1927–) and Mario Molina (1943–), discovered that chlorofluorocarbons (CFCs) could break down in the stratosphere, releasing chlorine atoms that could destroy thousands of ozone molecules. This discovery led to a ban on CFCs as a propellant in aerosols in the United States and other countries.

In 1984 British scientists at Halley Bay in Antarctica measured the ozone in the air column above them and discovered alarmingly low concentrations. Measurements indicated ozone levels about 50% lower than they had been in the 1960s.

Scientists report ozone concentrations in Dobson units. The unit is named after Gordon M. B. Dobson, a British scientist who invented an instrument for measuring ozone concentrations from the ground. One Dobson unit (DU) corresponds to a layer of atmospheric ozone that would be 0.001 millimeters thick if it was compressed into a layer at standard temperature and pressure at the Earth's surface. Atmospheric ozone is considered "thin" if its concentration falls below 220 DU. A thin spot in the ozone layer is commonly called an ozone hole.

The extreme cold and unique climate conditions over the poles are thought to make the ozone layers there particularly susceptible to thinning. Where cloud and ice particles are present, reactions that hasten ozone destruction also

FIGURE 4.1

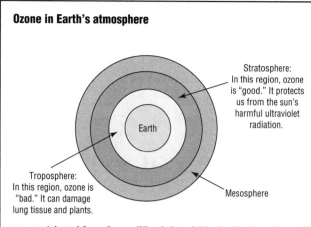

Ozone in Earth's atmosphere

Stratosphere:
In this region, ozone is "good." It protects us from the sun's harmful ultraviolet radiation.

Earth

Troposphere:
In this region, ozone is "bad." It can damage lung tissue and plants.

Mesosphere

SOURCE: Adapted from *Ozone: What Is It and Why Do We Care about It? NASA Facts*, National Aeronautics and Space Administration, Goddard Space Flight Center, May 1998

FIGURE 4.2

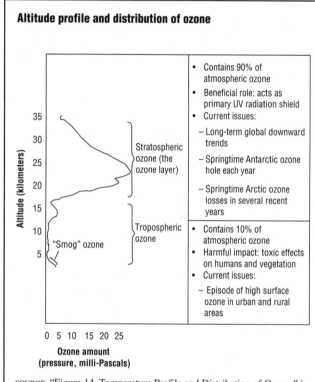

Altitude profile and distribution of ozone

- Contains 90% of atmospheric ozone
- Beneficial role: acts as primary UV radiation shield
- Current issues:
  - Long-term global downward trends
  - Springtime Antarctic ozone hole each year
  - Springtime Arctic ozone losses in several recent years

Stratospheric ozone (the ozone layer)

Tropospheric ozone

- Contains 10% of atmospheric ozone
- Harmful impact: toxic effects on humans and vegetation
- Current issues:
  - Episode of high surface ozone in urban and rural areas

"Smog" ozone

Altitude (kilometers)

Ozone amount (pressure, milli-Pascals)

0 5 10 15 20 25

SOURCE: "Figure 14. Temperature Profile and Distribution of Ozone," in *Reporting and Climate Change: Understanding the Science*, National Safety Council, Environmental Health Center, June 2000, http://www.nsc.org/public/ehc/climate/chaptr5.pdf (accessed September 30, 2007)

occur on the surface of ice particles. Since 1982 an ozone hole has appeared each year over Antarctica (the South Pole) beginning in August and lasting until November. The hole formation is linked to polar clouds that form during the dark Antarctic winter (May through September). These clouds provide reaction surfaces for chlorine-containing compounds to release their chlorine. As sunlight

returns in August or September, the released chlorine begins destroying ozone molecules.

The Antarctic ozone hole increased in size throughout the 1980s. By the early 1990s it was consistently larger than the area of Antarctica. Throughout most of the early 2000s the hole has been larger in size than the continent of North America. In 2002 the size of the hole dropped dramatically because of unusually warm weather at the South Pole. As shown in Figure 4.3, the 2006 hole measured twenty-six million square kilometers (ten million square miles) in size, constituting the largest area recorded since 1998.

In 1995 scientists first detected thinning of the ozone over the Arctic (the North Pole). Historically, Arctic winters have been warmer than those in Antarctica (the South Pole). This helped protect the northern pole from ozone depletion. However, during the 1990s and early 2000s scientists reported increasingly colder temperatures over the Arctic region and the formation of more polar clouds. In April 2005 European researchers reported the lowest Arctic levels of ozone since monitoring began decades ago.

The World Meteorological Organization (WMO) notes in *Scientific Assessment of Ozone Depletion: 2002* (2002, http://www.esrl.noaa.gov/csd/assessments/2002/) that the average total ozone column on a global-wide basis was approximately 3% lower between 1997 and 2001 when compared with pre-1980 average values. The most dramatic changes were recorded in the polar regions and midlatitudes (between the tropics and the poles). Most of the global population lives in the midlatitudes of the Northern and Southern Hemispheres. For instance, mainland United States lies approximately in the range of 30 degrees and 50 degrees north latitude.

CONSEQUENCES OF OZONE DEPLETION

The sun emits radiation at a variety of wavelengths. The ozone layer acts as a protective shield against UV radiation (i.e., radiation with wavelengths of approximately 290 to 400 nanometers; a nanometer is one billionth of a meter). As ozone diminishes in the upper atmosphere, the Earth could receive more UV radiation. In "Ozone Science: The Facts behind the Phaseout" (December 26, 2006, http://www.epa.gov/ozone/science/sc_fact.html), the U.S. Environmental Protection Agency (EPA) reports that the amount of UV radiation reaching the ground in Antarctica can double during the existence of its annual ozone hole.

Scientists are particularly worried about the increased exposure to radiation in the ultraviolet-B (UVB) spectrum (i.e., wavelengths of approximately 190 to 320 nanometers). This wavelength can be damaging to human health, because it is linked with adverse effects to deoxyribonucleic acid (DNA), skin, eyes, and the immune system.

FIGURE 4.3

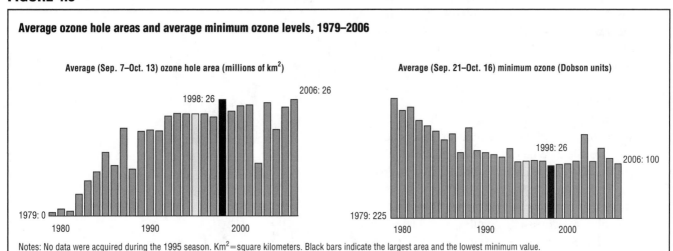

Average ozone hole areas and average minimum ozone levels, 1979–2006

Average (Sep. 7–Oct. 13) ozone hole area (millions of km²)

Average (Sep. 21–Oct. 16) minimum ozone (Dobson units)

Notes: No data were acquired during the 1995 season. Km²=square kilometers. Black bars indicate the largest area and the lowest minimum value.

SOURCE: "Annual Record Since 1979," in *Ozone Hole Watch*, National Aeronautics and Space Administration, Goddard Space Flight Center, December 31, 2006, http://ozonewatch.gsfc.nasa.gov/ (accessed June 14, 2007)

In addition, excessive exposure to UV radiation can negatively affect terrestrial and aquatic ecosystems and damage synthetic materials.

UV radiation alters photosynthesis, plant yield, and growth in plant species. Phytoplankton (one-celled organisms found in the ocean) are the backbone of the marine food web. According to the EPA, excessive exposure to UVB radiation reduces the productivity and survival rate for these organisms. Diminishing phytoplankton supplies would likely harm many fish species that depend on them for food. Studies performed in the mid-1990s blamed the rise in UV radiation caused by the thinning of the ozone layer for the decline in the number of frogs and other amphibians.

Increased UV radiation also affects synthetic materials. Plastics are especially vulnerable, tending to weaken, become brittle and discolored, and break.

OZONE-DEPLETING CHEMICALS

Most ozone destruction in the atmosphere is believed to be anthropogenic (caused by humans). In 1998 the WMO estimated in *Scientific Assessment of Ozone Depletion: 1998* (http://www.esrl.noaa.gov/csd/assessments/1998/Exec Sum98.pdf) that only 18% of the sources contributing to ozone depletion were natural. The remaining 82% of sources contributing to ozone depletion were industrial chemicals. The blame is largely placed on chemicals developed by modern society for use as refrigerants, air conditioning fluids, solvents, cleaning agents, and foam-blowing agents. These chemicals can persist for years in the atmosphere. Thus, there is a significant lag between the time that emissions decline at the Earth's surface and the time at which ozone levels in the stratosphere recover.

Table 4.1 lists the chemicals of particular concern to scientists. Each chemical is assigned a value called an ozone depletion potential (ODP) based on its harmfulness to the ozone layer. The most common depleters are the chlorofluorocarbons CFC-11, CFC-12, and CFC-13. Each of these

TABLE 4.1

Lifetime and ozone depletion potential of various chemicals

	Lifetime in years	Ozone depletion potential
Class I		
CFC-11	45	1
CFC-12	100	1
CFC-13	640	1
CFC-113	85	0.8–1
CFC-114	300	0.94–1
CFC-115	1,700	0.44–0.6
Halon 1211	16	3–6
Halon 1301	65	10–12
Halon 2402	20	6–8.6
Carbon tetrachloride	26	0.73–1.1
Methyl bromide	0.7	0.38–0.6
Methyl chloroform	5	0.1–0.12
Class II		
HCFC-21	1.7	0.04
HCFC-22	1.2	0.05–0.055
HCFC-123	1.3	0.02–0.06
HCFC-124	5.8	0.02–0.04
HCFC-141b	9.3	0.1–0.12
HCFC-142b	17.9	0.06–0.07
HCFC-225ca	1.9	0.02–0.025
HCFC-225cb	5.8	0.03–0.033

Notes: The ODP is the ratio of the impact on ozone of a chemical compared to the impact of a similar mass of CFC-11. Thus, the ODP of CFC-11 is defined to be 1.0. Other CFCs and HCFCs have ODPs that range from 0.01 to 1.0. CFC=Chlorofluorocarbon. HCFC=Hydrochlorofluorocarbon. ODP=Ozone-depleting potential.

SOURCE: Adapted from "Class I Ozone-Depleting Substances" and "Class II Ozone-Depleting Substances," in *Ozone Depletion Chemicals*, U.S. Environmental Protection Agency, February 12, 2004, http://www.epa.gov/ozone/ods.html and http://www.epa.gov/ozone/ods2.html (accessed July 20, 2007)

chemicals is arbitrarily assigned an ODP of 1. The ODPs for other chemicals are determined by comparing their relative harmfulness with that of CFC-11. In general, Class I chemicals are those with an ODP value greater than or equal to 0.2, and Class II chemicals have ODP values less than 0.2.

Class I Chemicals

Even though a number of chemicals can destroy stratospheric ozone, CFCs are the main offenders because they are so prevalent. When CFCs were invented in 1928, they were welcomed as chemical wonders. Discovered by Thomas Midgley Jr. (1889–1944), they were everything the refrigeration industry needed at the time: nontoxic, nonflammable, noncorrosive, stable, and inexpensive. Their artificial cooling provided refrigeration for food and brought comfort to warm climates. The compound was originally marketed under the trademark Freon.

Over time, new formulations were discovered, and the possibilities for use seemed endless. CFCs could be used as coolants in air conditioners and refrigerators, as propellants in aerosol sprays, in certain plastics such as polystyrene, in insulation, in fire extinguishers, and as cleaning agents. World production doubled every five years through 1970, and another growth spurt occurred in the 1980s as new uses were discovered—primarily as a solvent to clean circuit boards and computer chips.

CFCs are extremely stable; it is this stability that allows them to float intact through the troposphere and into the ozone layer. The National Aeronautics and Space Administration (NASA) estimates in "Peering into the Ozone Hole" (October 2, 2000, http://science.nasa.gov/headlines/y2000/ast02oct_1.htm) that it can take up to two years for CFC molecules to reach the stratosphere. Once there, some can survive for hundreds of years. CFCs do not degrade in the lower atmosphere but, after entering the stratosphere, they encounter the sun's UV radiation and eventually break down into chlorine, fluorine, and carbon. Many scientists believe it is the chlorine that damages the ozone layer. (See Figure 4.4.)

Even though CFCs are primarily blamed for ozone loss, other gases are also at fault. One of these gases is halon, which contains bromine. As shown in Table 4.1, halons have much higher ODP values than do CFCs. The bromine atoms in halons destroy ozone in a manner similar to that shown in Figure 4.4 for chlorine, but they are chemically more powerful. This means that the impact to ozone of a particular mass of halon is more destructive than a similar mass of a CFC. Halons are relatively long-lived in the atmosphere, lingering for up to sixty-five years before being broken down. Halon is used primarily for fighting fires. Civilian and military firefighting training accounts for much of the halon emission.

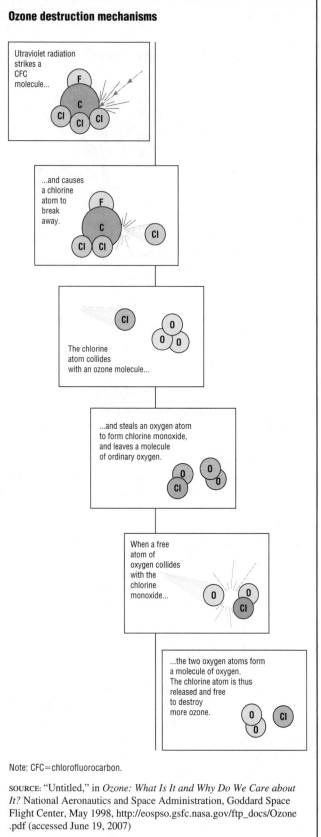

FIGURE 4.4

Ozone destruction mechanisms

Utraviolet radiation strikes a CFC molecule...

...and causes a chlorine atom to break away.

The chlorine atom collides with an ozone molecule...

...and steals an oxygen atom to form chlorine monoxide, and leaves a molecule of ordinary oxygen.

When a free atom of oxygen collides with the chlorine monoxide...

...the two oxygen atoms form a molecule of oxygen. The chlorine atom is thus released and free to destroy more ozone.

Note: CFC=chlorofluorocarbon.

SOURCE: "Untitled," in *Ozone: What Is It and Why Do We Care about It?* National Aeronautics and Space Administration, Goddard Space Flight Center, May 1998, http://eospso.gsfc.nasa.gov/ftp_docs/Ozone.pdf (accessed June 19, 2007)

Other Class I ozone destroyers include carbon tetrachloride, methyl bromide, and methyl chloroform. These chemicals are commonly used as solvents and cleaning agents.

Class II Chemicals

The most common Class II ozone-depleting chemicals are hydrochlorofluorocarbons (HCFCs). HCFCs contain hydrogen. This makes them more susceptible to atmospheric breakdown than CFCs. As shown in Table 4.1, most HCFCs have a lifetime of less than six years. The most long-lived, HCFC-142b, lasts for only 17.9 years. HCFCs have much lower ODP values than CFCs, halons, and industrial ozone depleters. HCFCs are considered good short-term replacements for CFCs. Even though HCFCs are less destructive to ozone than the chemicals they are replacing, scientists believe that HCFC use must also be phased out to allow the ozone layer to fully recover.

A LANDMARK IN INTERNATIONAL DIPLOMACY: THE MONTREAL PROTOCOL

CFCs and halons were widely used in thousands of products and represented a significant share of the international chemical industry, with billions of dollars in investment and hundreds of thousands of jobs. Ozone depletion was a global problem that necessitated international cooperation, but nations mistrusted one another's motives. As with the issues of global warming and pollution, developing countries resented being asked to sacrifice their economic development for a problem they felt the industrialized nations had created. To complicate matters, gaps in scientific proof led to disagreements over whether a problem actually existed.

In 1985, as the first international response to the ozone threat, twenty nations signed an agreement in Vienna, Austria, calling for data gathering, cooperation, and a political commitment to take action at a later date. In a 1987 negotiators meeting in Montreal, Canada, the participants finalized a landmark in international environmental diplomacy: the Montreal Protocol on Substances That Deplete the Ozone Layer. It is generally referred to as the Montreal Protocol. The protocol was signed by twenty-nine countries, including the United States, Canada, Mexico, Japan, Australia, all of western Europe, the Russian Federation, and a handful of other countries around the world.

The protocol called for industrial countries to cut CFC emissions in half by 1998 and to reduce halon emissions to 1986 levels by 1992. Developing countries were granted deferrals to compensate for their low levels of production. Industrial countries agreed to reimburse developing countries that complied with the protocol for "all agreed incremental costs," meaning all additional costs above any they would have expected to incur had they developed their infrastructure in the absence of the protocol. More important, the protocol also called for further amending as new data became available.

Throughout the 1990s and early 2000s new scientific information revealed that ozone depletion was occurring faster than expected. This news spurred calls to revise the

TABLE 4.2

Phase-out schedule under the Montreal Protocol for ozone-depleting substances

Ozone-depleting subtance	Developed countries must phase out by:	Developing countries must phase out by:
Halons	1994	2010
Carbon tetrachloride	1996	2010
Chlorofluorocarbons (CFCs)	1996	2010
Hydrobromofluorocarbons (HBFCs)	1996	1996
Methyl chloroform	1996	2015
Bromochloromethane	1999	1999
Methyl bromide	2005	2015
Hydrochlorofluorocarbons (HCFCs)	2030	2040

SOURCE: Created by Kim Masters Evans for Thomson Gale, 2007

treaty. In total, four amendments to the Montreal Protocol have been adopted. These are known as the London Amendment (effective 1992), the Copenhagen Amendment (effective 1994), the Montreal Amendment (effective 1999), and the Beijing Amendment (effective 2002). The final phaseout schedule for ozone-depleting substances is shown in Table 4.2.

According to the United Nations Environment Program (UNEP), in "Evolution of the Montreal Protocol: Status of Ratification" (August 6, 2007, http://ozone.unep.org/Ratification_status/index.shtml), as of 2007, 191 countries had ratified the original Montreal Protocol, whereas only 130 nations had ratified the Beijing Amendment. The United States has ratified all the amendments to the Montreal Protocol.

The Montreal Protocol has been hailed as a historic event—the most ambitious attempt ever to combat environmental degradation on a global scale. It ushered in a new era of environmental diplomacy. Some historians view the signing of the accord as a defining moment, the point at which the definition of international security was expanded to include environmental issues as well as military matters. In addition, an important precedent was established: that science and policy makers had a new relationship. Many observers thought that the decision to take precautionary action in the absence of complete proof of a link between CFCs and ozone depletion was an act of foresight that would now be possible with other issues.

MONTREAL PROTOCOL IMPLEMENTATION

In 2007 the UNEP marked the twentieth anniversary of the Montreal Protocol with issuance of the report *A Success in the Making* (http://ozone.unep.org/Publications/MP_A _Success_in_the_making-E.pdf), which details the progress made and the challenges remaining to be solved for complete implementation. According to the UNEP, the Montreal Protocol had been ratified by 191 countries by 2006, and those countries had phased out the production and consumption of more than 95% of the chemicals controlled by the agreement. The UNEP reports high levels of compliance in both developed and developing countries. The latter have been aided financially with money from the Multilateral Fund—a fund established under the protocol to assist developing nations with phaseout costs. The UNEP indicates that atmospheric levels of major ozone-depleting substances (ODS) have decreased and projects that full implementation of the protocol will return the ozone layer to pre-1980 levels by 2050 to 2075.

Despite these successes the UNEP recognizes that the program faces ongoing challenges to its full implementation. As shown in Table 4.2, developing nations must phase out CFCs, halons, and carbon tetrachloride by 2010. In *A Success in the Making*, the UNEP estimates that as of 2006 these countries had eliminated 72% of their usage, leaving sizable progress to be made within only four years. Furthermore, the UNEP notes in the press release "Backgrounder: Basic Facts and Data on the Science and Politics of Ozone Protection" (August 2003, http://www.unep.ch/ozone/pdf/Press-Backgrounder.pdf) that the use of CFCs is increasing, not decreasing, in many developing countries because of demand from growing middle-class populations for consumer products that use refrigerants. The UNEP complains that much of this demand is being met by the exportation of used and older refrigeration units that still use CFCs instead of acceptable alternatives. This is expected to make it much more difficult for the developing countries to reduce their demand for CFCs by the phaseout deadline.

Illegal Trade Problems

Illegal black market trading of ODS is another frequently mentioned challenge associated with implementing the Montreal Protocol. The Environmental Investigation Agency (EIA) is a London-based nonprofit organization that works to expose international environmental crimes. Tom Maliti notes in "Illegal Trade in Ozone-Depleting Substances Is Thriving over Three Continents, Says Report" (Associated Press, November 11, 2003) that in 2003 the EIA reported that international trade in illegal ozone-depleting substances was detrimental to achieving progress under the Montreal Protocol. The EIA noted that demand for illegal CFCs remained high in the United States, Russia, China, Vietnam, Cambodia, and Nepal. Ezra Clark of the EIA, in "Preventing Illegal Trade in ODS: Strengthening the Montreal Protocol Licensing System" (June 2007, http://www.eia-international.org/files/reports 138-1.pdf), indicates that weaknesses in the agreement's licensing system have allowed ODS smuggling to flourish. The EIA recommends tightening record keeping and enforcement requirements to help alleviate these problems.

THE U.S. BLACK MARKET. In 1996 the ban on CFCs was implemented in the developed countries, including the United States. The CFC called Freon was widely used in automobile air conditioners before that time. After the ban went into effect, there were still millions of Americans with cars that used Freon as a refrigerant. Even though alternative refrigerants were available, they were more expensive than Freon. The result was a black market for the product. This market expanded in the United States during the early 2000s with the boom in the illegal production of methamphetamine at so-called meth labs. Freon is commonly used in meth labs as part of the production process.

Several U.S. government agencies—the EPA, the U.S. Customs and Border Protection, the U.S. Departments of Commerce and Justice, and the Internal Revenue Service—began intensive antismuggling efforts. The Internal Revenue Service became involved because of the Revenue Reconciliation Act of 1989, which imposes an excise tax on most U.S. manufacturers, producers, and importers of ODS. During the early 2000s U.S. law enforcement officials broke up a massive Freon-smuggling ring based in Panama that operated during the 1990s to supply Freon to customers in southern Florida. The U.S. Department of Justice (DOJ) reports in "Defendant to Serve 17 Years in Prison for Smuggling Freon" (May 21, 2004, http://www.usdoj.gov/opa/pr/2004/May/04_tax_354.htm) that the ring leader was sentenced to seventeen years in prison and ordered to pay a $20.3 million fine. He also had to pay $6.5 million in restitution to the Internal Revenue Service for tax evasion. In another case, the DOJ notes in "Businessmen Sentenced to 88 Months in Prison for Scheme to Evade Taxes on Sales of Ozone-Depleting Chemical" (March 22, 2006, http://www.usdoj.gov/opa/pr/2006/March/06_enrd_164.html) that in 2005 two New York businessmen were convicted of dozens of counts in an ODS scheme. The two purchased large quantities of CFC-113 and avoided the excise tax by claiming that they intended to export the chemical. Instead, they sold it to U.S. buyers, including a laboratory supply company indicted in a separate investigation for selling CFC-113 to meth labs. In 2006 the two men received prison sentences of more than one year and were ordered to pay $1.9 million in restitution.

MONITORING DATA SHOW PROGRESS

The National Oceanic and Atmospheric Administration (NOAA) operates the Earth System Research Laboratory (ESRL), which is headquartered in Boulder, Colorado. The ESRL collects data at its observatories around the world and does research related to global trends in air quality.

Figure 4.5 shows atmospheric data collected by the ESRL for five ozone-depleting chemicals: CFC-11, CFC-12, CFC-113, methyl chloroform (CH_3CCl_3), and carbon tetrachloride (CCl_4). The data were collected at five ESRL observatories:

- Point Barrow, Alaska

- Niwot Ridge, Colorado

- Mauna Loa, Hawaii

FIGURE 4.5

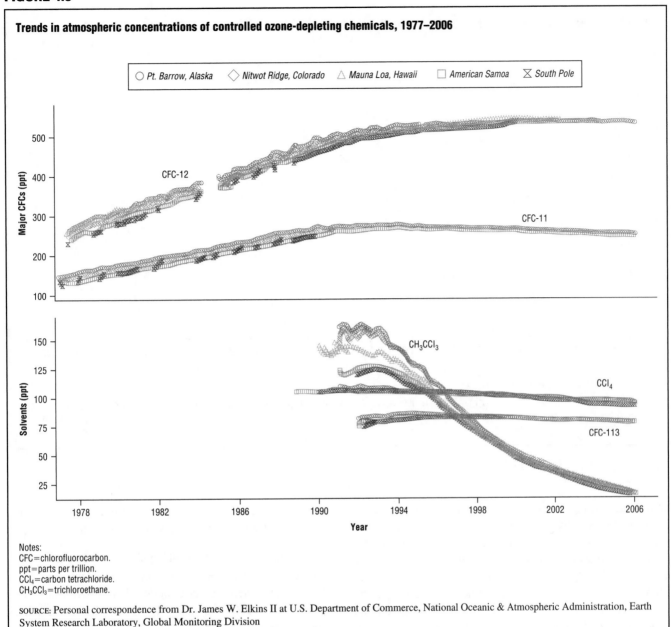

Trends in atmospheric concentrations of controlled ozone-depleting chemicals, 1977–2006

Notes:
CFC=chlorofluorocarbon.
ppt=parts per trillion.
CCl₄=carbon tetrachloride.
CH₃CCl₃=trichloroethane.

SOURCE: Personal correspondence from Dr. James W. Elkins II at U.S. Department of Commerce, National Oceanic & Atmospheric Administration, Earth System Research Laboratory, Global Monitoring Division

- Cape Matatula, American Samoa

- South Pole, Antarctica

After peaking in the 1990s, the atmospheric concentrations of CFC-11 began to decline. Concentrations of CFC-113, methyl chloroform, and carbon tetrachloride have declined dramatically since 1990. CFC-12 concentrations began to level off in 2002, after climbing steadily for decades. CFC-12 has the longest atmospheric lifetime (one hundred years) of the five compounds.

PREDICTING THE BENEFITS OF THE MONTREAL PROTOCOL

The EPA uses the model called the Atmospheric and Health Effects Framework (AHEF) to evaluate the human health impacts expected to be gained from mitigating (correcting) ozone depletion. Specifically, the model estimates the incidence and mortality of skin cancer cases in the United States for different control scenarios under the Montreal Protocol. According to the latest available AHEF report, *Human Health Benefits of Stratospheric Ozone Protection* (April 24, 2006, http://www.epa.gov/ozone/science/AHEFDEC2003D3.pdf), earlier versions of the model also estimated the incidence of cataracts (clouding of the natural eye lens). However, the EPA notes that the link between UV exposure and cataracts is now considered "weak." The AHEF uses stratospheric ozone levels from 1979 to 1980 as the baseline for its analysis.

Figure 4.6 presents AHEF predictions of stratospheric ozone column levels at 40 degrees to 50 degrees north

FIGURE 4.6

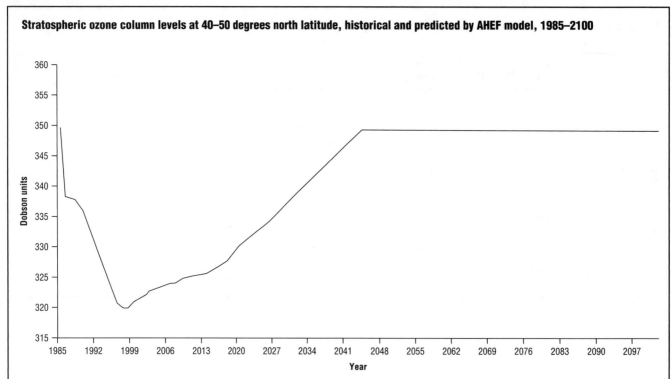

Stratospheric ozone column levels at 40–50 degrees north latitude, historical and predicted by AHEF model, 1985–2100

Note: AHEF=Atmospheric and health effects framework.

SOURCE: "Figure D-1. Stratospheric Ozone Column Levels at 40–50 Degrees North: AHEF Predictions, Montreal Adjustments," in *Human Health Benefits of Stratospheric Ozone Protection*, U.S. Environmental Protection Agency, April 24, 2006, http://www.epa.gov/ozone/science/AHEFDEC2003D3.pdf (accessed June 19, 2007)

latitude, assuming that the 1999 Montreal Amendment to the protocol is fully implemented. The EPA anticipates that ozone levels at this latitude range, which encompasses the northern U.S. mainland, will return to baseline levels by the 2040s. Figure 4.7 compares the original Montreal Protocol with its amendments in terms of the annual incidence of cutaneous malignant melanoma (CMM) cases. CMM is the least common but most dangerous form of skin cancer, because it can quickly spread to other parts of the body that are difficult to treat. As shown in Figure 4.7, the Montreal Amendment to the Montreal Protocol came closest to approaching the baseline incidence (for the period from 1979 to 1980), which is reflected in the y-axis. In other words, full implementation of the Montreal Amendment will come close to reducing the incidence of CMM to levels that occurred before 1980, when the ozone level had not yet been depleted. (Note that the Beijing Amendment is not included in the graph, because it would make only slight changes to the Montreal Amendment.)

THE LATEST SCIENTIFIC ASSESSMENT

Article 6 of the Montreal Protocol requires that the ratifying nations base their decision making on scientific information assessed and presented by an international panel of ozone experts. This panel includes the WMO, the UNEP, the European Commission, NOAA, and NASA.

In February 2007 the UNEP published the panel's latest findings in *Scientific Assessment of Ozone Depletion: 2006* (http://ozone.unep.org/Assessment_Panels/SAP/Scientific_Assessment_2006/index.shtml). This is the sixth scientific assessment of the world's ozone condition and is based on analysis of data collected from satellites, aircraft, balloons, and ground-based instruments and the results of laboratory investigations and computer modeling.

The following are the major findings:

• Global emissions of CFC-11 and CFC-12 in 2003 were approximately 25% of their maximum values reported back around 1986. CFC-113 emissions declined approximately 3% over the same time period. Emissions of all three ODS have declined since 2000.

• Stratospheric abundance of all ODS has declined since peaking in the late 1990s.

• Total column ozone values averaged globally for 2002–05 were 3.5% less than 1964–80 values. Ozone values over the Northern Hemisphere reached a minimum in the early 1990s and have been increasing since that

FIGURE 4.7

Projected annual incremental incidence of cutaneous malignant melanoma (CMM), based on various ozone depleting substance control policies, 1985–2100

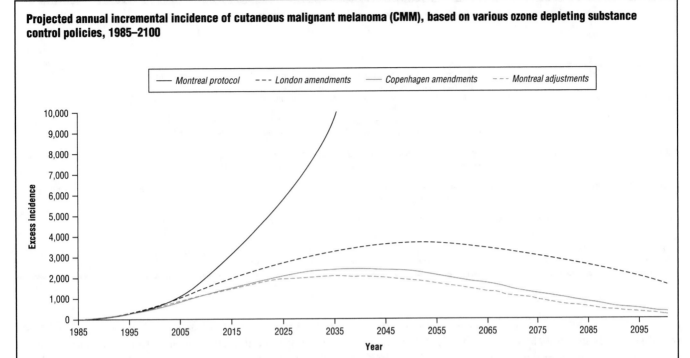

Notes: CMM=cutaneous malignant melanoma. Because this graph shows the incremental CMM incidence relative to the 1979–1980 baseline, the level of CMM incidence in the baseline is represented by zero on the y-axis.

SOURCE: "Figure 4. Annual Incremental U.S. CMM Incidence through 2100 Under Different ODS Control Policies (SCUP-h Action Spectrum)," in *Human Health Benefits of Stratospheric Ozone Protection*, U.S. Environmental Protection Agency, April 24, 2006, http://www.epa.gov/ozone/science/ AHEFDEC2003D3.pdf (accessed June 19, 2007)

time. In the Southern Hemisphere the levels decreased through the late 1990s before leveling off.

- Total column ozone is projected to increase by 1% to 2.5% between 2000 and 2020. By 2100 total column ozone should be approximately 5% greater than values recorded in 1980.

- Stratospheric chlorine levels are expected to return to pre-1980 levels by 2049 at the midlatitudes and by 2065 over Antarctica.

U.S. EFFORTS TO END OZONE DEPLETION

In April 2005 the U.S. Food and Drug Administration (FDA) adopted a final rule banning the use of such ozone-depleting substances as propellants in medical inhalers. This use was exempted from the general ban on CFCs that went into effect during the 1990s. The FDA rule prohibits the distribution of metered-dose inhalers (commonly used for the medical treatment of respiratory problems) using CFCs after December 31, 2008. The agency reports that alternative acceptable propellants for the devices are available on the market and should adequately serve patient needs.

Even though CFCs are no longer used in new applications in the United States, existing users can continue using them, provided they are maintained under strict regulation, such as being replenished and "reclaimed" by authorized technicians. The EPA Office of Enforcement and Compliance Assurance can levy civil fines and criminal prosecutions against companies and individuals who violate regulations regarding ODS.

Recycled halon and inventories produced before January 1, 1994, are the only supplies now available. It is legal under the Montreal Protocol and the U.S. Clean Air Act to import recycled halon, but each shipment requires approval from the EPA. Certain uses, such as fire protection, are classified as "critical use" and are permitted as long as supplies remain. The EPA also maintains a list of acceptable substitutes for halon.

SUBSTITUTES AND NEW TECHNOLOGIES

As pressure increased to discontinue the use of CFCs and halons, substitute chemicals and technologies began to be developed. One of the most popular substitutes is a class of compounds called hydrofluorocarbons (HFCs). HFCs do not contain chlorine, a potent ozone destroyer. Furthermore, they are relatively short-lived in the atmosphere— most survive intact for less than twelve years. This means that HFCs do not directly impact Earth's protective ozone layer. As a result, HFCs have ODP values of zero.

During the 1990s the use of HFCs increased dramatically. NASA reports that atmospheric levels of HFCs

TABLE 4.3

Global warming potential of common ozone-depleting substances and some alternatives

Substance	Uses	Global warming potential*
Chlorofluorocarbons (CFCs)	Refrigerants, cleaning solvents, aerosol propellants, and blowing agents for plastic foam manufacture.	4,680–10,720
Halons	Fire extinguishers/fire suppression systems, explosion protection.	1,620–7,030
Carbon tetrachloride (CCl_4)	Production of CFCs (feedstock), solvent/diluents, fire extinguishers.	1,380
Methyl chloroform ($CHCl_3$)	Industrial solvent for cleaning, inks, correction fluid.	144
Methyl bromide (CH_3Br)	Fumigant used to control soil-borne pests and diseases in crops prior to planting and in commodities such as stored grains. Fumigants are substances that give off fumes; they are often used as disinfectants or to kill pests.	5
Hydrochlorofluorocarbons (HCFCs)	Transitional CFC replacements used as refrigerants, solvents, blowing agents for plastic foam manufacture, and fire extinguishers. HCFCs deplete stratospheric ozone, but to a much lesser extent than CFCs; however, they are greenhouse gases.	76–2,270
Hydrofluorocarbons (HFCs)	CFC replacements used as refrigerants, aerosol propellants, solvents, and fire extinguishers. HFCs do not deplete stratospheric ozone, but they are greenhouse gases.	122–14,130

*Global warming potential (GWP) is the ratio of the warming caused by a substance compared to the warming caused by a similar mass of carbon dioxide. The GWP of carbon dioxide is 1.0.

SOURCE: Adapted from "Common Ozone-Depleting Substances and Some Alternatives," in *Achievements in Stratospheric Ozone Protection: Progress Report*, U.S. Environmental Protection Agency, April 2007, http://www.epa.gov/ozone/pdffile/spd-annual-report_final_highres_4-25-07.pdf (accessed June 19, 2007)

also surged during this time period. This is a concern to scientists studying global warming because HFCs are believed to enhance atmospheric heating. Also, HFC breakdown in the atmosphere produces a chemical called trifluoroacetic acid, large concentrations of which are known to be harmful to certain plants (particularly in wetlands). Continued heavy use of HFCs during the twenty-first century could introduce or aggravate other environmental problems.

The development of effective chemical substitutes with acceptable health and environmental effects is an enormous challenge. Some experts propose returning to the refrigerant gases used before the invention of CFCs. These include sulfur dioxide, ammonia, and various hydrocarbon compounds. However, these chemicals have their own issues; for example, most are highly toxic.

The EPA's Significant New Alternative Policy program evaluates alternatives to ozone-depleting substances and determines their acceptability for use. Submissions for evaluation include those that could be used in a variety of industrial applications, including refrigeration and air conditioning, foam blowing, and fire suppression and protection.

Many industrial engineers are pursuing new technologies for cooling, including semiconductors that cool down when charged with electricity, refrigeration that uses plain water as a refrigerant, and the use of thermoacoustics (sound energy). Extensive investment in research and development of new technologies will be required to produce cooling methods acceptable to industry and environmentalists.

THE GLOBAL WARMING CONNECTION

In *Scientific Assessment of Ozone Depletion: 2006*, the UNEP notes that "changes in ozone affect climate; and changes in climate affect ozone." As described in Chapter 3, the Earth's climate has been warming in recent decades and is expected to continue to do so. Many scientists blame this warming on a buildup in the atmosphere of anthropogenic emissions of chemicals, such as carbon dioxide. Many ODS are believed to contribute to this warming effect. Table 4.3 shows the global warming potential (GWP) of some common ODS and alternatives compared with a GWP value of 1 for carbon dioxide. CFCs and HFCs have GWP values that are several thousand times that of carbon dioxide. The Montreal Protocol has and will decrease emissions of CFCs. However, HFC emissions and their associated contribution to global warming are expected to increase as HFCs become common replacements for CFCs. Table 3.1 in Chapter 3 lists emissions of HFCs and other ODS substitutes for various years between 1990 and 2005.

On the other side of the equation, scientists are not completely sure how continued global warming will affect stratospheric ozone levels. The UNEP assessment predicts that future increases in greenhouse gas concentrations will contribute to cooling in the stratosphere. This could actually aid recovery of the ozone layer by slowing the rate of photochemical ozone destruction.

PUBLIC OPINION ABOUT THE OZONE LAYER ISSUE

In March 2007 the Gallup Organization conducted its annual poll of Americans' beliefs and attitudes about environmental issues. The results show that damage to the Earth's ozone layer ranks low on the list of environmental problems about which Americans are worried. (See Table 1.6 in Chapter 1.) Only 43% of those asked in 2007 expressed a great deal of worry about damage to the ozone layer. As shown in Figure 4.8, this percentage

FIGURE 4.8

Public concern about damage to the Earth's ozone layer, 1989–2007

	Great deal	Fair amount	Only a little	Not at all	No opinion
	%	%	%	%	%
2007 Mar 11–14	43	27	19	11	*
2006 Mar 13–16	40	28	19	13	*
2004 Mar 8–11	33	27	26	14	*
2003 Mar 3–5	35	31	21	12	1
2002 Mar 4–7	38	29	21	11	1
2001 Mar 5–7	47	28	16	8	1
2000 Apr 3–9	49	29	14	7	1
1999 Apr 13–14	44	32	15	8	1
1997 Oct 27–28	33	27	25	13	2
1991 Apr 11–14	49	24	16	8	4
1990 Apr 5–8	43	28	15	10	4
1989 May 4–7	51	26	13	8	2

*Less than 0.5%.

SOURCE: "I'm going to read you a list of environmental problems. As I read each one, please tell me if you personally worry about this problem a great deal, a fair amount, only a little, or not at all. First, how much do you personally worry about—Damage to the earth's ozone layer," in *Environment*, The Gallup Organization, 2007, http://www.galluppoll.com/content/?ci=1615&pg=1 (accessed June 19, 2007). Copyright © 2007 by The Gallup Organization. Reproduced by permission of The Gallup Organization.

is down from a peak of 51% in 1989. In 2007 another 27% expressed a fair amount of concern about the problem, whereas 19% felt only a little concern and 11% felt no concern at all.

CHAPTER 5
ACID RAIN

WHAT IS ACID RAIN?

Acid rain is the common name for acidic deposits that fall to Earth from the atmosphere. The term was coined in 1872 by the Scottish chemist Robert Angus Smith (1817–1884) to describe the acidic precipitation in Manchester, England. In the twenty-first century scientists study both wet and dry acidic deposits. Even though there are natural sources of acid in the atmosphere, acid rain is primarily caused by emissions of sulfur dioxide (SO_2) and nitrous oxide (N_2O) from electric utilities burning fossil fuels, especially coal. These chemicals are converted to sulfuric acid and nitric acid in the atmosphere and can be carried by the winds for many miles from where the original emissions took place. (See Figure 5.1.) Other chemicals contributing to acid rain include volatile organic compounds (VOCs). These are carbon-containing chemicals that easily become vapors or gases. VOC sources include paint thinners, degreasers, and other solvents and burning fuels such as coal, natural gas, gasoline, and wood.

Wet deposition occurs when the acid falls in rain, snow, or ice. Dry deposition is caused by tiny particles (or particulates) in combustion emissions. They may stay dry as they fall or pollute cloud water and precipitation. Moist deposition occurs when the acid is trapped in cloud or fog droplets. This is most common at high altitudes and in coastal areas. Whatever its form, acid rain can create dangerously high levels of acidic impurities in water, soil, and plants.

Measuring Acid Rain

The acidity of any solution is measured on a potential hydrogen (pH) scale numbered from zero to fourteen, with a pH value of seven considered neutral. (See Figure 5.2.) Values higher than seven are considered more alkaline or basic (the pH of baking soda is eight); values lower than seven are considered acidic (the pH of lemon juice is two).

The pH scale is a logarithmic measure. This means that every pH change of one is a tenfold change in acid content. Therefore, a decrease from pH seven to pH six is a tenfold increase in acidity; a drop from pH seven to pH five is a one hundredfold increase in acidity; and a drop from pH seven to pH four is a one thousandfold increase.

Pure, distilled water has a neutral pH of seven. Normal rainfall has a pH value of about 5.6. It is slightly acidic because it accumulates naturally occurring sulfur oxides (SO_x) and nitrogen oxides (NO_x) as it passes through the atmosphere. Acid rain has a pH of less than 5.6.

Figure 5.3 shows the average rainfall pH measured during 2005 at various locations around the country by the National Atmospheric Deposition Program (NADP), a cooperative project between many state and federal government agencies and private entities. Rainfall was most acidic in the mid-Atlantic region and upper Southeast, particularly Ohio, Pennsylvania, West Virginia, Maryland, Delaware, Virginia, eastern Tennessee, and Kentucky. The areas with the lowest rainfall pH contain some of the country's most sensitive natural resources, such as the Appalachian Mountains, the Adirondack Mountains, Chesapeake Bay, and Great Smoky Mountains National Park. Overall, precipitation is much more acidic in the eastern United States than in the western United States because of a variety of natural and anthropogenic (human-caused) factors that are discussed below.

SOURCES OF SULFATE AND NITRATE IN THE ATMOSPHERE
Natural Sources

Natural sources of sulfate in the atmosphere include ocean spray, volcanic emissions, and readily oxidized hydrogen sulfide, which is released from the decomposition of organic matter found in the Earth. Natural sources of nitrogen or nitrates include NO_x produced by microorganisms in soils, by lightning during thunderstorms,

FIGURE 5.1

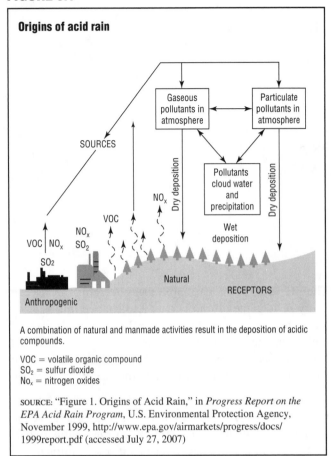

Origins of acid rain

A combination of natural and manmade activities result in the deposition of acidic compounds.

VOC = volatile organic compound
SO$_2$ = sulfur dioxide
No$_x$ = nitrogen oxides

SOURCE: "Figure 1. Origins of Acid Rain," in *Progress Report on the EPA Acid Rain Program*, U.S. Environmental Protection Agency, November 1999, http://www.epa.gov/airmarkets/progress/docs/1999report.pdf (accessed July 27, 2007)

FIGURE 5.2

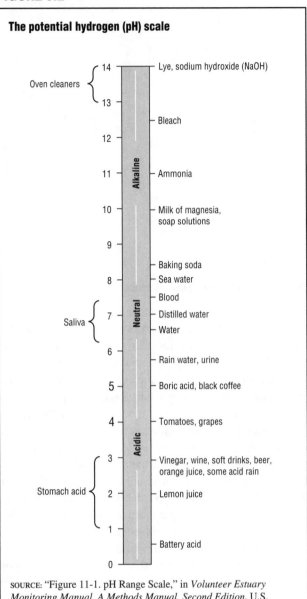

The potential hydrogen (pH) scale

SOURCE: "Figure 11-1. pH Range Scale," in *Volunteer Estuary Monitoring Manual, A Methods Manual, Second Edition*, U.S. Environmental Protection Agency, March 2006, http://www.epa.gov/nep/monitor/documents/chap11.pdf (accessed July 20, 2007)

and by forest fires. Scientists generally speculate that one-third of the sulfur and nitrogen emissions in the United States comes from these natural sources. (This is a rough estimate as there is no way to measure natural emissions as opposed to those that are manmade.)

Sources Caused by Human Activity

According to the U.S. Environmental Protection Agency (EPA), in "What Is Acid Rain?" (June 8, 2007, http://www.epa.gov/acidrain/what/index.html), the primary anthropogenic contributors to acid rain are SO$_2$ and NO$_x$, resulting from the burning of fossil fuels, such as coal, oil, and natural gas.

The EPA notes in "Clearinghouse for Inventories and Emissions Factors" (http://www.epa.gov/ttn/chief/trends/trends06/nationaltier1upto2006basedon2002finalv2.1.xls) that approximately 70% of SO$_2$ emissions produced in 2006 were because of fuel combustion by fossil-fueled electric utilities. Fuel combustion at industrial facilities contributed another 13%. Lesser sources included transportation vehicles and industrial processes. Highway vehicles were the primary source of NO$_x$ emissions, accounting for 36% of the total in 2006. Off-highway vehicles (such as bulldozers) contributed 22%. Fuel combustion in power plants was another major source,

accounting for 20% of the total. Lesser sources included industrial processes and waste disposal and recycling

NATURAL FACTORS THAT AFFECT ACID RAIN DEPOSITION

Major natural factors contributing to the impact of acid rain on an area include air movement, climate, and topography and geology. Transport systems—primarily the movement of air—distribute acid emissions in definite patterns around the planet. The movement of air masses transports emitted pollutants many miles, during which the pollutants are transformed into sulfuric and nitric acid by mixing with clouds of water vapor.

FIGURE 5.3

Laboratory measurements of pH values from the National Atmospheric Deposition Program/National Trends Network, 2005

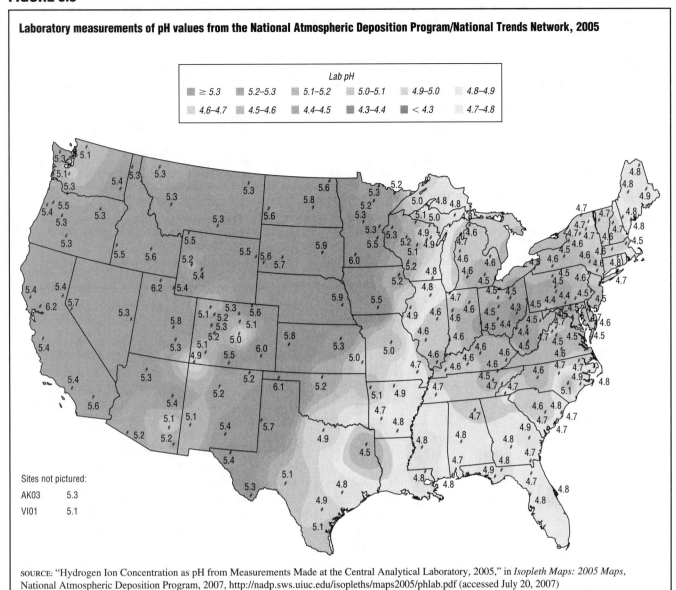

SOURCE: "Hydrogen Ion Concentration as pH from Measurements Made at the Central Analytical Laboratory, 2005," in *Isopleth Maps: 2005 Maps*, National Atmospheric Deposition Program, 2007, http://nadp.sws.uiuc.edu/isopleths/maps2005/phlab.pdf (accessed July 20, 2007)

In drier climates, such as those of the western United States, windblown alkaline dust moves more freely through the air and tends to neutralize atmospheric acidity. The effects of acid rain can be greatly reduced by the presence of basic (also called alkali) substances. Sodium, potassium, and calcium are examples of basic chemicals. When a basic and an acid chemical come into contact, they react chemically and neutralize each other. By contrast, in more humid climates where there is less dust, such as along the eastern seaboard, precipitation is more acidic.

Areas most sensitive to acid rain contain hard, crystalline bedrock and thin surface soils. When no alkaline-buffering particles are in the soil, runoff from rainfall directly affects surface waters, such as mountain streams. In contrast, a thick soil covering or soil with a high buffering capacity, such as flat land, neutralizes acid rain better. Lakes tend to be most susceptible to acid rain

because of low alkaline content in lake beds. A lake's depth, its watershed (the area draining into the lake), and the amount of time the water has been in the lake are also factors.

EFFECTS OF ACID RAIN ON THE ENVIRONMENT

In nature the combination of rain and oxides is part of a natural balance that nourishes plants and aquatic life. However, when the balance is upset by acid rain, the results to the environment can be harmful and destructive. (See Table 5.1.)

Aquatic Systems

Even though pH levels vary considerably from one body of water to another, a typical pH range for the lakes and rivers in the United States is six to eight. Low pH levels kill fish, their eggs, and fish food organisms. The

TABLE 5.1

Effects of acid rain on human health and selected ecosystems and anticipated recovery benefits

Human health and ecosystem	Effects	Recovery benefits
Human health	In the atmosphere, sulfur dioxide and nitrogen oxides become sulfate and nitrate aerosols, which increase morbidity and mortality from lung disorders, such as asthma and bronchitis, and impacts to the cardiovascular system.	Decrease emergency room visits, hospital admissions, and deaths.
Surface waters	Acidic surface waters decrease the survivability of animal life in lakes and streams and in the more severe instances eliminate some or all types of fish and other organisms.	Reduce the acidic levels of surface waters and restore animal life to the more severely damaged lakes and streams.
Forests	Acid deposition contributes to forest degradation by impairing trees' growth and increasing their susceptibility to winter injury, insect infestation, and drought. It also causes leaching and depletion of natural nutrients in forest soil.	Reduce stress on trees, thereby reducing the effects of winter injury, insect infestation, and drought, and reduce the leaching of soil nutrients, thereby improving overall forest health.
Materials	Acid deposition contributes to the corrosion and deterioration of buildings, cultural objects, and cars, which decreases their value and increases costs of correcting and repairing damage.	Reduce the damage to buildings, cultural objects, and cars, and reduce the costs of correcting and repairing future damage.
Visibility	In the atmosphere, sulfur dioxide and nitrogen oxides form sulfate and nitrate particles, which impair visibility and affect the enjoyment of national parks and other scenic views.	Extend the distance and increase the clarity at which scenery can be viewed, thus reducing limited and hazy scenes and increasing the enjoyment of national parks and other vistas.

SOURCE: "Appendix I. Effect of Acid Rain on Human Health and Selected Ecosystems and Anticipated Recovery Benefits," in *Acid Rain: Emissions Trends and Effects in the Eastern United States*, U.S. General Accounting Office, March 2000, http://www.gao.gov/archive/2000/rc00047.pdf (accessed July 27, 2007)

degree of damage depends on several factors, one of which is the buffering capacity of the watershed soil—the higher the alkalinity, the more slowly the lakes and streams acidify. The exposure of fish to acidified freshwater lakes and streams has been intensely studied since the 1970s. Scientists distinguish between sudden shocks and chronic (long-term) exposure to low pH levels.

Sudden, short-term shifts in pH levels result from snowmelts, which release acidic materials accumulated during the winter, or sudden rainstorms that can wash residual acid into streams and lakes. The resulting acid shock can be devastating to fish and their ecosystems. At pH levels below 4.9, fish eggs are damaged. At acid levels below 4.5, some species of fish die. Below pH 3.5, most fish die within hours. (See Table 5.2.)

TABLE 5.2

Generalized short-term effects of acidity on fish

pH range	Effect
6.5–9	No effect
6.0–6.4	Unlikely to be harmful except when carbon dioxide levels are very high ($>1,000$ mg l^{-1})
5.0–5.9	Not especially harmful except when carbon dioxide levels are high (>20 mg l^{-1}) or ferric ions are present
4.5–4.9	Harmful to the eggs of salmon and trout species (salmonids) and to adult fish when levels of Ca^{2+}, Na^+ and Cl^- are low
4.0–4.4	Harmful to adult fish of many types which have not been progressively acclimated to low pH
3.5–3.9	Lethal to salmonids, although acclimated roach can survive for longer
3.0–3.4	Most fish are killed within hours at these levels

SOURCE: "Generalized Short-Term Effects of Acidity on Fish," in *National Water Quality Inventory: 1998 Report to Congress*, U.S. Environmental Protection Agency, June 2000

Because many species of fish hatch in the spring, even mild increases in acidity can harm or kill the new life. Temporary increases in acidity also affect insects and other invertebrates, such as snails and crayfish, on which the fish feed.

Gradual decreases of pH levels over time affect fish reproduction and spawning. Moderate levels of acidity in water can confuse a salmon's sense of smell, which it uses to find the stream from which it came. Atlantic salmon are unable to find their home streams and rivers because of acid rain. In addition, excessive acid levels in female fish cause low amounts of calcium, thereby preventing the production of eggs. Even if eggs are produced, their development is often abnormal.

Increased acidity can also cause the release of aluminum and manganese particles that are stored in a lake or river bottom. High concentrations of these metals are toxic to fish.

Soil and Vegetation

Acid rain is believed to harm vegetation by changing soil chemistry. Soils exposed to acid rain can gradually lose valuable nutrients, such as calcium, magnesium, and potassium and become too concentrated with dissolved inorganic aluminum, which is toxic to vegetation. Long-term changes in soil chemistry may have already affected sensitive soils, particularly in forests. Forest soils saturated in nitrogen cannot retain other nutrients required for healthy vegetation. Subsequently, these nutrients are washed away. Nutrient-poor trees are more vulnerable to climatic extremes, pest invasion, and the effects of other air pollutants, such as ozone.

FIGURE 5.4

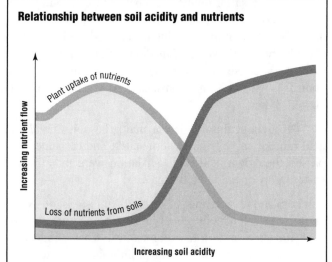

Relationship between soil acidity and nutrients

Increasing nutrient flow

Plant uptake of nutrients

Loss of nutrients from soils

Increasing soil acidity

Note: As soil and deposition acidity increases, nutrients, such as base cations, are leached from the soil and are not available for plant growth.

SOURCE: "Figure 18. Relationship between Soil Acidity and Nutrients," in *Progress Report on the EPA Acid Rain Program*, U.S. Environmental Protection Agency, Air and Radiation, November 1999, www.epa.gov/airmarkets/progress/docs/1999report.pdf (accessed July 27, 2007)

Some researchers believe that acid rain disrupts soil regeneration, which is the recycling of chemical and mineral nutrients through plants and animals back to the Earth. They also believe acids suppress decay of organic matter, a natural process needed to enrich the soils. Valuable nutrients such as calcium and magnesium are normally bound to soil particles and are, therefore, protected from being rapidly washed into groundwater. Acid rain, however, may accelerate the process of breaking these bonds to rob the soil of these nutrients. This, in turn, decreases plant uptake of vital nutrients. (See Figure 5.4.)

Acid deposition can cause leafy plants such as lettuce to hold increased amounts of potentially toxic substances such as the mineral cadmium. Research also finds a decrease in carbohydrate production in the photosynthesis process of some plants exposed to acid conditions. Research is under way to determine whether acid rain could ultimately lead to a permanent reduction in tree growth, food crop production, and soil quality. Effects on soils, forests, and crops are difficult to measure because of the many species of plants and animals, the slow rate at which ecological changes occur, and the complex interrelationships between plants and their environment.

TREES. The effect of acid rain on trees is influenced by many factors. Some trees adapt to environmental stress better than others; the type of tree, its height, and its leaf structure (deciduous or evergreen) influence how well it will adapt to acid rain. Scientists believe that acid rain directly harms trees by leaching calcium from their foliage and indirectly harms them by lowering their tolerance to other stresses.

According to the EPA, acid rain has also been implicated in impairing the winter hardening process of some trees, making them more susceptible to cold-weather damage. In some trees the roots are prone to damage because the movement of acidic rain through the soil releases aluminum ions, which are toxic to plants.

One area in which acid rain has been linked to direct effects on trees is from moist deposition via acidic fogs and clouds. The concentrations of acid and SO_x in fog droplets are much greater than in rainfall. In areas of frequent fog, such as London, significant damage has occurred to trees and other vegetation because the fog condenses directly on the leaves.

Birds

Increased freshwater acidity harms some species of migratory birds. Experts believe the dramatic decline of the North American black duck population since the 1950s is because of decreased food supplies in acidified wetlands. Acid rain leaches calcium out of the soil and robs snails of the calcium they need to form shells. Because titmice and other species of songbirds get most of their calcium from the shells of snails, the birds are also perishing. The eggs they lay are defective—thin and fragile. The chicks either do not hatch or have bone malformations and die.

In "Adverse Effects of Acid Rain on the Distribution of the Wood Thrush *Hylocichla mustelina* in North America" (*Proceedings of the National Academy of Sciences*, August 12, 2002), Ralph S. Hames et al. discuss the results of their large-scale study, which shows a clear link between acid rain and widespread population declines in the wood thrush, a type of songbird. Hames and his colleagues believe that calcium depletion has had a negative impact on this bird's food source, mainly snails, earthworms, and centipedes. The bird may also be ingesting high levels of metals that are more likely to leach out of overly acidic soils. Declining wood thrush populations are most pronounced in the higher elevations of the Adirondack, Great Smoky, and Appalachian mountains. Hames and his cohorts warn that acid rain may also be contributing to population declines in other songbird species.

Materials

Acid rain can also be harmful to materials, such as building stones, marble statues, metals, and paints. Elaine McGee of the U.S. Geological Service reports in *Acid Rain and Our Nation's Capital* (1997, http://pubs.usgs.gov/gip/acidrain/contents.html) that limestone and marble are particularly vulnerable to acid rain. Historical monuments and buildings composed of these materials in the eastern United States have been hit hard by acid rain.

Human Health

Acid rain has several direct and indirect effects on humans. Particulates are extremely small pollutant particles that can threaten human health. Particulates related to acid rain include fine particles of SO_x and nitrates. These particles can travel long distances and, when inhaled, penetrate deep into the lungs. Acid rain and the pollutants that cause it can lead to the development of bronchitis and asthma in children. Acid rain is also believed to be responsible for increasing health risks for those over the age of sixty-five; those with asthma, chronic bronchitis, and emphysema; pregnant women; and those with histories of heart disease.

THE POLITICS OF ACID RAIN

Scientific research on acid rain was sporadic and largely focused on local problems until the late 1960s, when Scandinavian scientists began more systematic studies. Acid precipitation in North America was not identified until 1972, when scientists found that precipitation was acidic in eastern North America, especially in northeastern and eastern Canada. In 1975 the First International Symposium on Acid Precipitation and the Forest Ecosystem convened in Columbus, Ohio, to define the acid rain problem. Scientists used the meeting to propose a precipitation-monitoring network in the United States that would cooperate with the European and Scandinavian networks and to set up protocols for collecting and testing precipitation.

In 1977 the Council on Environmental Quality was asked to develop a national acid rain research program. Several scientists drafted a report that eventually became the basis for the National Acid Precipitation Assessment Program (NAPAP). This initiative eventually translated into legislative action with the Energy Security Act of 1980. Title VII (Acid Precipitation Act of 1980) of the act produced a formal proposal that created NAPAP and authorized federally financed support.

The first international treaty aimed at limiting air pollution was the United Nations Economic Commission for Europe (UNECE) Convention on Long-Range Transboundary Air Pollution, which went into effect in 1983. It was ratified by thirty-eight of the fifty-four UNECE members, which included not only European countries but also Canada and the United States. The treaty targeted sulfur emissions, requiring that countries reduce emissions 30% from 1980 levels—the so-called Thirty Percent Club.

The early acid rain debate centered almost exclusively on the eastern United States and Canada. The controversy was often defined as a problem of property rights. The highly valued production of electricity in coal-fired utilities in the Ohio River Valley caused acid rain to fall on land in the Northeast and Canada. An important part of the acid rain controversy in the 1980s was the adversarial relationship between U.S. and Canadian government officials over emission controls of SO_2 and NO_2. More of these pollutants crossed the border into Canada than the reverse. Canadian officials very quickly came to a consensus over the need for more stringent controls, whereas this consensus was lacking in the United States.

Throughout the 1980s the major lawsuits involving acid rain all came from eastern states, and the states that passed their own acid rain legislation were those in the eastern part of the United States.

Legislative attempts to restrict emissions of pollutants were often defeated after strong lobbying by the coal industry and utility companies. These industries advocated further research for pollution-control technology rather than placing restrictions on utility company emissions.

The NAPAP Controversy

In 1980 Congress established NAPAP to study the causes and effects of acid deposition and recommend policy approaches for controlling acid rain effects. About two thousand scientists worked on this unique interagency program, which ultimately cost more than $500 million. Even though its first report was due in 1985, the program was plagued by problems that resulted in numerous delays. In 1985 the first executive director, Christopher Bernabo, resigned and was replaced by Lawrence Kulp. In 1987 the study group released to Congress *Interim Assessment: The Causes and Effects of Acidic Deposition*, a massive four-volume preliminary report that caused a storm of controversy. The report contained detailed scientific information in its technical chapters about acid rain. The executive summary, written by Kulp, was released to the public and widely criticized for misrepresenting the scientific findings of the report and downplaying the negative effects of acid rain. Philip Shabecoff notes in "Acid Rain Report Unleashes a Torrent of Controversy" (*New York Times*, March 20, 1990) that critics claimed Kulp had slanted the summary to match the political agenda of the administration of President Ronald Reagan (1911–2004), which advocated minimum regulation of business and industry.

Some of the scientific findings in the 1987 report included:

- Acid rain had adversely affected aquatic life in about 10% of eastern lakes and streams.

- Acid rain had contributed to the decline of red spruce at high elevations by reducing this species' cold tolerance.

- Acid rain had contributed to erosion and corrosion of buildings and materials.

- Acid rain and related pollutants had reduced visibility throughout the Northeast and in parts of the West.

The report concluded, however, that the incidence of serious acidification was more limited than originally feared. At that time the Adirondacks area of New York was the only region showing widespread, significant damage from acid. Furthermore, results indicated that electricity-generating power plants were responsible for two-thirds of SO_2 emissions and one-third of NO_x emissions.

Controversy over Kulp's role led to him being replaced by James Mulhoney. The new director ordered reassessments and revisions of the interim report. This was completed in 1991. However, by that time President George H. W. Bush (1924–) was in power, and he had made acid rain legislation a component of his election campaign. As a result, political forces, rather than NAPAP, largely drove the nation's emerging policy toward acid rain.

THE ACID RAIN PROGRAM—CLEAN AIR ACT AMENDMENTS, TITLE IV

Congress created the Acid Rain Program under Title IV (Acid Deposition Control) of the 1990 Clean Air Act Amendments. The goal of the program is to reduce annual emissions of SO_2 and NO_x from electric power plants nationwide. The program set a permanent cap on the total amount of SO_2 that could be emitted by these power plants. According to the EPA, in *Acid Rain Program: 2005 Progress Report* (October 2006, http://www.epa.gov/airmarkets/progress/docs/2005report.pdf), this cap was set at 8.9 million tons (approximately half the number of tons of SO_2 emitted by these plants during 1980). The program also established NO_x emissions limitations for certain coal-fired electric utility plants. The objective of these limitations was to achieve and maintain a two-million-ton reduction in NO_x emission levels by 2000 compared with the emissions that would have occurred in 2000 if the limitations had not been implemented.

In the *1999 Compliance Report: Acid Rain Program* (July 2000, http://www.epa.gov/airmarkets/progress/docs/1999compreport.pdf), the EPA indicates that the reduction was implemented in two phases. Phase I began in 1995 and covered 263 units at 110 utility plants in 21 states with the highest levels of emissions. Most of these units were at coal-burning plants located in eastern and midwestern states. They were mandated to reduce their annual SO_2 emissions by 3.5 million tons. An additional 182 units joined Phase I voluntarily, bringing the total of Phase I units to 445.

Phase II began in 2000. It tightened annual emission limits on the Phase I group and set new limits for more than two thousand cleaner and smaller units in all forty-eight contiguous states and the District of Columbia.

A New Flexibility in Meeting Regulations

Traditionally, environmental regulation has been achieved by the "command and control" approach, in which the regulator specifies how to reduce pollution, by what amount, and what technology to use. Title IV, however, gave utilities flexibility in choosing how to achieve these reductions. For example, utilities could reduce emissions by switching to low-sulfur coal, installing pollution-control devices called scrubbers, or shutting down plants.

Utilities took advantage of their flexibility under Title IV to choose less costly ways to reduce emissions—many switching from high- to low-sulfur coal—and as a result, they have been achieving sizable reductions in their SO_2 emissions.

Allowance Trading

Title IV also allows electric utilities to trade allowances to emit SO_2. Utilities that reduce their emissions below the required levels can sell their extra allowances to other utilities to help them meet their requirements.

Title IV allows companies to buy, sell, trade, and bank pollution rights. Utility units are allocated allowances based on their historic fuel consumption and a specific emissions rate. Each allowance permits a unit to emit one ton of SO_2 during or after a specific year. For each ton of SO_2 discharged in a given year, one allowance is retired and can no longer be used. Companies that pollute less than the set standards will have allowances left over. They can then sell the difference to companies that pollute more than they are allowed, bringing them into compliance with overall standards. Companies that clean up their pollution would recover some of their costs by selling their pollution rights to other companies.

The EPA holds an allowance auction each year. The sale offers allowances at a fixed price. This use of market-based incentives under Title IV is regarded by many as a major new method for controlling pollution.

From 1995 to 1998 there was considerable buying and selling of allowances among utilities. Because the utilities that participated in Phase I reduced their sulfur emissions more than the minimum required, they did not use as many allowances as they were allocated for the first four years of the program. Those unused allowances could be used to offset SO_2 emissions in future years. In *Acid Rain: Emissions Trends and Effects in the Eastern United States* (March 2000, http://www.gao.gov/archive/2000/rc00047.pdf), the U.S. General Accounting Office (now the U.S. Government Accountability Office) notes that from 1995 to 1998 a total of 30.2 million allowances were allocated to utilities nationwide; almost 8.7 million,

FIGURE 5.5

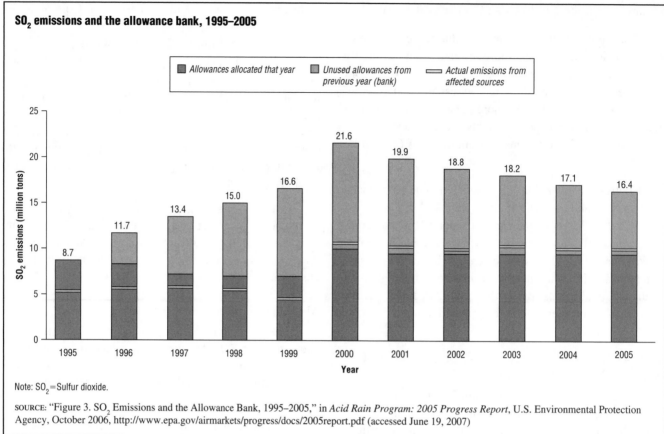

SO₂ emissions and the allowance bank, 1995–2005

Note: SO₂ = Sulfur dioxide.

SOURCE: "Figure 3. SO₂ Emissions and the Allowance Bank, 1995–2005," in *Acid Rain Program: 2005 Progress Report*, U.S. Environmental Protection Agency, October 2006, http://www.epa.gov/airmarkets/progress/docs/2005report.pdf (accessed June 19, 2007)

or 29%, of the allowances were not used but were carried over (banked) for subsequent years.

Figure 5.5 shows the status of the allowance bank from 1995 through 2005. Banked allowances increased dramatically in 2000 due to the addition of the Phase II sources to the Acid Rain Program. Over the next five years the allowance bank steadily decreased in size. The EPA reports in *Acid Rain Program: 2005 Progress Report* that in 2005 a total of 9.5 million allowances were allocated. Another 6.9 million banked allowances were carried over from previous years. The EPA expects that the allowance bank will eventually be depleted as SO₂ emissions are further restricted by the implementation of the Clean Air Interstate Rule.

PERFORMANCE RESULTS OF THE ACID RAIN PROGRAM

There are three quantitative measures that environmental regulators use to gauge the performance of the Acid Rain Program: emissions, atmospheric concentrations, and deposition amounts.

U.S. Progress Report

The following information comes from the EPA's *Acid Rain Program: 2005 Progress Report*.

SOURCES AND EMISSIONS. The report notes that in 2005 there were 3,456 electric generating units subject to the SO₂ provisions of the Acid Rain Program. Most emissions were associated with approximately 1,100 coal-fired units making up the total. In all, program sources emitted 10.2 million tons of SO₂ into the air. (See Figure 5.6.) The EPA expects that the 8.9-million-ton annual cap on emissions will be achieved by 2010. SO₂ emissions from sources covered by the program decreased by 41% between 1980 and 2005.

In 2005 the NOₓ portion of the Acid Rain Program applied to a subset of the 3,456 units mentioned earlier, specifically 982 operating coal-fired units generating at least 25 megawatts. Between 1990 and 2005 NOₓ emissions from power plants subject to the Acid Rain Program decreased from 5.5 million tons per year to 3.3 million tons per year. (See Figure 5.7.)

According to the report, in 2000 the program first achieved its goal of reducing emissions by at least 2 million tons; 8.1 million tons were originally predicted in 1990 to be emitted in 2000 without the program in place.

The report indicates that the SO₂ and NOₓ emission reductions were achieved even though the amount of fuel used to produce electricity in the United States increased by more than 30% between 1990 and 2005. Coal was the

FIGURE 5.6

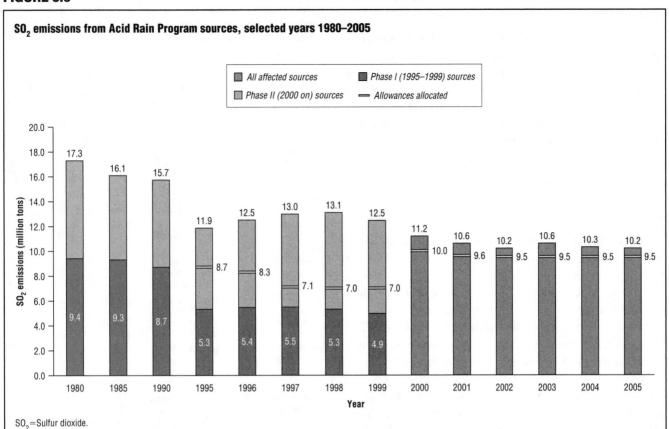

SO₂ emissions from Acid Rain Program sources, selected years 1980–2005

SO₂=Sulfur dioxide.

SOURCE: "Figure 2. SO₂ Emissions from Acid Rain Program Sources," in *Acid Rain Program: 2005 Progress Report*, U.S. Environmental Protection Agency, October 2006, http://www.epa.gov/airmarkets/progress/docs/2005report.pdf (accessed June 19, 2007)

FIGURE 5.7

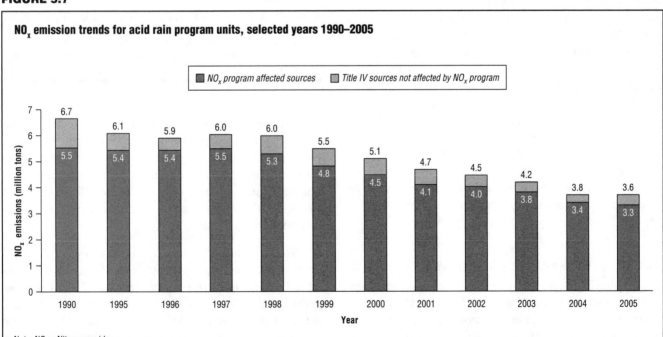

NOₓ emission trends for acid rain program units, selected years 1990–2005

Note: NOx=Nitrogen oxides.

SOURCE: "Figure 12. NOₓ Emission Trends for Acid Rain Program Units, 1990–2005," in *Acid Rain Program: 2005 Progress Report*, U.S. Environmental Protection Agency, October 2006, http://www.epa.gov/airmarkets/progress/docs/2005report.pdf (accessed June 19, 2007)

single-largest fuel source for U.S. electric generating plants in 2005, accounting for 50% of the total.

ATMOSPHERIC CONCENTRATIONS AND DEPOSITION AMOUNTS. The EPA's Acid Rain Program uses two complementary monitoring networks to track trends in regional air quality and acid deposition: the Clean Air Status and Trends Network and the NADP's National Trends Network. Additional monitoring data are provided by national, state, and local ambient monitoring systems.

As shown in Figure 2.14 and Figure 2.6 in Chapter 2, atmospheric levels of SO_2 and NO_2 averaged nationwide since 1990 have been well below the national standards for these pollutants.

Table 5.3 shows trends in atmospheric concentrations and deposition for four key regions in the Acid Rain Program: mid-Atlantic, Midwest, Northeast, and Southeast. Overall, concentrations of ambient SO_2 and wet sulfates averaged over the period 2003–05 declined in all these regions, compared with the period 1989–91. The most dramatic differences are evident in the Northeast, where ambient SO_2 concentrations decreased by more than 50%. The results for nitrogen and nitrate compound concentrations are mixed, with decreases in some areas and increases in others. The same is true for wet inorganic nitrogen deposition, which decreased in the mid-Atlantic, Midwest, and Northeast, but increased slightly in the Southeast.

Canadian Progress Report

In November 2006 Environment Canada released a report on progress made by Canada and the United States on cross-border air pollution. The study, *Canada–United States Air Quality Agreement: 2006 Progress Report* (http://www.ec.gc.ca/cleanair-airpur/caol/canus/report/2006canus/toc_e.cfm), is the eighth biennial report related to the 1991 agreement between the two countries. The report states that Canada has been successful at reducing SO_2 emissions below its national cap. Canada's total SO_2 emissions were 2.3 million tonnes (metric tons) in 2004, which is 28% below the national cap of 3.2 million tonnes. However, Environment Canada notes that the reductions have not been sufficient to reduce acid deposition below the levels needed to ensure the recovery of ecosystems damaged by excess acidity in its eastern provinces.

ARE ECOSYSTEMS RECOVERING?

Monitoring data clearly indicate decreased emissions and atmospheric concentrations of SO_2 and NO_x and some reductions in deposition amounts. These improvements have not necessarily resulted in recovery of sensitive aquatic and terrestrial ecosystems. This is due, in part, to the long recovery times required to reverse damage done by acidification. The EPA reports that ecosys-

TABLE 5.3

Regional changes in air quality and deposition of sulfur and nitrogen, 1989–91 and 2003–05

Measurement	Unit	Region	Average 1989–1991	Average 2003–2005	Percent change*
Wet sulfate deposition	kg/ha	Mid-Atlantic	27	20	−24
		Midwest	23	16	−32
		Northeast	23	14	−36
		Southeast	18	15	−19
Wet sulfate concentration	mg/L	Mid-Atlantic	2.4	1.6	−33
		Midwest	2.3	1.6	−30
		Northeast	1.9	1.1	−40
		Southeast	1.3	1.1	−21
Ambient sulfur dioxide concentration	μg/m³	Mid-Atlantic	13	8.4	−34
		Midwest	10	5.8	−44
		Northeast	6.8	3.1	−54
		Southeast	5.2	3.4	−35
Ambient sulfate concentration	μg/m³	Mid-Atlantic	6.4	4.5	−30
		Midwest	5.6	3.8	−33
		Northeast	3.9	2.5	−36
		Southeast	5.4	4.1	−24
Wet inorganic nitrogen deposition	kg/ha	Mid-Atlantic	5.9	5.5	−8
		Midwest	6.0	5.5	−8
		Northeast	5.3	4.1	−23
		Southeast	4.3	4.4	+2
Wet nitrate concentration	mg/L	Mid-Atlantic	1.5	1.0	−29
		Midwest	1.4	1.2	−14
		Northeast	1.3	0.9	−33
		Southeast	0.8	0.7	−9
Ambient nitrate concentration	μg/m³	Mid-Atlantic	0.9	1.0	+5
		Midwest	2.1	1.8	−14
		Northeast	0.4	0.5	+20
		Southeast	0.6	0.7	+17
Total ambient nitrate concentration (nitrate + nitric acid)	μg/m³	Mid-Atlantic	3.5	3.0	−14
		Midwest	4.0	3.5	−12
		Northeast	2.0	1.7	−13
		Southeast	2.2	2.1	−5

*Percent change is estimated from raw measurement data, not rounded; some of the measurement data used to calculate percentages may be at or below detection limits. Notes: kg=kilogram. ha=hectare. mg=milligram. L=liter. μg=microgram. m³=cubic meter.

SOURCE: "Table 4. Regional Changes in Air Quality and Deposition of Sulfur and Nitrogen, 1989–1991 Versus 2003–2005," in *Acid Rain Program: 2005 Progress Report*, U.S. Environmental Protection Agency, October 2006, http://www.epa.gov/airmarkets/progress/docs/2005report.pdf (accessed June 19, 2007)

tems harmed by acid rain deposition can take a long time to fully recover even after harmful emissions cease. The most chronic aquatic problems can take years to be resolved. Forest health is even slower to improve following decreases in emissions, taking decades to recover. Finally, soil nutrient reserves (such as calcium) can take centuries to replenish.

The most recent comprehensive analysis of acidified ecosystems was presented by NAPAP in the *National Acid Precipitation Assessment Program Report to Congress: An Integrated Assessment* (2003, http://www.cleartheair.org/documents/NAPAP_FINAL_print.pdf). The report presents a literature review summarizing findings from various government and academic studies. Overall, NAPAP finds that some ecosystems affected by acid deposition are showing limited signs of recovery. For example, one study shows that more than 25% of affected lakes and streams studied in the Adirondacks and northern Appalachians are no longer acidic. However, little to no improvement has been seen in examined water bodies in other regions, including New England and portions of Virginia. The report notes that even though chemical recovery has begun in some waterways, complete recovery for aquatic life forms, such as fish, is expected to take "significantly longer."

In regards to terrestrial ecosystems, NAPAP reports that forests are under many stresses besides acid rain, such as global warming, land use changes, and air pollution from urban, agricultural, and industrial sources. The combined effect of these stressors has greatly limited forest recovery from acidification. According to NAPAP, "There are as yet no forests in the U.S. where research indicates recovery from acid deposition is occurring." However, it is expected that reduced emissions under the Acid Rain Program will benefit forests in the long term.

The report acknowledges the future benefits of continued implementation of the Acid Rain Program, but it concludes that "the emission reductions achieved by Title IV are not sufficient to allow recovery of acid-sensitive ecosystems." Recent studies support the idea that additional emission cuts 40% to 80% beyond those of the existing program will be needed to protect acid-sensitive ecosystems. NAPAP modeling indicates that even virtual elimination of SO_2 emissions from power plants will be insufficient to provide this protection. It is believed that emission reductions from other sources (such as the industrial and transport sectors) will be necessary.

The Next Step: The Clean Air Interstate Rule

In 2005 the EPA issued the Clean Air Interstate Rule (CAIR; April 5, 2007, http://www.epa.gov/cair/) to address the transport of air pollutants across state lines in the eastern United States. CAIR puts permanent caps on emissions of SO_2 and NO_x in twenty-eight eastern states and the District of Columbia. It is expected to reduce SO_2 emissions by more than 70% and reduce NO_x emissions by more than 60% compared with 2003 levels. These measures should reduce the formation of acid rain and other pollutants, such as fine particulate matter and ground-level ozone.

The CAIR program will use a cap-and-trade system similar to that used in the SO_2 portion of the acid rain program. The EPA projects that complete implementa-

tion of CAIR in 2015 will result in up to $100 billion in annual health benefits and a substantial reduction in premature deaths because of air pollution in the eastern United States. It should also improve visibility in southeastern national parks that have been plagued by smog in recent years.

PUBLIC OPINION ABOUT ACID RAIN

Every year the Gallup Organization polls Americans about their attitudes regarding environmental issues. The most recent poll to assess acid rain was conducted in March 2007. Participants were asked to express their level of personal concern about various environmental issues, including acid rain, water pollution, soil contamination, air pollution, plant and animal extinctions, loss of tropical rain forests, damage to the ozone layer, and global warming. The results showed that acid rain ranked last among these environmental problems.

Analysis of historical Gallup poll results shows a dramatic decline in concern about acid rain since the late 1980s. (See Table 5.4.) In 1989 Gallup found that 41% of respondents felt a great deal of concern about acid rain and 11% felt none at all. By 2007 only 25% of people polled were concerned a great deal about acid rain and 20% expressed no concern about the acid rain issue.

TABLE 5.4

Public concern about acid rain, 1989–2007

	Great deal	Fair amount	Only a little	Not at all	No opinion
	%	%	%	%	%
2007 Mar 11–14	25	25	28	20	1
2006 Mar 13–16	24	28	24	23	1
2004 Mar 8–11	20	26	27	26	1
2003 Mar 3–5	24	26	27	21	2
2002 Mar 4–7	25	23	31	19	2
2001 Mar 5–7	28	28	26	16	2
2000 Apr 3–9	34	31	19	15	1
1999 Apr 13–14	29	35	23	11	2
1991 Apr 11–14	34	30	20	14	3
1990 Apr 5–8	34	30	18	14	4
1989 May 4–7	41	27	19	11	3

SOURCE: "I'm going to read you a list of environmental problems. As I read each one, please tell me if you personally worry about this problem a great deal, a fair amount, only a little, or not at all. First, how much do you personally worry about—Acid Rain," in *Environment*, The Gallup Organization, 2007, http://www.galluppoll.com/content/?ci=1615&pg=1 (accessed June 19, 2007). Copyright © 2007 by The Gallup Organization. Reproduced by permission of The Gallup Organization.

CHAPTER 6
NONHAZARDOUS WASTE

All waste materials not specifically deemed hazardous under federal law are considered nonhazardous wastes. The vast majority of waste produced in the United States is not inherently hazardous. It includes paper, wood, plastics, glass, metals, and chemicals, as well as other materials generated by industrial, commercial, agricultural, and residential sources. Even though these wastes are not defined as hazardous, improper management of them poses significant risks to the environment and human health. Therefore, the handling, transport, and disposal of nonhazardous wastes is regulated by the government, largely at the state and local level.

LAWS REGARDING WASTE

In 1965 the U.S. government passed the Solid Waste Disposal Act, the first of many solid waste management laws. It was amended several times, most notably in 1976, with the Resource Conservation and Recovery Act (RCRA). Its primary goal was to "protect human health and the environment from the potential hazards of waste disposal." The RCRA is also concerned with reducing the amount of waste generated, ensuring that wastes are managed properly, and conserving natural resources and energy. The RCRA primarily covers hazardous waste, which makes up only a small portion of all waste generated. State and local governments are mainly responsible for passing laws concerning nonhazardous waste, although the federal government will supply money and guidance to local governments so they can better manage their garbage systems. The RCRA consists of ten subtitles. (See Table 6.1.)

RCRA Subtitle D assigns to the states responsibility for permitting and monitoring landfills for municipal solid waste and other nonhazardous wastes. Regulations established under Subtitle D describe minimum federal standards for the design, location, and operation of solid waste landfills to protect the environment. The states can develop their own permitting programs, so long as they include the federal landfill criteria. The U.S. Environmental Protection Agency (EPA) has the authority to review and approve the state programs.

WASTE TYPES AND AMOUNT ESTIMATES

The RCRA definition of solid waste includes garbage and other materials ordinarily considered "solid," as well as sludges, semisolids, liquids, and even containers of gases. These wastes can come from many different sources. Table 6.2 lists various types of wastes that may be considered nonhazardous. It should be noted that these categories are not all-inclusive; for example, certain batteries and light-bulbs disposed by businesses fall under hazardous waste regulations. Thus, the extent to which a particular waste is deemed nonhazardous depends on both its physical and chemical nature and the source from which it comes.

It is difficult to calculate exactly how much non-hazardous waste is generated in the United States and what becomes of it. Under the RCRA the federal government collects data primarily on hazardous waste. In addition, the EPA estimates the production of municipal solid waste (or common garbage) each year using surveys, studies, population data, and other information. However, municipal solid waste composes only a small portion of all nonhazardous waste generated. The vast majority of nonhazardous waste produced in this country is not tracked or estimated by the federal government but falls under varying state and local regulatory schemes.

NONHAZARDOUS INDUSTRIAL WASTES

Nonhazardous industrial wastes are believed to be, by far, the largest single type of waste produced in the United States. The EPA (February 22, 2006, http://www.epa.gov/epaoswer/non-hw/industd/questions.htm) notes that "an old survey" estimates that 7.6 billion tons of this waste are produced annually. Approximately 97% of this amount is in the form of wastewaters. (Chapter 9

TABLE 6.1

Outline of the Resource Conservation and Recovery Act

Subtitle	Provisions
A	General provisions
B	Office of Solid Waste; authorities of the administrator and Interagency Coordinating Committee
C	Hazardous waste management
D	State or regional solid waste plans
E	Duties of the Secretary of Commerce in resource and recovery
F	Federal responsibilities
G	Miscellaneous provisions
H	Research, development, demonstration, and information
I	Regulation of underground storage tanks
J	Standards for the tracking and management of medical waste

SOURCE: "Figure 1-3. Outline of the Act," in *RCRA Orientation Manual*, EPA530-R-02-016, U.S. Environmental Protection Agency, Office of Solid Waste and Emergency Response, January 2003, www.epa.gov/epaoswer/general/orientat/romtoc.pdf (accessed July 27, 2007)

discusses wastewater management in detail.) Thus, approximately 228 million tons per year of nonwastewater industrial waste is generated.

Figure 6.1 shows an estimate made in 1997 of the breakdown of nonhazardous waste by industry in the United States. Major waste producers at that time included the pulp and paper, metal, chemical, and mining industries.

Many big manufacturing plants have sites on their own property where they dispose of waste or treat it so it will not become dangerous. Still others ship it to private disposal sites for dumping or for treatment. Smaller manufacturers might use private waste disposal companies or even the city garbage company.

The Texas Tracking System

State and local governments have regulatory responsibility for the management of most nonhazardous wastes. However, different states have different regulatory schemes. For example, Texas categorizes nonhazardous industrial

wastes into three classes based on their potential harm to the environment and human health. Class 1 wastes are the most tightly regulated. They include asbestos, ash, and various solids, sludges, and liquids contaminated with nonhazardous chemicals. The most recent report available on Texas industrial waste was published in August 2000 and includes data for 1997. According to *Needs Assessment for Industrial Class 1 Nonhazardous Waste Commercial Disposal Capacity in Texas (2000 Update)* (http://www.tceq.state.tx.us/assets/public/comm_exec/pubs/sfr/038_00.pdf), nearly eighty-three million tons of Class 1 waste were generated in Texas in 1997. The vast majority (96%) of the waste was liquid.

Class 2 wastes include containers that held Class 1 wastes, depleted aerosol cans, some medical wastes, paper, food wastes, glass, aluminum foil, plastics, Styrofoam, and food packaging resulting from industrial processes. Class 3 wastes include all other chemically inert and insoluble substances such as rocks, brick, glass, dirt, and some rubbers and plastics.

Texas industries do not have to report how much Class 2 or Class 3 wastes they generate or how they dispose of it. However, municipal solid waste landfills are required to report the receipt of all industrial waste.

AGRICULTURAL WASTES

Agricultural wastes are made up primarily of organic-based wastes, such as livestock manure, urine, and bedding material. According to the Agricultural Research Service, in "FY-2006 Annual Report Manure and Byproduct Utilization National Program" (2006, http://www.ars.usda.gov/SP2UserFiles/Program/206/NP206ManureandByproductUtilization.doc), more than one billion tons of organic agricultural wastes are produced annually in the United States. The management of livestock waste, particularly on large agricultural facilities, is an issue of concern because of the potential environmental impacts. (See Table 6.3.)

TABLE 6.2

Nonhazardous wastes

Agricultural waste	Nonhazardous components include animal manure, urine, and bedding materials.
Batteries	Contain heavy metals, such as mercury, lead, cadmium, and nickel, that can contaminate the environment if batteries are improperly disposed.
Construction & demolition debris	Materials generated during the construction, renovation, and demolition of buildings, roads, and bridges.
Industrial waste	Nonhazardous waste produced by industries in the United States.
Medical waste	Solid waste generated in the diagnosis, treatment, or immunization of human beings or animals.
Municipal solid waste	Trash or garbage generated by households and commercial institutions consisting of everyday items such as product packaging, grass clippings, furniture, clothing, bottles, food scraps, newspapers, appliances, paint and batteries.
Scrap tires	Used automotive tires that are destined for disposal.
Special wastes	Industrial wastes deemed nonhazardous by the EPA pending further study. Includes cement kiln dust, crude oil and natural gas wastes, fossil fuel combustion wastes, and certain mineral processing and mining wastes.

SOURCE: Adapted from "Nonhazardous Waste," in *Nonhazardous Waste*, U.S. Environmental Protection Agency, August 17, 2006, http://www.epa.gov/osw/non-haz.htm (accessed July 19, 2007) and "Special Waste," in *Special Waste*, U.S. Environmental Protection Agency, July 11, 2007, http://www.epa.gov/epaoswer/other/special/index.htm (accessed July 19, 2007)

FIGURE 6.1

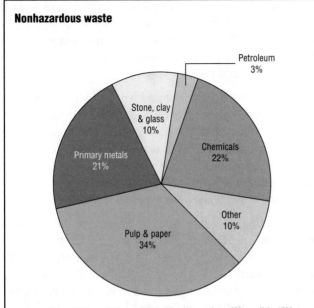

Nonhazardous waste

Petroleum 3%

Stone, clay & glass 10%

Chemicals 22%

Primary metals 21%

Other 10%

Pulp & paper 34%

SOURCE:Adapted from "Figure W-1. Non-hazardous Waste," in "Waste Generation," *Energy, Environmental and Economics (E³) Handbook*, U.S. Department of Energy, Office of Energy Efficiency and Renewable Energy, Office of Industrial Technology, September 1997, http://www .p2pays.org/ref/36/e3/www.oit.doe.gov/e3handbook/w.shtml.htm (accessed July 27, 2007)

Runoff of nutrients from manure collection and storage facilities poses a threat to the water quality of streams, lakes, and rivers. For this reason the waste management practices of certain agricultural operations are regulated by the federal government under the Clean Water Act. (Water issues are discussed in detail in Chapter 9.)

CONSTRUCTION AND DEMOLITION DEBRIS

Construction and demolition (C&D) debris is a non-hazardous waste stream generated from the construction, renovation, and demolition of buildings, roads, and bridges. According to the EPA (May 3, 2007, http://www.epa.gov/ epaoswer/non-hw/debris-new/index.htm), its constituents include the following:

- Concrete

- Wood (from buildings)

- Asphalt (from roads and roofing shingles)

- Gypsum (the main component of drywall)

- Metals

- Bricks

- Glass

- Plastics

- Salvaged building components (doors, windows, and plumbing fixtures)

- Trees, stumps, earth, and rock from clearing sites

TABLE 6.3

Major pollutants associated with agriculture

- **Nutrients**—Nitrogen and phosphorus are essential plant nutrients, but can degrade water quality by causing eutrophication.
- **Ammonia**—A pungent, colorless gas that can be a health hazard to humans and animals at high concentrations, and a precursor for fine particulates (haze) in the atmosphere. It also contributes to soil acidification and eutrophication.
- **Hydrogen sulfide**—A colorless gas also hazardous to humans and animals.
- **Methane**—A nontoxic, odorless gas that contributes to global warming (greenhouse gas).
- **Odor**—A nuisance associated with animal production facilities. Odorous gases consist of a host of compounds (over 160) that originate from manure in animal housing, manure storage units, and land application.
- **Pathogens**—Threats to human health that are often contained in manure. Some of the pathogens that pose a threat to human health include the protozoan parasites Cryptosporidium and Giardia and some bacteria species such as Salmonella, E. coli, and Campylobacter.

SOURCE: Marc Ribaudo and Noel Gollehon, "Text," in *Agricultural Resources and Environmental Indicators, 2006 Edition*, U.S. Department of Agriculture, Economic Research Service, July 2006, http://www.ers.usda .gov/publications/arei/eib16/eib16_4-5.pdf (accessed June 20, 2007)

Even though it is not specifically regulated by the federal government, the EPA, in "Construction and Demolition (C&D) Debris: Basic Information" (February 22, 2006, http://www.epa.gov/epaoswer/non-hw/debris-new/ basic.htm), reports that an estimated 136 million tons of C&D building-related debris was generated in 1996. Additional "significant" quantities are believed to be generated from the construction of roads and bridges and land clearing before construction. Most C&D debris is managed through disposal at specially designated landfills.

MEDICAL WASTE

Medical waste attracted widespread attention in the mid-1980s, when used needles and similar items washed up onto beaches in the Northeast. Even though most medical waste is regulated by state governments, Congress responded with the Medical Waste Tracking Act of 1988. This temporary act called for better tracking and disposal methods for medical waste. The act, which expired in 1999, defined medical waste as "any solid waste that is generated in the diagnosis, treatment, or immunization of human beings or animals, in research pertaining thereto, or in the production or testing of biologicals." Thus, sources include health care facilities, medical research facilities, veterinary clinics, and medical laboratories. In "Medical Waste" (January 31, 2007, http://www.epa.gov/epaoswer/ other/medical/), the EPA gives the following as examples of medical waste under the federal definition:

- Bloody bandages

- Used surgical gloves and instruments

- Used needles (medical sharps)

- Biological cultures and associated equipment, such as glassware and swabs

- Surgically removed body parts, such as tonsils and limbs
- Used lancets

The EPA notes that there are varying state definitions of medical waste that can include additional waste streams not previously specified. There are different regulatory categories of medical wastes, including infectious, hazardous, radioactive, and general wastes. The EPA estimates that infectious medical waste makes up only 10% to 15% of all medical wastes generated. Likewise, hazardous and radioactive wastes are believed to make up small fractions of the total medical waste stream. These two streams are regulated by the federal government. Infectious and general medical wastes are regulated at the state level. The EPA reports that more than 90% of infectious medical waste is incinerated. The federal government regulates emissions from medical waste incinerators.

SPECIAL WASTES

When the RCRA regulations were promulgated in 1987, the EPA included a list of six wastes deemed "special wastes" and exempted them from classification as hazardous wastes until further studies could be conducted. As of June 2007 many studies on the toxicity of these wastes have been conducted, and the following are considered special wastes under federal law:

- Cement kiln dust, which is the fine-grained highly alkaline dust removed by air pollution control devices during the production of cement

- Wastes generated during the exploration, development, and production of crude oil, natural gas, and geothermal energy

- Wastes produced from the burning of fossil fuels (coal, oil, and natural) and including all ash and slag (metal waste) and any particulates removed from flue gases

- Twenty waste streams that are generated during the processing of minerals to remove them from the native ore

- Most wastes generated from the extraction and beneficiation of "hardrock" (metal ores and phosphate rock) and twenty specific mineral processing wastes

These waste streams are also known as high-volume, low-toxicity wastes. Even though some components, particularly cement kiln dust, can be reused within the processes involved or sold for commercial purposes, most special wastes are disposed in land-based disposal units, such as landfills, waste piles, or surface impoundments.

MUNICIPAL SOLID WASTE

The EPA defines municipal solid waste (MSW) as "common garbage or trash." MSW includes items such as food scraps, paper, containers and packaging, appliances, batteries, and yard trimmings. These types of wastes are generally collected and managed by local municipal agencies. MSW does not include construction and demolition wastes, automobile bodies, sludge, combustion ash, and industrial process wastes.

Determining the amount and types of MSW generated in the United States is a difficult task. People are not required to track or report how much MSW they produce or what it contains. The EPA uses information supplied by trade groups and industrial sources, combined with estimated product life spans and population and sales data, to estimate how much and what types of MSW are generated.

According to Table 6.4, Americans produced 245.7 million tons of MSW in 2005, down slightly from 247.3 million tons in 2004. The tons of MSW generated annually increased dramatically between 1960 and 2000. Most of this increase occurred during the 1960s, 1970s, and 1980s. In 1960, 88.1 million tons of MSW were generated. Over the next three decades MSW generation increased on average by 33% per decade. However, the 1990s witnessed a slowdown in this rate of increase. MSW generation increased by only 16% between 1990 and 2000 and then began leveling off, increasing by only 3% between 2000 and 2005.

This trend is also reflected in the per capita (per person) values for MSW generation. In 1960 each American generated on average 2.68 pounds of MSW per day. This value steadily increased until 1990, when it reached 4.50 pounds per day. As shown in Figure 6.2, this rate leveled off during the 1990s, fluctuating between 4.50 and 4.63 pounds. In 2005 per capita generation was 4.54 pounds per day. This number has remained fairly constant since 1990.

MSW Composition

Figure 6.3 shows EPA estimates of the breakdown of MSW produced in 2005 by waste type. Paper was the largest single component by weight, composing 34.2% of the waste stream. It was followed by yard trimmings (13.1%), food scraps (11.9%), plastics (11.8%), metals (7.6%), rubber, leather, and textiles (7.3%), wood (5.7%), glass (5.2%), and other MSW (3.4%). The top five categories—paper, yard trimmings, food scraps, plastics, and metals—together made up 79% of the MSW generated in 2005.

PAPER. The EPA estimates in *Municipal Solid Waste in the United States: 2005 Facts and Figures* (October 2006, http://www.epa.gov/msw/pubs/mswchar05.pdf) that in 2005 there were eighty-four million tons of paper generated as MSW. The paper category includes many paper and paperboard (boxboard and containerboard) products. Corrugated boxes make up the bulk of this category in terms of the tons generated. In 2005 MSW included 30.9 million tons of corrugated boxes, representing 12.6% of paper waste.

TABLE 6.4

Municipal solid waste generation, materials recovery, composting, combustion with energy recovery, and discards, 1960–2005

[In millions of tons]

Activity	1960	1970	1980	1990	2000	2003	2004	2005
Generation	88.1	121.1	151.6	205.2	237.6	240.4	247.3	245.7
Recovery for recycling	5.6	8.0	14.5	29.0	52.7	55.8	57.2	58.4
Recovery for composting[a]	Neg.	Neg.	Neg.	4.2	16.5	19.1	20.5	20.6
Total materials recovery	5.6	8.0	14.5	33.2	69.1	74.9	77.7	79.0
Combustion with energy recovery[b]	0.0	0.4	2.7	29.7	33.7	33.7	34.1	33.4
Discards to landfill, other disposal[c]	82.5	112.7	134.4	142.3	134.8	131.9	135.5	133.3

[Percent of total generation]

Activity	1960	1970	1980	1990	2000	2003	2004	2005
Generation	100.0%	100.0%	100.0%	100.0%	100.0%	100.0%	100.0%	100.0%
Recovery for recycling	6.4%	6.6%	9.6%	14.2%	22.2%	23.2%	23.1%	23.8%
Recovery for composting[a]	Neg.	Neg.	Neg.	2.0%	6.9%	7.9%	8.3%	8.4%
Total materials recovery	6.4%	6.6%	9.6%	16.2%	29.1%	31.1%	31.4%	32.1%
Combustion with energy recovery[b]	0.0%	0.3%	1.8%	14.5%	14.2%	14.0%	13.8%	13.6%
Discards to landfill, other disposal[c]	93.6%	93.1%	88.6%	69.3%	56.7%	54.9%	54.8%	54.3%

[a]Composting of yard trimmings, food scraps and other municipal solid waste (MSW) organic material. Does not include backyard composting.
[b]Includes combustion of MSW in mass burn or refuse-derived fuel form, and combustion with energy recovery of source separated materials in MSW (e.g., wood pallets and tire-derived fuel).
[c]Discards after recovery minus combustion with energy recovery. Discards include combustion without energy recovery. Details may not add to totals due to rounding.

SOURCE: Adapted from "Table ES-1. Generation, Materials Recovery, Compositing, Combustion with Energy Recovery, and Discards of Municipal Solid Waste, 1960–2005 (in millions of tons)," and Table ES-2. Generation, Materials Recovery, Compositing, Combustion with Energy Recovery, and Discards of Municipal Solid Waste, 1960–2005 (in percent of generation) in *Municipal Solid Waste in the United States: 2005 Facts and Figures*, U.S. Environmental Protection Agency, October 2006, http://www.epa.gov/msw/pubs/mswchar05.pdf (accessed June 19, 2007)

Newspapers, office papers, commercial printing papers, milk cartons, and junk mail are other major contributors to the paper category. This category does not include gypsum wallboard facings (which are classified as construction and demolition debris) or toilet tissue (which goes to sewage treatment plants).

YARD TRIMMINGS. In *Municipal Solid Waste in the United States*, the EPA estimates show that in 2005 there were 32.1 million tons of yard trimmings generated as MSW. Yard trimmings include grass, leaves, and tree and brush trimmings from residential, commercial, and institutional sources. According to the EPA, yard trimmings are assumed to contain an average by weight of 50% grass, 25% leaves, and 25% brush.

In the past the EPA based its estimates of yard trimming generation on only sampling studies and population and housing data. During the 1990s it began to take into account the expected effects of local and state legislation on yard trimmings disposal in landfills. For example, in 1992 only eleven states and the District of Columbia had laws prohibiting or discouraging residents from disposing yard trimmings at landfills. In 2005 twenty-one states and the District of Columbia had such legislation in place. The EPA believes that this increased the use of mulching

lawnmowers and the practice of backyard composting of yard trimmings, thus reducing the amount of yard trimmings in MSW.

FOOD SCRAPS. The EPA, in *Municipal Solid Waste in the United States*, estimates that in 2005 there were 29.2 million tons of food waste generated in MSW. Included in the EPA's definition of food scraps are uneaten food and food preparation scraps from residences, commercial establishments (such as restaurants and grocery stores), institutional sources (such as school cafeterias and prisons), and industrial sources (such as factory cafeterias). Food scraps generated by industrial sources that produce and package food products are not included in MSW.

PLASTICS. The EPA estimates in *Municipal Solid Waste in the United States* that in 2005 there were 28.9 million tons of plastic materials in the MSW waste stream. The word "plastics" refers to materials made from particular chemical resins that can be molded or shaped into various products. Plastic materials are found in a wide variety of products, including containers, packaging, trash bags, milk jugs, cups, eating utensils, disposable diapers, sporting and recreational equipment, and many common household items (such as shower curtains). In addition,

FIGURE 6.2

Trends in total and per capita municipal solid waste (MSW) generation, 1960–2005

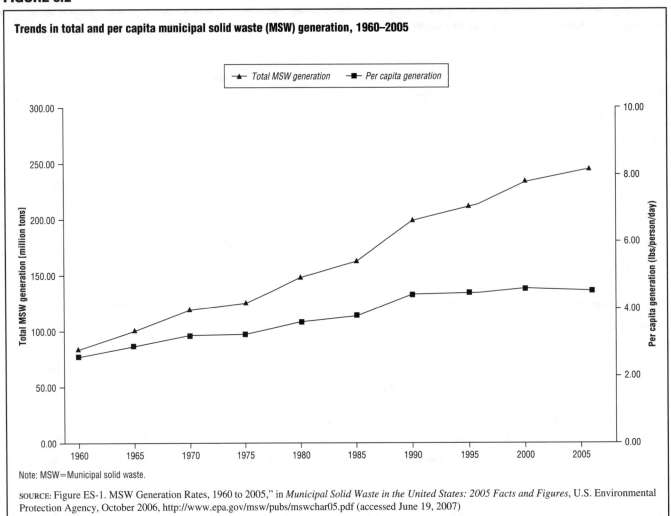

Note: MSW=Municipal solid waste.

SOURCE: Figure ES-1. MSW Generation Rates, 1960 to 2005," in *Municipal Solid Waste in the United States: 2005 Facts and Figures*, U.S. Environmental Protection Agency, October 2006, http://www.epa.gov/msw/pubs/mswchar05.pdf (accessed June 19, 2007)

there are plastic components in appliances, computers, furniture, luggage, and many other consumer products.

METALS. According to EPA estimates in *Municipal Solid Waste in the United States*, in 2005 there were 18.7 million tons of nonhazardous metals generated in MSW. Ferrous metals (iron and steel) made up 74% of this category by weight, followed by aluminum at 17% and other nonferrous (non-iron) metals at 9%. Ferrous metals are widely used in durable goods such as appliances and furniture. Ferrous metals used in transportation vehicles (such as automobiles) are not included in this category. Steel is also used to manufacture food cans, barrels, and drums. Aluminum found in MSW is most commonly in beer and soft drink cans, food cans, and as foil wrap.

CONSUMER ELECTRONICS. Consumer electronics include televisions, computers, videocassette recorders, compact disc and digital video disc players, digital and video cameras, radios, answering machines, telephones and cellular phones, fax machines, printers, scanners, and miscellaneous other equipment. Historically, the EPA has lumped such products under the category "other miscellaneous durable goods."

In 2000, for the first time, consumer electronics were categorized separately, and it was estimated that 2.1 million tons entered the MSW stream. In 2005 this value climbed to 2.6 million tons, representing 1.1% of the total MSW generated. Even though this percentage is small, it is expected to increase quickly during the 2000s as more electronic products reach the end of their useful lives.

Disposal of electronic goods in MSW poses environmental risks because of the presence of metals and other hazardous contaminants in the products. Some states, therefore, forbid electronic waste from MSW, as described in Chapter 8.

Historical Trends in MSW Composition

Since 1960 paper has consistently been the largest single component of MSW generated. The EPA notes in *Municipal Solid Waste in the United States* that paper's share of the total was virtually identical in 1960 and 2005: 34%.

FIGURE 6.3

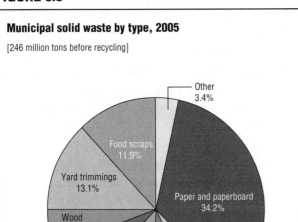

Municipal solid waste by type, 2005

[246 million tons before recycling]

Other 3.4%

Food scraps 11.9%

Yard trimmings 13.1%

Paper and paperboard 34.2%

Wood 5.7%

Rubber, leather & textiles 7.3%

Plastics 11.8%

Metals 7.6%

Glass 5.2%

SOURCE: "Figure ES-3. 2005 Total MSW Generation—246 Million Tons (Before Recycling)," in *Municipal Solid Waste in the United States: 2005 Facts and Figures*, U.S. Environmental Protection Agency, October 2006, http://www.epa.gov/msw/pubs/mswchar05.pdf (accessed June 19, 2007)

FIGURE 6.4

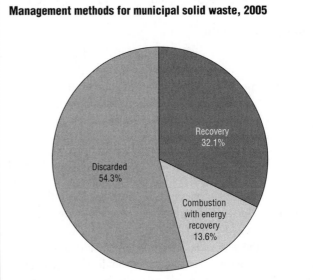

Management methods for municipal solid waste, 2005

Recovery 32.1%

Discarded 54.3%

Combustion with energy recovery 13.6%

SOURCE: "Figure ES-6. Management of MSW in the United States, 2005," in *Municipal Solid Waste in the United States: 2005 Facts and Figures*, U.S. Environmental Protection Agency, October 2006, http://www.epa.gov/msw/pubs/mswchar05.pdf (accessed June 19, 2007)

In 1960 plastics made up only 0.4% of the total MSW generated. By 2005 they made up 11.8% of the MSW total. Manufacturers are increasingly using plastic to package their products because plastic is so easy to use and shape. As a result, plastics are the fastest-growing proportion of MSW in the United States. The EPA predicts that the amount of plastic thrown away will continue to increase.

The total number of pounds of plastic in MSW increased from only 390,000 tons in 1960 to 28.9 million tons in 2005. Most of these plastics (a family of more than forty-five types) are nonbiodegradable and, once discarded, remain relatively intact for decades and even centuries. They do not break down through organic processes.

The percentage of yard trimmings in the MSW total decreased from 22.7% in 1960 to 13.1% in 2003. However, the tons of yard trimmings in MSW actually increased during this period.

MSW Management

The three primary methods for the management of MSW are:

- Land disposal

- Combustion (or incineration)

- Recovery through recycling or composting

Land disposal involves piling or burying waste materials on or below the ground surface. This is primarily

done at facilities called landfills. Incineration is a disposal method in which MSW is burned at high temperatures, while combustion is the burning of waste to produce energy. Recycling is the reuse of a material in another product or application. Composting is a method of decomposing yard trimmings and other biodegradable wastes for reuse as fertilizer. Recycling and composting are discussed at length in Chapter 7.

According to the EPA, in 2005 land disposal was the most common method used to manage MSW in the United States. (See Figure 6.4.) More than half (54.3%) of the MSW generated was discarded, going to land disposal, whereas 32.1% was recovered and 13.6% was combusted.

The EPA does not break down MSW disposal methods by region or state. However, Phil Simmons et al., in "The State of Garbage" (*BioCycle*, April 2006), provide regional information on disposal methods for 2004. Landfilling is most prevalent in the Rocky Mountain and midwestern states. In general, these states are less densely populated, thus they generate less MSW and have more space for landfills than many other states. Combustion and incineration were more common in the New England and mid-Atlantic states. These states are much more densely populated and have few areas available or suitable for landfilling.

The EPA reports in *Municipal Solid Waste in the United States* that the percentage of MSW landfilled has decreased dramatically from 93.6% in 1960 to 54.3% in 2005. In 1960 only 6.4% of MSW was recycled. This value was 23.8% in 2005. Composting and combusting of

MSW were virtually nonexistent in 1960. In 2005, 13.6% of MSW was combusted and 8.4% was composted.

Municipal Landfills

Municipal (or sanitary) landfills are areas where MSW waste is placed into and onto the land. Even though some landfilled organic wastes will decompose, many of the wastes in MSW are not biodegradable. Landfills provide a centralized location in which these wastes can be contained.

HOW ORGANIC MATTER DECOMPOSES IN LANDFILLS.

Organic material (material that was once alive, such as paper and wood products, food scraps, and clothing made of natural fibers) decomposes in the following way: first, aerobic (oxygen-using) bacteria use the material as food and begin the decomposition process. Principal by-products of this aerobic stage are water, carbon dioxide, nitrates, and heat. This stage lasts about two weeks. However, in compacted, layered, and covered landfills, the availability of oxygen may be low.

After the available oxygen is used, anaerobic bacteria (those that do not use oxygen) continue the decomposition. They generally produce carbon dioxide and organic acids. This stage can last up to one to two years. During a final anaerobic stage of decomposition lasting several years or decades, methane gas is formed along with carbon dioxide. The duration of this stage and the amount of decomposition depend on landfill conditions, including temperature, soil permeability, and water levels.

In "Five Major Myths about Garbage and Why They're Wrong" (*The Smithsonian*, July 1992), William Rathje and Cullen Murphy report on a twenty-year study called the Garbage Project. Conceived in 1971 and officially established at the University of Arizona in 1973, the Garbage Project was an attempt to apply archaeological principles to the study of solid waste. About 750 people processed more than 250,000 pounds of waste, excavating fourteen tons of it from landfills.

Among the Garbage Project's findings is the discovery that even though some degradation takes place initially (sufficient to produce large amounts of methane and other gases), it then slows to a virtual standstill. Study results reveal that an astonishingly high volume of old organic matter remained largely intact. Even after two decades, one-third to one-half of supposedly degradable organics remained in recognizable condition. Rathje and Murphy conclude that well-designed and well-managed landfills, in particular, seem more likely to preserve their contents than to transform them into humus or mulch.

Landfills and the Environment

METHANE. Methane, a flammable gas, is produced when organic matter decomposes in the absence of oxygen.

If not properly vented or controlled, it can cause explosions and underground fires that smolder for years. Methane is also deadly to breathe. The RCRA requires landfill operators to monitor methane gas.

Rathje and Murphy note that "for 15 or 20 years after a landfill has stopped accepting garbage, the wells vent methane in fairly substantial amounts. Then methane production drops off rapidly, indicating that the landfill has stabilized."

Methane gas can be recovered through pipes inserted into landfills, and the gas can be used to generate energy. According to the EPA, in *Municipal Solid Waste in the United States*, as of April 2007 there were 424 operational landfill gas-to-energy projects in the United States. (See Figure 6.5.) The EPA's Landfill Methane Outreach Program estimates that approximately 560 other landfill sites presented attractive opportunities for project development.

Landfill Design Standards

The RCRA standards require landfill operators to do several things to lessen the chance of polluting the underlying groundwater. Groundwater can become contaminated when liquid chemicals or contaminated rainfall runoff seep down through the ground underneath the landfill. This liquid is called leachate.

The RCRA requirements are as follows:

- Landfill operators must monitor the groundwater for pollutants. This is usually accomplished with a groundwater monitoring well system.

- Landfills must have plastic liners underneath their waste, as well as a leachate collection system. (See Figure 6.6.)

- Debris must be covered daily with soil to prevent odors and stop refuse from being blown away.

- Methane gas (a by-product of decomposition) must be monitored, which is usually accomplished with an explosive-gas monitoring well.

- Landfill owners are responsible for cleanup of any contamination.

Landfills are not open dumps but managed facilities in which wastes are controlled. MSW is often compacted before it is placed in a landfill and covered with soil. Modern landfills have liner systems and other safeguards to prevent groundwater contamination. When they are full, landfills are usually capped with a clay liner to prevent contamination. (See Figure 6.6.)

Imports and Exports of Garbage

Lack of landfill space has encouraged some municipalities to send their garbage to other states. Even though shipments do occur across the Mexican and Canadian borders, the vast majority of U.S. MSW is managed within the United States.

FIGURE 6.5

Status of landfill gas energy projects by state, April 2007

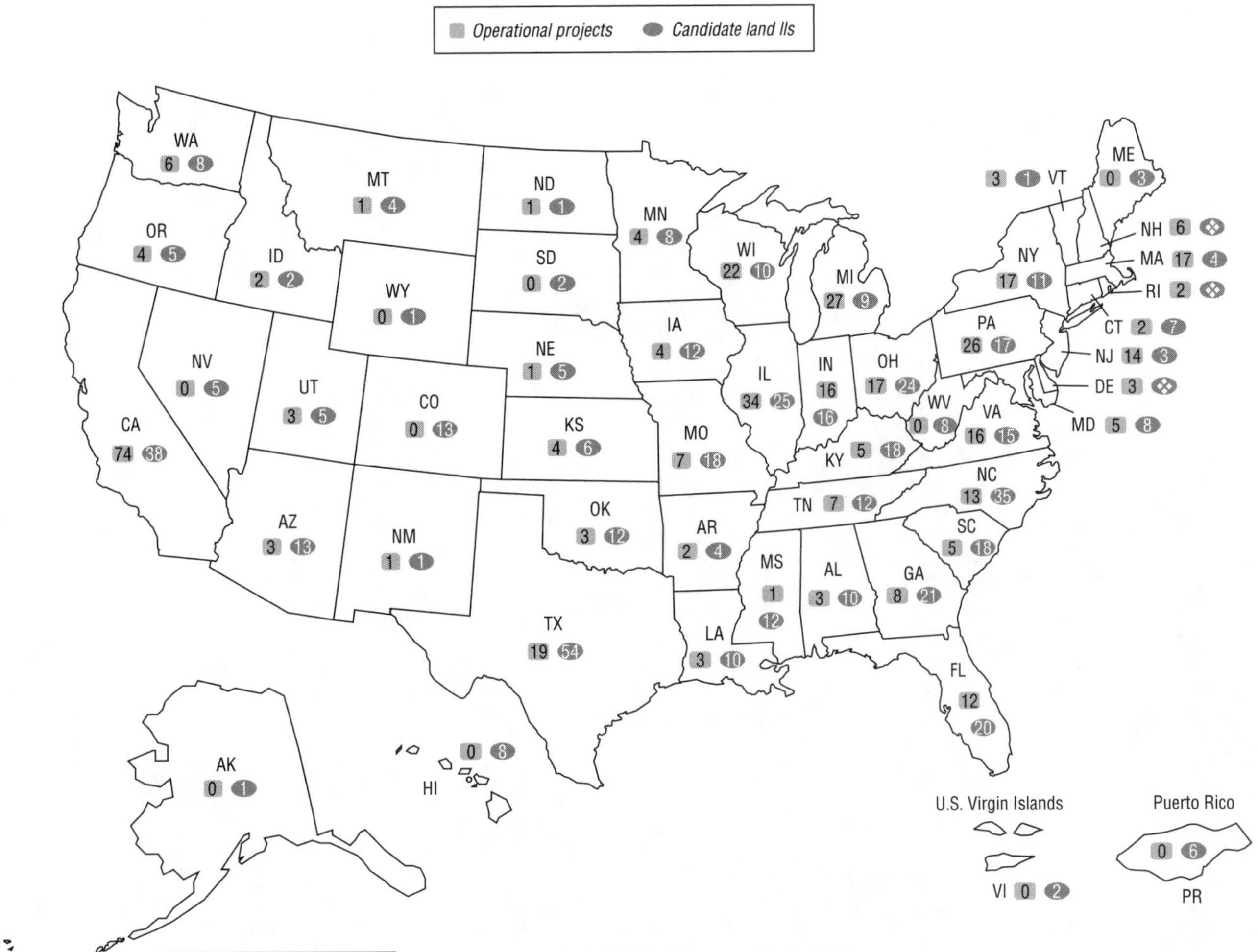

Operational projects
Candidate land lls
WA 6 8
OR 4 5
CA 74 38
NV 0 5
ID 2 2
MT 1 4
WY 0 1
UT 3 5
CO 0 13
AZ 3 13
NM 1 1
ND 1 1
SD 0 2
NE 1 5
KS 4 6
OK 3 12
TX 19 54
MN 4 8
IA 4 12
MO 7 18
AR 2 4
LA 3 10
WI 22 10
IL 34 25
MI 27 9
IN 16 16
OH 17 24
KY 5 18
TN 7 12
MS 1 12
AL 3 10
GA 8 21
FL 12 20
SC 5 18
NC 13 35
VA 16 15
WV 0 8
PA 26 17
NY 17 11
3 1 VT
ME 0 3
NH 6
MA 17 4
RI 2
CT 2 7
NJ 14 3
DE 3
MD 5 8
AK 0 1
HI 0 8
U.S. Virgin Islands
VI 0 2
Puerto Rico
PR 0 6

Nationwide summary
424 Operational projects (1,195 MW and 235 mmscfd)
~560 Candidate landfills (1,370 MW or 695 mmscfd, 16 MMTCE Potential)

These data are from LMOP's database as of April 2, 2007.

❖ LMOP does not have any information on candidate landfills in this state.

LMOP=Landfill methane outreach program.
MW=Megawatts.
mmscfd=Million square feet per day.
MMTCE=Million metric tons of carbon equivalent.

SOURCE: "Landfill Gas Energy and Candidate Landfills," in *Landfill Gas Energy Projects and Candidate Landfills*, U.S. Environmental Prptection Agency, April 2, 2007, http://www.epa.gov/outreach/lmop/docs/map.pdf (accessed June 19, 2007)

Simmons and his colleagues indicate that importing and exporting MSW from state to state is common. In 2004 Maryland exported the most MSW (2.6 million tons), followed by New Jersey (2.5 million tons) and New York (2.2 million tons). Other states exporting more than one million tons of MSW included Washington (1.5 million tons), Massachusetts (1.4 million tons), and North Carolina (1.1 million tons). The chief MSW importers were Pennsylvania (10.6 million tons), Michigan (6 million tons), Virginia (5.9 million tons), and Ohio (3.2 million tons). The vast majority of imported MSW was landfilled.

Several states have tried to ban the importing of garbage into their states. In 1992 the U.S. Supreme Court ruled in *Chemical Waste Management v. Hunt* (504 U.S. 334) that the constitutional right to conduct commerce across state borders protects such shipments. Experts point out that newer, state-of-the-art landfills with multiple liners and sophisticated pollution control equipment have to accept waste from a wide region to be financially viable.

Trends in Landfill Development

Before using landfills, cities used open dumps, areas in which garbage and trash were simply discarded in

FIGURE 6.6

Example of a properly closed landfill

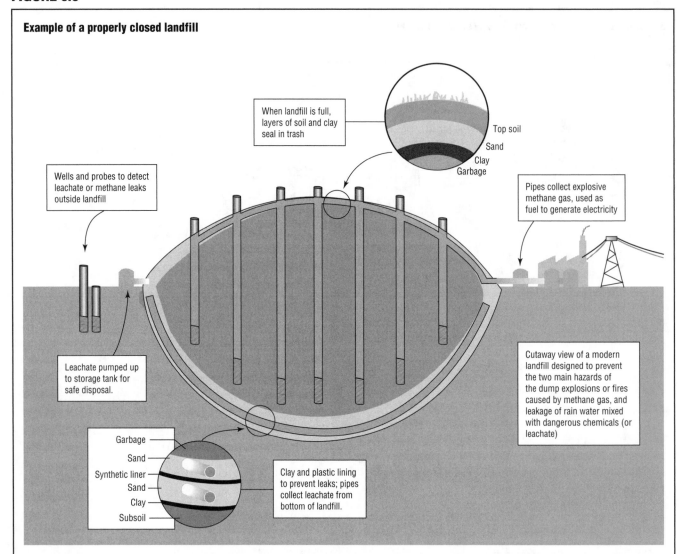

When landfill is full, layers of soil and clay seal in trash

Top soil
Sand
Clay
Garbage

Wells and probes to detect leachate or methane leaks outside landfill

Pipes collect explosive methane gas, used as fuel to generate electricity

Leachate pumped up to storage tank for safe disposal.

Cutaway view of a modern landfill designed to prevent the two main hazards of the dump explosions or fires caused by methane gas, and leakage of rain water mixed with dangerous chemicals (or leachate)

Garbage
Sand
Synthetic liner
Sand
Clay
Subsoil

Clay and plastic lining to prevent leaks; pipes collect leachate from bottom of landfill.

SOURCE: "Diagram 1. Example of a Properly Closed Landfill," in *Fact Flash 6: Resource Conservation and Recovery Act*, U.S. Environmental Protection Agency, Office of Solid Waste and Emergency Response, 1999, http://www.epa.gov/superfund/students/clas_act/haz-ed/ff_06.htm (accessed July 27, 2007)

huge piles. However, open dumps produced unpleasant odors and attracted animals. In the early 1970s the number of operating landfills in the United States was estimated at about twenty thousand. In 1979, as part of the RCRA, the EPA designated conditions under which solid waste disposal facilities and practices would not pose adverse effects to human health and the environment. As a result of the implementation of these criteria, open dumps had to be closed or upgraded to meet the criteria for landfills.

Additionally, many more landfills closed in the early 1990s because they could not conform to the new standards that took effect in 1993 under the 1992 RCRA amendment. Other landfills closed as they became full. According to the EPA, the number of landfills available for MSW disposal decreased dramatically from 7,924 in 1988 to 1,654 in 2005. (See Figure 6.7.)

Landfilling is expected to continue to be the single most predominant MSW management method. In the coming decades it will be economically prohibitive to develop and maintain small-scale, local landfills. There will likely be fewer, larger, and more regional operations. More MSW is expected to move away from its point of generation, resulting in increased import and export rates.

Landfill protection methods will likely become stronger in the future with more options for leachate and gas recovery. To make landfills more acceptable to neighborhoods, operators will likely establish larger buffer zones, use more green space, and show more sensitivity to land-use compatibility and landscaping.

Bioreactors: Accelerated Landfilling

Traditional landfills are often called dry tombs, because the waste is kept as dry as possible to reduce the

FIGURE 6.7

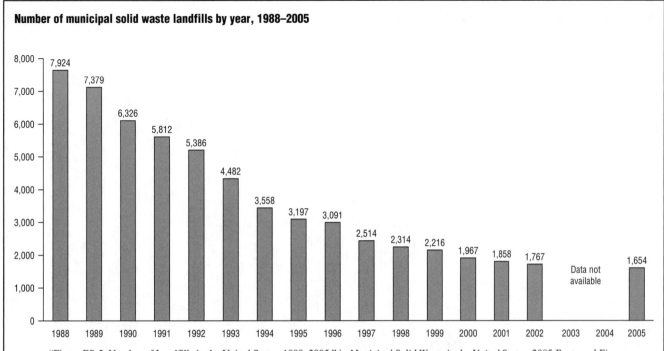

Number of municipal solid waste landfills by year, 1988–2005

SOURCE: "Figure ES-5. Number of Landfills in the United States, 1988–2005," in *Municipal Solid Waste in the United States: 2005 Facts and Figures*, U.S. Environmental Protection Agency, October 2006, http://www.epa.gov/msw/pubs/mswchar05.pdf (accessed June 19, 2007)

possibility of leaching contaminants to the environment. Biodegradation under these conditions can take decades. A new approach is offered in bioreactor landfills—landfills in which moisture is purposely added to accelerate biodegradation. Bioreactor landfills can operate using aerobic (oxygen-based) or anaerobic (oxygen-free) processes or a combination of the two. In aerobic bioreactor landfills oxygen as well as moisture are introduced to the waste pile.

The EPA (August 31, 2007, http://www.epa.gov/epao swer/non-hw/muncpl/landfill/bioreactors.htm) promotes the development of bioreactor landfills and touts research showing the following advantages for them over conventional landfills:

- Much faster decomposition and biological stabilization of waste, typically taking years, instead of decades

- Reduced toxicity of the waste

- Lower costs for leachate disposal

- Less space required because of the higher density of the waste

- Significant increase in landfill gases produced for energy production

- Lower costs for landfill care after closure

The primary disadvantage of bioreactor landfills is their higher capital (construction) costs compared with traditional landfills. Furthermore, particular attention must be paid to preventing leachates from escaping from the waste piles.

Bioreactor.org notes in "Bioreactors around the World" (February 5, 2007, http://www.bioreactor.org/world.html) that in 2007 the following thirteen bioreactor landfills were in operation in the United States:

- California—Yolo County

- Florida—Alachua County Southeast, Highlands County, New River Regional Landfill in Raiford, and Polk County Landfill in Lakeland

- Kentucky—Outer Loop Landfill

- Michigan—Clare County

- Mississippi—Plantation Oaks in Sibley

- Missouri—Columbia

- New Jersey—Haneman Environmental Park in Egg Harbor Township

- North Carolina—Buncombe County

- Virginia—Virginia Landfill Project XL Demonstration Project

INCINERATION AND COMBUSTION

Incineration and combustion are popular disposal choices for nonhazardous wastes. They both involve heating waste to high temperatures. In the past waste was burned in incinerators primarily to reduce its volume. During the 1980s

FIGURE 6.8

Waste combustion plant with pollution control system

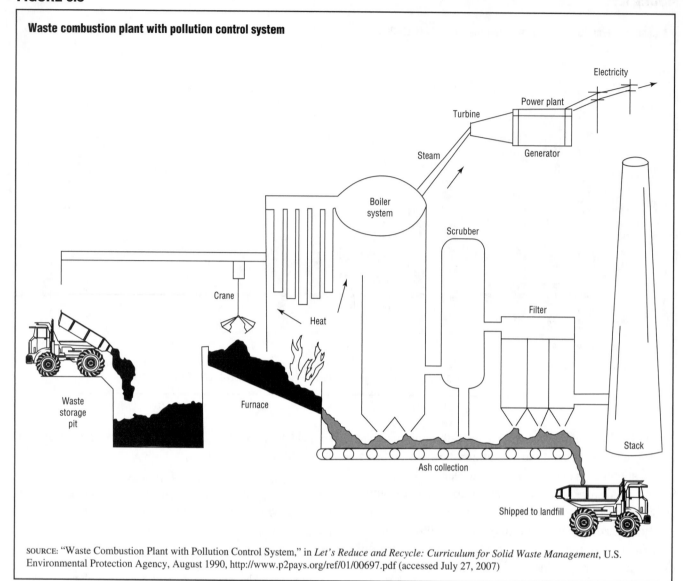

SOURCE: "Waste Combustion Plant with Pollution Control System," in *Let's Reduce and Recycle: Curriculum for Solid Waste Management*, U.S. Environmental Protection Agency, August 1990, http://www.p2pays.org/ref/01/00697.pdf (accessed July 27, 2007)

technology was developed that allowed waste to be burned for energy recovery. Use of waste as a fuel is more commonly called combustion; however, both terms are used interchangeably. The EPA refers to waste combustion as a waste-to-energy (WTE) process.

Figure 6.8 shows a typical WTE system. At this facility, the trucks dump waste into a pit. The waste is moved to the furnace by a crane. The furnace burns the waste at a high temperature, heating a boiler that produces steam for generating electricity and heat. Ash collects at the bottom of the furnace, where it is later removed and taken to a landfill for disposal. Figure 6.9 illustrates the combustion process, which produces both gaseous emissions and solid waste (in the form of ash).

Incineration of Various Wastes

According to the EPA, in *Municipal Solid Waste in the United States*, in 2005 there were 88 WTE facilities operating in the United States that incinerated 33.4 million tons of MSW, representing 13.6% of the total MSW generated that year. (See Figure 6.4.) In "Solid Waste Combustion/ Incineration" (August 17, 2007, http://www.epa.gov/epaoswer/non-hw/muncpl/landfill/sw_combst.htm), the EPA estimates that combusting MSW reduces the amount of waste by 90% in volume and 75% in weight. According to the U.S. Department of Energy (DOE), in 2006 waste-derived energy made up just over one-half of 1% of the nation's total energy supply, producing 404 trillion British thermal units (BTUs) of power. (See Figure 6.10.)

Scrap tires have always posed a disposal problem for the United States. Scrap tires accumulated in landfills or uncontrolled tire dumps can pose health and fire hazards. Scrap tires do not compress in landfills and provide breeding grounds for a variety of pests. In fact, some states ban the disposal of tires in landfills. In 1985 Minnesota passed the first state legislation dealing with scrap

FIGURE 6.9

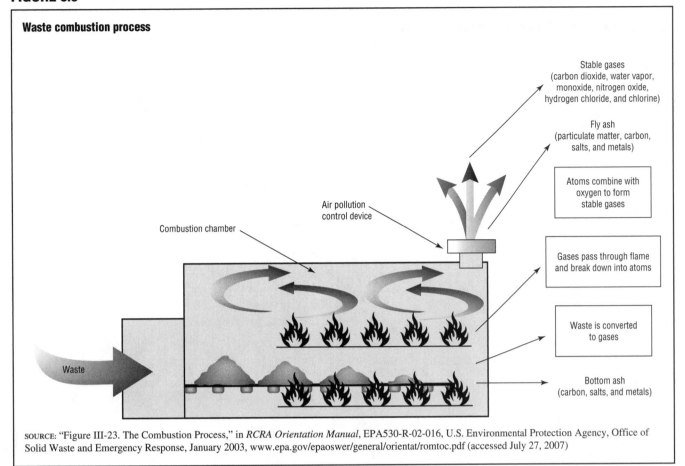

Waste combustion process

Stable gases
(carbon dioxide, water vapor,
monoxide, nitrogen oxide,
hydrogen chloride, and chlorine)

Fly ash
(particulate matter, carbon,
salts, and metals)

Atoms combine with
oxygen to form
stable gases

Air pollution
control device

Gases pass through flame
and break down into atoms

Combustion chamber

Waste is converted
to gases

Waste

Bottom ash
(carbon, salts, and metals)

SOURCE: "Figure III-23. The Combustion Process," in *RCRA Orientation Manual*, EPA530-R-02-016, U.S. Environmental Protection Agency, Office of Solid Waste and Emergency Response, January 2003, www.epa.gov/epaoswer/general/orientat/romtoc.pdf (accessed July 27, 2007)

tires. Other states followed suit. The Rubber Manufacturers Association reports in *Scrap Tire Markets in the United States* (November 2006, www.rma.org/getfile.cfm ?ID=894&type=publication) that several waste management companies invested in tire-to-fuel projects, and by 1990 up to twenty-five million scrap tires per year were burned for fuel. Furthermore, it notes that 155 million scrap tires were burned as fuel during 2005 in specialized WTE facilities.

Industries are increasingly choosing WTE as a means to reduce the amount of waste that requires disposal and for energy benefits. For example, Shaw Industries (2007, http:// www.shawfloors.com/Shaw-Environmental/Innovation), a major manufacturer of carpet and wood flooring, operates a WTE plant at its manufacturing facility in Dalton, Georgia. The WTE plant burns up to twenty-one million pounds of wood and carpet waste per year that ordinarily would be landfilled. It also produces heat that is used within the manufacturing process.

MSW Incineration Emissions

Incineration of MSW fell into disfavor during the 1980s because of concerns about air emissions from the combustion process. These emissions can include mercury and other heavy metals and acid gases (such as hydrochloric acid) from the burning of paints, lightbulbs, electronics, and so on. Chlorine-containing chemicals within MSW are of particular concern, because their combustion can produce dioxins and furans, two groups of complex organic and toxic compounds.

WTE facilities are required to use air pollution control equipment to reduce the emissions of toxic chemicals. In 1995, under Section 129 of the Clean Air Act, the EPA adopted emissions guidelines for municipal waste combustors (MWCs). These regulations were fully implemented by 2000. The EPA reports in the fact sheet "Standards of Performance for New Stationary Sources and Emission Guidelines for Existing Sources: Large Municipal Waste Combustors" (April 28, 2006, http://www.epa.gov/ttn/oarpg/t3/ fact_sheets/largeMWC_fsfinal.html) that these limits substantially reduced MWC emissions of dioxins and furans (more than a 99% reduction), metals (more than a 93% reduction), and acid gases (more than a 91% reduction) compared with 1990s levels. In April 2006 the EPA adopted even tighter emission limits for the largest MWCs: those processing more than 250 tons of MSW per day.

FIGURE 6.10

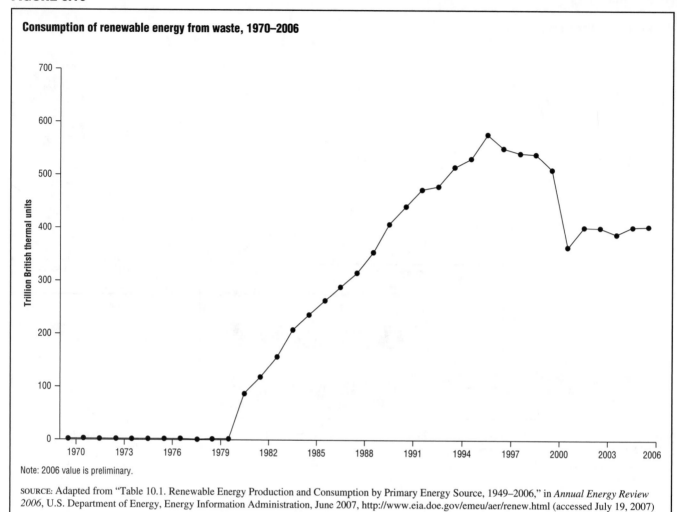

Consumption of renewable energy from waste, 1970–2006

Note: 2006 value is preliminary.

SOURCE: Adapted from "Table 10.1. Renewable Energy Production and Consumption by Primary Energy Source, 1949–2006," in *Annual Energy Review 2006*, U.S. Department of Energy, Energy Information Administration, June 2007, http://www.eia.doe.gov/emeu/aer/renew.html (accessed July 19, 2007)

FOCUS ON DIOXINS AND FURANS. In November 2006 the EPA released *An Inventory of Sources and Environmental Releases of Dioxin-Like Compounds in the United States for the Years 1987, 1995, and 2000* (http://cfpub .epa.gov/ncea/cfm/recordisplay.cfm?deid=159286). The report notes that MWCs were the largest single source of dioxin-like compounds in 1987, emitting 8,905 grams per year, or 64% of the total. (See Figure 6.11.) By 2000 these emissions had been substantially reduced to 84 grams per year, accounting for only 6% of total sources.

THE FEDERAL ROLE IN MSW MANAGEMENT

The federal government plays a key role in waste management. Its legislation has set landfill standards under the RCRA and incinerator and landfill emission standards under the Clean Air Act.

Some waste management laws have been controversial, resulting in legal challenges. Consequently, the federal government has also had an effect on waste management programs through federal court rulings. In a series of rulings, including Supreme Court decisions such as

Chemical Waste Management v. Hunt, federal courts have held that shipments of waste are protected under the interstate commerce clause of the Constitution. As a result, state and local governments may not prohibit landfills from accepting waste from other states, nor may they impose fees on waste disposal that discriminate on the basis of origin.

Flow Control Laws

Municipalities nationwide have upgraded waste management programs and attempted to deal with public concern over waste issues. In most areas of the country state and local governments have played the lead role in transforming solid waste management. Private waste management firms have also been involved, often under contract or franchise agreements with local governments. Private firms manage most of the commercial waste and increasingly collect residential waste.

Flow control laws require private waste collectors to dispose of their waste in specific landfills. State and local governments institute these laws to guarantee that any new landfill they build will be used. This way, when they

FIGURE 6.11

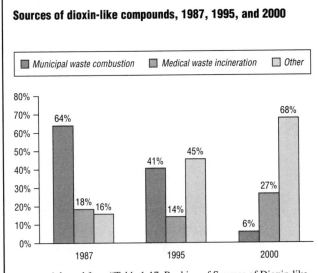

Sources of dioxin-like compounds, 1987, 1995, and 2000

- ■ Municipal waste combustion ■ Medical waste incineration □ Other

SOURCE: Adapted from "Table 1-17. Ranking of Sources of Dioxin-like Compounds Based on Environmental Releases (from High to Low) for Reference Years 2000, 1995, and 1987," in *An Inventory of Sources and Environmental Releases of Dioxin-Like Compounds in the United States for the Years 1987, 1995, and 2000*, U.S. Environmental Protection Agency, November 2006, http://cfpub.epa.gov/ncea/cfm/recordisplay.dfm?deid=159286 (accessed June 19, 2007)

sell bonds to get the money to build a new landfill, the bond purchasers will not worry that they will not be repaid. James E. McCarthy of the Congressional Research Service notes in "IB10002: Solid Waste Issues in the 106th Congress" (April 27, 2000, http://www.ncseonline.org/nle/crsreports/waste/waste-27.cfm) that "since 1980, about $10 billion in municipal bonds have been issued to pay for the construction of solid waste facilities. In many of these cases, flow control authority was used to guarantee the investment. Flow control also has benefited recycling facilities in cases where recycling was financed by fees collected at designated incinerators or landfills." In the process, however, a monopoly is created, prohibiting facilities outside a jurisdiction from offering competitive services. As a result, there have been a number of court challenges to flow control laws.

In 1994 the Supreme Court, in *C & A Carbone v. Clarkstown* (511 U.S. 383), held that flow control violates the interstate commerce clause. In response, however, many local governments have strongly pushed for the restoration of flow control authority. They have appealed to Congress, with its authority to regulate interstate commerce, to restore the use of flow control. As of September 2007, bills proposed to address flow control had failed.

CHAPTER 7
NONHAZARDOUS MATERIALS RECOVERY—RECYCLING AND COMPOSTING

Materials recovery is considered one of the most promising ways to reduce the amount of nonhazardous waste requiring disposal. The terms *recovery* and *recycling* are often used interchangeably. Both mean that a waste material is being reused rather than put in a landfill or incinerated. In general, reuse as a fuel does not fall under the definition of recovery, whereas composting does.

Recycling involves the sorting, collecting, and processing of wastes such as paper, glass, plastic, and metals, which are then refashioned or incorporated into new marketable products. Composting is the decomposition of organic wastes, such as food scraps and yard trimmings, in a manner that produces a humuslike substance for fertilizer or mulch.

Waste recovery offers many advantages. It conserves energy otherwise used to incinerate the waste; reduces the amount of landfill space needed for the disposal of waste; reduces possible environmental pollution because of waste disposal; generates jobs and small-scale enterprises; reduces dependence on foreign imports of raw materials; and replaces some chemical fertilizers with composting material, which further lessens possible environmental pollution. However, recycling sometimes requires more energy and water consumption than waste disposal. It depends on how far the materials must be transported and what is necessary to clean them before they can be reused. Demand for some recyclable materials is weak, making them economically unfeasible to recycle in a market-driven society.

Many Americans view waste recovery primarily as a way to help the environment. For example, if paper is recycled, fewer trees have to be cut down to make paper. State and local governments see recycling as a way to save money on waste disposal costs and prolong the life of landfill space. Thus, waste recovery has both environmental and economic components.

INDUSTRIAL WASTE RECOVERY

As noted in Chapter 6, industrial waste is believed to be the largest nonhazardous waste stream generated in the United States. Furthermore, the U.S. Environmental Protection Agency (EPA; February 22, 2006, http://www.epa.gov/epaoswer/non-hw/industd/questions.htm) estimates that 97% of it is in the form of wastewater. There are opportunities for the recycling of industrial wastewaters, including process rinse waters, cooling water, and scrubber water. Reuse often requires sophisticated treatment technologies to cleanse wastewaters of impurities. These technologies produce wastes, typically sludges, that contain the concentrated impurities stripped from the wastewaters. Nontoxic, industrial wastewater sludges can themselves be reused, for example, in agricultural applications or construction materials.

Nonwastewater industrial wastes can also be recycled either within a facility or between facilities and/or companies. The latter can be accomplished via materials exchange services operated throughout the country. For example, the King County government in Washington State operates IMEX, a free listing service that helps match industrial waste generators with industrial waste users. In 2007 IMEX (September 7, 2007, http://www.govlink.org/hazwaste/business/imex/browse.cfm) included "Available" and "Wanted" listings for a variety of materials, including acids, alkalis, laboratory chemicals, metals, sludges, paints, coatings, solvents, textiles, and wood. Links are provided to dozens of other material exchanges in North America.

The use of wastes from one facility as raw materials at another facility is called by-product synergy (BPS). In 2006 the EPA and the U.S. Business Council for Sustainable Development (a nonprofit association of businesses) began a series of projects intended to boost BPS collaboration between corporations. The projects will establish a system within which businesses can confidentially

TABLE 7.1

Industrial materials that can be recycled

Coal combustion products	**Can be recycled in**
• Fly and bottom ash	• Portland cement and concrete
• Boiler slag	• Flowable and structural fill
• Flue gas desulfurization material	• Wallboard
Construction and demolition debris	**Can be recycled in**
• Concrete gypsum from drywall	• Asphalt paving
• Metals	• Concrete
• Bricks	• Re-milled lumber
• Asphalt from roads and roofing shingles	• Wallboard
• Wood from buildings	
Foundry sand	**Can be recycled in**
• Spent sand used in metal casting	• Road embankments
	• Flowable and structural fill
	• Base and sub-base for road construction

SOURCE: "Industrial Materials," in *Industrial Materials Recycling: Managing Resources for Tomorrow: RCRA Fact Sheet*, U.S. Environmental Protection Agency, Office of Solid Waste and Emergency Response, January 2007, http://www.epa.gov/epaoswer/osw/conserve/resources/ind-mat.htm (accessed June 20, 2007)

exchange information on processes and waste production. It is believed this will encourage greater intercompany recycling of industrial waste streams.

EPA Focus Wastes

The EPA also promotes recycling of industrial wastes through its Resource Conservation Challenge (RCC) project and an industry-government partnership called the Industrial Resources Council (IRC). The RCC project focuses on three waste materials: coal combustion products, foundry sand, and construction and demolition (C&D) waste. Table 7.1 lists potential reuses for these materials. The IRC met in January 2007 to discuss recycling programs and potentials for six target wastes: coal combustion products, foundry sands and slags, iron and steel slags, C&D waste, tire shreds, and pulp and paper industry by-products.

COAL COMBUSTION PRODUCTS. Coal combustion products (CCP) include ash, boiler slag (molten ash that crystallizes as it cools), and fine solid materials collected in flue gas treatment equipment. As shown in Figure 7.1, approximately 120 million tons of CCP were generated in 2003, and more than 46 million tons (38.1%) were reused. The American Coal Ash Association reports that most reuse was in cement and concrete production. Other major applications included structural fills and embankments and use as a stabilizer or solidifier for liquid wastes. In 2006 the California Department of Transportation won an award from the EPA for using large amounts of CCP during construction and refurbishing of the Bay Bridge. The department actively supports the use of CCP, in part, because it helps reduce the high greenhouse gas emissions associated with traditional cement manufacture.

FOUNDRY SAND. Foundries are manufacturing plants in which metal parts are produced in molds. Large amounts of high-quality silica sands are used in the molding and casting operations. Even though the sand can be reused many times, eventually it becomes degraded and must be removed from the process. According to the industry group Foundry Industry Recycling Starts Today (FIRST; 2007, http://www.foundryrecycling.org/Home/IndustryOverview /FAQ/tabid/139/Default.aspx), approximately one hundred million tons of sand are used annually in foundries. About six million tons of sand per year become a waste product because of degradation. This sand can be reused in other industries. In *Foundry Sand Facts for Civil Engineers* (May 2004, http://isddc.dot.gov/OLP Files/FHWA/011435.pdf), the U.S. Department of Transportation notes that approximately five hundred thousand to seven hundred thousand tons of foundry sand are used each year in engineering applications, such as embankments, site development fills, and road bases. Additional amounts are used to produce commercially available topsoil.

METAL SLAGS. Metal slags are composed of minerals and other impurities separated from metals during melting. The slags are quickly cooled to form glassy granules that can be ground into a powder and reused, for example, in cement and concrete. According to the Slag Cement Association (2007, http://www.slagcement.org/ shared/), slag was a major component in the rebuilt 7 World Trade Center in New York City and the Georgia Aquarium in Atlanta. Metal slags are believed to be one of the most recycled industrial materials. In the undated report *Use of EPA's Industrial Waste Management Evaluation Model (IWEM) to Support Beneficial Use Determinations* (http://www.epa.gov/epaoswer/osw/conserve/ c2p2/pubs/iwem-report.pdf), Jeffrey S. Melton and Kevin H. Gardner of the University of New Hampshire indicate that up to 100% of blast furnace and steel-making slags were recycled in the United States in the late 1990s.

C&D WASTE. C&D wastes result from the construction, renovation, and demolition of buildings, roads, and bridges. Typical wastes include concrete, wood, asphalt, drywall, metals, bricks, and glass and cleared trees, stumps, and earth. For building projects the EPA recommends the recovery options shown in Table 7.2. Deconstruction—the careful dismantling of a building to salvage reusable materials—is touted by the EPA in lieu of demolition, which tends to produce waste that must be removed to a landfill. Table 7.3 lists components and materials with a high recovery potential that are typically found in buildings.

C&D debris from roads, bridges, and similar infrastructure is also reusable. According to the Recycled Materials Company, in "World's Largest Recycle Project" (March 2007, http://www.rmci-usa.com/stapleton.htm), in

FIGURE 7.1

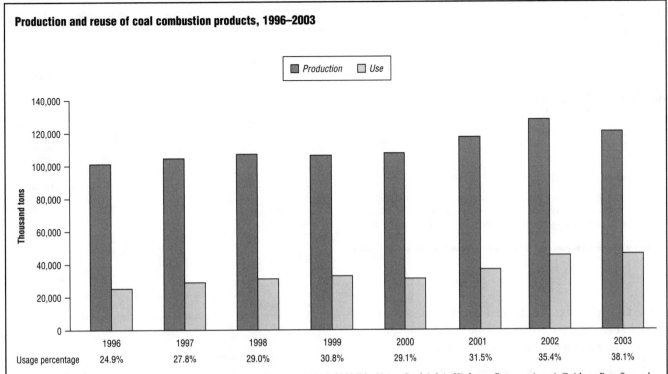

Production and reuse of coal combustion products, 1996–2003

Legend: ■ Production ☐ Use

Year	1996	1997	1998	1999	2000	2001	2002	2003
Usage percentage	24.9%	27.8%	29.0%	30.8%	29.1%	31.5%	35.4%	38.1%

SOURCE: "Figure 8. Production and Use of Coal Combustion Products, 1996–2003," in *Using Coal Ash in Highway Construction: A Guide to Benefits and Impacts*, U.S. Environmental Protection Agency, April 2005, http://www.epa.gov/epaoswer/osw/conserve/c2p2/pubs/greenbk508.pdf (accessed June 20, 2007)

2005 the company completed a six-year project in which 6.5 million tons of concrete, sand, and asphalt from the former Stapleton International Airport in Denver, Colorado, was reclaimed. The world's largest recycling project, as it has been dubbed, sold the materials to federal, state, and municipal governments for reuse in road construction and other applications. The company reports in "The Next 'World's Largest Recycle Project'" (February 2007, http://www.rmci-usa.com/eltoro.htm) that a similar project began in 2006 at the decommissioned El Toro Marine Corps Air Station in Orange County, California. Approximately 3.5 million tons of rubble (technically called hardscape) is expected to be salvaged from that site in a reclamation effort that could last eight years or more.

Some coastal communities have found unique and beneficial uses for C&D debris in artificial reefs. According to the article "Florida County Turns Trash into Artificial Reef" (*Waste Age*, June 15, 2007), authorities in Collier County, Florida, reported in 2007 that they were nearing completion of a two-thousand-ton artificial reef being constructed approximately nine miles off the coast

TABLE 7.2

Types of building projects

Construction: Putting together all or part of a structure. Most construction site debris is generated from packaging and when raw materials are cut or sized. Workers can save large scraps for use in other projects. Durable packaging can be returned to suppliers. Smaller scraps and non-durable packaging can be source separated when produced, and recycled.

Renovation: Partial removal of a building's interior and/or exterior followed by construction. Contractors can adapt the same recovery techniques as above for renovation projects.

Deconstruction: A "soft" demolition technique whereby workers dismantle a significant portion of a building in order to maximize recovery of materials for reuse and recycling.

Demolition: The complete removal of a building. On most demolition projects, after extracting easily removable materials for reuse or recycling, workers complete the demolition with sledgehammers, explosives, or heavy equipment. Additional recyclables are often sorted from the rubble generated during these demolition activities.

SOURCE: "This Fact Sheet Profiles Building Projects of Four Distinct Types," in *Building Savings: Strategies for Waste Reduction of Construction and Demolition Debris from Buildings*, U.S. Environmental Protection Agency, June 2000, http://www.ilsr.org/recycling/buildingdebris.pdf (accessed June 20, 2007)

TABLE 7.3

Building materials and components with a high recovery potential

Appliances	Dimensional lumber	Light fixtures	Plywood	Tile
Bathroom fixtures	Doors	Marble	Shelving	Trim
Bricks	Ductwork	Metal framing	Siding	Windows
Cabinets	Flooring	Paneling	Soil	Wood
Carpeting	Insulation	Pipes	Stairs	beams

SOURCE: "Table A4. Typical Components/Materials with a High Recovery Potential," in *Public Works Technical Bulletin 420-49-32: Selection of Methods for the Reduction, Reuse, and Recycling of Demolition Waste*, U.S. Corps of Engineers, July 16, 2001, http://www.wbdg.org/ccb/ARMYCOE/PWTB/pwtb_420_49_32.pdf (accessed June 20, 2007)

TABLE 7.4

Organic by-products

Animal manure and bedding
Biosolids
Food processing residuals (fruit and vegetable peelings, pulp, pits)
Food scraps
Hatchery wastes
Meat, seafood, poultry and dairy processing wastewater and solids
Mixed refuse (food scraps, paper etc.)
Pharmaceutical and brewery waste
Pulp and paper mill residues
Spent mushroom substrate
Textile residuals
Waste grain, silage
Wood ash
Yardwaste (leaves, grass clippings, woodchips)

SOURCE: Adapted from "Other Organic By-Products," in *Guide to Field Storage of Biosolids*, U.S. Environmental Protection Agency, July 2000, http://www.epa.gov/owm/mtb/biosolids/fsguide/fsguide.pdf (accessed June 20, 2007)

TABLE 7.5

Types of land onto which different types of biosolids may be applied

Biosolids options	Pathogen class	VAR[a] options	Type of land	Other restrictions
EQ	A	1–8	All[b]	None
	A	9 or 10	All except lawn and home gardens[c]	Management practices
PC	B	1–10	All except lawn and home gardens[c]	Management practices and site restrictions
	A	1–10	All except lawn and home garden[d]	Management practices
CPLR	B	1–10	All except lawn and home garden[c, d]	Management practices and site restrictions
APLR	A	1–8	All, but most likely lawns and home gardens	Labeling management practice

[a]VAR means vector attraction reduction.
[b]Agricultural land, forest, reclamation sites, and lawns and home gardens.
[c]It is not possible to impose site restrictions on lawns and home gardens.
[d]It is not possible to track cumulative additions of pollutants on lawns and home gardens.
Notes: EQ=Exceptional quality.
PC=Pollutant concentration.
CPLR=Cumulative pollutant loading rate.
APLR=Annual pollutant loading rate.

SOURCE: "Table 2-4. Types of Land onto Which Different Types of Biosolids May Be Applied," in *A Plain English Guide to the EPA Part 503 Biosolids Rule*, U.S. Environmental Protection Agency, September 1994, http://www.epa.gov/OWM/mtb/biosolids/503pe/503pe_2.pdf (accessed June 20, 2007)

in the Gulf of Mexico. The reef consists of clean C&D debris, such as culverts, telephone poles, and junction boxes, that was donated by construction companies.

TIRE SHREDS. As described in Chapter 6, scrap tires pose many disposal challenges and environmental risks. Because of their high petroleum content, tires are widely combusted in waste-to-energy facilities. The Rubber Manufacturers Association notes in *Scrap Tire Markets in the United States* (November 2006, www.rma.org/getfile .cfm?ID=894&type=publication) that just over half of the scrap tires generated in 2005 were used as fuel. However, civil engineering applications increasingly consume large amounts of recycled tires—an estimated forty-nine million tires in 2005, representing approximately 16% of all scrap tires produced that year. These applications use tire shreds in roads and landfills, septic tank leach fields, and other construction projects. In addition, ground rubber from scrap tires is used to produce new rubber products and as a surface material at playgrounds and sports arenas, such as running tracks. The association indicates that nearly thirty-eight million scrap tires in 2005 (12% of the total) were used in this manner.

ORGANIC BY-PRODUCT RECOVERY

Organic by-products encompass a variety of materials from industrial, commercial, and residential sources. (See Table 7.4.) Wastes with high organic contents can be recycled, most commonly in agricultural applications. Mulch, compost, and soil amendments are also produced from organic by-products.

Biosolids

Biosolids are organic by-products derived from wastewater treatment sludges. Sludges can come from municipal (sewage) plants or industrial facilities with organic-based

processes, such as pulp and paper mills. In either case, some sludge treatment and processing is typically required before biosolids can be reused.

SEWAGE-SOURCE BIOSOLIDS. The reuse of sewage-source biosolids is regulated by the federal government under Title 40 Part 503 (Standards for the Use or Disposal of Sewage Sludge), which went into effect in 1993. The EPA classifies and regulates biosolids based on their levels of metals and pathogens (disease-causing organisms), their intended reuses, and the extent to which the biosolids will attract vectors (flies, mosquitoes, etc.). There are two pathogen classes. Class A requires that no or virtually no pathogens be present in the biosolid. Class B allows limited levels of certain pathogens. Biosolids are categorized as shown in Table 7.5. Exceptional Quality (EQ) biosolids meet the strictest limits and are permitted for all types of land application with no legal restrictions on reuse. EQ-class biosolids can be sold to the public, for example, in lawn and garden stores.

In "Survey of Organic Wastewater Contaminant in Biosolids Destined for Land Application" (*Environmental Science and Technology*, vol. 40, no. 23, September 2006), which reports on the presence of nonbiological organic contaminants in biosolid samples, Chad A. Kinney et al. raise questions about the effectiveness of Part 503. Kinney and his colleagues tested nine different biosolids produced by sewage treatment plants in seven different states. More than fifty organic contaminants were detected in the samples, including disinfectants and fragrances. Even though the concentrations were not believed to be harmful, Kinney and his collaborators stress that additional study is needed to determine the level and fate of nonbiological organic chemicals in biosolids. Critics believe that the EPA's biosolid limits are outdated—they were crafted in the late 1980s—and need to be updated to reflect the range of complex organic chemicals found in sewage in the 2000s, such as disinfectants that are added to soaps.

PULP AND PAPER INDUSTRY BY-PRODUCTS. Pulp and paper industry by-products are one of the wastes targeted by the EPA via the IRC for greater recycling. Bill Thacker of the National Center for Air and Stream Improvement, in "Management of Byproduct Solids Generated in the Pulp and Paper Industry" (January 23, 2007, http://www.epa.gov/epaoswer/non-hw/imr/irc-meet/03-paper.pdf), states that approximately fifteen million dry tons of pulp and paper mill by-products are produced annually. This waste stream includes wastewater treatment plant sludge, boiler ash, fine materials collected in flue gas treatment equipment, causticizing residues, wood waste, and rejects from the pulping and papermaking processes. Thacker notes that only about a quarter of the by-products are recycled, primarily through land application. Most of the by-products go to disposal, for example, in landfills.

AGRICULTURAL WASTE. The Agricultural Research Service, in "FY-2006 Annual Report Manure and Byproduct Utilization National Program" (2006, http://www.ars.usd.gov/SP2UserFiles/Program/206/NP206ManureandByproductUtilization.doc), indicates that more than one billion tons of agricultural wastes are produced annually. Organic by-products within this waste stream include manure and animal bedding (e.g., hay). Manure is rich in nutrients, such as nitrogen and phosphorus, that have beneficial uses as fertilizing agents. Thus, land application is a common recovery method. Figure 7.2 shows waste handling practices, including land application, at a typical dairy farm.

The availability of sufficient and easily accessible land for application of organic agricultural wastes is a pressing concern. Noel Gollehon et al. note in "Confined Animal Production and Manure Nutrients" (*Agriculture Information Bulletin*, no. 771, June 2001) that in 2001 approximately one-fourth of the nation's livestock operations lacked adequate on-farm land for application of the waste stream at acceptable rates. Even though most counties in which these operations were located did contain sufficient crop acres on other farms for application of the excess manure, transport problems were widely reported. The U.S. Department of Agriculture recommends that acceptable alternatives, such as energy production, be developed to mitigate reusability challenges associated with manure.

MUNICIPAL SOLID WASTE RECOVERY

Municipal solid waste (MSW) is the everyday garbage produced by homes and businesses. The EPA conducts detailed tracking of the generation and recovery of this nonhazardous waste stream. The EPA notes that Americans recycled seventy-nine million tons of MSW in 2005, accounting for 32.1% of total MSW generated. (See Figure 7.3.) Recycling rates for various materials are shown in Table 7.6. The materials with the highest recovery rates were nonferrous metals excluding aluminum (72.4%), yard trimmings (61.9%), and paper and paperboard (50%). By contrast, recovery rates were low for food wastes (2.4%) and plastics (5.7%).

The EPA does not break down recovery rates by state. However, in "The State of Garbage" (*BioCycle*, April 2006), Phil Simmons et al. estimate the state-by-state recycling rates in 2004. According to Simmons and his coauthors, the states with the highest recycling rates in 2004 were Oregon (45.8%), Minnesota (43.2%), New York (43%), Tennessee (42.2%), and Washington (40.5%).

Municipal Solid Waste Components Recovered

PAPER. The paper industry has been at the leading edge of the recycling revolution. Used paper-based products can be de-inked in chemical baths and reduced to a fibrous slurry that can be reformulated into new paper products. Paper can undergo this process several times before the fibers become too damaged for reuse. Paper products vary greatly in the type (hardwood versus softwood) and length of fibers that are used to make them. Recycled papers must typically be sorted into particular usage categories (e.g., newsprint or fine writing papers) before being reprocessed.

Figure 7.4 shows EPA estimates of the tons of paper (and paperboard) products generated as municipal waste and the tons recovered between 1960 and 2005. Overall, the recovery rate for 2005 was 50%. However, according to the EPA, in *Municipal Solid Waste in the United States: 2005 Facts and Figures* (October 2006, http://www.epa.gov/msw/pubs/mswchar05.pdf), there were wide variations in rates for specific paper products. For example, the EPA states that newspaper had a recovery rate of 89.2%. This was the highest rate for any product within this category. Recovery rates were also high for corrugated boxes (71.5%) and office papers (62.6%). Most other paper products had moderate recovery rates falling within the 10% to 40% range. By contrast, paper products such as tissue papers and towels, milk cartons, and paper plates and cups had negligible recovery rates (less than 0.1%).

GLASS. Waste glass can be melted down and formed into new glass products over and over without losing its structural integrity. Virgin raw materials, such as sand, limestone, and soda ash, are added as needed to formulate new glass products. However, colored glass cannot be easily de-colored, as paper is de-inked. This means that glass products must be sorted by color before reprocessing.

FIGURE 7.2

Waste handling and reuse options for a dairy farm

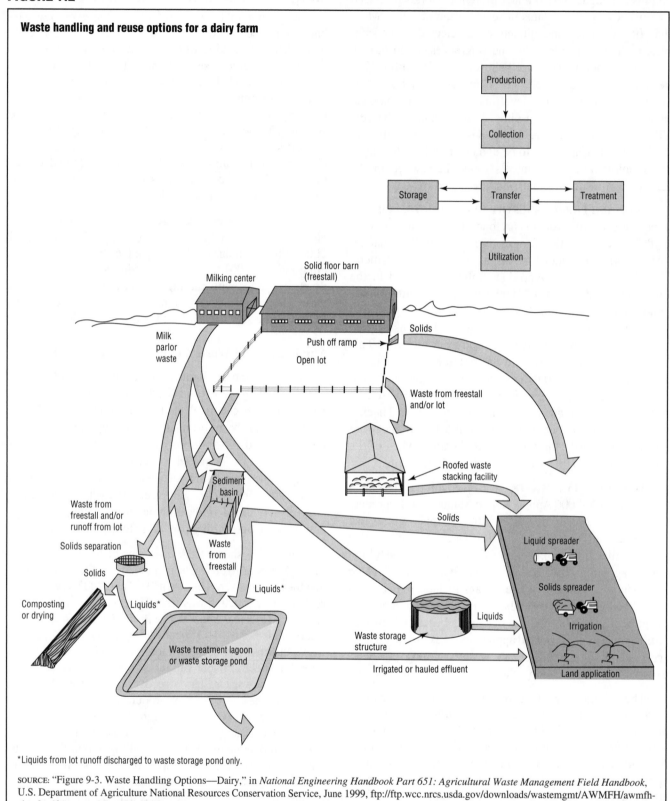

*Liquids from lot runoff discharged to waste storage pond only.

SOURCE: "Figure 9-3. Waste Handling Options—Dairy," in *National Engineering Handbook Part 651: Agricultural Waste Management Field Handbook*, U.S. Department of Agriculture National Resources Conservation Service, June 1999, ftp://ftp.wcc.nrcs.usda.gov/downloads/wastemgmt/AWMFH/awmfh-chap9.pdf (accessed June 20, 2007)

Figure 7.5 shows EPA estimates of the tons of glass products generated as municipal waste and the tons recovered between 1960 and 2005. Most glass that becomes MSW is from bottles and jars manufactured for food and drink prod-ucts. Glass generation rates generally declined between 1980 and 2003 because of competition from the plastics industry for these markets. Glass recovery increased throughout the 1980s and early 1990s and then experienced a slight decline.

FIGURE 7.3

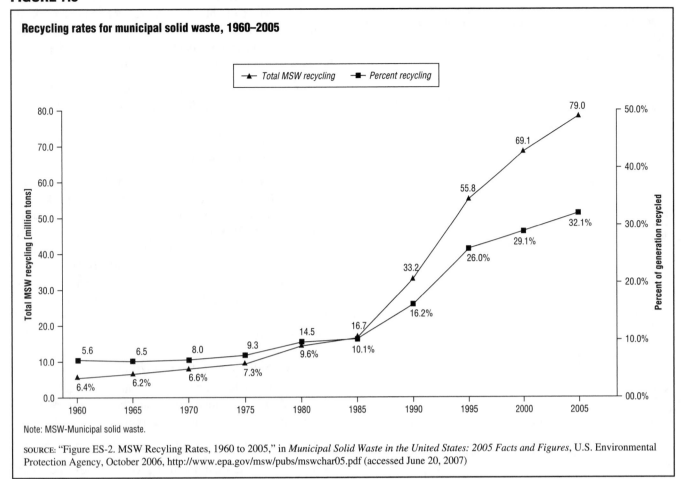

Recycling rates for municipal solid waste, 1960–2005

Note: MSW–Municipal solid waste.

SOURCE: "Figure ES-2. MSW Recyling Rates, 1960 to 2005," in *Municipal Solid Waste in the United States: 2005 Facts and Figures*, U.S. Environmental Protection Agency, October 2006, http://www.epa.gov/msw/pubs/mswchar05.pdf (accessed June 20, 2007)

METALS. Metal recycling is as old as metalworking. Coins and jewelry made of gold and silver were melted down in ancient times to make new coins with images of the current ruler. Metal objects were generally considered valuable and were frequently sold or given away, rarely simply discarded. When metal objects could not be repaired, they could be melted down and fashioned into something else. This practice continues in modern society. In general, metals must be sorted by composition before reprocessing.

Figure 7.6 shows EPA estimates of the tons of metal products generated as municipal waste and the tons recovered between 1960 and 2005. According to the EPA, ferrous metals (iron and steel) comprise the largest category of metals in MSW. They are primarily used in durable goods such as appliances, furniture, and tires. Aluminum is used extensively in drink and food cans and packaging materials. Lead, zinc, and copper fall under the category "other nonferrous metals." They are found in batteries, appliances, and consumer electronics.

Metals recovery was relatively flat until the mid-1980s, when it began increasing dramatically. Recovery leveled off during the late 1990s. Detailed EPA data in *Municipal Solid Waste in the United States* show that recovery rates differ greatly from metal to metal. More than 72% of nonferrous metals (excluding aluminum) in the 2005 municipal waste stream were recovered, compared with only 35.8% of ferrous metals and 21.5% of aluminum.

PLASTICS. Plastic products are manufactured from chemical resins molded into various shapes. There are dozens of different resins in common use, each with a different chemical formulation. Even though waste plastic products can be melted down and reformulated into new products, sorting by resin type must first be performed.

Figure 7.7 shows EPA estimates of the tons of plastic products generated as municipal waste and the tons recovered between 1960 and 2005. In 1960 there were virtually no plastic products in MSW. In *Municipal Solid Waste in the United States*, the EPA indicates that in 2005 MSW contained 28.9 million tons of plastic products. This massive increase in generation was accompanied by incredibly low rates of recovery. Only 5.7% of all plastic products generated in MSW during 2005 were recovered. This is about 1.6 tons of plastic recovered. The plastics recovery rate has hovered between 5% and 6% since 1995.

TABLE 7.6

Generation and recovery of materials in municipal solid waste by weight, 2005

[In millions of tons and percent of generation of each material]

Material	Weight generated	Weight recovered	Recovery as a percent of generation
Paper and paperboard	84.0	42.0	50.0%
Glass	12.8	2.76	21.6%
Metals			
Steel	13.8	4.93	35.8%
Aluminum	3.21	0.69	21.5%
Other nonferrous metals[a]	1.74	1.26	72.4%
Total metals	**18.7**	**6.88**	**36.8%**
Plastics	28.9	1.65	5.7%
Rubber and leather	6.70	0.96	14.3%
Textiles	11.1	1.70	15.3%
Wood	13.9	1.31	9.4%
Other materials	4.57	1.17	25.6%
Total materials in products	**180.7**	**58.4**	**32.3%**
Other wastes			
Food, other[b]	29.2	0.69	2.4%
Yard trimmings	32.1	19.9	61.9%
Miscellaneous inorganic wastes	3.69	Neg.	Neg.
Total other wastes	**65.0**	**20.6**	**31.6%**
Total municipal solid waste	**245.7**	**79.0**	**32.1%**

[a]Includes lead from lead-acid batteries.
[b]Includes recovery of other MSW organics for composting.
Notes: Includes waste from residential, commercial, and institutional sources. Details may not add to totals due to rounding.
Neg.=Less than 5,000 tons or 0.05 percent.
MSW=Municipal solid waste.

SOURCE: "Table ES-4. Generation and Recovery of Materials in MSW, 2005 (in millions of tons and percent of generation of each material)," in *Municipal Solid Waste in the United States: 2005 Facts and Figures*, U.S. Environmental Protection Agency, October 2006, http://www.epa.gov/msw/pubs/mswchar05.pdf (accessed June 20, 2007).

Detailed EPA data show that the recovery of some plastic products is much higher than others. In 2005, 34.1% of polyethylene terephthalate soft drink bottles were recovered from municipal waste. Nearly 29% of high-density polyethylene milk and water bottles were recovered. However, recovery rates for other plastic products were low.

ELECTRONIC EQUIPMENT. Computers and other electronic devices contain materials that are valuable for reuse, particularly metals, plastics, and glass. (See Figure 7.8.) The most common metals in personal computers are aluminum, steel, and copper. Small amounts of precious metals, such as gold, palladium, platinum, and silver, are also found in computer circuit boards. Some of the metals used in personal computers (antimony, arsenic, cadmium, chromium, cobalt, lead, mercury, and selenium) are classified as hazardous by the Resource Conservation and Recovery Act and cannot be disposed of in municipal solid waste landfills. This is discussed further in Chapter 8.

The primary source of plastics in electronic devices is computer casings. Plastic can be melted down to pro-duce new materials or used as a fuel in certain industrial processes. Most of the glass content of computers is in cathode ray tube monitors. This glass contains lead, which is a hazardous material. However, the glass can be reused to produce new cathode ray tubes.

Figure 7.9 provides generation and recovery data for electronic wastes in MSW for various years between 2000 and 2005. Over 2.6 million tons of electronic equipment were generated as municipal waste in 2005 and only 330,000 tons were recovered.

CONTAINERS AND PACKAGING. The EPA reports that in 2005, 76.6 million tons of containers and packaging were generated, comprising 31.2% of municipal solid waste. In 2005, 39.8% of containers and packaging were recovered, up slightly from 37.9% in 2000. The containers and packaging recovery rate was only 10.5% in 1960. The 2005 recovery figures for containers and packaging included 63.3% of steel, 58.8% of paper and paperboard, 36.3% of aluminum, 25.3% of glass, 15.4% of wood, and 9.4% of plastics.

Municipal Solid Waste Recycling Programs

The successful recycling of any product within municipal solid waste depends on the success of three key components in the recycling process:

- Collection and sorting of the products to be recycled
- Processing and manufacturing technologies to convert waste materials into new products
- Consumer demand for recycled products and those containing recycled materials

Lack of any one of these components seriously jeopardizes recovery efforts for a particular material within the MSW stream. These three factors are represented by the three arrows in the international symbols used to show that a product is recyclable or contains recycled materials. A discussion of the various MSW recycling programs follows.

CURBSIDE PROGRAMS. Curbside programs are those in which recyclable items are collected from bins placed outside residences. According to the EPA, in *Municipal Solid Waste in the United States*, there were more than eighty-five hundred curbside recycling collection programs in the United States in 2005. The EPA estimates that these programs served 79% of the population in the Northeast and 67% of the population in the West. Much smaller percentages were reported for the Midwest (43%) and South (23%). Overall, 48% of the U.S. population had access to curbside recycling programs in 2005.

DROP-OFF CENTERS. Drop-off centers for recyclable materials are operated by various entities, including cities, grocery stores, charitable organizations, and apartment complexes. Typically, they accept a broader range

FIGURE 7.4

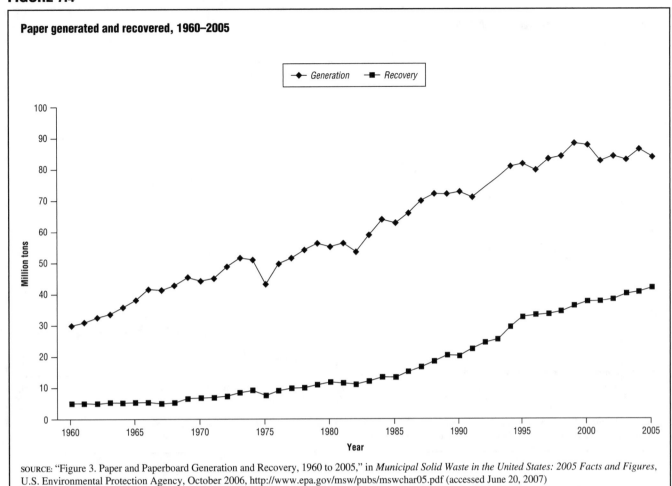

Paper generated and recovered, 1960–2005

SOURCE: "Figure 3. Paper and Paperboard Generation and Recovery, 1960 to 2005," in *Municipal Solid Waste in the United States: 2005 Facts and Figures,* U.S. Environmental Protection Agency, October 2006, http://www.epa.gov/msw/pubs/mswchar05.pdf (accessed June 20, 2007)

of materials than curbside collection programs. The number of drop-off centers around the country is unknown.

Buy-Back Centers and Deposit Systems

Two systems provide a cash incentive to encourage recycling. These are buy-back centers and deposit programs. Buy-back centers are typically businesses that pay cash for recovered materials, such as scrap metal, aluminum cans, or paper.

Deposit programs charge consumers a deposit or fee on beverage containers at the time of purchase, typically a few cents. The deposit can be redeemed if the container is returned empty for reuse. The EPA indicates in *Municipal Solid Waste in the United States* that in 2005 there were ten states operating deposit-type programs: Connecticut, Delaware, Hawaii, Iowa, Maine, Massachusetts, Michigan, New York, Oregon, and Vermont. Furthermore, in California consumers do not pay a deposit on containers, but they can redeem them. Deposit amounts vary by state. For example, in 2007 Californians could redeem bottles containing less than twenty-four ounces for five cents each. Larger bottles had a redemption value of ten cents each.

Materials Recovery Facilities

Materials recovery facilities (MRFs) sort collected recyclables, process them, and ship them to companies that can use them to produce new or reformulated products. For example, a materials recovery facility may sort and crush various types of glass recovered from curbside programs and then ship the processed glass to a bottle factory, where it can be used to produce new bottles.

MRFs vary widely in the types of materials they accept and the technology and labor they use to sort and process recyclables. Most MRFs are classified as low technology, meaning that most of the sorting is done manually. High-technology MRFs sort recyclables using eddy currents (swirling air or water), magnetic pulleys, optical sensors, and air classifiers.

The EPA indicates in *Municipal Solid Waste in the United States* that there were 504 materials recovery facilities operating in the United States in 2005, which processed a total of approximately 50,000 tons per day.

COMMERCIAL RECYCLABLES COLLECTION. According to the EPA, commercial establishments are responsible for

FIGURE 7.5

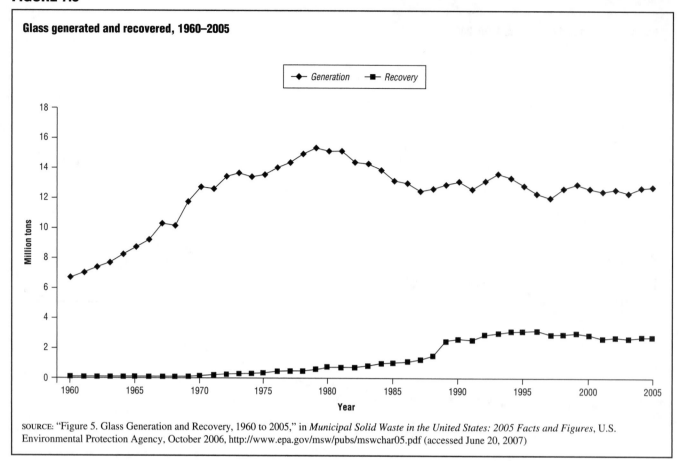

Glass generated and recovered, 1960–2005

SOURCE: "Figure 5. Glass Generation and Recovery, 1960 to 2005," in *Municipal Solid Waste in the United States: 2005 Facts and Figures*, U.S. Environmental Protection Agency, October 2006, http://www.epa.gov/msw/pubs/mswchar05.pdf (accessed June 20, 2007)

the largest quantity of municipal solid waste recycled in the United States. The most commonly recycled materials in the business sector are old corrugated containers and office papers. Grocery stores and other retail outlets are the primary recyclers of old corrugated containers, which are typically picked up by paper dealers. Likewise, many businesses collect used office paper for collection by paper dealers.

The Role of Government in Municipal Solid Waste Recycling

The oldest recycling law in the United States is the Oregon Recycling Opportunity Act, which was passed in 1983 and went into effect in 1986. The act established curbside residential recycling opportunities in large cities and set up drop-off depots in small towns and rural areas.

A growing number of states require that many consumer goods sold must be made from recycled products. In addition, many states have set recycling/recovery goals for their municipal waste. In 1989 Maine adopted a goal to achieve 50% recycling by 1994. The deadline has been extended several times, and in 2005 it was extended to 2009.

For recycling programs to work, there must be markets for recycled products. To help create demand, some states require that newspaper publishers use a minimum proportion of recycled paper. Many states require that recycled

materials be used in making products such as telephone directories, trash bags, glass, and plastic containers. All states have some kind of "buy recycled" program that requires them to purchase recycled products when possible.

The states also use other incentives for recycling. Some states provide financial assistance, incentive money, or tax credits or exemptions for recycling businesses. Furthermore, almost all states bar certain recyclable materials (such as car and boat batteries, grass cuttings, tires, used motor oil, glass, plastic containers, and newspapers) from entering their landfills.

The federal government also helps create a market for recycled goods. The Resource Conservation and Recovery Act requires federal procuring agencies to purchase recycled-content products designated by the EPA in its overall Comprehensive Procurement Guidelines (CPG). EPA guidance regarding the purchase of recycled-content products is also included in Recovered Materials Advisory Notices, which are published periodically and include recommended recycled-content ranges for CPG products that are commercially available.

COMPOSTING

Composting is a recovery method in which plant-based waste materials are isolated and allowed to decompose,

FIGURE 7.6

Metals generated and recovered, 1960–2005

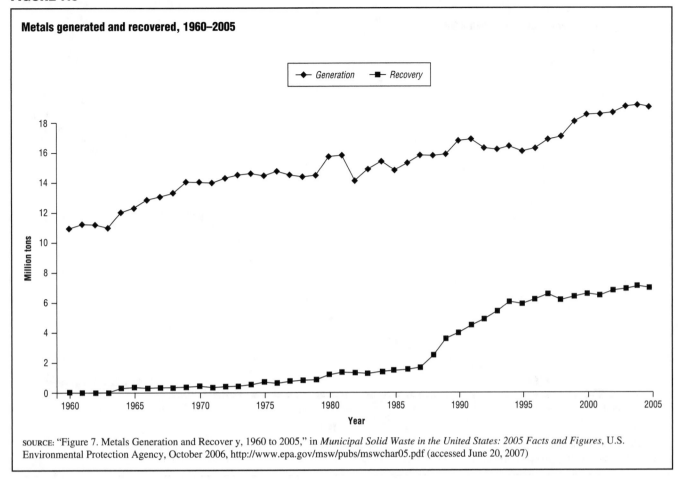

SOURCE: "Figure 7. Metals Generation and Recover y, 1960 to 2005," in *Municipal Solid Waste in the United States: 2005 Facts and Figures*, U.S. Environmental Protection Agency, October 2006, http://www.epa.gov/msw/pubs/mswchar05.pdf (accessed June 20, 2007)

producing an organic-rich substance suitable for use as a soil amendment. Typical compost wastes include grass and garden cuttings, leaves, and kitchen refuse, such as potato peels and coffee grounds. Meat scraps and other animal-based wastes are not recommended for composting, because they can attract scavenging animals.

Natural decomposition of a pile of organic waste can be a long process. Composters can accelerate the process through a variety of techniques, including layering plant wastes with manure or soil, watering the compost, and turning or churning it with garden implements to provide more oxygen. These methods can produce a usable compost material within a few months.

Gardeners mix compost with the soil to loosen the structure of the soil and provide it with nutrients, or spread it on top of the soil as a mulch to keep in moisture. Because compost adds nutrients to the soil, slows soil erosion, and improves water retention, it is an alternative to the use of chemical fertilizers. Compost created on a large scale is often used in landscaping, land reclamation, and landfill cover and to provide high-nutrient soil for farms and nurseries.

Yard waste is especially suitable for composting because of its high moisture content. Over the past few decades composting yard trimmings has become an accepted waste management method in many U.S. locations. The practice got a huge boost beginning in the late 1980s, when many states banned yard trimmings from disposal facilities. In *Municipal Solid Waste in the United States*, the EPA states that in 2005 there were 3,474 publicly operated yard-trimming composting programs operating in the United States. An unknown amount of backyard composting also takes place.

THE HISTORY AND CURRENT STRENGTH OF RECYCLING

For a quarter-century after the first Earth Day (April 22, 1970), recycling advocates pleaded their case to skeptical decision makers in the interest of environmental benefit. As with any business, recycling is subject to the cyclical highs and lows of supply and demand. In the early years of recycling the economy was unable to use all the plastic, paper, and other materials that were recovered. It was difficult for private recycling companies to make a profit. Instead of earning money from recycling, the programs cost them money. Some cities even started dumping their recycled materials into landfills because they could not sell them. Eventually, markets grew for some recycled materials, particularly in the paper sector.

FIGURE 7.7

Plastics generated and recovered, 1960–2005

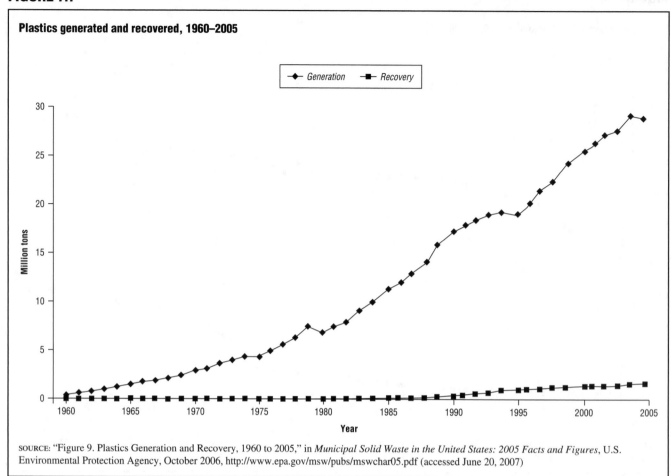

SOURCE: "Figure 9. Plastics Generation and Recovery, 1960 to 2005," in *Municipal Solid Waste in the United States: 2005 Facts and Figures*, U.S. Environmental Protection Agency, October 2006, http://www.epa.gov/msw/pubs/mswchar05.pdf (accessed June 20, 2007)

FIGURE 7.8

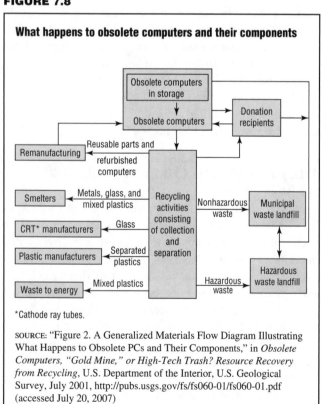

What happens to obsolete computers and their components

*Cathode ray tubes.

SOURCE: "Figure 2. A Generalized Materials Flow Diagram Illustrating What Happens to Obsolete PCs and Their Components," in *Obsolete Computers, "Gold Mine," or High-Tech Trash? Resource Recovery from Recycling*, U.S. Department of the Interior, U.S. Geological Survey, July 2001, http://pubs.usgs.gov/fs/fs060-01/fs060-01.pdf (accessed July 20, 2007)

Market growth has been helped by the widespread public support that recycling receives. Riley E. Dunlap of the Gallup Organization reports in "The State of Environmentalism in the U.S." (April 19, 2007, http://www.galluppoll.com/content/?ci=27256&pg=1) that 89% of survey participants reported voluntarily recycling such items as newspapers, aluminum cans, and glass. This value was 90% in 2000.

Some analysts believe that recycling rates for municipal solid waste have reached a plateau and cannot easily be increased because of the supply and demand imbalance in recycled-content markets. They prefer to focus on source reduction, that is, the reduction of the amount of municipal waste produced in the first place. One method for reducing MSW generation is a principle called Extended Producer Responsibility (EPR). EPR regulations require manufacturers and producers to take some responsibility for the final disposition of their products. This provides an incentive for products and their packaging to be more recoverable and contain less toxic materials. EPR is a cornerstone of recycling requirements in Canada, Japan, and the European Union.

FIGURE 7.9

Consumer electronics generated and recovered, 2000 and 2003–05

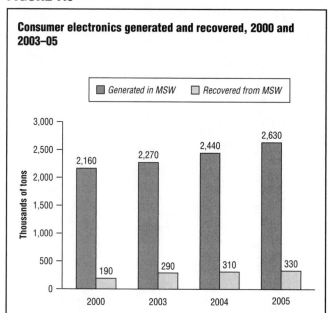

SOURCE: Adapted from "Table 12. Products Generated in the Municipal Waste Stream, 1960 to 2005 (with Detail on Durable Goods) (In Thousands of Tons and Percent of Total Generation)" and "Table 13. Recovery of Products in Municipal Solid Waste, 1960 to 2005 (with Detail on Durable Goods) (In Thousands of Tons and Percent of Generation of Each Product)," in *Municipal Solid Waste in the United States: 2005 Facts and Figures*, U.S. Environmental Protection Agency, October 2006, http://www.epa.gov/msw/pubs/mswchar05.pdf (accessed June 19, 2007)

CHAPTER 8
HAZARDOUS AND RADIOACTIVE WASTE

The most toxic and dangerous waste materials produced in the United States are those classified by the government as hazardous or radioactive.

WHAT IS HAZARDOUS WASTE?

Hazardous waste is dangerous solid waste. The government's definition of solid waste includes materials one would ordinarily consider solid, as well as sludges, semi-solids, liquids, and even containers of gases. The vast majority of hazardous waste is generated by industrial sources. Small amounts come from commercial and residential sources.

Officially, hazardous waste is defined by the federal government as a waste that is either listed as such in regulations issued by the U.S. Environmental Protection Agency (EPA) or that exhibits one or more of the following characteristics: corrosivity, ignitability, reactivity, or contains toxic constituents more than the federal standards. (See Figure 8.1.) In 2007 the EPA had a list of over fifteen hundred hazardous wastes. The list is published in the Code of Federal Regulations (CFR; September 13, 2007, http://ecfr.gpoacc ess.gov/cgi/t/text/text-idx?cecfr&tpl=%2Findex.tpl) under Title 40 §261.31–33.

Because of its dangerous characteristics, hazardous waste requires special care when being stored, transported, or discarded. Most hazardous wastes are regulated under Subtitle C of the Resource Conservation and Recovery Act (RCRA). The EPA has the primary responsibility for permitting facilities that treat, store, and dispose of hazardous waste. The states can adopt more stringent regulations if they wish.

Contamination of the air, water, and soil with hazardous waste can frequently lead to serious health problems. Exposure to some hazardous wastes is believed to cause cancer, degenerative diseases, mental retardation, birth defects, and chromosomal changes. Even though most scientists agree that exposure to high doses of hazardous waste is dangerous, there is less agreement on the danger of exposure to low doses.

INDUSTRIAL HAZARDOUS WASTE

Industrial hazardous wastes are usually a combination of compounds, one or more of which may be hazardous. For example, used pickling solution from a metal processor may contain acid, a hazardous waste, along with water and other nonhazardous compounds. (Pickling is a chemical method of cleaning metal and removing rust during processing.) A mixture of wastes produced regularly as a result of industrial processes generally consists of diluted rather than full-strength compounds. Often, the hazardous components are suspended or dissolved in a mixture of dirt, oil, or water.

Every two years the EPA, in partnership with the states, publishes the *National Biennial RCRA Hazardous Waste Report* (http://www.epa.gov/epaoswer/hazwaste/ data/br05/national05.pdf). The latest report available was published in December 2006 and includes data from 2005.

The EPA distinguishes between large- and small-quantity generators of hazardous waste. A large-quantity generator is one that:

- Generates at least 1,000 kilograms (2,200 pounds) of RCRA hazardous waste in any single month

- Generates in any single month or accumulates at any time at least 1 kilogram (2.2 pounds) of RCRA acute hazardous waste

- Generates or accumulates at any time at least 100 kilograms (220 pounds) of spill clean-up material contaminated with RCRA acute hazardous waste

In 2005 there were 14,984 large-quantity generators and 1,207 small-quantity generators in the United States.

FIGURE 8.1

Types of hazardous waste

- Corrosive—A corrosive material can wear away (corrode) or destroy a substance. For example, most acids are corrosives that can eat through metal, burn skin on contact, and give off vapors that burn the eyes.

- Ignitable—An ignitable material can burst into flames easily. It poses a fire hazard; can irritate the skin, eyes, and lungs; and may give off harmful vapors. Gasoline, paint, and furniture polish are ignitable.

- Reactive—A reactive material can explode or create poisonous gas when combined with other chemicals. For example, chlorine bleach and ammonia are reactive and create a poisonous gas when they come into contact with each other.

- Toxic—Toxic materials or substances can poison people and other life. Toxic substances can cause illness and even death if swallowed or absorbed through the skin. Pesticides, weed killers, and many household cleaners are toxic.

SOURCE: "What Kinds of Hazardous Waste Are There?" in *Fast Flash I: Hazardous Substances and Hazardous Waste*, U.S. Environmental Protection Agency, March 1, 2006, http://www.epa.gov/superfund/students/clas_act/haz-ed/ff_01.htm (accessed July 20, 2007)

Together, they generated 38.3 million tons of RCRA hazardous waste. In 2005 the five states with the largest generation of hazardous waste were Texas (15.2 million tons), Louisiana (5.4 million tons), Ohio (2.1 million tons), Mississippi (1.5 million tons), and Kentucky (1.1 million tons). Together, these states accounted for more than two-thirds (66%) of the total quantity generated.

The chemical industry was by far the largest producer, responsible for 21.1 million tons of hazardous waste, or 56% of the total. Petroleum and coal products manufacturers were responsible for 5.1 million tons (13% of the total), followed by the resin, synthetic rubber, and artificial synthetic fibers and filaments manufacturing industry with 1.8 million tons (5% of the total).

METHODS OF MANAGING HAZARDOUS WASTE

Before the 1970s most industrial hazardous waste was dumped in landfills, stored on-site, burned, or discharged into surface waters with little or no treatment. Since the Pollution Prevention Act of 1990, industrial waste management follows a hierarchy introduced by the EPA that advocates source reduction first, followed by recycling or reuse, and then treatment. Source reduction is an activity that prevents the generation of waste initially—for example, a change in operating practices or raw materials. The second choice is recycling, followed by energy recovery. If none of these methods is feasible, then treatment before disposal is recommended.

For example, a paper mill that changes its pulping chemicals might reduce the amount of toxic liquid left over after the paper is produced. If that is not possible, perhaps the pulping liquid could be recycled and reused in the process. If not, perhaps the liquid can be burned for fuel to recover energy. If not, and the liquid requires disposal, it should be treated as necessary to reduce its toxicity before being released into the environment.

A variety of chemical, biological, and thermal processes can be applied to neutralize or destroy toxic compounds in hazardous waste. (See Table 8.1.) For example, microorganisms and chemicals can remove hazardous hydrocarbons from contaminated water. State and federal regulations require the pretreatment of most hazardous wastes before they are discarded in landfills. These treated materials can only be placed in specially designed land disposal facilities. Besides land disposal, hazardous wastes may be injected deep underground under high pressure in wells thousands of feet deep. (See Figure 8.2.) Hazardous waste can also be burned in incinerators. However, as waste is burned, hot gases are released into the atmosphere, carrying toxic materials not consumed by the flames. In 1999 the federal government imposed a ban on new hazardous waste incinerators.

FEDERAL REGULATION OF HAZARDOUS WASTES

The Toxics Release Inventory

The Toxics Release Inventory (TRI) was established under the Emergency Planning and Community Right-to-Know Act of 1986. Under the program certain industrial facilities using specific toxic chemicals must report annually on their waste management activities and toxic chemical releases. These releases are to air, land, or water. More than 650 toxic chemicals are on the TRI list. In addition, the Pollution Prevention Act of 1990 requires the EPA to collect data on toxic chemicals that have been recycled, treated, or combusted for energy recovery.

Manufacturing facilities (called original industries) have had to report under the TRI program since 1987. In 1998 the TRI requirements were extended to a second group of industries called new industries. These include metal and coal mining, electric utilities burning coal or oil, chemical wholesale distributors, petroleum terminals, bulk storage facilities, RCRA Subtitle C hazardous water treatment and disposal facilities, solvent recovery services, and federal facilities. However, only facilities with

TABLE 8.1

Technologies to neutralize or destroy toxic compounds in hazardous waste

Technology	Description
Biodegradation	Biodegradation uses microorganisms to breakdown organic compounds to make a wasteless toxic.
Chemical reduction	Chemical reduction converts metal and inorganic constituents in wastewater into insoluble precipitates that are later settled out of the wastewater, leaving a lower concentration of metals and inorganics in the wastewater.
Combustion	Combustion destroys organic wastes or makes them less hazardous through burning in boilers, industrial furnaces, or incinerators.
Deactivation	Deactivation is treatment of a waste to remove the characteristic of ignitability, corrosivity, or reactivity.
Macroencapsulation	Macroencapsulation is the application of a surface coating material to seal hazardous constituents in place and prevent them from leaching or escaping.
Neutralization	Neutralization makes certain wastes less acidic or certain substances less alkaline.
Precipitation	Precipitation removes metal and inorganic solids from liquid wastes to allow the safe disposal of the hazardous solid portion.
Recovery of metals	Recovery of organics uses direct physical removal methods to extract metal or inorganic constituents from a waste.
Recovery of organics	Recovery of organics uses direct physical removal methods (e.g., distillation, steam stripping) to extract organic constituents from a waste.
Stabilization	Stabilization (also referred to as solidification) involves the addition of stabilizing agents (e.g., Portland cement) to a waste to reduce the leachability of metal constituents.

SOURCE: Adapted from "Figure III-21. Excerpts from the 40 CFR 268.42 Technology-Based Standards Table," in *RCRA Orientation Manual*, EPA530-R-02-016, U.S. Environmental Protection Agency, Office of Solid Waste and Emergency Response, January 2003, www.epa.gov/epaoswer/general/orientat/romtoc.pdf (accessed July 27, 2007)

ten or more full-time employees that use certain thresholds of toxic chemicals are included.

In the *2005 Toxics Release Inventory (TRI) Public Data Release Report* (March 2007, http://www.epa.gov/tri/tridata/tri05/pdfs/2005brochure.pdf), the EPA states that 25.1 billion pounds of TRI chemicals were waste managed during 2005. The breakdown by management method is shown in Figure 8.3. Thirty-six percent of the waste was recycled, and 34% was treated. Another 18% was released to the environment, and 12% was used for energy recovery. The EPA reports that 4.3 billion pounds of TRI chemicals were released during 2005 by 23,461 facilities. Most of the chemicals (88%) were released on-site. Figure 8.4 shows the distribution of releases to the environment.

A breakdown by industry is provided in Figure 8.5. The metal mining industry was responsible for more than a quarter (27%) of the releases, followed by electric utilities (25%) and chemicals production (12%). In the *2005 TRI Public Data Release eReport* (March 2007, http://www.epa.gov/tri/tridata/tri05/pdfs/eReport.pdf), the EPA notes that the states with the highest releases were Alaska (548.4 million pounds), Nevada (326.1 million pounds),

FIGURE 8.2

Typical class I injection well

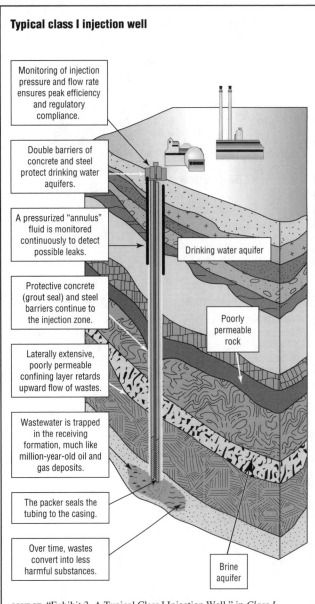

SOURCE: "Exhibit 3. A Typical Class I Injection Well," in *Class I Underground Injection Well Control Program: Study of the Risks Associated with Class I Underground Injection Wells*, U.S. Environmental Protection Agency, Office of Water, March 2001, http://www.epa.gov/safewater/uic/classonestudy.pdf (accessed July 27, 2007)

Ohio (276.9 million pounds), Texas (261.8 million pounds), and Indiana (249.2 million pounds). These five states accounted for more than 38% of all TRI releases in 2005. According to the EPA, total releases of the core set of TRI chemicals (those that were identified and tracked beginning in 1988) declined by 58% (1.7 billion pounds) between 1988 and 2005 from roughly 3 billion pounds to 1.3 billion pounds.

The Resource Conservation and Recovery Act

The RCRA, first enacted by Congress in 1976 and expanded by amendments in 1980, 1984, 1992, and 1996, was designed to manage the disposal, incineration, treatment,

FIGURE 8.3

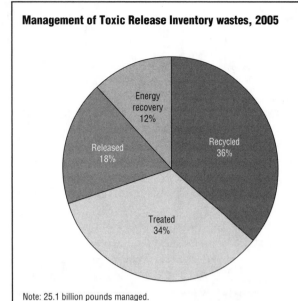

Management of Toxic Release Inventory wastes, 2005

Energy recovery 12%

Recycled 36%

Released 18%

Treated 34%

Note: 25.1 billion pounds managed.

SOURCE: Adapted from "Table 2. Production-related Waste Managed by Waste Management Activity, 2005," in *2005 Toxics Release Inventory (TRI) Public Data Release Report*, U.S. Environmental Protection Agency, March 2007, http://www.epa.gov/tri/tridata/tri05/pdfs/2005brochure.pdf (accessed June 28, 2007)

FIGURE 8.4

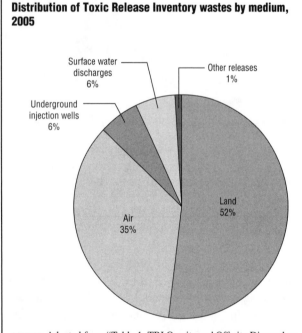

Distribution of Toxic Release Inventory wastes by medium, 2005

Surface water discharges 6%

Other releases 1%

Underground injection wells 6%

Land 52%

Air 35%

SOURCE: Adapted from "Table 1. TRI On-site and Off-site Disposal or Other Releases, 2005," in *2005 Toxics Release Inventory (TRI) Public Data Release Report*, U.S. Environmental Protection Agency, March 2007, http://www.epa.gov/tri/tridata/tri05/pdfs/2005brochure.pdf (accessed June 28, 2007)

FIGURE 8.5

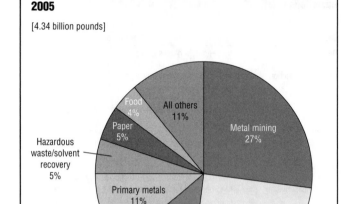

Distribution of Toxic Release Inventory wastes by industry, 2005

[4.34 billion pounds]

Food 4%

All others 11%

Paper 5%

Hazardous waste/solvent recovery 5%

Metal mining 27%

Primary metals 11%

Chemicals 12%

Electric utilities 25%

Note: This information does not indicate whether (or to what degree) the public has been exposed to toxic chemicals. Therefore, no conclusions on the potential risks can be made based solely on this information (including any ranking information). Does not include off-site disposal or other releases transferred to other Toxic Release Inventory facilities that reported the amounts as on-site disposal or other releases. Data as of March 2007.

SOURCE: "TRI Total Disposal or Other Releases, 2005," in *2005 TRI Public Data Release eReport*, U.S. Environmental Protection Agency, March 2007, http://www.epa.gov/tri/tridata/tri05/pdfs/eReport.pdf (accessed June 28, 2007)

guidelines and mandates to improve waste disposal practices. The EPA also has the authority under the RCRA to require businesses with hazardous waste operations to take corrective action to clean up the waste they have released into the environment.

The RCRA imposes design and maintenance standards for waste disposal facilities, such as the installation of liners to prevent waste from migrating into groundwater. Land disposal facilities in operation after November 1980 are regulated under the act and are required to meet RCRA standards or close. Owners of facilities that ceased operation before November 1980 are required to clean up any hazardous waste threats their facilities still pose. Abandoned sites and those that owners cannot afford to clean up under the RCRA are usually referred to the national Superfund program.

The Comprehensive Environmental Response, Compensation, and Liability Act and the Superfund

The Comprehensive Environmental Response, Compensation, and Liability Act (CERCLA) of 1980 established the Superfund program to pay for cleaning up highly contaminated hazardous waste sites that had been abandoned or where a sole responsible party could not be identified. Originally a $1.6 billion, five-year program,

and storage of waste in landfills, surface impoundments, waste piles, tanks, and container storage areas. It regulates the production and disposal of hazardous waste and provides

the Superfund was focused initially on cleaning up leaking dumps that jeopardized groundwater.

During the original mandate of the Superfund, only six sites were cleaned up. When the program expired in 1985, many observers viewed it as a billion-dollar fiasco rampant with scandal and mismanagement. Nonetheless, the negative publicity surrounding the program increased public awareness of the magnitude of the clean-up job in the United States. Consequently, in 1986 and later in 1990 the Superfund was reauthorized.

THE NATIONAL PRIORITIES LIST. CERCLA requires the government to maintain a list of hazardous waste sites that pose the highest potential threat to human health and the environment. This list is known as the National Priorities List (NPL) and includes hazardous waste sites in the country that are being cleaned up under the Superfund program. The NPL constitutes Appendix B to the National Oil and Hazardous Substances Pollution Contingency Plan, 40 CFR Part 300, which the EPA promulgated pursuant to Section 105 of CERCLA.

The NPL is constantly changing as new sites are officially added (finalized) and other sites are deleted (removed). Table 8.2 shows NPL site actions and milestones achieved by fiscal year (October through September) for 1992 through 2007. These data were reported in June 2007, so only data for nine months are included for fiscal year 2007.

According to the EPA (http://www.epa.gov/super fund/sites/npl/status.htm), as of August 27, 2007, there were 1,242 sites on the NPL. More than one thousand had been declared as "construction completed." The EPA determines construction completed when all physical construction of clean-up actions are completed, all immediate threats have been addressed, and all long-term threats are under control. This does not mean that a site has met its clean-up goals. It simply means that the engineering/construction phase of site clean-up is completed. The EPA has deleted 320 sites from the NPL. Sites are deleted when the EPA determines that "no further federal steps under CERCLA are appropriate."

As can be summed from Table 8.2, more sites were proposed to the NPL (406) than were deleted (282) between 1992 and 2007.

According to the EPA, the construction phase of clean-up was completed at more than three times as many Superfund sites between 1993 and 2000 as in all the previous years of the program combined. (See Figure 8.6.) However, many NPL sites are still years away from having all hazardous waste removed.

FUNDING FOR SUPERFUND. Funding for the Superfund program is derived through two major sources: the Superfund Trust Fund and monies appropriated from the federal government's general fund.

The Superfund Trust Fund was set up as part of the original Superfund legislation of 1980. It was designed to help the EPA pay for clean-ups and related program activities. Figure 8.7 shows the Superfund budget history between 1981 and 2005. Until 1995 the Superfund Trust Fund was financed primarily by dedicated taxes collected from companies in the chemical and crude oil industries. This system was extremely unpopular with many corporations arguing that environmentally responsible companies should not have to pay for the mistakes of others. In 1995 the tax was eliminated.

The Superfund Trust Fund is also financed through cost recoveries—money that the EPA recovers through legal settlements with responsible parties. The EPA is authorized to compel parties responsible for creating hazardous pollution, such as waste generators, waste haulers, site owners, or site operators, to clean up the sites. If these parties cannot be found, or if a settlement cannot be reached, the Superfund program finances the clean-up. After completing a clean-up, the EPA can take action against the responsible parties to recover costs and replenish the fund. According to the EPA, in many cases the polluters cannot be located or are unable to pay. In other cases the agency lacks the staff or evidence to proceed with lawsuits.

TABLE 8.2

National Priorities List (NPL) site actions and milestones, 1992–2007

Action	1992	1993	1994	1995	1996	1997	1998	1999	2000	2001	2002	2003	2004	2005	2006	2007
Sites proposed to the NPL	30	52	36	9	27	20	34	37	40	45	9	14	26	12	10	5
Sites finalized on the NPL	0	33	43	31	13	18	17	43	39	29	19	20	11	18	11	5
Sites deleted from the NPL	2	12	13	25	34	32	20	23	19	30	17	9	16	18	7	5
Milestone																
Partial deletions*	—	—	—	—	0	6	7	3	5	4	7	7	7	5	3	2
Construction completions	88	68	61	68	64	88	87	85	87	47	42	40	40	40	40	4

*These totals represent the total number of partial deletions by fiscal year and may include multiple partial deletions at a site. Currently, there are 56 partial deletions at 46 sites.
Notes: A fiscal year is October 1 through September 30. Fiscal year 2007 data are from October 1, 2006 through June 28, 2007. Partial deletion totals are not applicable until fiscal year 1996, when the policy was first implemented.

SOURCE: "Number of NPL Site Actions and Milestones by Fiscal Year," in *National Priorities List*, U.S. Environmental Protection Agency, June 28, 2007, http://www.epa.gov/superfund/sites/query/queryhtm/nplfy.htm (accessed June 28, 2007)

FIGURE 8.6

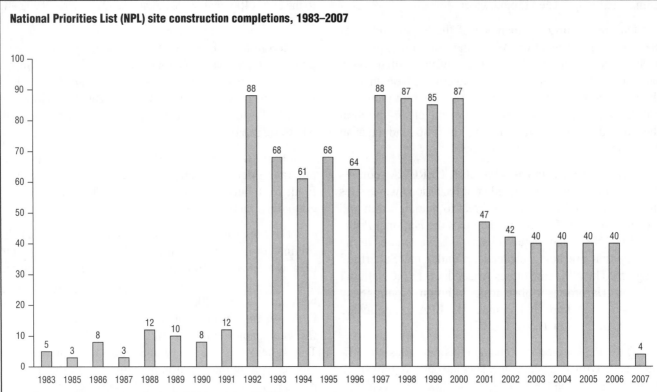

National Priorities List (NPL) site construction completions, 1983–2007

Note: Fiscal year 2007 data are from October 1, 2006 through June 28, 2007.

SOURCE: Adapted from "Figure V-1. Superfund Construction Completions by Fiscal Year," in *Final Report: Superfund Subcommittee of the National Advisory Council for Environmental Policy and Techology*, U.S. Environmental Protection Agency, Washington, DC, April 12, 2004, http://www.epa.gov/ swerrims/docs/naceptdocs/NACEPTsuperfund-Final-Report.pdf (accessed August 4, 2005) and "Number of NPL Site Actions and Milestones by Fiscal Year," in *National Priorities List*, U.S. Environmental Protection Agency, June 28, 2007, http://www.epa.gov/superfund/sites/query/queryhtm/nplfy .htm (accessed June 28, 2007)

All these factors have resulted in only modest amounts of money being collected for the Superfund Trust Fund through cost recoveries. Total revenue into the fund dropped substantially beginning in 2000. (See Figure 8.7.) However, the EPA has continued to add sites to the NPL that require clean-up.

In recent years the EPA has increasingly relied on money appropriated from the federal government's general fund to pay for NPL clean-ups. During the early 2000s the general fund accounted for roughly half of all appropriations to the Superfund program, as shown in Figure 8.7. The budgets for 2004 and 2005 were based entirely on the general fund. This means that all American taxpayers are assuming the financial burden to clean up hazardous waste sites under the Superfund program. Some critics have called for the federal government to reinstate dedicated taxes against petroleum and chemical corporations to fund the Superfund program, instead of burdening tax-paying individuals.

HAZARDOUS WASTE FROM SMALL BUSINESSES AND HOUSEHOLDS

A small percentage of hazardous waste comes from thousands of small-quantity generators—businesses that pro-

duce less than 1,000 kilograms (2,205 pounds) of hazardous waste per month. Common generators are dry-cleaning facilities, furniture-making plants, construction companies, and photo processors. Typical hazardous wastes include spent solvents, leftover chemicals, paints, and unused cleaning chemicals. Hazardous wastes from small-quantity generators and households are regulated under Subtitle D of RCRA.

Household hazardous waste (HHW) includes solvents, paints, cleaners, stains, varnishes, pesticides, motor oil, and car batteries. The EPA reports in "Household Hazardous Waste" (August 9, 2007, http://www.epa.gov/garbage/hhw .htm) that Americans generate 1.6 million tons of household hazardous waste every year. The average home can have as much as 100 pounds of these wastes in basements, garages, and storage buildings. Because of the relatively low amount of hazardous substances in individual products, HHW is not regulated as a hazardous waste. Since the 1980s many communities have held special collection days for household hazardous waste to ensure that it is disposed of properly.

Universal Wastes

Universal wastes are a federally defined subset of hazardous wastes that are produced in small amounts by

FIGURE 8.7

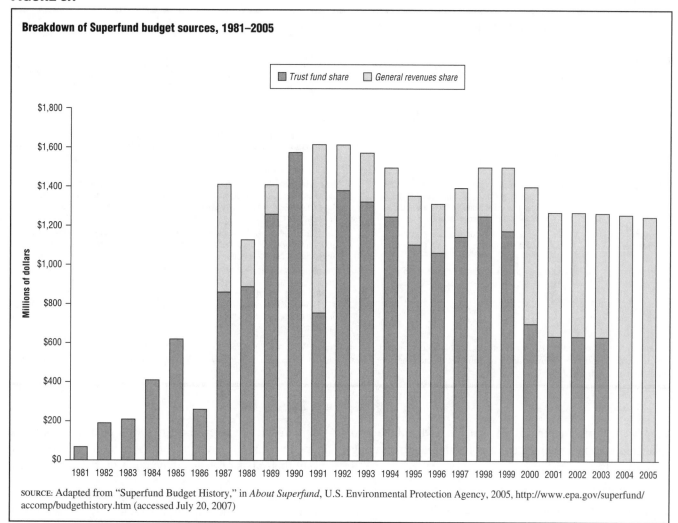

Breakdown of Superfund budget sources, 1981–2005

□ Trust fund share □ General revenues share

Millions of dollars

SOURCE: Adapted from "Superfund Budget History," in *About Superfund*, U.S. Environmental Protection Agency, 2005, http://www.epa.gov/superfund/accomp/budgethistory.htm (accessed July 20, 2007)

many generators. As of 2007 the federal list of universal wastes includes batteries, pesticides, mercury-containing equipment (e.g., thermostats), and lamps (e.g., fluorescent bulbs). Even though these wastes sometimes wind up in the municipal waste stream, they contain worrisome components, such as heavy metals, that pose an environmental hazard. Thus, the EPA regulates them separately from other hazardous wastes with simpler streamlined requirements designed to encourage generators to recycle or dispose of the wastes properly. The EPA's universal waste regulations are published in 40 CFR 273 and apply only to businesses, not residential generators. The states are allowed to adopt the federal universal waste regulations or add to them, as they see fit. For example, California's list of universal wastes as of June 2007 included nonempty aerosol cans, batteries (excluding automotive), cell phones, electronic devices (computers, monitors, televisions, etc.), and mercury-containing items, such as fluorescent lamps.

FOCUS ON ELECTRONIC WASTE. Improper disposal of electronic goods poses environmental risks because of the presence of hazardous metals and other contaminants in the products, as noted in Table 8.3. Concern about the environmental hazards of electronic waste disposal has prompted action by state governments around the country. These measures are discussed by Denise Griffin of the National Conference of State Legislatures, in "Electronic Waste" (July 2005, http://www.ncsl.org/programs/environ/cleanup/elecwaste.htm). Griffin describes legislation crafted in Arkansas, California, Maine, Maryland, and Virginia. Overall, California and Maine have incorporated the strictest regulatory actions designed to achieve maximum recycling results.

In 2003 California passed legislation called the Electronic Waste Recycling Act. This act requires electronic manufacturers to reduce the amount of hazardous substances used in specific electronic products sold in California. It also established a funding mechanism to ensure that these products are properly collected and recycled at the end of their useful lives. In 2005 retailers began collecting fees from consumers purchasing certain electronic products (primarily monitors and other display products with cathode ray tubes). The fees range from $6 to $10 per item, depending on the size of the item. The

TABLE 8.3

Contaminants of concern in old electronics

Contaminant	Source	Hazards
Cadmium	Chip resistors, infrared detectors, and semiconductors	Cadmium can accumulate in, and negatively impact, the kidneys. Cadmium is persistent, bioaccumulative, and toxic. The principal exposure pathway is through respiration and through our food.
Lead	Glass panels in computer monitors and in lead soldering of printed circuit boards	Lead can cause damage to the central and peripheral nervous systems, blood systems, and kidneys in humans. Lead has also been shown to have negative effects on the development of children's brains. Lead can accumulate in the environment and have a detrimental effect on plants, animals, and humans. Consumer electronics may be responsible for 40% of the lead found in landfills. The principal pathway of concern is lead leaching from landfills and contaminating drinking water supplies.
Mercury	Thermostats, position sensors, relays and switches (e.g., on printed circuit boards), discharge lamps, batteries, medical equipment, data transmission, telecommunications, and mobile phones.	When mercury makes its way into waterways, it is transformed into methylated mercury in the sediments. Methylated mercury accumulates in living organisms and travels up the food chain. Methylated mercury can cause brain damage. The principal exposure pathway is through our food.
Hexavalent chromium (chromium VI)	Used to protect against corrosion of untreated and galvanized steel plates	Chromium VI can damage DNA and has been linked to asthmatic bronchitis. The major pathways are through landfill leachate or from fly ash generated when materials containing Chromium VI are incinerated.
Brominated flame retardants	Printed circuit boards, components such as plastic covers and cables as well as plastic covers of televisions	Although less is known about BFRs than some other contaminants of concern, but research has shown that one of these flame retardants, polybrominated diphenylethers (PDBE) might act and an endocrine disrupter. Flame retardant polybrominated biphenyls (PBB) may increase cancer risk to the of the digestive and lymph systems. Once released into the environment through landfill leachate and incineration they are concentrated in the food chain.

SOURCE: Adapted from "What Are the Contaminants of Concern in Old Electronics and What Are Their Pathways?" in *eCycling: Frequent Questions*, U.S. Environmental Protection Agency, Office of Solid Waste and Emergency Response, April 18, 2006, http://www.epa.gov/epaoswer/hazwaste/recycle/ecycling/faq .htm (accessed June 20, 2007).

money is turned over to the state and distributed to qualified companies engaged in collecting and recycling the products.

In 2004 California passed the Cell Phone Recycling Act, which forbids retailers from selling cell phones unless they have a collection, reuse, and recycling program in place for them. The recycling programs must not charge a fee to consumers. The act went into effect in July 2006.

RADIOACTIVE WASTE

What Is Radioactivity?

Radioactivity is the spontaneous emission of energy and/or high-energy particles from the nucleus of an unstable atom. The three primary types of radiation are alpha, beta, and gamma. Isotopes are atoms of an element that have the same number of protons but different numbers of neutrons in their nuclei. For example, the element carbon has twelve protons and twelve neutrons comprising its nucleus. One isotope of carbon, C-14, has twelve protons and fourteen neutrons in its nucleus. This is a radioactive isotope or radioisotope.

Radioisotopes are unstable and their nuclei decay, or break apart, at a steady rate. Decaying radioisotopes produce other isotopes as they emit energy and/or high-energy particles. If the newly formed nuclei are radioactive too, they emit radiation and change into other nuclei. The final products in this chain are stable, non-radioactive nuclei. The amount of time it takes for half the radioactive nuclei in a sample to decay is called the half-life. Half-lives range from a fraction of a second to many thousands of years, depending on the substance.

Radioactivity is measured in units called curies. One curie represents the quantity of radioactive material that will undergo thirty-seven billion disintegrations per second. The biological effect of radiation on human tissue is defined using a unit called the roentgen equivalent man or rem. A rem is the dosage of ionizing radiation that will cause the same biological effect as one roentgen of x-ray or gamma radiation.

Radioisotopes reach our bodies daily, emitted from sources in outer space, and from rocks and soil on Earth. Radioisotopes are also used in medicine and provide useful diagnostic tools.

Energy can be released by artificially breaking apart atomic nuclei. Such a process is called nuclear fission. The fission of uranium 235 (U-235) releases several neutrons that can penetrate other U-235 nuclei. In this way the fission of a single U-235 atom can begin a cascading chain of nuclear reactions. If this series of reactions is regulated to occur slowly, as it is in nuclear power plants, the energy emitted can be captured for a variety of uses, such as generating electricity. If this series of reactions is allowed to occur all at once, as in a nuclear (atomic) bomb, the energy emitted is explosive. (Plutonium-239 can also be used to generate a chain reaction similar to that of U-235.)

FIGURE 8.8

Locations of commercial operating nuclear power reactor, 2005

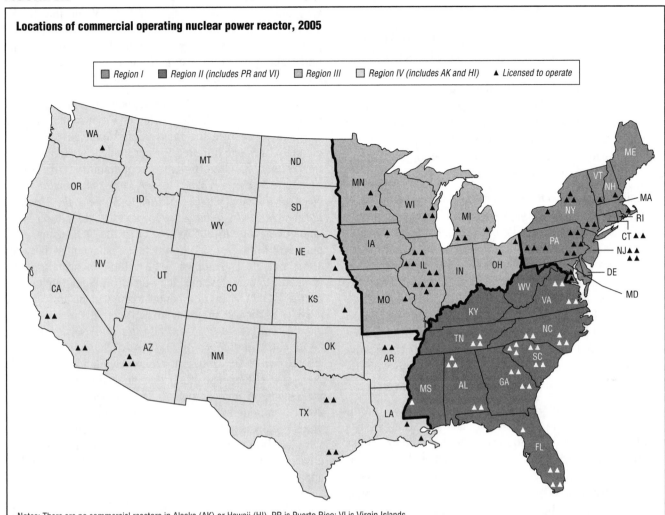

Notes: There are no commercial reactors in Alaska (AK) or Hawaii (HI). PR is Puerto Rico; VI is Virgin Islands.

SOURCE: "Map of the United States Showing Locations of Operating Nuclear Power Reactors," in *Find Operating Nuclear Power Reactors by Location or Name*, U.S. Nuclear Regulatory Commission, April 17, 2007, http://www.nrc.gov/info-finder/reactor/ (accessed July 20, 2007)

Sources of Radioactive Waste

Radioactive waste results from the mining, processing, and use of radioactive materials for commercial, military, medical, and research purposes. In general, the U.S. Department of Energy (DOE) is responsible for managing radioactive waste associated with the nation's military and defense operations. The Nuclear Regulatory Commission (NRC) has primary responsibility for managing radioactive wastes produced by other sources. Some state agencies have also been authorized to regulate aspects of radioactive waste management within their jurisdictions. The EPA regulates the release of radioactive materials to the environment.

NUCLEAR POWER PLANTS. The primary commercial source of radioactive waste is associated with electricity generation at nuclear power plants. These plants rely on controlled slow fission reactions with nuclear fuel pellets to produce heat to create steam. Figure 8.8 shows the locations of operational nuclear power reactors in the United States as of 2005. At that time just over one hundred reactors were operating at more than sixty facilities. According to the DOE's Energy Information Administration, in "Generation" (May 16, 2003, http://www.eia.doe.gov/cneaf/electricity/epav1/generation.html#N_39_), nuclear power has accounted for approximately 18% to 20% of power generation in the United States since the 1990s.

No new nuclear power plants have been ordered since the late 1970s. The decline is attributed to a variety of factors including construction and regulatory difficulties, availability of cheap supplies of natural gas, and public opposition to nuclear power. Opposition grew dramatically following an emergency at the Three Mile Island nuclear power plant near Harrisburg, Pennsylvania. On March 28, 1979, equipment failures, design problems, and operator errors led to a partial meltdown in the nuclear core of one of the reactors. A meltdown occurs when cooling of the nuclear fuel rods is inadequate and the fuel overheats and melts, releasing radioactivity to the atmosphere.

Even though no one was directly injured or killed by the accident, it did expose a substantial population of nearby residents to radioactive gases. The NRC indicates in the fact sheet "Three Mile Island Accident" (February 20, 2007, http://www.nrc.gov/reading-rm/doc-collections/fact-sheets/3mile-isle.pdf) that approximately two million people in the area were exposed to an average dose of one millirem. This is roughly one-sixth the amount of radiation associated with a full set of chest x-rays.

Public fears about nuclear power were rekindled in 1986, when an explosion occurred at a nuclear power plant near the town of Chernobyl in the Soviet Union (now Ukraine). In the early morning hours of April 26, 1986, operators decided to test one of the reactors to see what would happen if the station lost electrical power. A combination of design flaws and operator errors during the test resulted in a massive power surge that overheated and ruptured some of the fuel rods. The resulting explosions destroyed the nuclear reactor core and ripped the roof off the reactor building, sending radioactive debris and smoke into the atmosphere.

Dozens of people, mostly plant workers, died during the explosion or soon thereafter of acute radiation poisoning. Hundreds, possibly thousands, more people died later as a result of exposure to radiation released by the accident. More than one hundred thousand people were evacuated from nearby areas. The Chernobyl disaster left a long-lasting negative public perception about nuclear power.

MILITARY AND DEFENSE SOURCES. The U.S. government maintained an active program for nuclear weapons development from the early 1940s through the 1980s. As scientists raced to develop an atomic bomb during World War II (1939–1945), wartime concern for national security led to a "culture of secrecy" that became characteristic of agencies dealing with nuclear power. On July 16, 1945, the first bomb was exploded above ground in Alamogordo, New Mexico. A few weeks later, two nuclear bombs were dropped on Japan. World War II ended and the Cold War began.

The Atomic Energy Act of 1946 put the responsibility for nuclear weapons development and production under the authority of a new agency called the Atomic Energy Commission (AEC). The AEC developed a nationwide complex of facilities that engaged in research, manufacturing, and testing of nuclear weapons. In 1975 the AEC was abolished, and the DOE assumed responsibility for atomic energy activities.

During the first three decades following the development of the atomic bomb, nuclear waste management received little attention from government policy makers. Beginning in the 1970s public concern about the environmental and health risks of stockpiled nuclear materials

led to political action. Over the next decade nuclear weapons production was curtailed. When the Soviet Union collapsed in 1991, the DOE ceased nearly all production of new nuclear weapons. In addition, a major undertaking began to dismantle and destroy many of the nuclear weapons that had been created.

In 1989 the DOE formed a new program that was eventually directed by the Office of Environmental Management to oversee the massive and expensive effort to clean up over one hundred former nuclear weapons facilities. The U.S. Government Accountability Office estimates in *Nuclear Waste: Better Performance Reporting Needed to Assess DOE's Ability to Achieve the Goals of the Accelerated Cleanup Program* (July 2005, http://www.gao.gov/new.items/d05764.pdf) that the DOE spent more than $60 billion on environmental management between 1989 and 2001. Another $192 billion in spending was projected to complete the clean-up effort. Spending outlays by the DOE for environmental management are reported each year for the previous fiscal year in the president's annual *Budget of the United States Government*. The DOE notes in *Budget of the United States Government, Fiscal Year 2008* (2007, http://www.whitehouse.gov/omb/budget/fy2008/energy.html) that an estimated $6 billion was spent on environmental management in fiscal year 2007. Summing actual spending from the budgets for previous fiscal years shows that, between 2001 and 2007, more than $40 billion was spent. This brings the total spent on environmental management between 1989 and 2007 to approximately $100 billion.

The DOE notes in *Five-Year Plan: FY 2007–FY 2011* (March 15, 2006, http://www.science.doe.gov/Budget_and_Planning/Five-Year%20Plan/FYP%20Vol%20I%20-%20final%20version.pdf) that for fiscal years 2008 through 2011 an average of $6.9 billion is expected to be requested each year for environmental management. In *Cleaning up the Nuclear Weapons Complex: Internet Resources* (March 30, 2001, http://www.rff.org/nuclearcleanup/), Resources for the Future, an environmental research organization, states that the majority of the program costs will be devoted to facilities in Savannah River, South Carolina; Hanford, Washington; Idaho Falls, Idaho; and Oak Ridge, Tennessee.

Classes of Radioactive Waste

Federal and state agencies classify radioactive wastes based on their radioactivity, sources, and methods of management. These classifications differ from agency to agency, and there is sometimes overlap between classes. Major classes defined by the federal government include uranium mill tailings, high-level radioactive wastes, low-level radioactive wastes, and transuranic waste. (See Table 8.4.)

URANIUM MILL TAILINGS. Uranium mining was extensively practiced in the western United States in the decades following World War II. This resulted in the

TABLE 8.4

Primary categories of nuclear waste

Type	Description
Uranium mill tailings	Byproducts and residues resulting from the processing of natural ores to extract uranium and thorium. Tailings are usually in the form of fine sand particles. These wastes contain radium, which has a half-life of thousands of years and decays to produce radon gas. Tailings emit low levels of radiation for long periods of time.
Spent nuclear fuel	Fuel elements and irradiated targets that have been removed from nuclear reactors. These spent fuels are highly radioactive and must be stored in special facilities that shield and cool the materials.
High-level waste	Highly radioactive byproduct associated with use and reprocessing of nuclear fuel in nuclear reactors. Sources include commercial reactors producing electricity and reactors operated at government and university research institutions and on nuclear-powered submarines and ships. This designation is also applied to solids made when liquid high-level waste is treated. This waste typically contains highly radioactive, short-lived fission products as well as long-lived isotopes, hazardous chemicals, and toxic heavy metals. High-level waste must be isolated from the environment for thousands of years.
Transuranic waste	Transuranic elements are radioactive elements with an atomic number (number of protons) greater than that of uranium (ninety-two) and therefore beyond ("trans-") uranium ("-uranic") on the periodic chart of the elements. The vast majority of transuranic elements does not exist in nature, but are synthesized (created) during the production of nuclear weapons. Plutonium is an example of a transuranic element. Transuranic waste is contaminated with transuranic elements at a concentration higher than 100 nanocuries per gram. This includes soil and chemicals as well as contaminated tools, equipment, and clothing. Transuranic waste is generated during nuclear weapons production and other activities involving long-lived transuranic elements, such as plutonium. Some of these isotopes have half-lives of tens of thousands of years, thus requiring long-term isolation.
Low-level waste	Any radioactive waste that does not fall into one of the above categories regardless of content, activity level, or longevity. Most low-level waste contains small amounts of radioactivity in large volumes of material. Examples include contaminated items such as protective clothing and shoe covers, tools and equipment, discarded reactor parts and filters, rags, mops, reactor water treatment residues, luminous dials, laboratory and medical supplies, and animal carcasses used in radiation research.

SOURCE: Adapted from "Table 1. Primary Categories of Environmental Waste and Byproducts," in *2006 Environmental Liabilities: Long-Term Fiscal Planning Hampered by Control Weaknesses and Uncertainties in the Federal Government's Estimates*, U.S. Government Accountability Office, March 2006, http://www.gao.gov/new.items/d06427.pdf (accessed June 19, 2007)

generation of large amounts of mill tailings. In 1978 Congress passed the Uranium Mill Tailings Radiation Control Act (UMTRCA) of 1978 to regulate mill-tailing operations. The law established programs for the clean-up of abandoned mill sites, primarily at federal expense, although owners of still-active mines were financially responsible for their own clean-up.

By the 1980s the United States imported most of the uranium it needed for nuclear power and weapons production. As a result, the vast majority of domestic uranium mines and processing facilities ceased operating.

Under UMTRCA Title I the DOE is responsible for cleaning up abandoned mill-tailings sites that were associated primarily with nuclear weapons production. The NRC oversees the clean-up operations to ensure that they meet environmental standards set by the EPA. Title I is funded jointly by federal and state sources. According to the fact sheet "Uranium Mill Tailings" (April 9, 2007, http://www.nrc.gov/reading-rm/doc-collections/fact-sheets/mill-tailings.pdf), the NRC states that Title I reclamation was ongoing at nineteen tailings disposal sites in 2006. These piles range in size from approximately 60,000 to 4.6 million cubic yards of material. Nearly all the inactive sites are located in western states.

Title II of UMTRCA applies to uranium mill sites licensed by the NRC or by approved state agencies since 1978. The NRC notes in "Uranium Mill Tailings" that sixteen sites fell under this program as of 2006. The vast majority of the sites were inactive and had completed or were completing clean-up activities.

HIGH-LEVEL RADIOACTIVE WASTE. High-level radioactive wastes (HLW) associated with the nation's defense operations are generally managed by the DOE. Other sources of HLW fall under NRC jurisdiction. The NRC manages two major types of HLW. The first type is spent reactor fuel from commercial reactors that is ready for disposal. Spent fuel, the used uranium that has been removed from a nuclear reactor, is far from being completely spent. It contains highly penetrating and toxic radioactivity and requires isolation from living things for thousands of years.

As of 2007 no permanent long-term storage facility existed for HLW; therefore, it was stored on-site at the locations where it was generated or transported to other approved sites for temporary storage. Figure 8.9 shows a map of the dozens of sites around the country at which HLW was being temporarily stored in 2005.

According to the NRC, in "Transportation of Spent Nuclear Fuel" (July 3, 2007, http://www.nrc.gov/waste/spent-fuel-transp.html), thousands of shipments of spent nuclear fuel have taken place in the United States since the early 1970s. Utility companies that operate multiple reactors are permitted to transport spent fuel between their facilities. In addition, spent fuel can be transported to research laboratories for testing purposes. Transportation of spent nuclear fuel is regulated by the NRC and the U.S. Department of Transportation.

High-level radioactive waste also results when spent fuel is reprocessed. This is a chemical process in which radioactive isotopes, primarily uranium and plutonium, are extracted from spent fuel for reuse as reactor fuel. As of 2007 there were no reprocessing operations in the United States devoted to commercial nuclear fuel.

During the Cold War the DOE reprocessed spent nuclear fuel at several locations for defense purposes. In 1992 the agency discontinued the program because of lack of demand for the fuel. As a result, significant amounts of

FIGURE 8.9

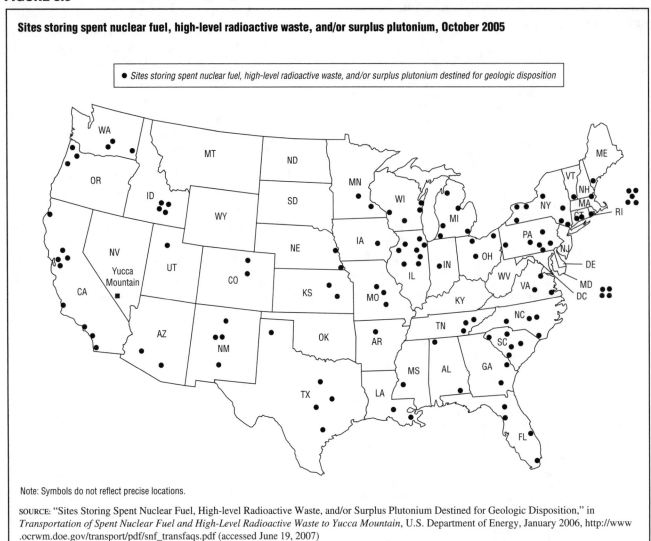

Sites storing spent nuclear fuel, high-level radioactive waste, and/or surplus plutonium, October 2005

● *Sites storing spent nuclear fuel, high-level radioactive waste, and/or surplus plutonium destined for geologic disposition*

Note: Symbols do not reflect precise locations.

SOURCE: "Sites Storing Spent Nuclear Fuel, High-level Radioactive Waste, and/or Surplus Plutonium Destined for Geologic Disposition," in *Transportation of Spent Nuclear Fuel and High-Level Radioactive Waste to Yucca Mountain*, U.S. Department of Energy, January 2006, http://www.ocrwm.doe.gov/transport/pdf/snf_transfaqs.pdf (accessed June 19, 2007)

spent nuclear fuel remain in storage at some DOE facilities. The DOE reports in "National Spent Nuclear Fuel Program" (July 24, 2007, http://nsnfp.inel.gov/snfData.asp) that as of December 2006 it maintained more than twenty-four hundred containers of spent nuclear fuel at locations around the country, including the Hanford Site in Washington State, and the Idaho National Laboratory in Idaho Falls, Idaho.

The Office of Civilian Radioactive Waste Management (OCRWM) is in charge of developing and managing a federal system for the disposal of spent nuclear fuel from commercial nuclear reactors and high-level radioactive waste from national defense activities.

LOW-LEVEL RADIOACTIVE WASTE. Until the 1960s the United States dumped low-level radioactive wastes (LLW) into the ocean. The first commercial site to house such waste was opened in 1962, and by 1971 six sites were licensed for disposal. The volume of LLW increased until the Low-Level Radioactive Waste Policy Act of 1980 and its amendments in 1985. In "Low-Level Waste Disposal Statistics" (March 21, 2007, http://www.nrc.gov/waste/llw-disposal/statistics.html), the NRC reports that in 2005 LLW disposal totaled 4 million cubic feet.

According to the NRC, in "Locations of Low-Level Waste Disposal Facilities" (April 5, 2007, http://www.nrc.gov/waste/llw-disposal/locations.html), there were only three commercial low-level waste sites still operating in 2007. Facilities in Richland, Washington, and Barnwell, South Carolina, accept a broad range of LLW, whereas a facility in Clive, Utah, operates a disposal site that accepts some types of LLW as well as other non-HLW wastes.

In 1980 Congress called for the establishment of a national system of LLW disposal facilities under the Low-Level Radioactive Waste Policy Act. Every state became responsible for finding a low-level disposal site for wastes generated within its borders by 1986. The act encouraged states to organize themselves into compacts to develop new radioactive waste facilities. In "Low-Level Waste Compacts" (March 21, 2007, http://www.nrc.gov/waste/llw-disposal/compacts.html), the NRC notes that as of 2007 there were eleven compacts that encompassed forty states.

No compact or state has, however, successfully developed a new disposal facility for LLW. Compacts and unaffiliated states have confronted significant barriers to developing disposal sites, including public health and environmental concerns, antinuclear sentiment, substantial financial requirements, political issues, and "not in my backyard" campaigns by citizen activists.

TRANSURANIC WASTE. Transuranic wastes are those with an atomic number greater than that of uranium (92) and therefore beyond ("trans-") uranium. Until 1999 all transuranic wastes were in temporary storage at various DOE facilities around the country. Because transuranic waste contains isotopes with half-lives that reach into the tens of thousands of years, the DOE had to develop a permanent storage plan. In 1999 it began moving the wastes to a storage facility in southern New Mexico called the Waste Isolation Pilot Plant (WIPP).

Geologic Repositories for Radioactive Waste

The United States has been working for decades to establish permanent storage facilities for high-level radioactive waste and transuranic waste. Historically, these wastes have been kept in temporary storage at nuclear power plants and DOE facilities around the country. Permanent storage sites are geological repositories, that is, storage facilities constructed deep underground in ancient geological formations that are relatively dry and not subject to earthquakes or other stresses.

Engineers working on permanent storage facilities have designed barrier systems that combine multiple physical barriers with chemical controls to provide a high level of long-term containment for radioactive waste. Radioactive waste is chemically treated for long-term storage and placed into steel drums. The drums are then placed in a concrete container. Many of these drum-filled concrete containers, surrounded with a special chemically treated backfill material, are placed in a larger concrete container deep in the ground. The rock surrounding this large concrete container must have low groundwater flow. The multiple barriers, chemical conditions, and geologic conditions under which the wastes are stored ensure that the wastes dissolve slowly and pose little danger to the groundwater. The Waste Isolation Pilot Plant in southeastern New Mexico has begun processing transuranic (defense) waste and, when it opens, the proposed Yucca Mountain facility in Nevada will process waste from nuclear power plants.

THE WASTE ISOLATION PILOT PLANT. The Waste Isolation Pilot Plant became the world's first deep depository for nuclear waste when it received its first shipment in March 1999. The large facility is located in a desert region near Carlsbad, New Mexico. It was designed for permanent storage of the nation's transuranic waste. WIPP is 2,150 feet below the surface in the salt beds of the Salado Formation. The layout is depicted in Figure 8.10.

According to WIPP (September 10, 2007, http://www.wipp.energy.gov/shipments.htm), 50,345 cubic meters (1.8 million cubic feet) of transuranic waste had been deposited at the facility by September 2007. Over six thousand shipments had been received at that time, most from Idaho National Laboratory and the Rocky Flats Environmental Technology Site (Colorado). The total amount of transuranic waste that can be deposited at WIPP is capped by the Waste Isolation Pilot Plant Land Withdrawal Act (1992) at 175,570 cubic meters (6.2 million cubic feet).

As transuranic waste is transported to WIPP, it is tracked by satellite and moved at night when traffic is light. It can be transported only in good weather and must be routed around major cities.

Every five years the DOE must submit to the EPA a recertification application that documents WIPP's compliance with radioactive waste disposal regulations. The DOE (http://www.wipp.energy.gov/library/CRA/index.htm) submitted the first such application in March 2004.

YUCCA MOUNTAIN. The centerpiece of the federal government's geologic disposal plan for spent nuclear fuel and other high-level waste is the Yucca Mountain site in Nevada. The site is approximately one hundred miles northwest of Las Vegas on federal lands within the Nevada Test Site in Nye County. As shown in Figure 8.11, the mountain is located in a remote desert region.

The Nuclear Waste Policy Act of 1982 required the secretary of energy to investigate the site and, if it was suitable, to recommend to the president that the site be established. In February 2002 President George W. Bush (1946–) received such a recommendation and approved it. Despite opposition from Nevada's governor, the project was subsequently approved by the U.S. House of Representatives and the U.S. Senate. In July 2002 President Bush signed the Yucca Mountain resolution into law.

The DOE must next submit a license application to the NRC to receive permission to begin construction. The DOE must satisfactorily demonstrate that the combination of the site and the repository design complies with standards set forth by the EPA for containing radioactivity within the repository. The DOE (April 30, 2007, http://www.ocrwm.doe.gov/ym_repository/license/index.shtml) reported in 2007 that the application was being prepared and was scheduled to be submitted in mid-2008. In addition, the Yucca site was anticipated to open in 2017.

FIGURE 8.10

Layout of the Waste Isolation Pilot Plant in New Mexico

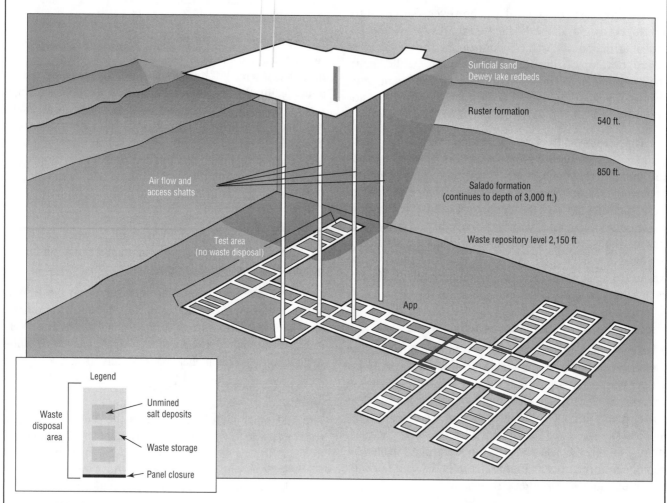

SOURCE: "This Diagram Shows Underground Orientation of the WIPP Repository 2,150 Feet Beneath the Surface," in *2005 EPA WIPP Recertification Fact Sheet No. 1*, U.S. Environmental Protection Agency, Office of Air and Radiation, June 2005, http://www.epa.gov/radiation/docs/wipp/recertification/fs1-recert.pdf (accessed July 20, 2007)

Development of the Yucca Mountain repository has been plagued by legal setbacks and political controversy. Nevada lawmakers have waged a massive and often successful campaign to stop the project from proceeding. Their ultimate goal is to stifle it completely.

As part of the licensing effort, the DOE is required to develop a massive electronic database that is available to the public and that includes all DOE documents supporting the license application. The Licensing Support Network (http://www.lsnnet.gov/) is expected to contain millions of pages when it is completed.

FIGURE 8.11

An aerial view of Yucca Mountain, Nevada. Yucca Mountain is the proposed site for a major, long-term, nuclear waste storage facility. *(U.S. Department of Energy, Office of Civilian Radioactive Waste Management.)*

CHAPTER 9
WATER ISSUES

Water is precious for many reasons. It is an essential resource for sustaining human, animal, and vegetable life. Agriculture is absolutely dependent on water to produce food crops and livestock. Water is crucial to tourism, navigation, and industry. Enormous amounts are used to generate power, mine materials, and produce goods. Water is an ingredient, a medium, and a means of conveyance or cooling in most industrial processes. Water supplies a vital habitat for many of Earth's creatures, from the whale to the tadpole. There are entire ecosystems that are water-based.

All these competing uses put an enormous strain on Earth's water supply. Overall, the amount of water on Earth remains constant, simply passing from one stage to another in a circular pattern known as the hydrologic cycle. Water in the atmosphere condenses and falls to Earth as precipitation, such as rain, sleet, or snow. Precipitation seeps into the ground, saturating the soil and refilling underground aquifers; it is drawn from the soil by vegetation for growth and returned into the air by plant leaves through the process of transpiration; and some precipitation flows into surface waters such as rivers, streams, lakes, wetlands, and oceans. Moisture evaporates from surface water back into the atmosphere to repeat the cycle. (See Figure 9.1.)

Humans have interrupted the cycle to accommodate the many water demands of modern life. Flowing rivers and streams are dammed up. Groundwater and surface water are pumped from their sources to other places. Water is either consumed or discharged back to the environment, usually not in the same condition. Water quality becomes increasingly important. There are two primary issues when it comes to water: availability and suitability.

WATER AVAILABILITY

Even though water covers nearly three-fourths of the planet, the vast majority of it is too salty to drink or nourish crops and too corrosive for many industrial processes. In general, saline water is defined as water that contains at least one thousand milligrams of salt per liter of water. No cheap and effective method for desalinating large amounts of ocean water has been discovered. This makes freshwater an extremely valuable commodity. Even though the overall water supply on Earth is enormous, freshwater is not often in the right place at the right time in the right amount to serve all the competing needs.

Overall Water Use in 2000

For reporting purposes, water use in the United States is classified as in-stream or off-stream. In-stream use means the water is used at its source, usually a river or stream, for example, for the production of hydroelectric power at a dam. Off-stream use means the water is conveyed away from its source, although it may be returned later.

WATER USERS. Susan S. Hutson et al., in *Estimated Use of Water in the United States in 2000* (April 2004, http://pubs.usgs.gov/circ/2004/circ1268/pdf/circular1268.pdf), find that in 2000 an estimated 408 billion gallons of water per day (Bgal/d) were withdrawn from surface and groundwater sources for off-stream use in 2000. (See Table 9.1.) Of this total, 195 Bgal/d was withdrawn for generation of thermoelectric power, 137 Bgal/d was used for irrigation, and 43.3 Bgal/d went to public water supply. Together, these three uses accounted for 375.3 Bgal/d, or about 92% of the total water used.

Minor uses included miscellaneous industrial (including commercial and mining), livestock and aquaculture, and self-supplied domestic (from private wells). Complete data were not available for all minor uses in 2000.

Together, only three states—California, Texas, and Florida—accounted for 25% of all off-stream water withdrawals in 2000. Irrigation and thermoelectric power generation were the primary uses in these states.

FIGURE 9.1

The water cycle

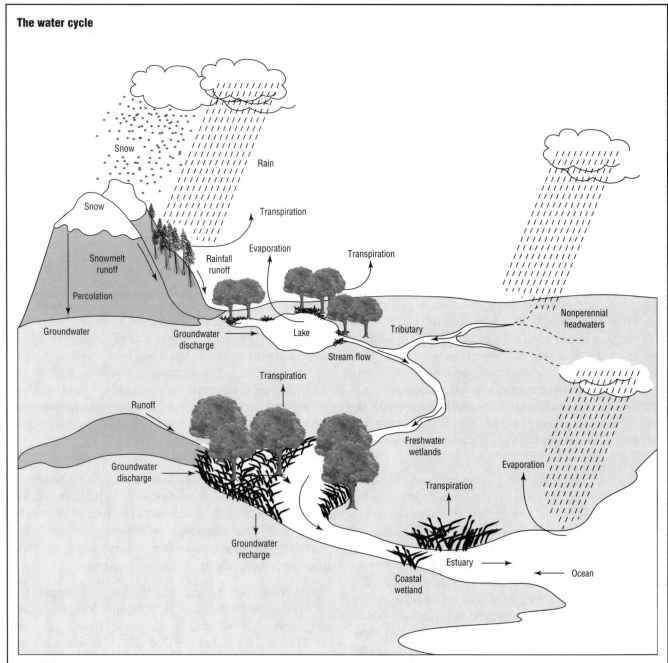

SOURCE: "The Water Cycle," in *National Water Quality Inventory: 1998 Report to Congress*, U.S. Environmental Protection Agency, June 2000, http://www.epa.gov/305b/98report/chap1.pdf (accessed July 27, 2007)

In-stream water use for the generation of hydroelectric power at dams was not reported by Hutson and her collaborators for 2000, but according to Wayne B. Solley, Robert R. Pierce, and Howard A. Perlman, in *Estimated Use of Water in the United States in 1995* (1998, http://water.usgs.gov/watuse/pdf1995/pdf/circular1200.pdf), it totaled 3.2 million gallons of water per day in 1995. In-stream water usage was highest at dams along the Columbia River in the Pacific Northwest and along the Niagara and St. Lawrence River systems in New York. The U.S. Department of Energy (DOE) notes in "Types of Hydropower Plants" (September 8, 2005, http://www1.eere.energy.gov/windandhydro/hydro_plant_types.html) that in 2005 there were approximately twenty-four hundred dams with hydroelectric-generating capacity in the United States.

FRESHWATER AND SALINE. Hutson and her colleagues note that freshwater accounted for 345 Bgal/d, or 85% of total off-stream water withdrawals in 2000. Freshwater is used exclusively for public water supply, domestic self-supply (private wells), irrigation, livestock watering, and aquaculture. It is also an important source

TABLE 9.1

Trends in estimated water use, selected years 1950–2000

[Billion gallons per day]

	1950[a]	1955[b]	1960[c]	1965[d]	1970[d]	1975[e]	1980[e]	1985[e]	1990[e]	1995[e]	2000[e]	Percentage change 1995–2000
						Year						
Population, in millions	150.7	164.0	179.3	193.8	205.9	216.4	229.6	242.4	252.3	267.1	285.3	17
Offstream use:												
Total withdrawals	180	240	270	310	370	420	440	399	408	402	408	12
Public supply	14	17	21	24	27	29	34	36.5	38.5	40.2	43.3	18
Rural domestic and livestock:												
Self-supplied domestic	2.1	2.1	2.0	2.3	2.6	2.8	3.4	3.32	3.39	3.39	3.59	16
Livestock and aquaculture	1.5	1.5	1.6	1.7	1.9	2.1	2.2	4.47[e]	4.50	5.49	[f]	—
Irrigation	89	110	110	120	130	140	150	137	137	134	137	12
Industrial:												
Thermo electric power use	40	72	100	130	170	200	210	187	195	190	195	13
Other industrial use	37	39	38	46	47	45	45	30.5	29.9	29.1	[g]	—
Source of water:												
Ground:												
Fresh	34	47	50	60	68	82	83	73.2	79.4	76.4	83.3	19
Saline	[h]	0.6	0.4	0.5	1.0	1.0	0.9	0.65	1.22	1.11	1.26	114
Surface:												
Fresh	140	180	190	210	250	260	290	265	259	264	262	11
Saline	10	18	31	43	53	69	11	59.6	68.2	59.7	61	12

[a]48 states and District of Columbia, and Hawaii.
[b]48 states and District of Columbia.
[c]50 states and District of Columbia, Puerto Rico, and U.S. Virgin Islands.
[d]50 states and District of Columbia, and Puerto Rico.
[e]From 1985 to present this category includes water use for fish farms.
[f]Data not available for all states; partial total was 5.46.
[g]Commercial use not available; industrial and mining use totaled 23.2.
[h]Data not available.

SOURCE: Susan S. Hutson et al., "Table 14. Trends in Estimated Water Use in the United States, 1950–2000," in *Estimated Use of Water in the United States in 2000* (Circular 1268), U.S. Department of the Interior, U.S. Geological Survey, April 2004, http://water.usgs.gov/pubs/circ/2004/circ1268/ (accessed July 20, 2007)

for thermoelectric power plants, industry, and mining. Most freshwater is obtained from surface water sources (rivers and lakes), as shown in Figure 9.2.

According to Hutson et al., in 2000 irrigation and thermoelectric power plants were the largest users of off-stream water, using 137 Bgal/d (34%) and 195 Bgal/d (48%) of total freshwater and salt water withdrawals. However, the vast majority (around 91%) of the water withdrawn for thermoelectric power generation was used for cooling purposes and then discharged, meaning the actual amount of water consumed was only approximately 18 Bgal/d. Thus, irrigation was actually the largest consumer of off-stream freshwater in 2000.

Far less saline water than freshwater was used in 2000. Only 15% of all water used was saline. Hutson and her coauthors indicate that 98% of the saline water used in 2000 came from surface water sources. Thermoelectric power plants are the largest user of saline water. They accounted for 96% of all saline water use in 2000. Again, most of this water was used and returned to the environment. Industry and mining each accounted for 2% of saline water use. Saline water is unsuitable for drinking and other domestic purposes, irrigation, aquaculture, or livestock watering.

Water Use Trends (1950–2000)

According to Hutson and the other researchers, total off-stream water withdrawals in the United States climbed steadily from 1950 to 1980, declined through 1985, and have remained relatively stable since then.

Table 9.1 shows trends in U.S. population and off-stream water withdrawals between 1950 and 2000. The population rose from 150.7 million in 1950 to 285.3 million in 2000, an increase of 89%, whereas water withdrawals went from 180 Bgal/d in 1950 to 408 Bgal/d in 2000, an increase of 127%. In 1950 the per capita (per person) off-stream water withdrawal was around twelve hundred gallons per day. This value climbed steadily over the years, reaching a peak in 1975 of 1,940 gallons per day per person. Per capita use has since declined and was at 1,430 gallons per day per person in 2000.

FIGURE 9.2

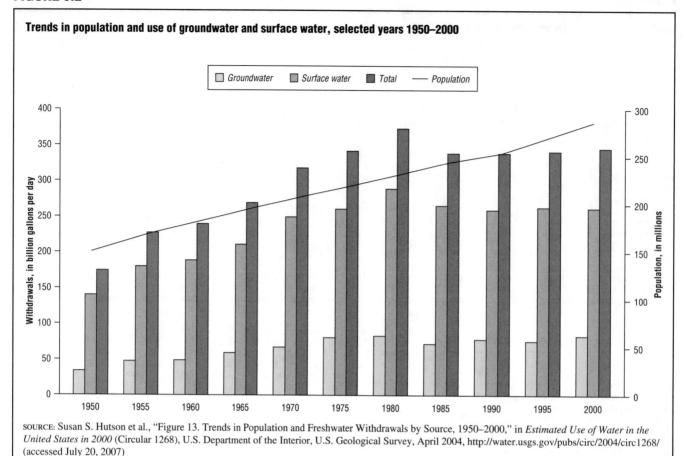

Trends in population and use of groundwater and surface water, selected years 1950–2000

Legend: ☐ Groundwater ☐ Surface water ■ Total — Population

SOURCE: Susan S. Hutson et al., "Figure 13. Trends in Population and Freshwater Withdrawals by Source, 1950–2000," in *Estimated Use of Water in the United States in 2000* (Circular 1268), U.S. Department of the Interior, U.S. Geological Survey, April 2004, http://water.usgs.gov/pubs/circ/2004/circ1268/ (accessed July 20, 2007)

Historically, freshwater has accounted for 85% to 95% of all water used. (See Table 9.1.) The percentage was at the high end during the 1950s and has gradually decreased, leveling off around 85% from 1980 through 2000. The nation's saline water withdrawals have consistently been 98% to 99% from surface water sources.

Even though in-stream water use for hydroelectric power is not covered by Hutson et al., Solley, Pierce, and Perlman note that in-stream withdrawals declined 4% between 1990 and 1995, from 3,290 Bgal/d to 3,160 Bgal/d.

Groundwater

Groundwater is water that fills pores or cracks in subsurface rocks. When rain falls or snow melts on the Earth's surface, water may run off into lower land areas or lakes and streams. Some is caught and diverted for human use. What is left absorbs into the soil where it can be used by vegetation, seeps into deeper layers of soil and rock, or evaporates back into the atmosphere. (See Figure 9.3.)

An aquifer is an underground formation that contains enough water to yield significant amounts when a well is sunk. Aquifers vary from a few feet thick to tens or hundreds of feet thick. They can be located just below the

Earth's surface or thousands of feet beneath it, and one aquifer may be only a part of a large system of aquifers that feed into one another. They can cover a few acres of

FIGURE 9.3

Groundwater in the hydrologic cycle

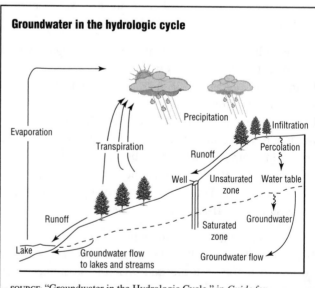

SOURCE: "Groundwater in the Hydrologic Cycle," in *Guide for Industrial Waste Management*, U.S. Environmental Protection Agency, Office of Solid Waste, June 1999, http://www.p2pays.org/ref/03/02001.pdf (accessed July 27, 2007)

land or many thousands of square miles. Because runoff water can easily seep down to the water table, aquifers are susceptible to contamination.

Modern technological developments allow massive quantities of water to be pumped out of the ground. When large amounts of water are removed from the ground, underground aquifers can become depleted much more quickly than they can naturally be replenished. Removal of groundwater also disturbs the natural filtering process that occurs as water travels through rocks and sand.

Focus on Irrigation

In 2000 irrigation accounted for 137 Bgal/d (34%) of all the water withdrawn that year. (See Table 9.1.) It was by far the largest single user of groundwater and the second-highest user of surface water (behind thermoelectric power plants). Because irrigation consumes more withdrawn water than do thermoelectric power plants, irrigation is actually the largest consumer of both surface water and groundwater.

Large-scale irrigation is concentrated in the Midwestern farm belt, southern Florida, the fertile valleys of California, and along the Mississippi River.

WATER SUITABILITY

Water is a fundamental need in every society. Families use water for drinking, cooking, and cleaning. Industry needs it to make chemicals, prepare paper, and clean factories and equipment. Cities use water to fight fires, clean streets, and fill public swimming pools. Farmers water their livestock, clean barns, and irrigate crops. Hydroelectric power stations use water to drive generators, whereas thermonuclear power stations need it for cooling. Water quality is important to all users, as differing levels of quality are required for different uses. Even though some industrial users can tolerate water containing high levels of contaminants, drinking water requirements are extremely strict.

Clean Water Act

On June 22, 1969, the Cuyahoga River in Cleveland, Ohio, burst into flames, the result of oil and debris that had accumulated on the river's surface. This episode thrust the problem of water pollution into the public consciousness. Many people became aware—and wary—of the nation's polluted waters, and in 1972 Congress passed the Federal Water Pollution Control Act, commonly known as the Clean Water Act.

The objective of the Clean Water Act was to "restore and maintain the chemical, physical, and biological integrity of the nation's waters." It called for ending the discharge of all pollutants into the navigable waters of the United States to achieve "wherever attainable, an interim goal of water quality which provides for the protection and propagation of fish, shellfish, and wildlife and provides for recreation in and on the water."

Section 305(b) of the Clean Water Act requires states to assess the condition of their waters and report the extent to which the waters support the basic goals of the Clean Water Act and state water quality standards. Water quality standards are designed to protect designated uses (such as recreation, protection and propagation of aquatic life, fish consumption, and drinking water supply) by setting criteria (e.g., chemical-specific limits on discharges) and preventing any waters that do meet standards from deteriorating from their current condition.

Each state reports to the U.S. Environmental Protection Agency (EPA) data indicating:

1. The water quality of all navigable waters in the state

2. The extent to which the waters provide for the protection and propagation of marine animals and allow recreation in and on the water

3. The extent to which pollution has been eliminated or is under control

4. The sources and causes of the pollution

The act stipulates that the states must submit this information to the EPA on a biennial basis (every two years). Under Section 303(d) of the Clean Water Act, states are required to submit to the EPA a separate list of waters considered impaired and requiring pollution controls.

National Water Quality Databases

Before 2002 the EPA issued a biennial report called the *National Water Quality Inventory* that summarized the state reports required under Section 305(b) of the Clean Water Act. In 2002 the EPA began electronic collection of state water quality data and urged states to combine data required under Sections 305(b) and 303(d). This information is incorporated into the EPA's Watershed Assessment, Tracking, and Environmental Results information system as shown in Table 9.2. The EPA, in "Overview of WATERS" (May 17, 2006, http://www.epa.gov/waters/about/overview.html), provides a list of interactive databases that allow users to access water quality data for individual states. As of September 2007 not all data were included for all states. In "Status of Water Program Features (Linked to the NHD) by State, Tribe, and Territory" (September 17, 2007, http://iaspub.epa.gov/waters/eventstatus), the EPA indicates which data types were available in 2007.

The EPA also cautions against using state data to form conclusions about national trends in water quality. This is because the states use differing monitoring and assessment methods.

In general, the states assess surface water quality in rivers and streams, lakes, ocean shoreline, and estuaries. Estuaries are areas where ocean and freshwater come

TABLE 9.2

Overview of EPA's Office of Water Programs databases

How is water quality determined under the Clean Water Act?	Scope	Database	Description of database
Step 1-Every state adopts goals or standards that need to be met for its waters, based on the intended uses of the waterbodies. Different goals are set for different waterbody uses.	Goals and uses	Water quality standards database (WQSDB)	Information on the uses that have been designated for waterbodies. Examples of such uses are: drinking water supply, recreation, and fish protection. As part of a state's water quality standards, these designated uses provide a regulatory goal for the waterbody and define the level of protection assigned to it.
Step 2-Scientists monitor the waters and . . .	Monitoring results	Storage and retrieval database (STORET)	Repository for water quality, biological, and physical data dating back to the early part of the 20th century.
Step 3-give them one of the following scores: GOOD-The waterbody fully supports its intended uses. IMPAIRED-The waterbody does not support one or more of its intended uses.	Assessment scores	National assessment database (NAD)	Contains information on the attainment of water quality standards. Assessed waters are classified as either fully supporting, threatened, or not supporting their designated uses. This information is under section 305(b) of the Clean Water Act.
Step 4-The impaired waters are then targeted by pollution control programs to reduce the discharge of pollutants into those waters.	Impaired waters	Total maximum daily load (TMDL) tracking system	Contains information on waters that are not supporting their designated uses. These waters are listed by the state as impaired under section 303(d) of the Clean Water Act. The status of TMDLs are also tracked. TMDLs are pollution control measures that reduce the discharge of pollutants into impaired waters.

SOURCE: Adapted from "Office of Water Programs," in *Office of Water Programs*, U.S. Environmental Protection Agency, August 21, 2006, http://www.epa .gov/waters/data/prog.html (accessed June 19, 2007) and "Overview of WATERS," in *Overview of WATERS*, U.S. Environmental Protection Agency, May 17, 2006, http://www.epa.gov/waters/about/overview.html (accessed June 30, 2007)

together. Because of the tremendous resources required to assess all water bodies, only a small portion of each water body type is actually assessed for each reporting period.

Water bodies meeting applicable water quality standards for criteria and designated uses are rated "good." Those water bodies meeting water quality standards but expected to degrade in the near future are rated "good, but threatened." Water bodies that do not meet water quality standards are rated "impaired."

National Water Quality Reports

For a better picture of the nation's overall water quality, the EPA recommends probability-based studies conducted at various sites using nationally consistent methods and designs. This approach was used in the *EPA's 2007 Report on the Environment: Science Report* (http://cfpub.epa.gov/ncea/cfm/recordisplay.cfm?deid=140917), which was released in draft form in May 2007 for public comment. The report presents "indicators" to gauge important aspects of water quality and track trends over time. The EPA acknowledges that data do not exist, or have shortcomings, for some indicators and should be addressed in future research and monitoring efforts.

In the draft report the EPA relies on many sources of water quality data and information, including the following reports:

• The H. John Heinz III Center for Science, Economics, and the Environment's *The State of the Nation's Ecosys-*

tems: Measuring the Lands, Waters, and Living Resources of the United States (2002, http://www.heinzctr.org/ecosystems/pdf_files/sotne_complete.pdf)

• The EPA's *Wadeable Streams Assessment: A Collaborative Survey of the Nation's Streams* (December 2006, http://www.epa.gov/owow/streamsurvey/pdf/WSA_Assessment_May2007.pdf)

• The U.S. Geological Survey's (USGS) *The Quality of Our Nation's Waters: National Water-Quality Assessment Program Pesticides in the Nation's Streams and Ground Water, 1992–2001* (Robert J. Gilliom et al., February 15, 2007, http://pubs.usgs.gov/circ/2005/1291/pdf/circ1291.pdf)

• The EPA's *National Coastal Condition: Report II (2005)* (December 2004, http://www.epa.gov/owow/oceans/nccr/2005/downloads.html)

The latter report was supplemented by the EPA in June 2007 with publication of *National Estuary Program Coastal Condition Report* (http://www.epa.gov/owow/oceans/nepccr/index.html).

THE STATE OF THE NATION'S ECOSYSTEMS. The H. John Heinz III Center for Science, Economics, and the Environment is a nonprofit organization based in Pennsylvania that researches environmental issues of importance to national policy makers. In 2002 the center published *The State of the Nation's Ecosystems*, which presented and assessed various indicators that gauge the condition of natural ecosystems, including water resources. Some portions of the report were updated in 2005.

At the national level the report examines two core indicators related to water quality—nitrogen load/movement and chemical contamination—for which sufficient data exist for analysis. Nitrogen load and movement are important, because excess nitrogen can stimulate algae growth in water bodies, which can reduce oxygen concentrations to dangerous levels for aquatic creatures, such as fish and shellfish. The center found that the Mississippi River carried approximately twice as much nitrate (a form of nitrogen) in the 1990s as it did in the 1950s. Significant nitrogen sources include wastewater treatment plants, runoff from agricultural land and fertilized lawns, and certain industrial discharges. Nitrogen also makes its way into water systems through atmospheric deposition of air pollutants.

In regards to chemical contamination, the report notes that data collected between 1992 and 1998 indicate that multiple contaminants (such as pesticides and other complex organic compounds) were found in high percentages of tested water sources as follows:

- Streams—more than 80% of sites sampled had five or more contaminants detected.

- Streambed sediments—more than 90% of sites sampled had five or more contaminants detected.

- Groundwater—more than 80% of sites sampled had five or more contaminants detected.

WADEABLE STREAMS ASSESSMENT. The EPA describes *Wadeable Streams Assessment: A Collaborative Survey of the Nation's Streams* as "the first nationally consistent baseline of the condition of the nation's streams." It resulted from a sampling effort conducted between 2000 to 2004, in which 1,392 wadeable streams and small rivers in the lower 48 states were sampled. According to the report, wadeable streams and rivers make up 90% of all stream and river miles in the United States.

The assessment examined various physical, chemical, and biological indicators of stream health, including acidification, sedimentation (i.e., the presence of excess particles of soil in the water because of erosion), fish habitat, riparian (streambank) vegetative cover, and biological condition (as indicated by populations of benthic macroinvertebrates, such as dragonflies, mayflies, midges, and beetles). As shown in Figure 9.4, nearly all the stream length examined was in "good" condition in regards to acidification. Approximately half of the stream length was rated "good" with respect to sedimentation levels, fish habitat, and riparian vegetative cover. However, less than 30% of stream length showed a "good" biological condition. A greater percentage of stream length (42%) was rated in "poor" biological condition.

Figure 9.5 shows the most widespread or common stressors of wadeable streams determined from the

assessment. These include high concentrations of nitrogen and phosphorus in the streams, high levels of riparian disturbance (e.g., from human modifications), and poor streambed sediment characteristics.

THE QUALITY OF OUR NATION'S WATERS. Since 1991 the USGS has operated the National Water-Quality Assessment (NAWQA) program to assess the condition of the nation's water resources and help policy makers make water management decisions. Data and findings have been disseminated through a series of publications known as *The Quality of Our Nation's Waters*. The latest report, *The Quality of Our Nation's Waters: National Water-Quality Assessment Program Pesticides in the Nation's Streams and Ground Water, 1992–2001*, is described by Gilliom et al. as "the most comprehensive analysis to date of pesticides in streams and ground water at the national scale."

Gilliom and his associates include data for water samples collected from 186 streams and 5,047 wells. In addition, 700 stream sites were sampled for fish and 1,052 streams were sampled for streambed sediments. Sampling was conducted in various land-use areas, such as agricultural, urban, undeveloped, and mixed use.

As shown in the left hand side of Figure 9.6, pesticides or their degradation products were detected in water samples more than 90% of the time from streams in agricultural, urban, and mixed land use areas. They were detected 65% of the time in streams in undeveloped areas. With regard to groundwater, pesticides were detected in more than half of the samples taken in agricultural and urban areas, and in one-third or less of the samples from mixed land use and undeveloped area. The right hand side of Figure 9.6 shows the surprisingly high occurrence of organochlorine compounds in fish and sediment samples taken from streams. Most organochlorine pesticides, such as dichloro-diphenyl-trichloroethane (DDT) and chlordane, have not been used in the United States for decades, yet they continue to linger in the environment.

Even though Gilliom and his collaborators find pesticides to be widespread in streams and groundwater, the detected levels were seldom greater than human-health benchmarks set by the EPA. (See Figure 9.7.) A troublesome result from a human-health standpoint is that nearly 10% of the stream water samples in agricultural areas contained one or more pesticides that exceeded the benchmarks. However, none of the stream sites sampled were sources of public drinking water. Gilliom et al. express concern regarding benchmark exceedances in groundwater because many of the wells sampled do supply domestic or public water supplies.

COASTAL CONDITION REPORTS. The *National Coastal Condition: Report II* presents data from assessments of 100% of the estuaries in the contiguous United States (the lower forty-eight states) and Puerto Rico. The estuary

FIGURE 9.4

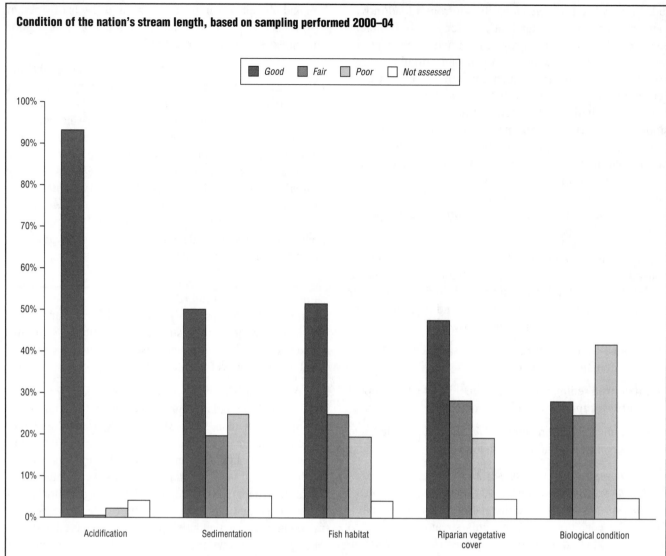

Condition of the nation's stream length, based on sampling performed 2000–04

Legend: ■ Good ■ Fair □ Poor □ Not assessed

SOURCE: Adapted from "Figure 13. Biological Condition of Streams Based on Macroinvertebrate Index of Biotic Condition," "Figure 18. Acidification in U.S. Streams," "Figure 19. Streambed Sediments in U.S. Streams," "Figure 20. In-stream Fish Habitat in U.S. Streams," and "Figure 21. Riparian Vegetative Cover in U.S. Streams," in *Wadeable Streams Assessment: A Collaborative Survey of the Nation's Streams*, U.S. Environmental Protection Agency, December 2006, http://www.epa.gov/owow/streamsurvey/pdf/WSA_Assessment_May2007.pdf (accessed June 30, 2007)

waters were assessed for five parameters: water quality, sediment quality, benthic community quality, coastal habitat loss, and fish tissue contamination. The data were collected between 1997 and 2000. Overall, the nation's coastal waters were rated as fair, the same as in the first report issued in 2001.

Section 320 of the Clean Water Act concerns the National Estuary Program (NEP), in which threatened "nationally significant" estuaries receive special protection and restoration efforts. In 2007 the EPA issued a report on the condition of the nation's twenty-eight NEPs in the *National Estuary Program Coastal Condition Report*. The estuaries were rated based on four of the five parameters used in the 2004 report. The results are shown in Table 9.3 using a scale of one to five, where higher scores indicate better quality. Overall, the EPA rates the

quality of the nation's NEPs as 2.7, which is considered "fair" condition.

Beach Closings

In 2000 Congress passed the Beaches Environmental Assessment and Coastal Health Act. It requires the EPA to collect information from coastal states regarding beach closings because of environmental problems. In 2004 the states began electronic submission of the data, which were compiled into a database called the Beach Advisory and Closing On-line Notification (BEACON; http://oaspub .epa.gov/beacon/beacon_national_page.main). For the 2006 swimming season, the EPA (June 5, 2007, http://www.epa .gov/waterscience/beaches/seasons/2006/national.html) indicates that data were collected on 3,771 beaches. The EPA reports that 1,201 of these beaches (32% of the total) were

FIGURE 9.5

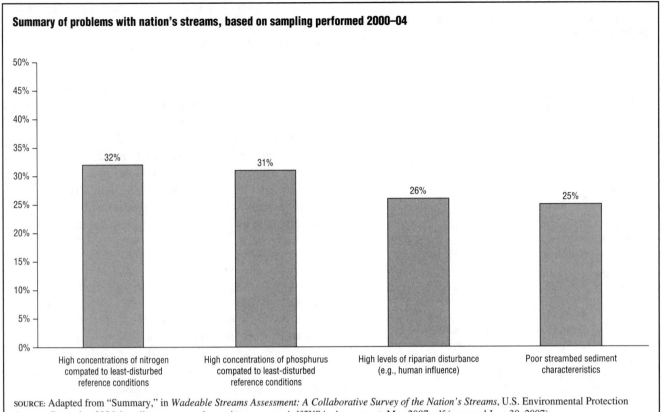

Summary of problems with nation's streams, based on sampling performed 2000–04

SOURCE: Adapted from "Summary," in *Wadeable Streams Assessment: A Collaborative Survey of the Nation's Streams*, U.S. Environmental Protection Agency, December 2006, http://www.epa.gov/owow/streamsurvey/pdf/WSA_Assessment_May 2007.pdf (accessed June 30, 2007)

FIGURE 9.6

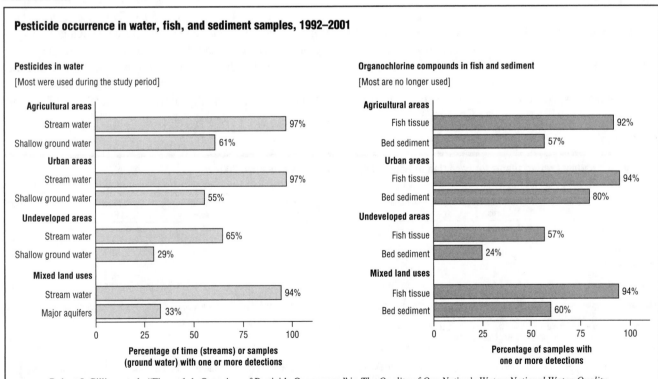

Pesticide occurrence in water, fish, and sediment samples, 1992–2001

SOURCE: Robert J. Gilliom et al., "Figure 1-1. Overview of Pesticide Occurrence," in *The Quality of Our Nation's Waters National Water-Quality Assessment Program Pesticides in the Nation's Streams and Ground Water, 1992–2001*, U.S. Geological Survey, February 15, 2007, http://pubs.usgs.gov/circ/2005/1291/pdf/circ1291.pdf (accessed June 30, 2007)

FIGURE 9.7

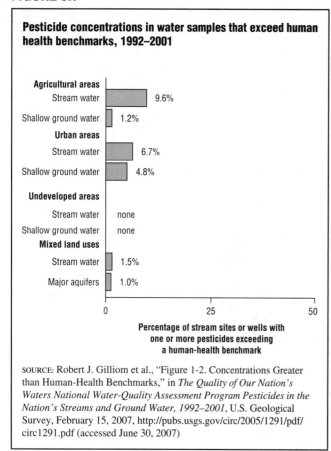

Pesticide concentrations in water samples that exceed human health benchmarks, 1992–2001

SOURCE: Robert J. Gilliom et al., "Figure 1-2. Concentrations Greater than Human-Health Benchmarks," in *The Quality of Our Nation's Waters National Water-Quality Assessment Program Pesticides in the Nation's Streams and Ground Water, 1992–2001*, U.S. Geological Survey, February 15, 2007, http://pubs.usgs.gov/circ/2005/1291/pdf/circ1291.pdf (accessed June 30, 2007)

closed or issued warnings to swimmers because of high bacteria levels.

FOCUS ON WATER POLLUTION SOURCES. The main reason that a body of water cannot support its designated uses is that it has become polluted. There are a vast number of pollutants that can make water "impaired," but to control a specific pollutant, it is necessary to find out where it is coming from. Even though there are many ways in which contaminants can enter waterways, sources of pollution are generally categorized as point sources and nonpoint sources.

Point sources are those that disperse pollutants from a specific source or area, such as a sewage drain or an industrial discharge pipe. (See Figure 9.8.) Pollutants commonly discharged from point sources include bacteria (from wastewater treatment plants and sewer overflow), toxic chemicals, and heavy metals from industrial plants. Point sources are regulated under the National Pollutant Discharge Elimination System (NPDES). Any facility using point sources to discharge to receiving waters must obtain an NPDES permit for them.

Nonpoint sources are those that are spread out over a large area and have no specific outlet or discharge point. These include agricultural and urban runoff, runoff from mining and construction sites, and accidental or deliberate spills. Agricultural runoff is primarily associated with nutrients from fertilizers, pathogens from animal waste operations, and pesticides. Urban runoff can contain a variety of contaminants, including pesticides, fertilizers, chemicals and metals, oil and grease, sediment, salts, and atmospheric deposits. Nonpoint sources are much more difficult to regulate than point sources and may require a new approach to water protection.

The Future of Water Management

In June 2001 the EPA issued *Protecting and Restoring America's Watersheds: Status, Trends, and Initiatives in Watershed Management* (http://www.epa.gov/owow/protecting/restore725.pdf). A watershed is defined as a "land area that drains to a body of water such as a stream, lake, wetland, or estuary." In other words, a watershed is determined geologically and hydrologically, rather than

TABLE 9.3

Regional and national rating scores for condition of National Estuary Program estuaries, 2007

Index	Northeast coast	Southeast coast	Gulf coast[a]	West coast	Puerto Rico[b]	United States[c]
Water quality index	3	5	3	3	3	3.6
Sediment quality index	1	4	2	1	1	2.1
Benthic index	1	3	2	5	1	2.7
Fish tissue contaminants index	1	4	4	1	1	2.6
Overall condition	**1.5**	**4.0**	**2.75**	**2.5**	**1.5**	**2.7**

Note: Rating scores are based on a 5-point system, where a score of less than 2.0 is rated poor; 2.0 to less than 2.3 is rated fair to poor; 2.3 to 3.7 is rated fair; greater than 3.7 to 4.0 is rated good to fair; and greater than 4.0 is rated good.
[a]This rating score does not include the impact of the hypoxic zone in offshore Gulf Coast waters.
[b]This rating score includes only San Juan Bay Estuary, Puerto Rico.
[c]The U.S.score is based on an a really weighted mean of the regional index scores.

SOURCE: "Table ES-2. Regional and National Rating Scores for Indices of Estuarine Condition and Overall Condition for the Nation's National Estuary Program estuaries," in *National Estuary Program Coastal Condition Report*, U.S. Environmental Protection Agency, June 2007, http://www.epa.gov/owow/oceans/nepccr/pdf/nepccr_exec_summ.pdf (accessed June 30, 2007)

FIGURE 9.8

Examples of point and nonpoint sources of pollution

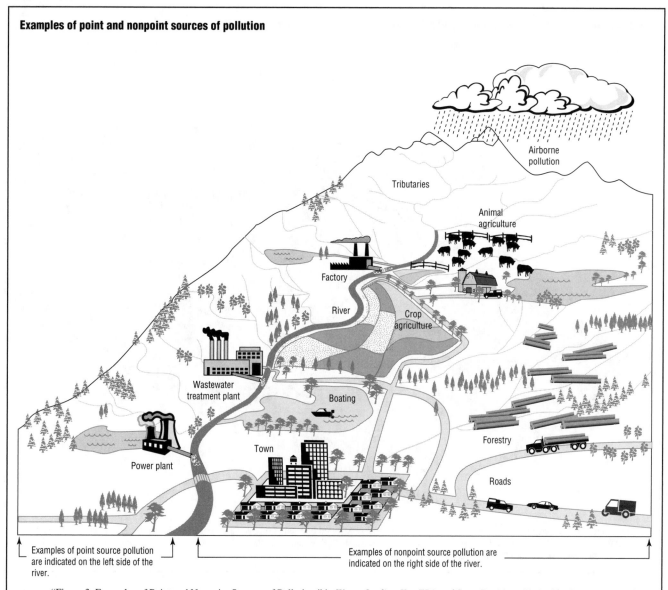

Examples of point source pollution are indicated on the left side of the river.

Examples of nonpoint source pollution are indicated on the right side of the river.

SOURCE: "Figure 3. Examples of Point and Nonpoint Sources of Pollution," in *Water Quality: Key EPA and State Decisions Limited by Inconsistent and Incomplete Data*, U.S. General Accounting Office, March 2000, http://www.gao.gov/archive/2000/rc00054.pdf (accessed July 27, 2007)

politically. Figure 9.9 shows a watershed example and the many issues and processes that affect it.

Watersheds are delineated by the USGS and identified with unique eight-digit numbers. There are more than two thousand individual watersheds around the country that are recognized by the USGS and the EPA.

The EPA believes that the nation's water quality problems cannot be solved by further regulating point-source discharges. Instead, the agency advocates a comprehensive approach that crosses jurisdictional boundaries and addresses all the air, water, land, social, and economic issues that affect a particular watershed. The watershed approach would balance competing needs for drinking water, recreation, navigation and flood control, agriculture and forestry, aquatic ecosystems, hydropower, and other uses. Currently,

these uses are managed by a variety of agencies at the federal, state, and local levels. The EPA actively encourages the participation of private environmental and conservation groups in the watershed approach.

The EPA operates the program Adopt Your Watershed (http://www.epa.gov/adopt/). This program provides a database that provides information about each of the nation's watersheds. The database identifies thousands of local and regional groups that engage in activities to further watershed protection and improvement.

OCEAN PROTECTION

Throughout history humans have used the oceans virtually as they pleased. Ocean waters have long served as highways and harvest grounds. Now, however, humankind

FIGURE 9.9

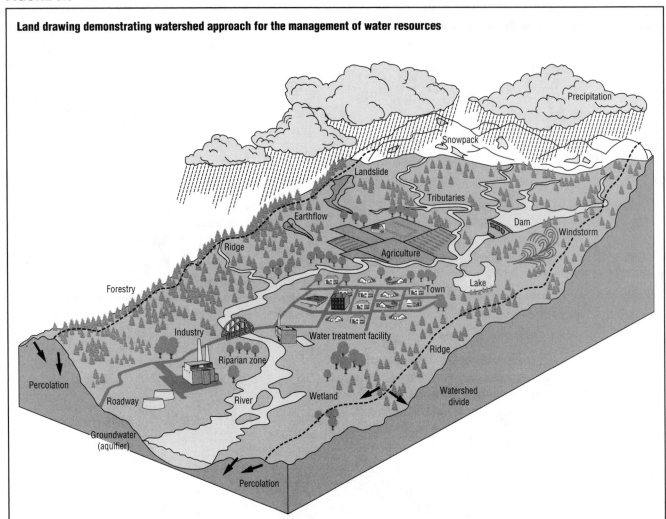

Land drawing demonstrating watershed approach for the management of water resources

SOURCE: "Figure 1. The Area Hydrologically Defined by a Watershed Is Affected by Many Processes and Issues. A 'Watershed Approach' Coordinates Their Management," in *Protecting and Restoring America's Watersheds*, U.S. Environmental Protection Agency, Office of Water, June 2001, http://www.epa.gov/owow/protecting/restore725.pdf (accessed July 27, 2007)

is at a threshold. Marine debris (garbage created by humans) is a problem of global proportions and is extremely evident in countries such as the United States, where there is extensive recreational and commercial use of coastal waterways.

International Convention for the Prevention of Pollution from Ships

Established in 1973, the International Convention for the Prevention of Pollution from Ships regulates many materials that are dumped at sea. The international treaty has been in effect in the United States only since its ratification in 1998. Even though eighty-three countries have ratified the treaty, they have not necessarily complied, as evidenced by the current level of marine debris.

Ocean Dumping Act

Congress enacted the Marine Protection, Research, and Sanctuaries Act in 1972 to regulate intentional ocean disposal of materials and to authorize research. Title 1 of the act, known as the Ocean Dumping Act, contains permit and enforcement provisions for ocean dumping. Four federal agencies have authority under the act: the EPA, the U.S. Army Corps of Engineers, the National Oceanic and Atmospheric Administration, and the U.S. Coast Guard. Title 1 prohibits all ocean dumping, except that allowed by permits, in any ocean waters under U.S. jurisdiction by any U.S. vessel or by any vessel sailing from a U.S. port. The act bans dumping of radiological, chemical, and biological warfare agents, high-level radioactive waste, and medical wastes. In 1997 Congress amended the act to ban dumping of municipal sewage sludge and industrial waste.

Oil Pollution Act

In 1989 the oil freighter *Exxon Valdez* ran into a reef in Prince William Sound, Alaska, spilling more than eleven million gallons of oil into one of the richest and most ecologically pristine areas in North America. An oil slick the size of Rhode Island killed wildlife and marine species. A $5 billion damage penalty was levied against Exxon, whose ship captain was found to be at fault in the wreck.

In response to the *Valdez* oil spill, Congress passed the Oil Pollution Act of 1990, which went into effect in 1993. The law requires companies involved in storing and transporting petroleum to have standby plans for cleaning up oil spills on land or in water. Under the act a company that does not adequately take care of a spill is vulnerable to almost unlimited litigation and expense. The law makes the Coast Guard responsible for approving clean-up plans and procedures for coastal and seaport oil spills, whereas the EPA oversees clean-ups on land and in inland waterways. The law also requires that oil tankers be built with double hulls to better secure the oil in the event of a hull breach.

DRINKING WATER
Drinking Water Legislation

Almost any legislation concerning water affects drinking water, either directly or indirectly. The following pieces of legislation are aimed specifically at providing safe drinking water for the nation's residents.

SAFE DRINKING WATER ACT OF 1974. The Safe Drinking Water Act (SDWA) of 1974 mandated that the EPA establish and enforce minimum national drinking water standards for all public water systems—community and noncommunity—in the United States. The law also required the EPA to develop guidelines for water treatment and to set testing, monitoring, and reporting requirements.

To address pollution of surface water supplies to public systems, the EPA established a permit system requiring any facility that discharges contaminants directly into surface waters (lakes and rivers) to apply for a permit to discharge a set amount of materials—and that amount only. It also created groundwater regulations to govern underground injection of wastes.

Congress intended that, after the EPA had set regulatory standards, each state or U.S. territory would run its own drinking water program. The EPA established the Primary Drinking Water Standards by setting maximum contaminant levels (MCLs) for contaminants known to be detrimental to human health. All public water systems in the United States are required to meet primary standards. Secondary standards cover nonhealth-threatening aspects of drinking water, such as odor, taste, staining properties, and color. Secondary standards are recommended but not required.

1986 AMENDMENTS TO THE SDWA. The 1986 amendments to the SDWA required that the EPA set maximum containment levels for an additional fifty-three contaminants by June 1989, twenty-five more by 1991, and twenty-five every three years thereafter. The amendments also required the EPA to issue a maximum contaminant level goal (MCLG) along with each MCL. An MCLG is a health goal equal to the maximum level of a pollutant not expected to cause any health problems over a lifetime of exposure. The EPA is mandated by law to set MCLs as close to MCLGs as technology and economics will permit.

The 1986 amendments banned the use of lead pipe and lead solder in new public drinking water systems and in the repair of existing systems. In addition, the EPA had to specify criteria for the filtration of surface water supplies and to set standards for the disinfection of all surface and groundwater supplies. The EPA was required to take enforcement action, including filing civil suits against violators of drinking water standards, even in states granted primacy if those states did not adequately enforce regulations. Violators became subject to fines up to $25,000 daily until violations were corrected.

WATER QUALITY CONTROL ACT OF 1987. Section 304 (1) of the revised Clean Water Act of 1987 determines the state of the nation's water quality and reviews the effectiveness of the EPA's regulatory programs designed to protect and improve that water quality. Section 308—known as the Water Quality Control Act—requires that the administrator of the EPA report annually to Congress on the effectiveness of the water quality improvement program.

The main purpose of the Water Quality Control Act is to identify water sources that need to be brought up to minimum standards and to establish more stringent controls where needed. States are now required to develop lists of contaminated waters as well as lists of the sources and amounts of pollutants causing toxic problems. In addition, each state is required to develop "individual control strategies" for dealing with these pollutants.

LEAD CONTAMINATION CONTROL ACT OF 1988. The Lead Contamination Control Act of 1988 strengthened the controls on lead contamination set out in the 1986 amendments to the SDWA. It requires the EPA to provide guidance to states and localities in testing for and remedying lead contamination in drinking water in schools and day care centers. The act also contains requirements for the testing, recall, repair, and/or replacement of water coolers that have lead-lined storage tanks or parts containing lead. It attaches civil and criminal penalties to the manufacture and sale of water coolers containing lead.

The ban on lead states that plumbing must be lead-free. In addition, each public water system must identify and notify anyone whose drinking water may be contaminated with lead, and the states must enforce the lead ban through plumbing codes and the public-notice requirement. The federal government gave the EPA the power to enforce the lead ban law by authorizing the agency to withhold up to 5% of federal grant funds to any state that does not comply with the new rulings.

REINVENTING DRINKING WATER LAW—1996 AMENDMENTS TO THE SDWA. In 1996 Congress passed a number of significant amendments to the SDWA. The law changed the relationship between the federal government and the states in administering drinking water programs, giving states greater flexibility and more responsibility.

The centerpiece of the law is the State Revolving Fund (SRF), a mechanism for providing low-cost financial aid to local water systems to build the treatment plants necessary to meet state and federal drinking water standards. The law also requires states to train and certify operators of drinking water systems. If they do not, states risk losing up to 20% of their federal grants. The law requires states to approve the operation of any new water supply system, making sure it complies with the technical, managerial, and financial requirements. The 1996 SDWA gives the EPA discretion in regulating only those contaminants that may be harmful to health, and it requires the EPA to select at least five contaminants every five years for consideration for new standards. A further change is that the EPA, when proposing a regulation, must now determine—and publish—whether or not the benefits of a new standard justify the costs.

Furthermore, the law affirms Americans' right to know the quality of their drinking water and mandates notification. Water suppliers must promptly (within twenty-four hours) alert consumers if water becomes contaminated by something that can cause illness and must advise as to what precautions can be taken. In 1998 states began to compile information about individual systems, which the EPA now summarizes in an annual compliance report. As of October 1999 water systems have been required to make that data available to the public. Large suppliers have to mail their annual safety reports to customers, whereas smaller systems can post the reports in a central location or publish them in local newspapers.

Sources of Drinking Water—Public and Private Supply

According to the EPA, there were 156,675 public water supply systems in operation in fiscal year 2006, serving 301.7 million people. (See Table 9.4.) These included systems that served homes, businesses, schools, hospitals, and recreational parks. Those who did not get their water from a public system were for the most part in rural areas and got their water from private wells. Even though most systems obtain their water from groundwater, most people receive drinking water from surface water sources. This is because a relatively small number of public systems using surface water sources serve large metropolitan areas.

TABLE 9.4

Public drinking water sources and violations, 2006

Community water system[a]	No. of systems	52,349
	Population served	281,705,494
Non-transient non-community water system[b]	No. of systems	19,048
	Population served	6,010,721
Transient non-community water system[c]	No. of systems	85,278
	Population Served	13,982,371
Total no. of systems		**156,675**
Total population served		**301,698,586**
Total violations		**194,428**
No. of systems reporting violations		**50,102**
Population served by systems reporting violations		**89,375,580**

[a]Community water system: A public water system that supplies water to the same population year round.
[b]Non-transient non-community water system: A public water system regularly supplies water to at least 25 of the same people at least six months per year, but not year-round. Some examples are schools, factories, office buildings, and hospitals which have their own water systems.
[c]Transient non-community water system: A public water system that provides water in a place such as a gas station or campground where people do not remain for long periods of time.

SOURCE: Adapted from "EPA's Drinking Water Data," in *Summary Inventory, Violations, and GPRA MS Excel PivotTables*, U.S. Environmental Protection Agency, May 29, 2007, http://www.epa.gov/safewater/data/zips/annualtrends.zip (accessed June 30, 2007)

The EPA and state health or environmental departments regulate public water supplies. Public supplies are required to ensure that the water meets certain government-defined health standards. The SDWA governs this regulation. The law mandates that all public suppliers test their water regularly to check for the existence of contaminants and treat their water supplies constantly to take out or reduce certain pollutants to levels that will not harm human health.

Private water supplies, usually wells, are not regulated under the SDWA. System owners are solely responsible for the quality of the water provided from private sources. However, many states have programs designed to help well owners protect their water supplies. Usually, these state-run programs are not regulatory but provide safety information. This type of information is vital because private wells are often shallower than those used by public suppliers. The shallower the well the greater the potential for contamination.

How Clean Is Our Drinking Water?

Safe drinking water is a cornerstone of public health. In accordance with the 1996 SDWA amendments, public water systems are mandated to submit compliance reports to the EPA (March 29, 2007, http://www.epa.gov/safewater/data/pivottables.html) regarding the quality of their drinking water. The EPA indicates that 89% of the nation's community water systems achieved health-related water quality levels or treatment standards in fiscal year 2006.

FIGURE 9.10

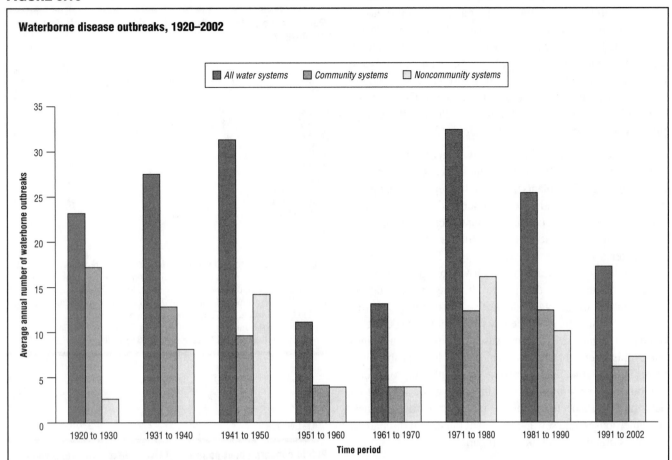

Waterborne disease outbreaks, 1920–2002

SOURCE: Michael F. Craun, Gunther F. Craun, Rebecca L. Calderon and Michael J. Beach, "Figure 1. Reported Waterborne Outbreaks, 1920 to 2002," in *Waterborne Outbreaks Reported in the United States*, U.S. Environmental Protection Agency, July/August 2006, http://www.epa.gov/nheerl/articles/2006/waterborne_disease/waterborne_outbreaks.pdf (accessed July 2, 2007)

According to the EPA, in "Public Drinking Water Systems: Facts and Figures" (February 28, 2006, http://www.epa.gov/safewater/pws/factoids.html), community water systems are defined as those that provide drinking water on a year-round basis. Two other classifications are non-transient noncommunity water systems—public water systems that regularly supply water to at least twenty-five of the same people at least six months per year, but not year-round (e.g., schools and hospitals with their own water systems)—and transient noncommunity water systems—public water systems that provide water to places where people remain for only short periods of time (e.g., campgrounds). The number of water systems and the population served during fiscal year 2006 are shown in Table 9.4.

Incidence of Disease Caused by Tainted Water—CDC Surveillance Report

It is difficult to know how many illnesses are caused by contaminated water. People may not know the source of many illnesses and may attribute them to food (which may also have been in contact with polluted water), chronic illness, or other infectious agents. Since 1971 the

Centers for Disease Control and Prevention (CDC) and the EPA have collected and reported data that relate to waterborne-disease outbreaks. These historical data are presented and analyzed by Michael F. Craun et al. in "Waterborne Outbreaks Reported in the United States" (*Journal of Water and Health*, vol. 4, supp. 2, 2006). Craun and his associates define an outbreak as an incident in which at least two people develop a similar illness that evidence indicates was probably caused by ingestion of drinking water or exposure to water in recreational or occupational settings.

Figure 9.10 shows the average annual number of waterborne outbreaks by decade from 1920 through 2002. According to Craun and his coauthors, there were 207 outbreaks (averaging 17 per year) that caused 433,947 illnesses between 1991 and 2002.

Milwaukee—"The Nation's Worst Drinking Water Disaster"

In April 1993 more than four hundred thousand residents of Milwaukee, Wisconsin, became victims of what is considered the worst drinking water disaster the nation has experienced. Microscopic parasites called *Cryptosporidium* flourished in the city water supply, causing an outbreak of cryptosporidiosis, a diarrheal disease. At least forty deaths resulted. City and state public health officials conducted an extensive review of the outbreak's effects and causes, and their results were published by William R. Mac Kenzie et al. in "A Massive Outbreak in Milwaukee of *Cryptosporidium* Infection Transmitted through the Public Water Supply" (*New England Journal of Medicine*, July 21, 1994).

According to the article, the city was served by two water treatment plants in 1993, both of which accessed water from Lake Michigan. Both plants used a multi-step treatment process including chlorination, other chemical treatments, and filtration. *Cryptosporidium* are resistant to chlorine and other typical chemical treatments, because the parasites have a very hard outer shell. They also require very fine filtration for removal. Thus, they were able to move unimpeded through the system and into the public drinking water supply. Although one of the plants did notice unusually high levels of turbidity (cloudiness) in the raw water before the outbreak, biological organisms were not suspected as the cause until later. This oversight and mechanical problems at the plant were later blamed for allowing the outbreak to occur. Although the original source of the parasites could not be determined, suspected sources included cattle ranches, slaughterhouses, and sewage treatment plants that discharged to waters draining into Lake Michigan.

PUBLIC OPINION ABOUT WATER ISSUES

Each year the Gallup Organization conducts an annual poll on environmental topics. The last poll was *Environment* poll (2007, http://www.galluppoll.com/content/?ci=1615 &pg =1). As described in Chapter 1, the pollsters found that water issues dominate the list of Americans' environmental concerns. The percentage of people expressing a great deal of worry about a particular environmental problem was highest for pollution of drinking water (58%), followed by pollution of rivers, lakes, and reservoirs (53%). Maintenance of the nation's freshwater supply for household needs ranked fourth (51%). Concern over polluted drinking water has diminished since peaking in 2000. (See Table 9.5.) As shown in Table 9.6, concern about polluted surface waters has decreased dramatically since the question was first asked in 1989. By contrast, concern about the nation's freshwater supply for household needs was slightly elevated in 2007 when compared with historical levels. (See Table 9.7.)

TABLE 9.5

Public concern about pollution of drinking water, selected years 1990–2007

	Great deal	Fair amount	Only a little	Not at all	No opinion
	%	%	%	%	%
2007 Mar 11–14	58	24	12	5	*
2006 Mar 13–16	54	27	12	7	*
2004 Mar 8–11	53	24	17	6	*
2003 Mar 3–5	54	25	15	6	—
2002 Mar 4–7	57	25	13	5	*
2001 Mar 5–7	64	24	9	3	*
2000 Apr 3–9	72	20	6	2	*
1999 Apr 13–14	68	22	7	3	*
1991 Apr 11–4	67	19	10	3	1
1990 Apr 5–8	65	22	9	4	*

*Less than 0.5%.
— No answers.

SOURCE: "I'm going to read you a list of environmental problems. As I read each one, please tell me if you personally worry about this problem a great deal, a fair amount, only a little, or not at all. First, how much do you personally worry about—Pollution of drinking water?" in *Environment*, The Gallup Organization, 2007, http://www.galluppoll.com/content/?ci=1615 &pg =1 (accessed June 19, 2007). Copyright © 2007 by The Gallup Organization. Reproduced by permission of The Gallup Organization.

TABLE 9.6

Public concern about pollution of rivers, lakes, and reservoirs, selected years 1989–2007

	Great deal	Fair amount	Only a little	Not at all	No opinion
	%	%	%	%	%
2007 Mar 11–14	53	31	13	3	—
2006 Mar 13–16	51	33	11	5	*
2004 Mar 8–11	48	31	16	5	*
2003 Mar 3–5	51	31	13	5	—
2002 Mar 4–7	53	32	12	3	*
2001 Mar 5–7	58	29	10	3	*
2000 Apr 3–9	66	24	8	2	*
1999 Apr 13–14	61	30	7	2	*
1999 Mar 12–14	55	30	12	3	*
1991 Apr 11–14	67	21	8	3	1
1990 Apr 5–8	64	23	9	4	—
1989 May 4–7	72	19	5	3	1

*Less than 0.5%.

SOURCE: "I'm going to read you a list of environmental problems. As I read each one, please tell me if you personally worry about this problem a great deal, a fair amount, only a little, or not at all. First, how much do you personally worry about—Pollution of rivers, lakes, and reservoirs," in *Environment*, The Gallup Organization, 2007, http://www.galluppoll.com/content/?ci=1615&pg=1 (accessed June 19, 2007). Copyright © 2007 by The Gallup Organization. Reproduced by permission of The Gallup Organization.

TABLE 9.7

Public concern about the nation's supply of fresh water, selected years 2000–07

	Great deal	Fair amount	Only a little	Not at all	No opinion
	%	%	%	%	%
2007 Mar 11–14	51	27	16	5	*
2006 Mar 13–16	49	27	14	9	1
2004 Mar 8–11	47	25	20	8	*
2003 Mar 3–5	49	28	15	8	*
2002 Mar 4–7	50	28	17	5	*
2001 Mar 5–7	35	34	19	10	2
2000 Apr 3–9	42	31	14	12	1

*Less than 0.5%.

SOURCE: "I'm going to read you a list of environmental problems. As I read each one, please tell me if you personally worry about this problem a great deal, a fair amount, only a little, or not at all. First, how much do you personally worry about—Maintenance of the nation's supply of fresh water for household needs?" in *Environment*, The Gallup Organization, 2007, http://www.galluppoll.com/content/?ci=1615&pg=1 (accessed June 19, 2007). Copyright © 2007 by The Gallup Organization. Reproduced by permission of The Gallup Organization.

CHAPTER 10
TOXINS IN EVERYDAY LIFE

The Swiss chemist Paracelsus (1493–1541) once stated that "it is the dose that makes the poison." Many of the substances naturally found in the environment or released by modern, industrialized society are poisonous at certain dosages. These substances may be found in the home, workplace, or backyard, in the food and water people eat and drink, and in medications and consumer products.

WHY ARE TOXINS TOXIC?

A toxin is a substance—bacterial, viral, chemical, metal, fibrous, or radioactive—that poisons or harms a living organism. A toxin may cause immediate, short-term symptoms such as gastroenteritis, or cause harm after long-term exposure such as living in a lead- or radon-contaminated home for many years. Some toxins can have both immediate and long-term effects: living in an environment with poor air quality may trigger an acute asthma attack, or, after many years of exposure, it may contribute to lung cancer. Even though the effects of a toxin may not show up for years, these effects may, nevertheless, be serious.

Toxins are often grouped according to their most harmful effect on living creatures. These categories include carcinogens, mutagens, and teratogens:

- A carcinogen is any substance that causes cancerous growth.

- A mutagen is an agent capable of producing genetic change.

- A teratogen is a substance that produces malformations or defective development.

The risks posed by environmental contamination may not be blatantly obvious. For example, people or animals that are exposed to contaminants may suffer damage to their immune systems and have difficulty recovering from infectious diseases. Tracing the problem to environmental pollutants, however, can be difficult.

GOVERNMENT LEGISLATION

Toxins that can be encountered in everyday life are regulated under a variety of federal and state legislation. The following are the major pieces of federal legislation.

The Pure Food and Drug Act was originally passed in 1906 and substantially strengthened in 1938 by passage of its replacement, the Federal Food, Drug, and Cosmetic Act. This act was amended during the 1950s and 1960s to tighten restrictions on pesticides, food additives, and drugs. Responsibility for enforcement of the act lies with the U.S. Food and Drug Administration (FDA) under the U.S. Department of Health and Human Services. The FDA oversees food supplies, human and veterinary drugs, biological products (such as vaccines and blood supplies), medical devices, cosmetics, and electronic products that emit radiation.

In 1947 Congress passed the Federal Insecticide, Fungicide, and Rodenticide Act (FIFRA). Even though it was originally enforced by the U.S. Department of Agriculture (USDA), authority passed to the U.S. Environmental Protection Agency (EPA) after its creation in 1970. FIFRA was strengthened and expanded by major amendments over the next few decades, particularly in 1996. The act provides the EPA with primary control over pesticide distribution, sale, and use. The states also have authority to regulate pesticides and can do so at more restrictive levels than used by the EPA. The EPA studies the environmental and health effects of pesticide usage and requires some users to register when purchasing pesticides. All pesticides used in the United States must be registered with the EPA and the state and be properly labeled before distribution.

The Federal Hazardous Substances Labeling Act was passed in 1960. The U.S. Consumer Product Safety Commission administers the law as it applies to household products. The commission has jurisdiction over approximately fifteen thousand consumer products that pose a fire, electrical, chemical, or mechanical hazard. House-hold products (such as cleaners) that contain hazardous chemicals must warn consumers about their potential hazards.

The Toxic Substances Control Act (TSCA) was enacted by Congress in 1976. It gives the EPA authority to track the thousands of industrial chemicals produced or imported into the United States. The EPA screens the chemicals and can require that industries test chemicals that may pose a hazard to the environment or human health. The EPA can ban chemicals it deems too risky. In "What Is the TSCA Chemical Substance Inventory?" (September 18, 2006, http://www.epa.gov/opptintr/newchems/pubs/invntory.htm), the EPA states that approximately seventy-five thousand chemicals are tracked and controlled by the EPA under the TSCA. Primary responsibility for administering the TSCA lies with the EPA's Office of Prevention, Pesticides, and Toxic Substances.

In 1984 a deadly cloud of chemicals was released from the Union Carbide pesticide plant in Bhopal, India, following an explosion in the plant. The methyl isocyanate gas killed approximately three thousand people and injured two hundred thousand others. Shortly after, a similar chemical release occurred in West Virginia, where a cloud of gas sent 135 people to the hospital with eye, throat, and lung irritation complaints. There were no fatalities. Such incidents fueled the demand by workers and the general public for information about hazardous materials in their areas. As a result, Congress passed the Emergency Planning and Community Right-to-Know Act of 1986.

The act established, among other things, the Toxics Release Inventory (TRI; September 5, 2007, http://www.epa.gov/tri), a public database that contains information on toxic chemical releases by various facilities. More than 650 toxic chemicals are on the TRI list.

RISK MANAGEMENT

In general, the risks associated with toxin exposures are assessed by scientists using the following five-step approach:

1. Identify the hazard—Gather and evaluate data on the hazards to human health of exposure to specific substances. This step typically involves research into the ways in which substances affect living tissues and cells, for example, using laboratory animals.

2. Determine the dose response—Calculate a numerical relationship between the amount of exposure (the dose) and the extent of harm. There may be many different dose responses for a single substance, depending on how the exposure occurs. The duration and pathway of exposure are key variables. Pathways include inhalation into the lungs, dermal (skin) contact, and ingestion (swallowing).

3. Assess the exposure—Ascertain information about the population that has been or will likely be exposed to particular substances.

4. Characterize the risk—Use data from the first three steps to determine the likelihood that harm is going to occur to a population from a particular exposure to a particular substance.

5. Manage the risk—Impose regulatory or other control measures to minimize the known risks associated with particular exposures to toxic substances by vulnerable populations.

The science of risk management is quite complex. Table 10.1 presents some of the common terms and

TABLE 10.1

Exposure and risk management terms

Acronym (If any)	Term	Definition
	Acute exposure	Exposure by the oral, dermal, or inhalation route for 24 hours or less.
	Short-term exposure	Repeated exposure by the oral, dermal, or inhalation route for more than 24 hours, up to 30 days.
	Subchronic exposure	Repeated exposure by the oral, dermal, or inhalation route for more than 30 days, up to approximately 10% of the life span in humans
	Chronic exposure	Repeated exposure by the oral, dermal, or inhalation route for more than approximately 10% of the life span in humans
NOAEL	No-observed-adverse-effect level	The highest exposure level at which there are no biologically significant increases in the frequency or severity of adverse effect between the exposed population and its appropriate control; some effects may be produced at this level, but they are not considered adverse or precursors of adverse effects.
NOEL	No-observed-effect level	An exposure level at which there are no statistically or biologically significant increases in the frequency or severity of any effect between the exposed population and its appropriate control.
RfC	Reference concentration	An estimate (with uncertainty spanning perhaps an order of magnitude) of a continuous inhalation exposure to the human population (including sensitive subgroups) that is likely to be without an appreciable risk of deleterious effects during a lifetime.
RfD	Reference dose	An estimate (with uncertainty spanning perhaps an order of magnitude) of a daily oral exposure to the human population (including sensitive subgroups) that is likely to be without an appreciable risk of deleterious effects during a lifetime.

SOURCE: Adapted from "Glossary of Integrated Risk Information System Terms," in *Glossary of IRIS Terms*, U.S. Environmental Protection Agency, April 5, 2007, http://www.epa.gov/iris/gloss8.htm#1 (accessed July 2, 2007)

acronyms used by the EPA to characterize exposure and risk data.

Sources of Public Data

The prevalence and biological effects of some chemical toxins have been studied extensively. However, experts acknowledge that there are many toxins for which little data are available. In general, data on the generation, usage, and levels of chemicals in the environment (air, water, soil, etc.) are much more plentiful than data on the known effects of chemicals to human health. This raises difficulties for regulatory agencies that wish to set health-based limits on particular toxins. It also makes it harder for the public to determine whether a particular exposure is harmful or not.

TOXICS RELEASE INVENTORY. In the *2005 Toxics Release Inventory (TRI) Public Data Release Report* (March 2007, http://www.epa.gov/tri/tridata/tri05/pdfs/2005broch ure.pdf), the EPA states that 4.3 billion pounds of TRI chemicals were released during 2005 by 23,461 facilities. Figure 8.4 in Chapter 8 shows the distribution of releases to the environment, and Figure 8.5, also in Chapter 8, shows the breakdown by industry. The primary releasers were the metal mining industry, electric utilities, and chemicals production. These three industries accounted for nearly two-thirds of the releases.

AMERICAN ASSOCIATION OF POISON CONTROL CENTERS. Since 1983 the American Association of Poison Control Centers (AAPCC) has maintained a database called the Toxic Exposure Surveillance System (TESS) that presents information from dozens of poison control centers around the country. These centers receive their funding from a variety of federal and state agencies and private sources (primarily hospitals and universities). TESS data are reported annually. The most recent data are from 2005 and were published in *Clinical Toxicology* (vol. 44, nos. 6–7, 2006).

According to the AAPCC, there were 2.4 million human exposures to toxic substances reported to poison control centers in 2005. Approximately 84% of these exposures (two million) were unintentional. One hundred seventy-two of the unintentional exposures resulted in fatalities. Sixteen were children less than six years old, though approximately half of all exposures reported during 2005 occurred in children less than six years old. The substances most frequently involved in all unintentional exposures were analgesics, cosmetics, personal care products, and household cleaning substances. Among children younger than six years of age, cosmetics and personal care products were the substances involved in most exposures.

THE NATIONAL REPORT ON HUMAN EXPOSURE TO ENVIRONMENTAL CHEMICALS. The Centers for Disease Control and Prevention (CDC) releases a report every two years that assesses the exposure of the U.S. population to environmental chemicals based on biomonitoring results. Biomonitoring involves collecting and analyzing bodily samples, such as blood, urine, breast milk, or hair, to measure the concentrations of particular chemical substances. This is also known as determining the "body burden" of chemicals.

The CDC defines environmental chemicals as chemicals present in air, water, food, soil, dust, or other environmental media (including consumer products). The report includes data on the blood and urine levels of various chemical substances. The *First National Report on Human Exposure to Environmental Chemicals* was published in 2001 and covers twenty-seven chemicals. The *Second National Report on Human Exposure to Environmental Chemicals*, released in 2003, provides data for 116 chemicals. The *Third National Report on Human Exposure to Environmental Chemicals* (http://www.cdc.gov/exposure report/pdf/thirdreport.pdf) was published in 2005 and includes biomonitoring data for 155 chemicals in the following categories:

- Metals (such as lead and mercury)

- Pesticides, insecticides, and herbicides

- Phthalates (a class of chemicals used in many consumer products, including adhesives, detergents, oils, solvents, soaps, shampoos, and plastics)

- Phytoestrogens (naturally occurring plant-based chemicals with hormonal effects)

- Polycyclic aromatic hydrocarbons (chemicals resulting from incomplete combustion of fossil fuels)

- Polychlorinated compounds (chlorine-containing organic chemicals used in a wide variety of industrial and commercial products)

- Cotinine (a component of tobacco smoke)

In 2006 and 2007 CDC researchers published supplemental articles providing biomonitoring results for two additional chemicals believed to be widely present in the environment: perchlorate (a chemical found in rocket fuel, explosives, and fireworks) and perfluorinated compounds (a class of compounds used in many consumer products, but most notable for imparting stain resistance to carpets and fabrics and nonstick properties to cookware).

The CDC notes that its reports do not assess the potential harmfulness of the chemicals examined. The reports provide scientists with biomonitoring data so that research priorities can be set to determine human health effects for particular exposure levels.

PRIVATE BIOMONITORING STUDIES. Biomonitoring has become a popular tool for environmental advocates to publicize their concerns about the widespread nature of toxins. In 2001 the journalist Bill Moyers had his chemical body burden measured by researchers at the Mount Sinai School of Medicine in New York. Blood and urine samples were tested for dozens of chemicals in the following categories: dioxins and furans, polychlorinated biphenyls (PCBs), phthalates, organochlorine pesticides (such as dichloro-diphenyl-trichloroethane [DDT]), organophosphate pesticides, and volatile and semivolatile organic compounds. The results indicated the presence of eighty-four of these chemicals, including DDT, dioxins, and xylene. Moyers's body burden results are presented in *Trade Secrets* (2001, http://www.pbs.org/tradesecrets/index.html), a documentary on the chemical industry.

In 2005 the Commonweal Biomonitoring Resource Center collected biosamples from eleven Californians and had the samples tested for more than twenty-five chemicals, including phthalates, perfluorochemicals, polybrominated diphenyl ethers (commonly used in flame retardants), mercury, and pesticides. At least six of the chemicals were detected in every participant. The results were published in *Taking It All In: Documenting Chemical Pollution in Californians through Biomonitoring* (2005, http://www.commonweal.org/programs/download/TIAI_1205.pdf).

In *Pollution in People: A Study of Toxic Chemicals in Washingtonians* (2006, http://www.pollutioninpeople.org/results/report), the Toxic-Free Legacy Coalition presents biomonitoring results obtained from blood, urine, and hair samples provided by ten people in Washington State. The samples were tested for phthalates, flame-retardants, heavy metals, perfluorinated chemicals, and pesticides. The study detected at least two dozen of the chemicals in every person tested.

INTEGRATED RISK INFORMATION SYSTEM. The most sophisticated source of publicly available data regarding human exposure to toxins is the EPA electronic database Integrated Risk Information System (IRIS; http://www.epa.gov/iris/index.html). IRIS contains information on the human health effects associated with exposure to environmental substances. Even though the EPA estimates that there are more than eighty-five thousand chemicals in use in the United States, the IRIS database includes health hazard information for less than six hundred chemicals.

CHEMICAL TOXINS

Chemical toxins are the broadest and most common type of toxic substances that people are likely to encounter in their daily lives. They can be found in a variety of products. The following are the primary sources:

- Household cleansers, solvents, adhesives, and paints
- Fertilizers, pesticides, herbicides, and insecticides

- Metal, fibrous, and wooden building materials
- Plastics and electronics

In addition, people can be exposed daily to chemicals that are purposely introduced to their environment. These releases may have beneficial purposes (e.g., chlorination and fluoridation of public water supplies) or they may be consequences of industrial, commercial, or residential processes.

Information on some selected chemical toxins follows.

Lead

Lead is a naturally occurring metal. It was commonly used in many industries before the 1970s. Exposure to even low levels of lead can cause severe health effects in humans. Lead was once commonly used in many products, including gasoline and paint. Even though these uses have been phased out, millions of older residences around the country are believed to have been painted at one time with lead-containing paints. Painted surfaces pose little danger as long as the paint remains undamaged. The greatest hazard is when chips of paint flake off or when renovations are performed that involve sanding or stripping paint.

Other products that may contain unacceptable levels of lead include ceramics and crystal ware, mini-blinds, weights used for draperies, wheel balances, fishing lures, seams in stained-glass windows, linoleum, batteries, solder, ammunition, and plumbing. Test kits and laboratories that test for lead can check questionable items and locations for the presence of the heavy metal.

Most of the lead in water comes from lead pipes and lead solder in plumbing systems. Mary Tiemann of the Congressional Research Service notes in "Lead in Drinking Water: Washington, DC: Issues and Broader Regulatory Implications" (October 7, 2004, http://www.law.umaryland.edu/marshall/crsreports/crsdocuments/RS21831_10072004.pdf) that in 1992 EPA monitoring revealed that nearly 20% of the nation's largest public water supply systems (i.e., those serving at least fifty thousand people) exceeded the EPA's action level for lead of fifteen parts per billion. By 1993 all large public water supply systems were required to add substances such as lime or calcium carbonate to their water lines to reduce the corrosion of older pipes, which releases lead.

REDUCING LEAD EXPOSURE. As early as the late 1890s medical reports concerning problems with lead began to appear. In 1914 the first U.S. case of lead poisoning was reported, although the cause was undetermined. Scientists eventually began to link lead poisoning to lead paints and, as World War II (1939–1945) ended, began to address the problem. Medical reports documented the connection of lead poisoning to both auto emissions and paint beginning in the mid-1960s.

In 1971 Congress passed the Lead-Based Poisoning Prevention Act, restricting residential use of lead paint in structures constructed or funded by the federal government. The phaseout of leaded fuel in automobiles began during the 1970s.

The Lead Contamination Control Act of 1988 banned the sale of lead-lined drinking water coolers and authorized the CDC to create and expand programs at the state and local levels for screening lead blood levels in infants and children and referring those with elevated levels for treatment.

In 1992 Congress amended the TSCA to add Title IV (Lead Exposure Reduction). Title IV directs the EPA to address the general public's exposure to lead-based paint through regulations, education, and other activities. A particular concern of Congress and the EPA is the potential lead exposure risk associated with housing renovation. The law directs the EPA to publish lead hazard information and make it available to the general public, especially to those undertaking renovations.

Also in 1992 Congress passed the Residential Lead-Based Paint Hazard Reduction Act, which is known as Title X. The law requires sellers and landlords to disclose information about lead-based paint hazards to buyers and leasers. The law also stopped the use of lead-based paint in federal structures and set up a framework to evaluate and remove paint from buildings nationwide. In 1996 Congress once again amended the TSCA, adding Section 402a to establish and fund training programs for lead abatement and to set up requirements and training of technicians and lead-abatement professionals.

In 2000 the EPA announced its goal to eliminate childhood lead poisoning by 2010. The plan for achieving this goal is described in *Eliminating Childhood Lead Poisoning: A Federal Strategy Targeting Lead Paint Hazards* (February 2000, http://www.hud.gov/offices/lead/reports/fedstrategy2000.pdf) by the President's Task Force on Environmental Health Risks and Safety Risks to Children. The report recommends federal grants for lead education programs and renovations at low-income housing projects.

BLOOD LEAD LEVELS. Lead is highly toxic, causing harm to the brain, kidneys, bone marrow, and central nervous system. Infants, children, and pregnant women can experience serious health effects with levels as low as ten micrograms of lead per deciliter of blood. (See Figure 10.1.) At high levels of exposure (now rare in the United States), lead can cause mental retardation, convulsions, and even death.

The CDC monitors blood lead levels (BLLs) of children and adults. Between the mid-1970s and early 2000s the concentrations of lead measured in blood samples of children aged five and under declined dramatically, though thousands were still affected by lead in 2005.

FIGURE 10.1

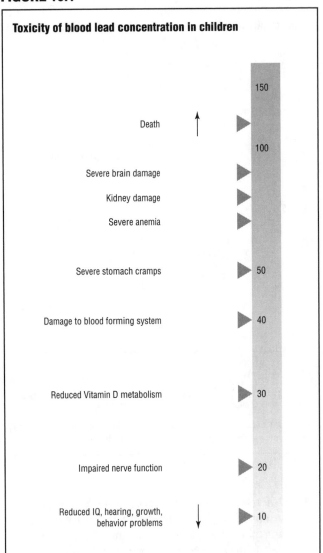

Toxicity of blood lead concentration in children

SOURCE: "Figure 3. Toxicity of Blood Lead Concentration in Children," in *Eliminating Childhood Lead Poisoning: A Federal Strategy Targeting Lead Paint Hazards*, U.S. Environmental Protection Agency, President's Task Force on Environmental Health Risks and Safety Risks to Children, February 2000, http://www.hud.gov/offices/lead/reports/fedstrategy2000.pdf (accessed July 27, 2007)

(See Figure 10.2.) Figure 10.3 shows the number of children aged six or younger tested in 2005 and determined to have elevated BLLs (i.e., more than ten micrograms per deciliter). The graph illustrates that thousands of children had BLLs greater than twenty micrograms per deciliter, the level at which impaired nerve function occurs. Eighty-eight children had BLLs more than seventy micrograms per deciliter, a level at which dangerous organ damage can occur.

LEAD DISCLOSURE LAW VIOLATIONS. In March 2000 a two-year-old girl in New Hampshire died of lead poisoning. It was the first pediatric fatality attributed to lead poisoning since 1990. Authorities found that the

FIGURE 10.2

Concentrations of lead measured in blood of children aged 5 and under, selected years 1976–2004

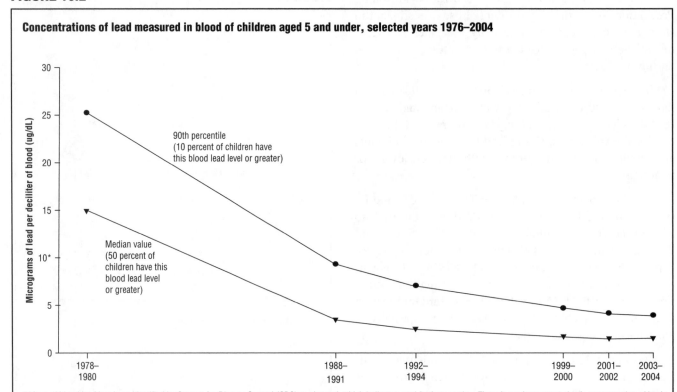

*10 µg of blood lead has been identified by Centers for Disease Control (CDC) as elevated, which indicates need for intervention. There is no demonstrated safe concentration of lead in blood. Adverse effects may occur at lower concentrations.

SOURCE: "Concentrations of Lead in Blood of Children Ages 5 and Under," in *America's Children and the Environment: Body Burdens*, U.S. Environmental Protection Agency, July 2, 2007, http://www.epa.gov/envirohealth/children/body_burdens/b1.htm (accessed July 4, 2007)

girl and her family were refugees from Sudan that had recently moved to the United States from Egypt. Lead-containing paint and dust in the family's New Hampshire apartment were blamed for the poisoning. Family members reported that the girl had been seen chewing on paint chips.

In 2001 the building's property manager was sentenced to fifteen months in jail for failing to provide the family with the lead hazard warning required by the Residential Lead-Based Paint Hazard Reduction Act. Prosecutors alleged that the man falsified documents indicating that the family had received the warning.

During the early 2000s the New England EPA office launched a massive effort to ensure that federal lead disclosure laws were being met throughout the region. Hundreds of inspections and investigations were conducted. In "Manchester, N.H. Landlord Charged with Failing to Warn Tenants about Lead Paint" (June 19, 2007, http://yosemite.epa.gov/opa/admpress.nsf/names/r01_2007-6-19_nh-pb), the EPA reports that in 2007 it charged a landlord in Manchester, New Hampshire, with failure to notify tenants about the dangers of lead paint in older rental units. The apartments were in buildings constructed during the late 1800s and early 1900s. The landlord faced fines in excess of $90,000 for the violations.

Pesticides

Pesticides are chemicals used to kill pests. These pests include insects, rodents, snails and slugs, mites, nematodes, algae, fungi, microorganisms, and unwanted plants (such as weeds). Insecticides are a subset of pesticides used against insects (such as mosquitoes). Herbicides are chemicals designed to target plant life. Pesticides are unique, because they are specifically formulated to be toxic (to some living things) and are deliberately introduced into the environment. Because of these two facts, they are closely regulated. The EPA reviews every pesticide for every particular use.

From an environmental and health hazard standpoint, pesticides of major concern include organochlorine and organophosphate insecticides. Both types can cause damage to the human nervous system.

The use of organophosphates as insecticides developed during the 1930s. Some of these chemicals were used during World War II as nerve agents. Despite their toxicity, organophosphates are not typically persistent in the environment.

Pesticide use in the 1960s centered around organochlorines, including DDT, aldrin, and chlordane. Scientists soon discovered that these chemicals were extremely persistent in the environment. Many were removed from the

FIGURE 10.3

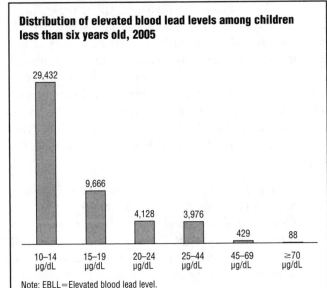

Distribution of elevated blood lead levels among children less than six years old, 2005

Note: EBLL=Elevated blood lead level.

SOURCE: Adapted from "Number of Children Tested and Confirmed EBLLs by State, Year, and BLL Group, Children <72 Months Old," in *Lead Program: CDC Surveillance Data, 1997–2005*, U.S. Department of Health and Human Services, Centers for Disease Control and Prevention, May 25, 2007, http://www.cdc.gov/nceh/lead/surv/database/State_Confirmed_byYear_1997_to_2005.xls (accessed July 4, 2007)

market and gradually replaced with other types of pesticides, mainly pyrethroids. Pyrethroid pesticides use synthetic forms of pyrethrin, a naturally occurring pesticide found in chrysanthemums. According to the EPA, some types of pyrethroids are toxic to the nervous system.

In general, the level of persistent toxins, including pesticides, has declined in humans and wildlife since the 1970s. Newer pesticide compounds are often more toxic than the older types of pesticides, but they are generally designed to be less persistent in the environment and tend to cause fewer chronic problems such as birth defects. However, even pesticides originally believed safe are sometimes found to be harmful later on. In 1998 the EPA began reexamining some older pesticides (those registered before November 1984) to assess their environmental and health effects based on new scientific findings. The program is called the Reregistration Review Process.

In 2000 researchers announced that recent tests of the pesticide chlorpyrifos, a commonly used chemical in residences, found the substance to be harmful, and many applications were withdrawn from the market. Ironically, chlorpyrifos was often used as a substitute for chlordane, a chemical also withdrawn from use after being discovered to be harmful.

CHROMATED COPPER ARSENIC. Chromated copper arsenic (CCA) is a wood preservative, a pesticide designed to protect wood from damage by insects, fungi, and other pests. Wood preservatives are widely used in the developed world on pressure-treated lumber intended for building purposes.

Industrial wood preservatives include creosote-based formulations, oil-borne preservatives (such as copper naphthenate), and waterborne preservatives (primarily CCA). Creosote preservatives contain a mixture of hundreds of chemicals and have been widely used in the United States for decades. However, improper disposal has led to environmental problems and health concerns. The EPA reports that dozens of sites around the country are contaminated with creosotes, which tend to linger in the environment and can be absorbed by plants and animals.

CCA has been widely used on lumber since the 1940s. Beginning in the 1970s CCA became the main preservative used to protect wood for residential outdoor applications, such as decks and playground equipment. In 2001 the EPA decided to reassess the safety of CCA under its Reregistration Review Process. Scientists found that inorganic arsenic in CCA could migrate from treated wood into the surrounding soil and even transfer to skin via direct contact. Because arsenic poses a known health hazard, the EPA initiated a labeling program for CCA-treated lumber as part of a public information campaign. Pesticide manufacturers agreed to a voluntary phaseout of CCA for residential lumber. The ban became mandatory at the end of 2003 with only a few exceptions.

In 2005 the EPA and the U.S. Consumer Product Safety Commission released interim reports on studies they conducted to test the effectiveness of various sealants at preventing the release of arsenic from CCA-treated wood (both old and new). The studies showed that the use of oil- or water-based penetrating sealant or stain at least once a year reduced arsenic migration. Paint was not recommended, because it tended to chip or flake off. The EPA lists these interim studies in "Chromated Copper Arsenate (CCA)" (May 11, 2005, http://www.epa.gov/oppad001/reregistration/cca/#general).

Endocrine Disrupters—Environmental Hormones

Medical and scientific researchers are increasingly linking some environmental chemicals to the endocrine systems of humans and wildlife. The endocrine system—also called the hormone system—consists of glands located throughout the body, hormones that are synthesized and secreted by the glands into the bloodstream, and receptors in the various target organs and tissues. The receptors recognize and respond to the hormones. The function of the system is to regulate the many bodily processes, including control of blood sugar, growth and function of the reproductive systems, regulation of metabolism, brain and nervous system development, and development of the organism from conception through adulthood and old age.

Substances that interfere with these processes are called endocrine disrupters. Some effects of certain estrogenic compounds have been well known for some time. Among these are the eggshell thinning and cracking that led to the population decline of the American bald eagle; the reproductive abnormalities of fetuses exposed to diethylstilbestrol, a synthetic estrogen prescribed between 1948 and 1971 to prevent miscarriages; and reported declines in the quantity and quality of sperm in men.

Only recently, however, have researchers begun to realize how many compounds in the environment are estrogenic. Dozens of these endocrine-disrupting chemicals have been observed to disrupt the hormone or reproductive system, but many thousands of chemicals currently in use remain to be studied. Among them are many herbicides, pesticides, insecticides, and industrial cleaning compounds. Many such compounds have been banned in the United States. Nonetheless, they persist in the food chain for many years and accumulate in animal tissue. Moreover, many of these chemicals continue to be used in developing countries.

Because of the potentially serious consequences of human exposure to endocrine-disrupting chemicals, Congress included specific language on endocrine disruption in the Food Quality Protection Act of 1996 and Safe Drinking Water Act Amendments of 1996. The first mandated the EPA to develop an endocrine-disrupter screening program (EDSP), whereas the latter authorized the EPA to screen endocrine disrupters found in drinking water. In June 2007 the EPA (http://www.epa.gov/scipoly/oscpendo/pubs/prioritysetting/draftlist.htm) published for public comment a draft list of seventy-three chemicals proposed for Tier 1 screening. The chemicals included pesticides and high-production volume chemicals (i.e., chemicals produced or imported into the United States in amounts exceeding one million pounds per year). Tier 1 substances found to interact with the endocrine system will undergo Tier 2 testing to determine their specific effects and establish the dose at which the effects occur.

ASBESTOS

Asbestos is the generic name for several fibrous minerals that are found in nature. Long and thin fibers are bundled together to make asbestos. First used as a coating for candlewicks by the ancient Greeks, asbestos was developed and manufactured in the twentieth century as an excellent thermal and electrical insulator. The physical properties that give asbestos its resistance to heat and decay have long been linked to adverse health effects in humans. Asbestos is found in mostly older homes and buildings, primarily in indoor insulation.

Asbestos tends to break into microscopic fibers. These tiny fibers can remain suspended in the air for long periods of time and can easily penetrate body tissues when inhaled. Because of their durability, these fibers can lodge and remain in the body for many years. No safe exposure threshold for asbestos has been established, but the risk of disease generally increases with the length and amount of exposure. Diseases associated with asbestos inhalation include asbestosis (scarring of the lungs), lung and throat cancers, malignant mesothelioma (a tissue cancer in the chest or abdomen), and nonmalignant pleural disease (accumulation of bloody fluid around the lungs).

Asbestos was one of the first substances regulated under Section 112 of the Clean Air Act of 1970 (CAA) as a hazardous air pollutant. The discovery that asbestos is a strong carcinogen has resulted in the need for its removal or encapsulation (sealing off so that residue cannot escape) from known locations, including schools and public buildings. Many hundreds of millions of dollars have been spent in such clean-ups.

Under the CAA asbestos-containing materials must be removed from demolition and renovation sites without releasing asbestos fibers into the environment. Among other safeguards, workers must wet asbestos insulation before stripping the material from pipes and must seal the asbestos debris while it is still wet in leak-proof containers to prevent the release of asbestos dust. The laws of most states have specific requirements for asbestos workers. A number of legal convictions have resulted from improper and illegal asbestos removal.

The Asbestos Hazard Emergency Response Act was signed into law in 1986. It requires public and private primary and secondary schools to inspect their buildings for asbestos-containing building materials. In "Schools Learn to Protect Students, Staff from Exposure to Asbestos Hazards" (*Enforcement Alert*, vol. 7, no. 1, September 2004), the EPA notes that it conducted inspections between 2002 and 2003 in Puerto Rico schools, which resulted in a $5.6 million penalty against the Puerto Rico Department of Education (PRDOE) for violating the act. Inspectors found widespread instances of asbestos dust in buildings where asbestos had been removed improperly. In addition, people not properly trained in asbestos removal had been allowed to perform some removals. The PRDOE was required to use the penalty money to fund a program to identify and reduce or eliminate asbestos in the island's schools.

In 1989 the EPA banned the importation, production, processing, and distribution of many asbestos-containing products in the United States. The ban was challenged in court and partially overturned. As a result, only a handful of asbestos-containing products remain banned. However, the use of asbestos is banned in products that have not traditionally contained it.

FIGURE 10.4

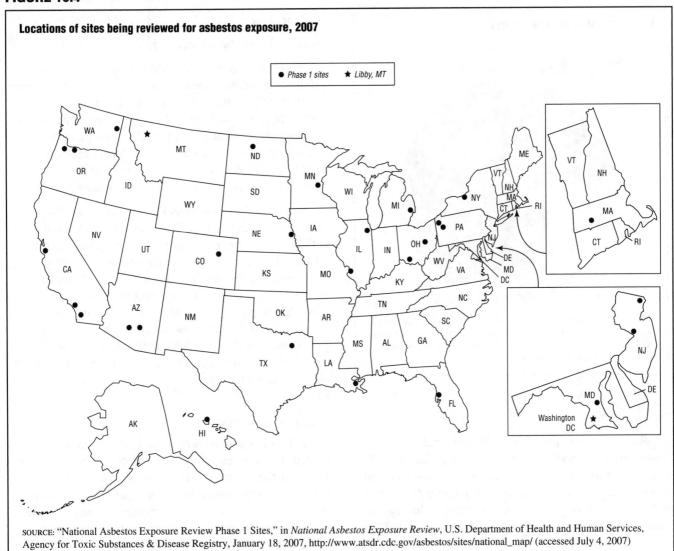

Locations of sites being reviewed for asbestos exposure, 2007

● Phase 1 sites   ★ Libby, MT

SOURCE: "National Asbestos Exposure Review Phase 1 Sites," in *National Asbestos Exposure Review*, U.S. Department of Health and Human Services, Agency for Toxic Substances & Disease Registry, January 18, 2007, http://www.atsdr.cdc.gov/asbestos/sites/national_map/ (accessed July 4, 2007)

Vermiculite

Vermiculite is a natural ore occurring underground that is mined and used to produce insulation, lawn and garden products, and fireproofing material. Scientists have learned that vermiculite mined from Libby, Montana, from the 1920s until 1990 was contaminated with naturally occurring asbestos fibers. The Agency for Toxic Substances and Disease Registry (ATSDR) has tracked most of the vermiculite mined in Libby from 1964 to 1980 to twenty-eight sites around the country, where it was processed into consumer products. These sites are known as Phase 1 sites and are depicted in Figure 10.4, as is the location of the Libby mine (which is now closed). The ATSDR's National Asbestos Exposure Review (January 18, 2007, http://www.atsdr.cdc .gov/asbestos/sites/national_map/index.html) has conducted assessments at the Phase 1 sites to evaluate the human health effects associated with past or current exposure to asbestos-contaminated vermiculite. This information will be used in Phase 2 to determine the specific public health actions needed to minimize further exposure.

RADIATION

Radiation is energy that travels in waves or particles. Radiation exposure comes from natural and human-made sources. People are exposed to natural radiation from outer space (cosmic radiation), the earth (terrestrial radiation and radon), and their own bodies (from naturally occurring radioactive elements). According to the U.S. Nuclear Regulatory Commission, these sources account for about 82% of the average person's radiation exposure. (See Figure 10.5.) Radon is, by far, the largest source of radiation exposure, at 55%. Human-made sources, such as medical devices, electromagnetic equipment, and consumer products, account for 18% of a person's average radiation exposure.

FIGURE 10.5

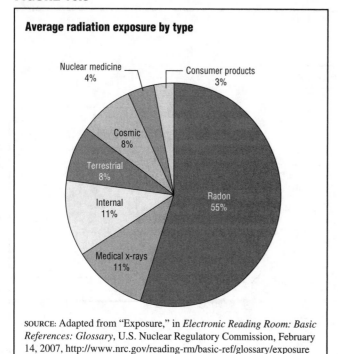

Average radiation exposure by type

SOURCE: Adapted from "Exposure," in *Electronic Reading Room: Basic References: Glossary*, U.S. Nuclear Regulatory Commission, February 14, 2007, http://www.nrc.gov/reading-rm/basic-ref/glossary/exposure.html (accessed July 5, 2007)

Radon

Radon is an invisible, odorless radioactive gas formed by the decay of uranium in rocks and soil. This gas seeps from underground rock into the basements and foundations of structures via cracks in foundations, pipes, and sometimes through the water supply. Because it is naturally occurring, it cannot be entirely eliminated from the environment. Radon inhaled into the lungs undergoes radioactive decay, releasing particles that damage the deoxyribonucleic acid in lung tissue.

The EPA notes in "Radiation Information: Radon" (October 6, 2006, http://www.epa.gov/radiation/radiob nuclides/radon.htm) that in 1988 the agency and the U.S. Surgeon General recommended that radon testing be performed in all U.S. homes and schools. The recommendation applied to all levels beneath the third floor. The EPA set a national voluntary action level for radon at four picoCuries per liter (pCi/L). The radon content in most homes can be reduced to two pCi/L or less with devices such as specially designed fans that prevent radon from seeping into a house.

The Indoor Radon Abatement Act of 1988 directed the EPA to identify areas of the country with the potential for elevated levels of indoor radon. The EPA assessed more than three thousand counties in terms of geology, aerial radioactivity, soil permeability, foundation type, and indoor radon measurements. Each county was assigned to one of three zones based on its predicted average indoor radon screening level:

- Zone 1—predicted level greater than four pCi/L
- Zone 2—predicted level of two to four pCi/L
- Zone 3—predicted level less than two pCi/L

According to the EPA (May 23, 2007, http://www.epa.gov/iaq/radon/zonemap.html), these zones are not intended to indicate which homeowners should test their homes for radon but to provide a general guide to state and local organizations dealing with radon abatement. The EPA cautions that homes with elevated levels of radon have been found in all three zones. The EPA and the National Safety Council both recommend home testing for radon.

In the *EPA Assessment of Risks from Radon in Homes* (June 2003, http://www.epa.gov/radon/pdfs/402-r-03-003.pdf), the EPA estimates that radon caused an estimated 21,800 deaths from lung cancer during 1995, making radon the second-leading cause of lung cancer after smoking. A synergistic effect has been noted: when radon levels are high in a home where a smoker resides, the likelihood of that person contracting lung cancer is greatly increased. The EPA estimates that an average of 13.4% of U.S. lung cancer deaths in 1995 were attributable to radon exposure.

INDOOR AIR TOXINS

Indoor pollution has become a serious problem in the United States. Even though most people think of outdoor air when they think of air pollution, studies now reveal that indoor environments are not safe havens from air pollution. Modern indoor environments contain a variety of pollution sources, including building materials and consumer products. People and pets also contribute to airborne pollution. Improvements in home and building insulation and the widespread use of central air conditioning and heating systems have largely ensured that any contaminant present indoors will not be diluted by outside air and, therefore, will become more concentrated.

The EPA indicates in *The Inside Story: A Guide to Indoor Air Quality* (August 27, 2007, http://www.epa.gov/iaq/pubs/insidest.html) that the following are the most common pollutants contributing to poor indoor air quality:

- Radon
- Smoke from tobacco use
- Biological pollutants (animal dander, bacteria, cat saliva, cockroaches, mildew, mites, mold, pollen, and viruses)
- Combustion products, such as carbon monoxide, nitrogen dioxide, and particulates
- Chemicals in household products used for cleaning, repairs and maintenance, personal care, and hobbies
- Formaldehyde and pressed wood products
- Pesticides

- Asbestos
- Lead

Health Hazards

Exposure to some indoor air pollutants is directly linked to severe health problems and even death. The dangers of asbestos, lead, pesticides, and radon have already been discussed. The potentially deadly effects of second-hand tobacco smoke are also well known. Another indoor pollutant known to be life threatening is carbon monoxide.

Carbon monoxide (CO) is a colorless, odorless gas that results from incomplete combustion of fossil fuels, such as natural gas and oil. Madhavi Vajani et al. note in "Unintentional Non-fire-related Carbon Monoxide Exposures—United States, 2001–2003" (*Morbidity and Mortality Weekly Report*, vol. 54, no. 2, January 21, 2005) that an average of 15,200 people annually were treated in emergency rooms in the United States between 2001 and 2003 for confirmed or possible CO poisoning not related to fires. Between 2001 and 2002 an average of 480 people per year died of CO poisoning not related to fires. Nearly one-fourth (23.5%) of the deaths were in

patients aged sixty-five or older. Even though the exact source of CO was not reported for all cases, Vajani and his coauthors cite faulty furnaces as the main identifiable source of CO exposures. Other sources include motor vehicles, gas stoves and water heaters, leaky gas lines, generators, space heaters, and miscellaneous machinery.

Most exposures to indoor air pollution are associated with respiratory problems. Many of the pollutants listed earlier can cause or aggravate respiratory conditions, such as asthma. Asthma is a chronic lung disease characterized by episodes (attacks) of wheezing, shortness of breath, coughing, and chest tightness. Environmental irritants are known to be one of the triggers for asthma attacks.

According to CDC data, the prevalence of asthma among the U.S. population increased dramatically between 1980 and 2004. (See Figure 10.6.) Approximately 12% of American children had suffered from asthma at some time in their lifetime as of 2004. The Asthma and Allergy Foundation of America notes in "Asthma Facts and Figures" (2007, http://www.aafa.org/display.cfm?id=8&sub=42) that every year about four thousand Americans die from asthma. Health and environmental agencies urge people to educate

FIGURE 10.6

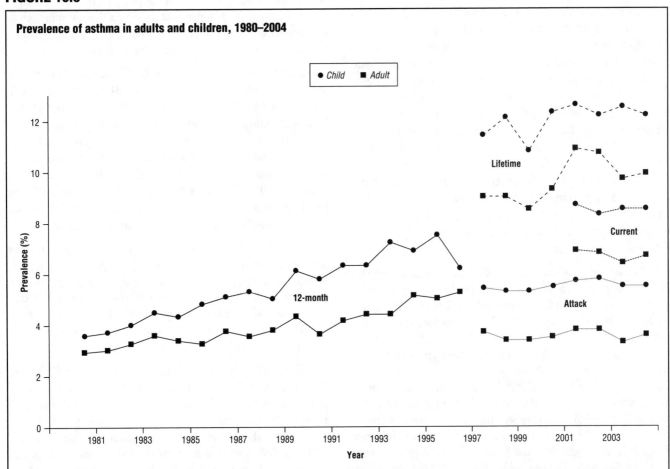

Prevalence of asthma in adults and children, 1980–2004

SOURCE: "Child and Adult Asthma Prevalence, United States, 1980-2004," in *Asthma Surveillance Data: Prevalence Slides*, U.S. Department of Health and Human Services, Centers for Disease Control and Prevention, 2005, http://www.cdc.gov/asthma/slides/prevalence06.ppt (accessed july 9, 2007)

themselves about possible asthma irritants in their homes and take measures to control or eliminate them.

TOXINS IN FOOD

The presence of environmental toxins in food has become a topic of major concern in recent years. Chemical pollutants that wind up in food can come from air and wastewater emissions or from land sources, such as landfills or farms. Food can also pose a danger to human health if it is contaminated by biological organisms.

Persistent and Bioaccumulative Chemicals

The most worrisome chemical contaminants in food are those that are persistent (i.e., resistant to biodegradation) and bioaccumulative, meaning that they are absorbed by lower life forms and become concentrated as they work their way up the food chain. There are four chemical toxins found in food that are particularly noted for their persistent bioaccumulative properties: mercury, pesticides, dioxins, and PCBs.

MERCURY. Mercury is a naturally occurring inorganic element. It is also released by human activities, primarily via waste incineration and fossil fuel combustion. In the environment inorganic mercury can convert to an organic form called methylmercury. It accumulates in fish and shellfish and works its way up the food chain. The highest concentrations of mercury in fish are found in large predator species, such as pike, bass, and shark. Methylmercury accumulates in human tissue when people eat contaminated fish. At certain dosages it can damage the central nervous system, cause severe neurological impairment, and be fatal. Figure 10.7 shows the distribution of women of childbearing age between 1999 and 2002 by the level of mercury in their blood. The EPA's reference dose for methylmercury is 0.1 micrograms per kilogram of body weight. This equates to approximately 5.8 parts per billion mercury in blood. As illustrated in Figure 10.7, small percentages of women of childbearing age tested higher than the reference dose for mercury.

During the 1990s and early 2000s the EPA and the FDA conducted extensive monitoring to determine the levels of contaminants, particularly mercury, in fish. The agencies issued the brochure "What You Need to Know about Mercury in Fish and Shellfish" (March 2004, http://www.cfsan.fda.gov/~dms/admehg3b.html), a joint recommendation regarding fish consumption by women of childbearing age and young children. The brochure warns against any consumption of shark, swordfish, king mackerel, and tilefish because of high levels of mercury commonly found in these fish. The public is urged to consult local and state fish advisories regarding the safety of fish caught in their area. In "Fish Advisories" (August 8, 2007, http://www.epa.gov/waterscience/fish/states.htm), the EPA provides links to state advisories. State advisories typically list major

FIGURE 10.7

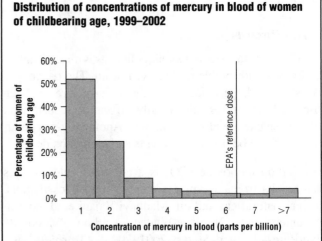

Distribution of concentrations of mercury in blood of women of childbearing age, 1999–2002

Note: EPA's reference dose (RID) for methylmercury is 0.1 micrograms per kilogram body weight per day. This is approximately equivalent to a concentration of 5.8 parts per billion mercury in blood.

SOURCE: "Distribution of Concentrations of Mercury in Women of Childbearing Age, 1999–2002," in *America's Children and the Environment: Body Burdens*, U.S. Environmental Protection Agency, July 2, 2007, http://www.epa.gov/envirohealth/children/body_burdens/b4.htm (accessed July 9, 2007)

water bodies and provide consumption restrictions (if any) for fish caught from those waters. Even though mercury is the subject of most restrictions, other contaminants are also a concern, including pesticides and dioxins.

PESTICIDES. Chlordane and DDT are insecticides that were once widely used in the United States. In 1972 DDT was banned by the EPA after scientists found the chemical was damaging wildlife. Chlordane was banned in 1988. Both pesticides are toxic, extremely persistent, and bioaccumulative, making them a threat to the environment and human health. Both are linked to severe neurological problems. Chlordane also adversely affects the liver and digestive system in animals and humans. DDT is classified as a probable human carcinogen.

The prevalence of pesticides in surface water bodies and groundwater was discussed at length in Chapter 9. Water contamination is a primary pathway for pesticides to reach food sources, particularly fish. Other foods can be affected via the use of contaminated irrigation waters. Pesticides are also spread directly on and around ground-grown foods, such as crops and fruit trees.

Since 1991 the USDA has conducted the Pesticide Data Program (PDP) in which a wide range of edible or drinkable commodities are tested for pesticide content. Testing is performed on fresh and processed foods. Table 10.2 shows the results obtained by the PDP for 2005 on foods obtained from twelve states: California, Colorado, Florida, Maryland, Michigan, Minnesota, Montana, New York, Ohio, Texas, Washington, and Wisconsin. Pesticides were detected in at least 90% of the samples

TABLE 10.2

Results from the Pesticide Data Program, 2005

	Number of samples analyzed	Samples with residues detected	Percent of samples with detections	Different pesticides detected	Different residues detected	Total residue detections
Fresh fruit and vegetables:						
Apples	743	727	98	36	43	2,643
Cantaloupe	558	288	52	22	27	445
Cauliflower	741	650	88	16	17	816
Eggplant	736	172	23	15	18	315
Grapefruit	742	470	63	11	13	643
Grapes	739	520	70	31	34	1,250
Green beans	181	166	92	18	22	536
Lettuce	743	696	94	43	52	2,475
Oranges	741	670	90	14	16	1,195
Pears	555	473	85	25	29	979
Plums	573	426	74	16	16	652
Strawberries	737	685	93	30	39	1,938
Watermelon	182	70	38	12	14	101
Winter squash	731	313	43	25	30	452
Total fresh	**8,702**	**6,326**	**73**			**14,440**
Processed fruit and vegetables:						
Green beans, frozen	555	431	78	18	19	756
Orange juice	744	430	58	9	10	459
Plums, dried (prunes)	153	20	13	7	7	25
Total processed	**1,452**	**881**	**61**			**1,240**

Fruit and vegetables totals:
Number of samples analyzed=10,154
Number of samples with residues detected=7,207
Percent with residue detections=71.0%

Total number of different pesticides detected=105
Total number of different residues detected=118
Total number of residue detections=15,680

	Number of samples analyzed	Samples with residues detected	Percent of samples with detections	Different pesticides detected	Different residues detected	Total residue detections
Grain product:						
Soybeans	668	144	22	9	9	150
Wheat	674	508	75	18	18	750
Total grain	**1,342**	**652**	**49**			**900**
Dairy Product:						
Heavy cream	369	366	99	9	11	901
Milk	746	738	99	12	12	1,857
Total dairy	**1,115**	**1,104**	**99**			**2,758**
Meat tissues:						
Pork, adipose	352	40	11	7	8	50
Pork, muscle	352	18	5	2	3	20
Total meat	**704**	**58**	**8**			**70**
Water product:						
Bottled water	378	59	16	7	14	105

All commodities (excludes 750 drinking water samples and 306 soybean rust/aphid special survey samples):
Number of samples analyzed=13,693
Number of samples with residues detected=9,080
Percent with residue detections=66.3%

Total number of different pesticides detected=166
Total number of different residues detected=178
Total number of residue detections=19,513

SOURCE: "Table 3. Number of Samples Analyzed and Summary of Residues Detected by Commodity," in *Pesticide Data Program: Annual Summary Calendar Year 2005*, U.S. Department of Agriculture, Agricultural Marketing Service, November 2006, http://www.ams.usda.gov/science/pdp/Summary2005.pdf (accessed July 6, 2007)

taken from the following foods: heavy cream (99%), milk (99%), fresh apples (98%), fresh lettuce (94%), fresh strawberries (93%), fresh green beans (92%), and fresh oranges (90%). In most cases dozens of different pesticides were detected for each food group. Pesticides also appeared in bottled water. Sixteen percent of the sampled bottled waters tested positive for pesticides.

Figure 10.8 shows USDA data collected between 1994 and 2004 on the percentage of fruits, vegetables, and grains containing detectable residues of organophosphate pesticides. In 2004 nearly 20% of the samples had detectable residues of these contaminants. However, there is some good news on pesticide usage. According to the EPA, in *America's Children and the Environment* (July 2, 2007, http://www.epa.gov/enviro health/children/contaminants/e8.htm), the amount of organophosphate pesticides used on foods most often eaten by children decreased by 52% between 1993 and 2004.

FIGURE 10.8

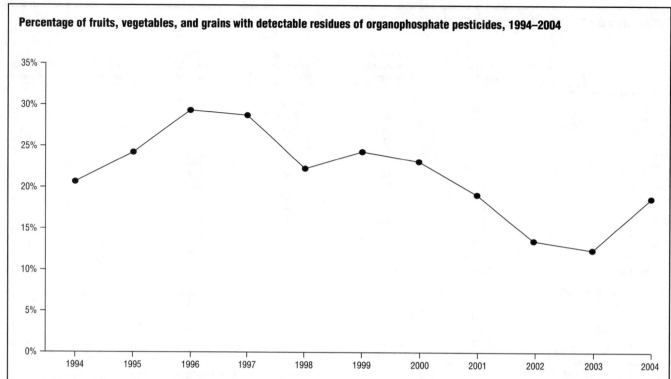

Percentage of fruits, vegetables, and grains with detectable residues of organophosphate pesticides, 1994–2004

SOURCE: "Percentage of Fruits, Vegetables, and Grains with Detectable Residues of Organophosphate Pesticides," in *America's Children and the Environment: Environmental Contaminants,* U.S. Environmental Protection Agency, July 2, 2007, http://www.epa.gov/envirohealth/children/contaminants/e8.htm (accessed July 9, 2007)

Fear of agricultural pesticide usage has contributed to a rise in the interest in organic foods. The federal government's National Organic Program defines organic agriculture as that which excludes the use of synthetic fertilizers and pesticides. More important, it strives for low environmental impact and enlists natural biological systems—cover crops, crop rotation, and natural predators—to increase fertility and decrease the likelihood of pest infestation.

DIOXINS AND PCBS. Dioxins are a group of several hundred chlorinated organic compounds with similar chemical structures and biological effects. In laboratory animal tests dioxins caused damage to major organs and systems. The chemicals are also linked with adverse effects to the skin and liver in humans. Dioxins are classified as probable human carcinogens.

Dioxin categories include chlorinated dibenzo-p-dioxins, chlorinated dibenzofurans, and some PCBs. PCBs are a group of synthetic organic chemicals that were primarily used as lubricants and coolants in electrical equipment before the 1970s. The manufacture of PCBs was halted in the United States in 1977 because of concerns about their effects on the environment and human health. PCBs are known to cause a wide variety of serious health problems, including liver cancer, in laboratory animals. They are classified as possible carcinogens in humans.

Dioxins are most commonly associated with the burning or combustion of other substances. Certain industrial processes, such as chlorine bleaching of pulp and paper, also produce dioxins. They are generated by natural sources, primarily forest fires, and are introduced to the environment by humans through a variety of activities. Table 10.3 lists the top ten anthropogenic (human-related) sources of dioxin compounds in 2000. Backyard burning of garbage and refuse is the largest offender, accounting for 35.1% of the total. Incineration of medical wastes is another culprit, contributing 26.6% of the total. Together, the top ten anthropogenic sources accounted for nearly 92.6% of the total in 2000.

Table 10.4 provides the EPA's estimates of the average U.S. adult's exposure to dioxins in food daily. Beef and freshwater fish and shellfish are the major sources of exposure. These levels are associated with adverse health effects but are below the levels associated with cancer. Levels of exposure are thought to be even greater in people who have diets high in fat content.

Total Diet Study on Chemical Contaminants

The FDA conducts its own analyses of the U.S. food supply through the Total Diet Study (TDS; http://www.cfsan.fda.gov/~comm/tds-toc.html). The TDS program was begun in 1960 to test foods for radioactive

TABLE 10.3

Sources of dioxin-like compounds, 2000

Source (released to)	2000 Releases (grams)	Percent of total
Backyard barrel burning of refuse (air)	498.5	35.1
Medical waste/pathological incineration (air)	378.0	26.6
Municipal wastewater treatment sludge, land application and incineration (land, air)	89.7	6.3
Municipal waste combustion (air)	83.8	5.9
Coal-fired utility boilers (air)	69.5	4.9
Diesel heavy-duty trucks (air)	65.4	4.6
Industrial wood combustion (air)	41.5	2.9
Diesel off-road equipment, ships, trains, tractors (air)	33.1	2.3
Ethylene dichloride/ vinyl chloride production (water, land, air)	30.0	2.1
Sintering plants (air)	27.6	1.9

SOURCE: Adapted from "Table 1-17. Ranking of Sources of Dioxin-like Compounds Based on Environmental Releases (from High to Low) for Reference Years 2000, 1995, and 1987," in *An Inventory of Sources and Environmental Releases of Dioxin-Like Compounds in the United States for the Years 1987, 1995, and 2000*, U.S. Environmental Protection Agency, November 2006, http://cfpub.epa.gov/ncea/cfm/recordisplay.cfm?deid=159286 (accessed July 10, 2007)

TABLE 10.4

EPA's estimates of the average adult's daily exposure to dioxins from dietary intake

[Picograms per day]

Food type	Dietary exposure to CDDs and CDFs	Dietary exposure to PCBs	Total dietary exposure to dioxins
Beef	9.0	4.2	13.2
Freshwater fish and shellfish	5.9	7.1	13.0
Dairy products (cheese, yogurt, etc.)	6.6	3.2	9.8
Other meats (lamb, baloney, etc.)	4.5	1.0	5.5
Marine fish and shellfish	2.5	2.4	4.9
Milk	3.2	1.5	4.7
Pork	4.2	0.2	4.4
Poultry	2.4	0.9	3.3
Eggs	1.4	1.7	3.1
Vegetable fat (oils, margarine, etc.)	1.0	0.6	1.6
Total	**40.7**	**22.8**	**63.5**

Note: The average adult is assumed to weigh 70 kilograms (154 pounds). A picogram is one-trillionth of a gram.
CDDs=Chlorinated dibenzo-p-dioxins.
CDFs=Chlorinated dibenzofurans.
PCBs=Polychlorinated biphenyls.

SOURCE: "Table 1. EPA's Estimates of the Average U.S. Adult's Daily Exposure to Dioxins from Dietary Intake, Picograms per Day," in *Information on EPA's Draft Reassessment of Dioxins*, GAO-02-515, U.S. General Accounting Office, April 2002, http://www.gao.gov/new.items/d02515.pdf (accessed July 27, 2007)

contamination. Since then, it has grown to include a wide variety of analyzed substances, both good (nutrients) and bad (pesticides, metals, and organic contaminants). Hundreds of food items are tested in ready-to-eat form. Examples include macaroni and cheese prepared from box mix, peanut butter, fruit-flavored breakfast cereal, frozen green peas, and fast-food hamburgers. An extensive assortment of baby foods are also tested.

The most recent update was performed in December 2006 and includes data collected through 2004. For each food the database shows the number of analyses for each chemical, the number of samples with amounts greater than or equal to the level of quantification (detectable amount) or trace (minute) amounts, and the minimum, mean (average), and maximum levels in parts per million. A search of the database in September 2007 revealed the list of chemicals shown in Table 10.5 for a plain milk chocolate candy bar. More than a dozen contaminants were detected, including 1,2,4-trimethylbenze, chloroform, DDT, lindane (a pesticide), styrene, and toluene.

Biological Contaminants

According to federal officials, food-borne illnesses due to pathogens (disease-causing biological organisms) pose "a substantial health burden" in the United States.

Even though the U.S. food supply is among the safest in the world, Americans do experience episodes of food poisoning and disease.

Food-borne illnesses became the object of intense public scrutiny following an outbreak of *Escherichia coli* (*E. coli*) in 1993 that killed four people and sickened hundreds. The illness was attributed to undercooked hamburgers from fast-food restaurants. The FDA responded by raising the recommended internal temperature for cooked hamburgers to 155 degrees Fahrenheit. A sampling program was begun to test for *E. coli* in raw ground beef. New labels containing food-handling instructions were required on consumer packages of raw meats and poultry.

In 1996 more illnesses were attributed to *E. coli*, this time in unpasteurized apple juice. The FDA proposed new regulations to improve the safety of fresh and processed juices. *E. coli* again became the focus of a food safety campaign following a widespread outbreak that affected consumers in twenty-six states in September 2006. The contaminant originated in cattle feces that tainted bagged spinach that had been grown and packaged by Natural Selection Foods LLC in San Juan Bautista, California. The outbreak sickened more than two hundred people and killed three. In "Nationwide *E. Coli* O157:H7 Outbreak: Questions & Answers" (October 20, 2006; http://

TABLE 10.5

Chemicals found in a plain milk chocolate candy bar

Food #	Description	Number of			Level in ppm		
		Analyses	$ LQ	Traces	Mean	Min	Max
187	**Candy bar, milk chocolate, plain**						
	1,1,1-trichloroethane	44	0	4	0.00032	0.0030	0.0040
	1,2,4-trimethylbenzene	44	15	1	0.00964	0.0060	0.0640
	Benzene*	44	5	5	0.00227	0.0010	0.0280
	BHC, alpha	44	1	19	0.00051	0.0001	0.0050
	Bromodichloromethane	44	0	1	0.00009	0.0040	0.0040
	Butylbenzene, A	44	0	2	0.00014	0.0030	0.0030
	Chlorobenzene	44	0	3	0.00041	0.0020	0.0120
	Chloroform	44	4	5	0.00214	0.0020	0.0360
	Chlorpyrifos	44	0	7	0.00015	0.0002	0.0030
	DDE, p,p'	44	1	32	0.00078	0.0002	0.0030
	DDT, p,p'	44	2	18	0.00097	0.0002	0.0090
	Dichlorobenzene, p-	44	2	3	0.00068	0.0020	0.0120
	Dieldrin	44	0	4	0.00002	0.0001	0.0004
	Diphenyl 2-ethylhexyl phosphate	44	1	0	0.01727	0.7600	0.7600
	Endosulfan I	44	0	6	0.00005	0.0003	0.0005
	Endosulfan II	44	0	3	0.00001	0.0002	0.0002
	Endosulfan sulfate	44	0	11	0.00017	0.0002	0.0010
	Ethyl benzene	44	3	14	0.00230	0.0020	0.0150
	Lindane	44	21	22	0.00167	0.0001	0.0060
	Malathion	44	1	0	0.00014	0.0060	0.0060
	Pentachlorophenyl methyl ether	44	0	1	0.00000	0.0002	0.0002
	Pirimiphos-methyl	44	0	1	0.00002	0.0010	0.0010
	Propylbenzene, A	44	0	1	0.00007	0.0030	0.0030
	Styrene	44	23	4	0.01302	0.0030	0.0760
	TDE, p,p'	44	0	14	0.00034	0.0003	0.0030
	Tetrachloroethylene	44	17	2	0.00952	0.0020	0.0700
	Toluene	44	30	0	0.02305	0.0090	0.0780
	Trichloroethylene	44	1	10	0.00098	0.0020	0.0090
	Xylene, m- and/or p-	44	13	14	0.01286	0.0030	0.0540
	Xylene, o	44	6	3	0.00307	0.0020	0.0150

LQ=Limit of quantification.
ppm=Parts per million.
* Benzene data are undergoing further review.

SOURCE: Adapted from "U.S. Food and Drug Administration—Total Diet Study, Market Baskets 1991–3 through 2003–4," in *US Food and Drug Administration—Total Diet Study: Market Baskets 1991–3 through 2003–4*, U.S. Food and Drug Administration, Center for Food Safety and Applied Nutrition, December 2006, http://www.cfsan.fda.gov/~acrobat/tds1byfd.pdf (accessed July 6, 2007)

www.cfsan.fda.gov/~dms/spinacqa.html#brands), the FDA reports that between 1995 and 2006 there had been nineteen outbreaks of foodborne illness traced back to lettuce or other leafy greens grown in the Salinas Valley in California, although the exact growers were not known in all cases.

To better protect consumers from such outbreaks, federal and state agencies established a surveillance program called FoodNet to monitor laboratory-identified food-borne diseases related to seven pathogens in parts of five states. Olga L. Henao of the CDC notes in *Foodborne Diseases Active Surveillance Network (FoodNet)* (2006, http://www.cdc.gov/foodsafety/PFSE/foodnet.pdf) that by 2006 the program had grown to monitor 11 pathogens and syndromes in 10 states, encompassing 44.9 million people (15% of the U.S. population). Preliminary FoodNet data for 2006 were published in 2007 and are presented in Table 10.6.

In "Preliminary FoodNet Data on the Incidence of Infection with Pathogens Transmitted Commonly

through Food—10 States, 2006" (*Morbidity and Mortality Weekly Report*, vol. 56, no. 14, April 13, 2007), Duc Vugia et al. note that the FoodNet identified 17,252 cases of food-borne illnesses related to monitored pathogens in 2006. *Salmonella* accounted for 39% of cases, followed by *Campylobacter* (33%) and *Shigella* (16%).

The incidence of diseases attributed to *Yersinia*, *Shigella*, *Listeria*, and *Campylobacter* decreased dramatically between 1996 and 2006. The CDC attributes the decline to several factors, including increased public awareness about food-borne diseases and food safety, new pathogen reduction measures implemented by the USDA at meat and poultry slaughterhouses and processing plants, egg quality assurance programs, better agricultural practices that ensure produce safety, increased regulation of imported foods and fruit and vegetable juices, and the introduction of hazard-reduction measures in the seafood industry. However, there is still much work to do. Table 10.6 lists rate goals for five

TABLE 10.6

Cases of bacterial and parasitic infection under surveillance, by site, compared with national health objectives, 2006

[Per 100,000 population.]

Pathogen/condition	California	Colorado	Connecticut	Georgia	Maryland	Minnesota	New Mexico	New York	Oregon	Tennessee	Overall 2006	National health objective[a]
Bacteria												
Campylobacter	26.82	18.52	15.16	6.27	7.61	17.51	18.77	12.07	17.14	7.40	12.71	12.30
Listeria	0.25	0.19	0.54	0.22	0.50	0.14	0.26	0.51	0.30	0.22	0.31	0.25
Salmonella	15.19	13.84	14.41	20.04	13.86	14.05	13.83	11.44	11.01	14.04	14.81	6.80
Shigella	7.55	6.96	1.91	15.01	2.18	4.99	8.71	1.11	2.58	3.30	6.09	NA[b]
STEC[c] O157	1.31	1.35	1.20	0.45	0.70	2.86	1.04	1.23	2.28	1.48	1.31	1.00
STEC non-O157	0.22	0.62	0.94	0.20	0.61	0.86	1.19	0.42	0.25	0.12	0.46	NA
Vibrio	1.15	0.12	0.54	0.28	0.59	0.08	0.10	0.28	0.27	0.15	0.34	NA
Yersinia	0.31	0.23	0.48	0.35	0.18	0.39	0.26	0.32	0.41	0.49	0.35	NA
Parasites												
Cryptosporidium	1.50	1.43	1.08	2.98	0.32	4.66	1.76	1.23	2.06	0.79	1.91	NA
Cyclospora	0	0	0.26	0.21	0.04	0.08	0.05	0	0.05	0.07	0.09	NA
HUS[d]	3.26	2.02	0.95	0.72	0.52	2.08	—	2.96	2.66	1.80	1.63	0.90

Note: Survillance populations (in millions): California (3.21), Colorado (2.59), Connecticut (3.51), Georgia (9.07), Maryland (5.60), Minnesota (5.13), New Mexico (1.93), New York (4.31), Oregon (3.64), Tennessee (5.96), and overall (44.95).

[a]Healthy People 2010 objectives for incidence of *Campylobacter, Salmonella,* and *Shiga* toxin-producing Escherichia coli O157 infections for year 2010 and for incidence of *Listeria* infections for year 2005.

[b]Not applicable because no national health objective exists regarding infection with this pathogen.

[c]*Shiga* toxin-producing *Escherichia* coli.

[d]Incidence rate for HUS in chldren aged <5 years; rate calculation is based on surveillance population aged <5 years in the nine sites that conducted hospital discharge data review; HUS data from 2005.

SOURCE: "Table. Incidence of Bacterial and Parasitic Infection in 2006 and Hemolytic Uremic Syndrome (HUS) in 2005, by Site and Pathogen/Condition, compared with National Health Objectives," in *Preliminary FoodNet Data on the Incidence of Infection with Pathogens Transmitted Commonly Through Food— 10 States, 2006,* U.S. Department of Health and Human Services, Centers for Disease Control and Prevention, April 13, 2007, http://www.CDC.gov/mmwr/preview/mmwrhtml/mm5614a4.htm (accessed July 6, 2007)

food-borne pathogens and syndromes that the federal government hopes to achieve by 2010. Rates of infection in 2006 per one hundred thousand population were higher than the national objectives.

CHAPTER 11
DEPLETION AND CONSERVATION OF NATURAL RESOURCES

Throughout history humans have relied on the world's natural resources for survival. Early civilizations were dependent on sources of clean water, soils suitable for growing crops to feed people and livestock, and wild animals that could be hunted for meat, skins, and fur. As time passed, societies learned to harvest and use other natural resources, primarily wood, metals, minerals, and fossil fuels. For centuries there was little thought given to the consequences of depleting these resources. The supply appeared to be never-ending.

The early American colonists were impressed by the country's abundance of natural resources. Settlers migrated west and south, building towns and developing land for agriculture and industry. New modes of transportation allowed access to areas that had previously been undisturbed by humans. Widespread development and demand for food, water, lumber, and other goods began to stress some natural resources. Massive areas of forest were cleared of trees. Passenger pigeons and heath hens were driven to extinction. Buffalo, elk, and beaver stocks were nearly wiped out.

During the nineteenth century awareness grew in the United States about the scarcity and value of natural resources. In 1892 John Muir (1838–1914) established the Sierra Club, an organization devoted to recreation, education, and conservation. President Theodore Roosevelt (1858–1919) set aside millions of acres of land under federal control for national refuges, forests, and parks. Over the next century people began to notice the environmental toll of mining, agriculture, timber harvesting, urban development, and pollution. The availability and condition of natural resources became a national priority.

Despite many technological advances, humans of the twenty-first century are still dependent on some of the same natural resources that sustained the first civilizations: clean water and productive soils. In addition, there is enormous demand for wood, metals, minerals, and other natural materials from which goods are manufactured. Finally, fossil fuels (coal, oil, petroleum, and natural gas) provide the bulk of the world's power. Since the latter half of the twentieth century, scientists have been aware that these natural resources have limits in terms of quantity and quality.

Natural resources are important not only for their practical value and economic worth but also for their contribution to environmental health. For example, forests and wetlands provide habitat for a wide variety of plant and animal life. These ecosystems are also appreciated by humans for their aesthetic appeal and recreational purposes. However, developers and industrial entities have an interest in using these lands for different purposes. To balance competing interests, the government has developed a number of agencies with responsibility for overseeing the management of natural resources. A list of federal agencies is provided in Table 11.1.

LAND USE

According to W. Brad Smith et al. in *Forest Resources of the United States, 2002* (2004, http://nrs.fs.fed.us/pubs/gtr/gtr_nc241.pdf), the United States encompasses 2.3 billion acres of land. The usage of this land has profound effects on the economic and environmental well-being of the nation. According to the U.S. Environmental Protection Agency's (EPA) "Draft Report on the Environment" (2007, http://www.epa.gov/indicators/roe/html/roeTOC.htm), nearly two-thirds (64%) of U.S. land is in private hands. (See Figure 11.1.) The federal government manages 27% of the total, and state and local governments manage the remaining 9% of the total. Most federal lands are located in the western United States and Alaska. They are managed by a variety of federal agencies, primarily the U.S. Department of Agriculture's (USDA) Forest Service, the Bureau of Land Management, the National Park Service, the U.S. Fish and Wildlife Service (USFWS), and the U.S. Department of Defense.

TABLE 11.1

Federal agencies that oversee natural resources

Federal agency	Founded	Description
U.S. Army Corps of Engineers	1802	Grants permits for dredging and filling in certain waterways, including many wetlands.
U.S. Department of Agriculture		
Forest Service	1905	Manages more than 190 million acres of public lands in national forests and grasslands.
Natural Resources Conservation Service	1935*	Helps private land owners/managers conserve their natural resources. Participation is voluntary.
U.S. Department of the Interior		
Bureau of Indian Affairs	1824	Manages 55.7 million acres of land held in trust for American Indians, Indian tribes, and Alaska Natives.
Bureau of Land Management	1812*	Manages 262 million acres of public lands (mostly in the West) and 300 acres of subsurface mineral resources.
Bureau of Reclamation	1902	Provides water and energy to more than 30 million people via hundreds of dams, reservoirs, canals, and power plants it has constructed in 17 western states.
Fish and Wildlife Service	1871*	Conserves, protects and enhances fish, wildlife, plants and their habitats for the benefit of the public.
Minerals Management Service	1982	Manages the nation's natural gas, oil and other mineral resources on the outer continental shelf.
National Park Service	1916	Preserves the resources of more than 80 million acres comprising the national park system.
Office of Surface Mining	1977	Oversees surface mining on federal lands and some tribal and state lands.
U.S. Geological Survey	1879	Provides data related to Earth sciences, natural disasters, and management of natural resources.
U.S. Environmental Protection Agency	1970	Develops and enforces regulations that implement environmental laws enacted by Congress.

*Date of founding of predecessor agency that evolved into current agency.

SOURCE: Created by Kim Masters Evans for Thomson Gale, 2007

FIGURE 11.1

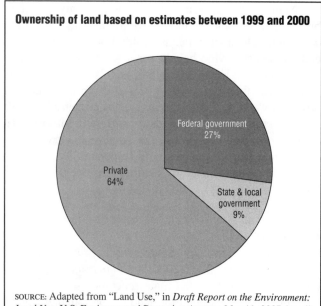

Ownership of land based on estimates between 1999 and 2000

Federal government 27%

Private 64%

State & local government 9%

SOURCE: Adapted from "Land Use," in *Draft Report on the Environment: Land Use*, U.S. Environmental Protection Agency, May 11, 2007, http://www.epa.gov/indicators/roe/html/roeLandU.htm (accessed July 10, 2007)

Figure 11.2 shows a breakdown of U.S. land usage in 2002 for the contiguous forty-eight states and for all states. Overall, for all states forest use comprised the largest category (29%), followed by grassland, pasture, and range (26%). Table 11.2 provides a detailed breakdown of land use categories in 2002. The split between agricultural and nonagricultural uses was nearly equal, with 51.8% of U.S. land devoted to agricultural purposes, such as crops, livestock grazing, farmsteads, and farm

roads. The remaining 48.2% of the United States had a variety of uses, including recreation, wildlife, forests, national defense, and urban development.

FORESTS

Forests are one of the world's most important natural resources. They not only offer a source of wood but also they perform a wide range of social and ecological functions. They provide a livelihood for forest workers, protect and enrich soils, regulate the hydrologic cycle, affect local and regional climate through evaporation, and help stabilize the global climate. Through the process of photosynthesis, they absorb carbon dioxide and release the oxygen humans and animals breathe. They provide habitat for many plant and animal species, are the main source of wood for industrial and domestic heating, and are widely used for recreation.

Forests play a particularly crucial role in the global cycling of carbon. When trees are cleared, the carbon they contain is oxidized and released into the air, adding to the atmospheric store of carbon dioxide. Many scientists believe that carbon dioxide contributes to global warming. This release happens slowly if the trees are used to manufacture lumber or are allowed to decay naturally. However, if they are burned as fuel or to clear forestland for farming, almost all their carbon is released rapidly.

The Natural Resources Defense Council, a private organization that supports environmental protection, reports in "Forest Facts" (April 27, 2004, http://www.nrdc.org/land/forests/fforestf.asp) that nearly half of the forests on the planet have been decimated. Exacerbating this problem, global wood consumption is set to double by 2050, further stressing the survival of global forests.

FIGURE 11.2

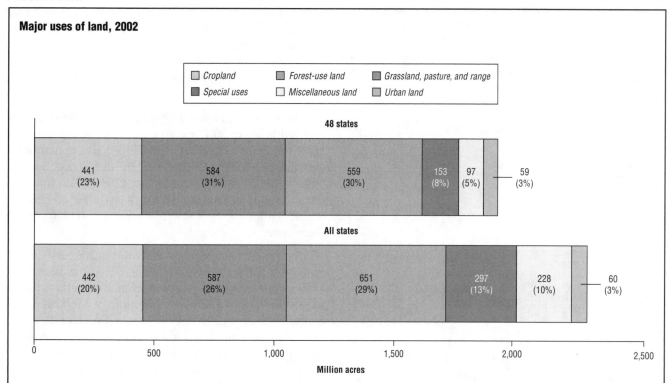

Major uses of land, 2002

☐ Cropland   ■ Forest-use land   ■ Grassland, pasture, and range
■ Special uses   ☐ Miscellaneous land   ■ Urban land

48 states

441 (23%)   584 (31%)   559 (30%)   153 (8%)   97 (5%)   59 (3%)

All states

442 (20%)   587 (26%)   651 (29%)   297 (13%)   228 (10%)   60 (3%)

0   500   1,000   1,500   2,000   2,500
Million acres

Notes: The area of each major land use is listed in millions of acres with the corresponding share of the total land base in parentheses. Urban uses are listed as a separate category and are not included under the special uses category as was done in previous Major Land Uses reports. The land base includes streams and canals less than one-eighth mile wide, and ponds, lakes, and reservoirs covering less than 40 acres. Distributions by major use may not add to totals due to rounding.

SOURCE: Ruben N. Lubowsk et al., "Figure 1. Major Uses of Land, 2002," in *Major Uses of Land in The United States, 2002*, U.S. Department of Agriculture, Economic Research Service, May 2006, http://www.ers.usda.gov/publications/EIB14/eib14.pdf (accessed July 10, 2007)

Tropical Rain Forests

Tropical forests lie in a broad belt centered at the Earth's equator, extending as far north as Mexico and as far south as northern Australia. They cover much of South America, central Africa, and Southeast Asia. In *Global Forest Resource Assessment 2000* (2001, ftp://ftp.fao.org/docrep/fao/003/Y1997E/FRA%202000%20Main%20report.pdf), the Food and Agriculture Organization (FAO) of the United Nations estimates that in 2000 tropical forests accounted for nearly half (47%) of the world's forest coverage of 3.8 billion hectares (9.6 billion acres). Rain forests are a subset of tropical forests that receive a large amount of precipitation. The hot moist conditions are conducive to plant and animal growth. Scientists believe that tropical rain forests are home to thousands and perhaps even millions of different species.

Despite their ecological importance, tropical forests are being cleared for timber production and agricultural development. The FAO notes that approximately 14.2 million hectares (35.1 million acres) of tropical forests were cleared annually during the 1990s. This means that an area nearly the size of Alaska was deforested over that decade.

Rain forests also play an essential role in the weather. They absorb solar energy, which affects wind and rainfall worldwide. Regionally, they reduce erosion and act as buffers against flooding. Tropical trees contain huge amounts of carbon, which, when the trees are destroyed, is released into the atmosphere as carbon dioxide.

Species in tropical rain forests possess a high degree of mutuality, in which two species are completely dependent on one another for survival; for example, a species of wasp and a species of fig tree. Such relationships are believed to evolve as a result of the relatively constant conditions in the tropics. Therefore, any species dependent on trees becomes imperiled when a tree is cut down.

THE AMAZON—AN EXAMPLE. The Amazon rain forests, located in South America, are the most famous of the Earth's tropical forests. They serve as a good example of the controversies surrounding rain forests worldwide. This controversy generally centers on the competing interests of environmentalists, who want to protect the rain forests from further exploitation, and populations in the developing world who want to utilize the forests for fuel and livelihood. Most developing nations claim that these needs are too great to be set aside for the sake of the environment. They also resent the industrialized world's disdain of practices the developed countries once followed themselves in building their own nations. These poorer, developing countries also wonder why they are

TABLE 11.2

Agricultural and non-agricultural uses of land, 2002

Land use	Acreage		Proportion of total	
	48 states	U.S.	48 states	U.S.
	Million acres		Percent	
Agricultural				
Cropland:				
Cropland used for crops[a]	340	340	18.0	15.0
Idle cropland	40	40	2.1	1.8
Cropland used only for pasture	62	62	3.3	2.7
Grass land pasture and range	584	587	30.8	25.9
Forest-use land:				
Forest land grazed	134	134	7.1	5.9
Special uses:				
Farmsteads, farm roads[b]	11	11	0.6	0.5
Total agricultural land[b]	1,171	1,174	61.8	51.8
Nonagricultural				
Forest-use land:				
Forest-use land not grazed[c]	425	517	22.4	22.8
Special uses:				
Transportation uses[d]	27	27	1.4	1.2
Recreation and wildlife areas[e]	100	242	5.3	10.7
National defense areas[f]	15	17	0.8	0.8
Urban land	59	60	3.1	2.6
Miscellaneous other land[g]	97	22 8	5.1	10.1
Total nonagricultural land[b]	723	1,091	38.2	48.2
Total land area[b]	**1,894**	**2,264**	**100.0**	**100.0**

[a]Cropland harvested, crop failure, and cultivated summer fallow.
[b]Breakdown of land uses may not add to totals due to rounding.
[c]Excludes 98 million acres of forest land in parks and other special uses.
[d]Rural highways, roads and railroad rights-of-way, and rural airports.
[e]National and state parks and related recreational areas, national and state wildlife refuges, and national wilderness and primitive areas.
[f]Federal land administered by the Department of Defense for military purposes and land administered by the Department of Energy.
[g]Includes miscellaneous uses not inventoried, and areas of little surface use such as marshes, open swamps, bare rock areas, desert, and tundra.

SOURCE: Ruben N. Lubowski et al., "Table 1. Agricultural and Nonagricultural Uses of Land, United States, 2002," in *Major Uses of Land in The United States, 2002*, U.S. Department of Agriculture, Economic Research Service, May 2006, http://www.ers.usda.gov/publications/EIB14/eib14.pdf (accessed July 10, 2007)

expected to pay for the clean-up of a world that they did not contaminate.

There are also international incentives for continuing to cut down the rain forests. Foreign countries, especially Asian nations, are increasingly eyeing the Amazon forests as a source of ancient trees to make plywood, ornamental moldings, and furniture. Granting logging rights to these nations may seem an appealing option for those South American countries desperate for money.

STATUS OF U.S. FORESTS

Smith and his coauthors note that the United States has 749 million acres of forested lands, comprising roughly one-third of the nation's total land area. (See Figure 11.3.) The forests contain more than eight hundred species of trees. Smith et al. estimate that in 1630 the land that would become the United States contained approximately a billion acres of forests. As shown in Figure 11.4, widespread deforestation occurred during the nineteenth century when forestland was converted to agricultural use. Most of this conversion was completed by the early 1900s. Since that time forest loss has slowed considerably and even been reversed in the northern part of the country. Overall, forestland area increased from 747 million acres to 749 million acres between 1997 and 2002.

As shown in Figure 11.5, almost half (49%) of U.S. forested lands in 2003 were in the hands of private owners with no ties to industry. Another 20% were part of the national forest system overseen by the Forest Service. Other federal agencies controlled 13% of the country's forestlands. Industrial entities (such as timber companies) owned 10% of U.S. forests, whereas the remaining 8% were under state control.

Smith and his collaborators report that approximately seventy-seven million acres of forestland (or 10% of all U.S. forestland) were reserved from commercial timber harvest in 2002. These are forests in wilderness areas, parks, or other legally reserved areas. Smith et al. define timberland as unreserved forestland capable of producing more than twenty cubic feet of timber per acre per year. An estimated 504 million acres of forest was classified as timberland in 2002, mostly located in the East and Pacific Northwest.

Human uses combined with natural environmental stresses (such as disease and drought) pose a constant threat to the health and vitality of the nation's forests.

Stresses on U.S. Forests

In *America's Forests: 2003 Health Update* (May 2003, http://www.fs.fed.us/publications/documents/forest-health-update2003.pdf), a comprehensive assessment on the health and well-being of the nation's forests, the Forest Service notes that there are five key areas of concern:

- Wildfires

- Outbreaks of native insects

- Nonnative invasive insects and pathogens (diseases)

- Invasive plant species

- Ecologically damaging changes in forest type

WILDFIRES. The Forest Service (January 5, 2007, http://www.fs.fed.us/aboutus/meetfs.shtml) manages 155 national forests across the country, covering 193 million acres. Management practices in the past called for the Forest Service to put out all wildfires in the national forests. In recent years scientists have put forward the idea that wildfires are necessary for forest health. They point out that wildfires are natural occurrences that serve to remove flammable undergrowth without greatly damaging larger trees.

Before pioneers settled the West, fires occurred frequently, keeping the forest clear of undergrowth. Fuels seldom accumulated, and the fires were generally of low intensity, consuming undergrowth but not igniting the tops

FIGURE 11.3

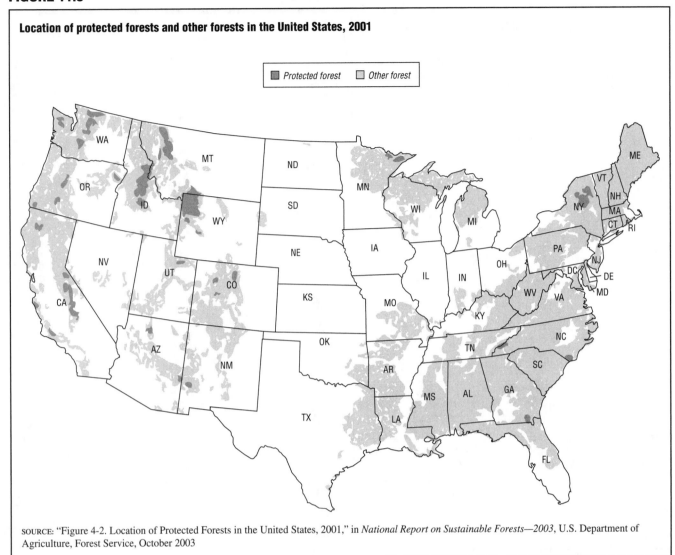

Location of protected forests and other forests in the United States, 2001

■ Protected forest   ☐ Other forest

SOURCE: "Figure 4-2. Location of Protected Forests in the United States, 2001," in *National Report on Sustainable Forests—2003*, U.S. Department of Agriculture, Forest Service, October 2003

of large trees. Disrupting this normal cycle of fire has produced an accumulation of vegetation capable of feeding an increasing number of large, uncontrollable, and catastrophic wildfires. Thus, the number of large wildfires has increased over the past decade, as have the costs of attempting to put them out.

Besides the risk fires pose to nearby inhabitants, smoke from such fires contains substantial amounts of particulate matter that contaminates the air for many hundreds of miles. In addition, forest soils become subject to erosion and mud slides after fires, further threatening the ecosystem and those who live near the forests.

In his statement before the Subcommittee on Forests and Forest Health, *Western National Forests: Catastrophic Wildfires Threaten Resources and Communities* (September 28, 1998, http://www.gao.gov/archive/1998/rc98273t.pdf), Barry T. Hill of the U.S. General Accounting Office (now the U.S. Government Accountability Office) stated that in 1997 the Forest Service began an attempt to improve forest health by reducing, through

controlled burns, the amount of accumulated vegetation, a program to be completed by 2015.

According to annual end-of-year reports compiled by state and federal fire agencies, the summer of 2000 was one of the most devastating fire seasons in fifty years in the United States. More than 92,000 wildland fires burned nearly 7.4 million acres. (See Table 11.3.) Ironically, one of these fires resulted when a controlled burn near Los Alamos, New Mexico, raged out of control, sweeping across hundreds of acres of land and destroying homes and businesses for miles. Following the disastrous 2000 fire season, the Forest Service collaborated with other agencies to develop the National Fire Plan (http://www.forestsand rangelands.gov/), a long-term strategy for more effectively dealing with fire threats and preventing future wildfires.

In 2002 the administration of George W. Bush (1948–) presented its plan for wildfire management in *Healthy Forests: An Initiative for Wildfire Prevention and Stronger Communities* (August 22, 2002, http://www.whitehouse .gov/infocus/healthyforests/Healthy_Forests_v2.pdf). The

FIGURE 11.4

Forest area by major region, 1630–2002

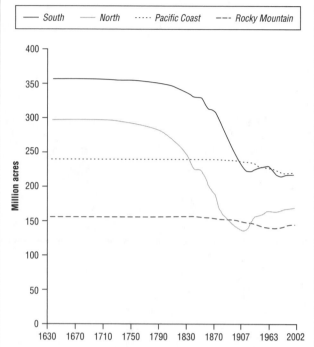

SOURCE: W. Brad Smith, Patrick D. Miles, John S. Vissage, and Scott A. Pugh, "Figure 4. Forest Area of the United States by Major Region, 1630–2002," in *Forest Resources of the United States, 2002*, U.S. Department of Agriculture, U.S. Forest Service, 2005, http://ncrs.fs.fed .us/pubs/gtr/gtr_nc241.pdf (accessed July 11, 2007)

FIGURE 11.5

Ownership of U.S. forests, 2003

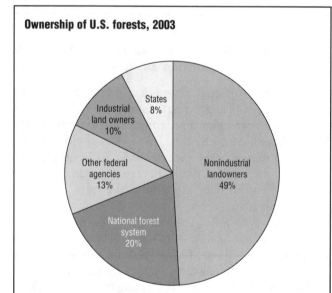

SOURCE: Adapted from data in *America's Forests: 2003 Health Update*, U.S. Department of Agriculture, Forest Service, May 2003, http://www .fs.fed.us/foresthealth/publications/foresthealthupdate2003.pdf (accessed July 27, 2007)

TABLE 11.3

Total wildland fires and acres burned, 1960–2006

Year	Fires	Acres
2006	96,385	9,873,745
2005	66,753	8,689,389
2004	65,461	*8,097,880
2003	63,629	3,960,842
2002	73,457	7,184,712
2001	84,079	3,570,911
2000	92,250	7,393,493
1999	92,487	5,626,093
1998	81,043	2,329,704
1997	66,196	2,856,959
1996	96,363	6,065,998
1995	82,234	1,840,546
1994	79,107	4,073,579
1993	58,810	1,797,574
1992	87,394	2,069,929
1991	75,754	2,953,578
1990	122,763	5,452,874
1989	121,714	3,261,732
1988	154,573	7,398,889
1987	143,877	4,152,575
1986	139,980	3,308,133
1985	133,840	4,434,748
1984	118,636	2,266,134
1983	161,649	5,080,553
1982	174,755	2,382,036
1981	249,370	4,814,206
1980	234,892	5,260,825
1979	163,196	2,986,826
1978	218,842	3,910,913
1977	173,998	3,152,644
1976	241,699	5,109,926
1975	134,872	1,791,327
1974	145,868	2,879,095
1973	117,957	1,915,273
1972	124,554	2,641,166
1971	108,398	4,278,472
1970	121,736	3,278,565
1969	113,351	6,689,081
1968	125,371	4,231,996
1967	125,025	4,658,586
1966	122,500	4,574,389
1965	113,684	2,652,112
1964	116,358	4,197,309
1963	164,183	7,120,768
1962	115,345	4,078,894
1961	98,517	3,036,219
1960	103,387	4,478,188

*2004 fires and acres do not include state lands for North Carolina.

SOURCE: "Total Wildland Fires and Acres (1960–2006)," in *Fire Information—Wildland Fire Statistics*, National Interagency Fire Center, 2007, http://www.nifc.gov/fire_info/fires_acres.htm (accessed July 9, 2007)

Healthy Forests Initiative implements core strategies of the National Fire Plan.

The Forest Service, in *A Collaborative Approach for Reducing Wildland Fire Risks to Communities and the Environment* (December 2006, http://www.forestsandran gelands.gov/plan/documents/10-YearStrategyFinal_Dec 2006.pdf), an update on its progress in implementing the National Fire Plan and Healthy Forests Initiative, lists the following four goals:

• Improve fire prevention and suppression

• Reduce hazardous fuels

- Restore fire-adapted ecosystems and ensure recovery of them after fires

- Promote community assistance

Table 11.3 shows the number of acres burned by wildland fires between 1960 and 2006. Over 9.8 million acres of wildlands burned in 2006, the most of any year on record.

OUTBREAKS OF NATIVE INSECTS. Native insects of concern in U.S. forests include bark beetles and southern pine beetles. Under certain conditions these insects can infest huge areas of forests and kill thousands of trees. This is damaging alone and exaggerates other threats to forests, such as wildfires. Wildfires are more likely to spread quickly and burn hotter when forests contain large amounts of trees that have been weakened or killed by insect damage.

NONNATIVE INVASIVE INSECTS AND PATHOGENS. Another major threat to U.S. forests is the spread of nonnative invasive insects and pathogens. Nonnative (or exotic) species can be harmful because they do not have natural predators in their new environment. This allows them to "invade" their new territory and spread quickly. Species of major concern to forest health include insects, such as gypsy moths, hemlock wooly Adelgids, and emerald ash borers, a fungus called white pine blister rust, and a disease caused by the pathogen *Phytophthora ramorum*.

The Forest Service employs a variety of measures to combat nonnative invasive pests, including the application of insecticides and the release of biological control agents. These agents include insects and pathogens found to prey on the nonnative invasive pests. For example, Carole Cheah et al. report in *Biological Control of Hemlock Woolly Adelgid* (2004, http://www.invasive.org/hwa/) that since 1995 more than one million ladybird beetles have been released into forests infested with hemlock woolly Adelgids. The beetles, which are native to the United States, feed on the Adelgids and their eggs. Experts hope this measure will wipe out nearly all the Adelgid population in the treated forests.

INVASIVE PLANT SPECIES. Insects and pathogens are not the only invaders causing damage to U.S. forests. Certain plants (native and nonnative) become a threat when they grow out of control and overpower regular forest vegetation. Invasive plants of major concern include leafy spurge in northern states (particularly in the West), kudzu in the South, and mile-a-minute weed in the Northeast and mid-Atlantic states.

Even though these plants are most often a problem in rangelands, they are increasingly affecting forests. Invasive plants strangle and smother young seedlings and gobble up resources, such as water and nutrients needed by other plants. They also contribute to the buildup of highly combustible undergrowth, making forests more susceptible to hot-burning wildfires. This is one of the reasons that the

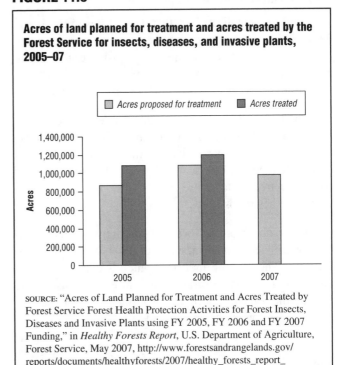

FIGURE 11.6

Acres of land planned for treatment and acres treated by the Forest Service for insects, diseases, and invasive plants, 2005–07

SOURCE: "Acres of Land Planned for Treatment and Acres Treated by Forest Service Forest Health Protection Activities for Forest Insects, Diseases and Invasive Plants using FY 2005, FY 2006 and FY 2007 Funding," in *Healthy Forests Report*, U.S. Department of Agriculture, Forest Service, May 2007, http://www.forestsandrangelands.gov/reports/documents/healthyforests/2007/healthy_forests_report_05142007.pdf (accessed July 9, 2007)

National Fire Plan targets invasive plants for reduction. In addition, there is the Federal Interagency Committee for the Management of Noxious and Exotic Weeds. This is a collaboration of seventeen agencies working to develop control techniques for invasive plants across the country. The Forest Service is working on a variety of measures, primarily biological agents (such as insects or fungi known to attack invasive plants).

Figure 11.6 shows the breakdown by acreage of the pests and diseases targeted for treatment by the Forest Service during fiscal years 2005, 2006, and 2007 and the acres treated in fiscal years 2005 and 2006.

ECOLOGICALLY DAMAGING CHANGES IN FOREST TYPE. U.S. forests have been changed over the years by many human and natural factors. This has led to ecological changes in entire forest types. For example, before the 1900s the forests of the Appalachian Mountains were dominated by the American chestnut. A fungus introduced from Europe virtually wiped out the chestnut population by the 1950s. Other species of trees soon became predominant. In the twenty-first century scientists consider this type of forest change to be harmful from an ecological standpoint. Major changes in forest type have profound effects on the overall health of a forest, wildlife habitat, and even soil conditions. The Forest Service worries that a combination of stressors, including fire, drought, destructive pests, and human activities, pose major dangers to forests. Human activities that can negatively affect forests include agriculture and residential development.

Timber Harvesting and Replanting

Environmentalists fear that U.S. forests are being depleted by clear-cutting practices—a method of logging in which all the trees in an area are cut—rather than being maintained by selective management techniques, in which only certain trees are removed from an area.

The lumber industry continually battles with environmentalists and the Forest Service over the right to clear-cut ancient forests, particularly in the Northwest. Experts believe that North American old growth forests (stands of old, large trees) may store more carbon than any of the world's other repositories.

Many observers believe that the biggest threat from this logging technique is the loss of diversity of species in the area. The logging industry contends that restrictions on logging devastate rural communities by causing the loss of thousands of jobs and leading to an increase in retail prices for lumber nationwide.

Logging roads are increasingly blamed for contributing to landslides, floods, and changes in rivers and streams. The Roadless Area Conservation Rule was adopted in January 2001 to protect nearly sixty million acres of national forests from further road building and logging, while keeping them open for recreational uses. The rule had both environmental and economic goals. In *Summary of Public Comment: Roadless Area Conservation Proposed Rule and DEIS 2000* (October 6, 2000, http://roadless.fs.fed.us/documents/csumm/summary .pdf), the Forest Service reports that it oversees 386,000 miles of roads and that their upkeep costs billions of dollars. The high cost of building and maintaining these roads is often cited as a reason many national forests lose money on timber sales.

In an effort to counteract tree loss, forests are often replanted or replaced. Most experts contend that when a natural forest is clear-cut and replanted with commercially valuable trees, the plot becomes a tree farm, not a forest, and the biological interaction is damaged. Primary forests represent centuries, perhaps a millennium, of undisturbed growth. Trees will rebound after clear-cutting within 70 to 150 years but, researchers find, the plants and herbs of the understory (growth under the canopy of the trees) never regain the richness of species diversity and complexity of their predecessors.

The Effects of Pollution

Many biologists believe that regional air pollution is a serious anthropogenic (human-made) threat to temperate forest ecosystems. The most dangerous impact on forests comes from ozone, heavy metals, and acid deposition. The effects of air pollution on forests and trees are discussed in detail in Chapter 2.

WETLANDS—FRAGILE ECOSYSTEMS

Marshes, swamps, bogs, estuaries, and bottomlands are specific biosystems with sometimes distinctive characteristics; however, they are commonly grouped together under the term *wetlands*. Wetlands are always or often saturated by enough surface or groundwater to sustain vegetation that is typically adapted to saturated soil conditions, such as cattails, bulrushes, red maples, wild rice, blackberries, cranberries, and peat moss. The Florida Everglades and the coastal Alaskan salt marshes are examples of wetlands, as are the sphagnum-heath bogs of Maine. Because some varieties of wetlands are rich in minerals and nutrients and provide many of the advantages of both land and water environments, they are often dynamic systems that teem with a diversity of species, including many insects—a basic link in the food chain.

Once regarded as useless swamps, good only for breeding mosquitoes and taking up otherwise valuable space, wetlands have become the subject of increasingly heated debate. Many people want to use them for commercial purposes such as agricultural and residential development. Others want them left in their natural state because they believe that wetlands and their inhabitants are indispensable parts of the natural cycle of life on Earth.

Wetland Types

There are several distinct forms of wetlands, each with its own unique characteristics. The main factors that distinguish each type of wetland are location (coastal or inland), source of water (precipitation, rivers and streams, groundwater), salinity (freshwater or salt water), and the dominant type of vegetation (peat mosses, soft-stemmed, or woody plants). Wetlands are a continuum in which plant life changes gradually from predominantly aquatic to predominantly upland species. The difficulty in defining the exact point at which a wetland ends and upland begins results in much of the confusion as to how wetlands should be regulated.

The Many Roles of Wetlands

Productive wetlands are rich ecosystems that support diverse forms of plant and wildlife. They provide food and habitat for many animals and breeding and nesting areas for aquatic life. They also serve as way stations for migrating birds. Wetlands can temporarily or permanently trap pollutants such as excess nutrients, toxic chemicals, suspended materials, and disease-causing microorganisms—thus cleansing the water that flows over and through them. Some pollutants that become trapped in wetlands are biochemically converted to less harmful forms; other pollutants remain buried there; still others are absorbed by wetland plants and are either recycled through the wetland or carried away from it. (See Figure 11.7.) Wetlands support commercial fishing

FIGURE 11.7

Wetlands' contribution to improving water quality and reducing storm water runoff

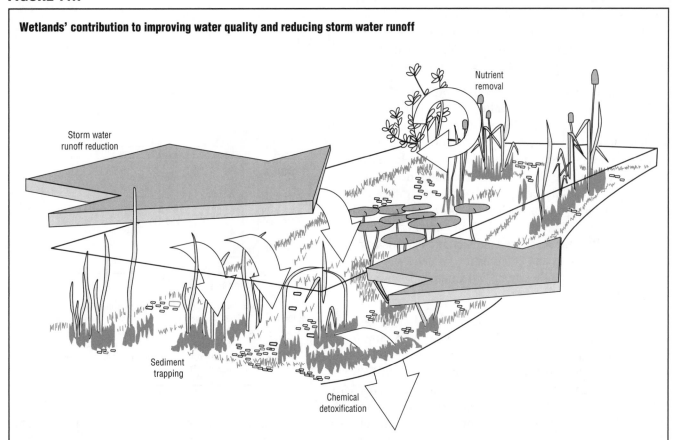

SOURCE: "Figure 5. Wetlands' Contribution to Improving Water Quality and Reducing Storm Water Runoff," in *Federal Incentives Could Help Promote Land Use That Protects Air and Water Quality*, GAO-02-12, U.S. General Accounting Office, October 2001, http://www.gao.gov/new.items/d0212.pdf (accessed July 27, 2007)

and are useful for floodwater reduction, shoreline stabilization, and recreational activities.

Wetlands Regulation

Wetlands use is affected by two major pieces of federal legislation: the Clean Water Act (CWA) and the Rivers and Harbors Appropriation Act (RHA) of 1899. Regulations carrying out the intent of these acts are promulgated by the EPA and the U.S. Army Corps of Engineers.

Sections of the CWA regulate activities that affect wetlands, particularly discharges to them of dredged or fill material. These discharges are subject to the requirements of Sections 401 and 404 of the CWA. They are also regulated under many state regulations. The RHA regulates activities that could obstruct navigation of the country's waterways. For example, the building of dams, bridges, wharves, and piers is regulated, as are excavation and fill activities. The creation of any obstruction requires the approval of the Army Corps of Engineers. The restrictions of the RHA apply only to wetlands that are navigable. The federal government defines navigable as a body of water that is subject to tides and/or has

been, is, or could likely be used to transport interstate or foreign commerce.

There are other federal laws and programs designed to protect wetlands through the use of incentives (such as grants) or disincentives (denial of federal funding for certain projects that affect wetlands). In addition, wetlands are regulated by a host of state and local agencies. Overall, there is no one federal program that oversees all aspects of wetland protection. Furthermore, the existing federal legislation regulates the filling of wetlands, but not other activities that could damage them. Critics complain that these policies do not provide adequate protection for wetlands. However, many private landowners, farmers, and developers believe that existing legislation is too restrictive.

Status of the Nation's Wetlands

The USFWS has been monitoring trends in the extent of the nation's wetlands since the 1950s. At that time centuries of development had resulted in massive losses in wetlands acreage to agriculture, mining, forestry, oil and gas extraction, and urbanization. Some loss also resulted from natural causes such as erosion, sedimentation (the buildup of soil by the settling of fine particles over a long period), subsidence (the sinking of land because of diminishing underground water supplies), and a rise in the sea level. However, experts estimate that the vast majority of the wetland conversions were for agricultural purposes.

During the late 1980s President George H. W. Bush (1924–) set a national goal for eliminating wetland losses in the short term and achieving net gains in wetlands over the long term. The concept is called no-net-loss. Land developers were encouraged to offset wetland losses by developing or buying shares in wetland mitigation banks. For example, a utility company that wanted to destroy wetlands in one location to build a power plant could develop a larger acreage of wetlands in another suitable location to offset the loss. Wetland banking became popular during the 1990s and 2000s as the no-net-loss policy was endorsed by both Presidents Bill Clinton (1946–) and George W. Bush.

In *Status and Trends of Wetlands in the Conterminous United States 1998 to 2004* (December 2005, http://wetlandsfws.er.usgs.gov/status_trends/national_reports/trends_2005_report.pdf), Thomas E. Dahl of the USFWS indicates that in 2004 there were an estimated 107.7 million acres of wetlands in the conterminous United States (the lower forty-eight states). Approximately 95% of these acres were freshwater wetlands. The remaining 5% were estuarine or marine (sea) systems. Overall, wetlands comprised 5.5% of the total land surface of the conterminous United States.

Figure 11.8 illustrates the enormous losses in wetland acreage that occurred between the 1950s and the 1990s. From the 1950s through the 1970s, 458,000 acres were lost annually. Losses slowed over the following two decades, and in 2004—for the first time—the USFWS measured a gain in wetland acreage. Wetland extent increased on average by thirty-two thousand acres per year between 1998 and 2004. Nearly 192,000 acres of wetlands were gained over this time period because of restoration and creation efforts. Dahl notes that this is a net gain obtained by summing all losses and gains. Nearly all the gained wetlands were the freshwater type, particularly in forested areas. The extent of intertidal wetlands (i.e., coastal wetlands influenced by tides) actually declined during this same period. Most were lost to the open ocean.

SOILS

The nation's soils are another major natural resource. Good soil conditions are crucial for healthy ecosystems and productive agriculture. Soil abundance and health are affected by many factors, both natural and anthropogenic. Major examples include pollution and erosion. The effects on soil of acid rain, water pollution, toxic releases,

FIGURE 11.8

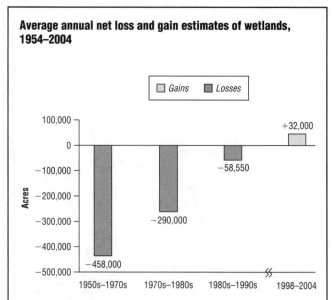

Average annual net loss and gain estimates of wetlands, 1954–2004

SOURCE: Thomas E. Dahl, "Figure 26. Average Annual Net Loss and Gain Estimates for the Conterminous United States, 1954 to 2004," in *Status and Trends of Wetlands in the Conterminous United States 1998 to 2004*, U.S. Fish and Wildlife Service, December 2005, http://wetlandsfws.er.usgs.gov/status_trends/national_reports/trends_2005_report.pdf (accessed July 11, 2007)

and waste disposal have already been addressed. This section focuses on the effects of erosion.

Erosion

Erosion is the process in which the materials of the Earth's crust are worn and carried away by wind, water, and other natural forces. The destruction of forests and native grasses has allowed water and wind greater opportunity to erode the soil. Changes in river flow and seepage from human technology have shifted the runoff patterns of water and the sediment load of rivers that, in turn, deposit into lakes and oceans. Erosion has become a problem in much of the world in areas that are over-farmed or where topsoil cannot be protected, such as on coasts, which are often overdeveloped.

Soil Erosion and Agriculture

Agricultural lands are the principal source of eroded soil. Agriculture depends primarily on the top six to eight inches of topsoil. Fields planted in rows, such as corn, are most susceptible to soil runoff. In 2002 corn comprised 22% of total acres used for crops in the United States. (See Figure 11.9.) Cover crops, such as hay, provide more soil cover to hold the land. Hay crops accounted for 17% of total acres used for crops in 2002.

As shown in Figure 11.10, the amount of erosion occurring nationally on cropland in the conterminous United States has declined in recent years. In 1982 more than three billion tons of soil were lost to erosion both from water runoff (sheet and rill erosion) and wind. The

FIGURE 11.9

Farm acres by crop, 2002

Other vegetables
2%

Cotton
4%

Fruits & nuts
1%

Corn
22%

Hops
8%

Other field
crops
10%

Soybeans
20%

Wheat
16%

Hay
17%

SOURCE: Adapted from "Field Crops: Acreage, Yield, Production, Price, and Value," "Fresh Vegetables: Acreage, Yield, Production, Price, and Value," "Fruits and Nuts: Noncitrus Fruit Acreage, Utilized Production, Price, and Value," "Fruits and Nuts: Citrus Fruit Acreage, Utilized Production, Price, and Value," and "Fruits and Nuts: Nut Acreage, Utilized Production, Price, and Value," in *Statistical Highlights of United States Agriculture, 2002/2003*, U.S. Department of Agriculture, National Agricultural Statistics Service, June 2003, http://www.usda.gov/nass/pubs/stathigh/2003/stathi03.pdf (accessed July 27, 2007)

FIGURE 11.10

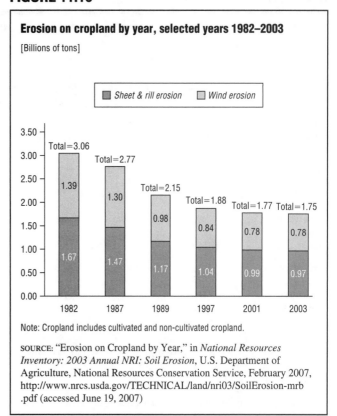

Erosion on cropland by year, selected years 1982–2003

[Billions of tons]

Note: Cropland includes cultivated and non-cultivated cropland.

SOURCE: "Erosion on Cropland by Year," in *National Resources Inventory: 2003 Annual NRI: Soil Erosion*, U.S. Department of Agriculture, National Resources Conservation Service, February 2007, http://www.nrcs.usda.gov/TECHNICAL/land/nri03/SoilErosion-mrb.pdf (accessed June 19, 2007)

USDA attributes the decline to the Federal Conservation Reserve Program, which pays farmers to take land out of production for ten years, and to the Conservation Compliance Program. As part of the 1985 Farm Act, the Conservation Compliance Program was initiated as a major policy tool. To be eligible for agricultural program benefits, farmers must meet minimum levels of conservation on highly erodible land.

Historically, when most of the topsoil was lost, farmers would abandon the land. Now, however, farmers continue to plow the soil, even when it consists of as much subsoil as topsoil. It costs more money to raise crops on such land than on land where topsoil is present. Farmers often use more fertilizer to make up for the decreasing productivity of the soil, and that, in turn, adds to environmental pollution.

COASTAL EROSION. In *Evaluation of Erosion Hazards* (April 2000, http://www.heinzctr.org/NEW_WEB/PDF/erosnrpt.pdf#pagemode=bookmarks&view=Fit), the H. John Heinz III Center for Science, Economics, and the Environment, a nonprofit research organization, finds that approximately 25% of structures within five hundred feet of the U.S. coastline will suffer the effects of coastal erosion within sixty years.

The nation's highest average erosion rates—up to six feet or more per year—occur along the Gulf of Mexico.

The average erosion rate on the Atlantic coast is two to three feet per year. A major storm can erode one hundred feet of coastline in a day. The Heinz Center estimates that roughly ten thousand structures are within the estimated ten-year erosion zone closest to the shore. This does not include structures in the densest areas of large coastal cities, such as New York, Chicago, Los Angeles, and Miami, which are heavily protected against erosion.

Erosion of beaches on the East Coast is becoming a more serious problem as development inches closer to the ocean. The Army Corps of Engineers has been rebuilding eroded beaches since the 1950s. Many experts, however, believe that beach replenishment is a futile effort and that funds could be better spent elsewhere.

BIODIVERSITY

Biological diversity, or biodiversity, refers to the full range of plant, animal, and microbial life and the ecosystems that house them. Environmentalists began using this term during the 1980s, when biologists increasingly warned that human activities were causing a loss of plant and animal species.

No one knows how many species of plants and animals exist in the world. By the beginning of the twenty-first century scientists had named and documented more than one million species. Educated guesses of the total number of different species range from five million to

TABLE 11.4

Number of threatened and endangered species, U.S. and foreign, as of July 20, 2007

Group	United States			Foreign			Total listings (US and foreign)	Listings with recovery plans*
	Endangered	Threatened	Total listings	Endangered	Threatened	Total listings		
Mammals	69	12	81	256	20	276	357	54
Birds	75	14	89	176	6	182	271	79
Reptiles	13	24	37	65	16	81	118	35
Amphibians	13	10	23	8	1	9	32	17
Fishes	74	65	139	11	1	12	151	98
Clams	62	8	70	2	0	2	72	69
Snails	65	11	76	1	0	1	77	29
Insects	47	10	57	4	0	4	61	33
Arachnids	12	0	12	0	0	0	12	6
Crustaceans	19	3	22	0	0	0	22	18
Animal subtotal	**449**	**157**	**606**	**523**	**44**	**567**	**1173**	**438**
Corals	0	2	2	0	0	0	2	0
Flowering plants	570	143	713	1	0	1	714	607
Conifers and cycads	2	1	3	0	2	2	5	3
Ferns and allies	24	2	26	0	0	0	26	26
Lichens	2	0	2	0	0	0	2	2
Plant subtotal	**598**	**148**	**746**	**1**	**2**	**3**	**749**	**638**
Grand total	**1047**	**305**	**1352**	**524**	**46**	**570**	**1922**	**1076**

Notes: 32 animal species (16 in the U.S. and 16 foreign) are counted more than once in the above table, primarily because these animals have distinct population segments (each with its own individual listing status).
There are a total of 551 distinct approved recovery plans. Some recovery plans cover more than one species, and a few species have separate plans covering different parts of their ranges. This count includes only plans generated by the United States Fish and Wildlife Service (USFWS) (or jointly by the USFWS and National Marine Fisheries Service), and only listed species that occur in the United States.
*This column includes only U.S. listings.

SOURCE: Adapted from "Summary of Listed Species: Listed Populations and Recovery Plans as of 07/20/2007," in *Threatened and Endangered Species System (TESS)*, U.S. Fish and Wildlife Service, July 20, 2007, http://ecos.fws.gov/tess_public/Boxscore.do (accessed July 20, 2007)

one hundred million. Just as the health of a nation is promoted by a diverse economy, the health of the biosphere is promoted by a diverse ecology.

The loss of diversity leads to problems beyond the simple loss of animal and plant variety. When local populations of species are wiped out, the genetic diversity within that species that enables it to adapt to environmental change is diminished, resulting in a situation of biotic impoverishment. Those organisms that do survive are likely to be hardy, opportunistic organisms that tolerate a wide variety of conditions—characteristics often associated with pests. Experts suggest that, as some species dwindle, their places may be taken by a disproportionate number of pest or weed species that, whereas a natural part of life, will be less beneficial to human beings.

The loss of habitats, the contamination of water and food supplies, poaching, and indiscriminate hunting and fishing have depleted the population of many species. Most scientists agree that prospects for the survival of many species of wildlife, and hence biodiversity, are worsening.

Endangered Species Act

The 1973 Endangered Species Act (ESA), passed into law during the administration of President Richard Nixon (1913–1994), was originally intended to protect creatures such as grizzly bears and whales with whose plight Ameri-

cans found it easy to identify. In the words of its critics, however, it has become the "pit bull of environmental laws," policing the behavior of entire industries. In three decades the ESA has gone from being one of the least controversial laws passed by Congress, to one of the most contentious.

The ESA regulates industries that can cause fish and wildlife populations to decline. It also determines the criteria to decide which species are endangered. Since the act was first passed, the pendulum has periodically swung between increased protection and the need to soften the law's economic impact.

There were 1,352 species in the United States listed as endangered or threatened as of July 2007. (See Table 11.4.) Another 570 species were listed for foreign countries. The number of endangered or threatened species listed in the United States has increased dramatically since 1980, when 223 species were listed.

Species Loss—Crisis or False Alarm?

As with most environmental questions, not all experts agree about the threat to species diversity. Some observers believe that extensive damage to species diversity has not been proven and claim that, even though wild habitats are disappearing because of human expansion, the seriousness of extinction has been exaggerated and is not supported by scientific evidence. They point to the fact that the total number of species and their geographic distribution are unknown. How, they ask, can forecasts be made based on such sketchy data?

Other observers contend that extinctions, even mass ones, are inevitable and occur as a result of great geological and astronomical events that humans cannot affect. They do not believe that disruptions caused by human activity are enough to create the mega-extinction prophesied by people they consider "alarmists."

Furthermore, some critics of the environmental movement believe that the needs of humans are being made secondary to those of wildlife. They contend that the ESA protects wildlife regardless of the economic cost to human beings.

Environmentalists have long argued with government and industry over the question of logging in the Pacific Northwest. Environmentalists claim that the biological health of the ecosystem is in decline and that more than one hundred species of plants and animals are threatened with extinction, whereas the timber industry responds that the forest provides jobs for thousands of Americans and lumber for millions of people.

The argument came to a head in 1990, when the spotted owl—which lived only in this particular region—was added to the list of endangered species. The owl's presence halted logging there—following protests by environmental groups—at considerable economic loss to communities and families in the area. A succession of lawsuits was filed against the Forest Service and the U.S. Department of the Interior. In 1992 President Bush grudgingly restricted logging in that area but, at the same time, moved to amend the law to allow economic considerations to be taken into account. In 1994 President Clinton worked out what was claimed to be a compromise between environmentalists and business interests, allowing logging to resume with restrictions on the size, number, and distribution of trees to be cut.

Critics contend that halting development because it threatens a species whose whole population occupies only a few acres and numbers only in the hundreds is simply nonsense.

Earth Summit Biodiversity Treaty

At the 1992 Earth Summit in Rio de Janeiro, Brazil, 156 nations signed a pact to conserve species, habitats, and ecosystems. This Biodiversity Treaty is regarded as one of two main achievements of the United Nations Conference on Environment and Development, the other being a treaty on global warming. The Biodiversity Treaty makes nations responsible for any environmental harm in other countries produced by companies headquartered in their country.

One provision of the treaty concerns biotechnology, a term referring to the ownership of genetic material. Plants, seeds, and germplasm have historically been in the public

domain (belonging to the general public), rather than belonging to any particular government. Therefore, anyone could exploit or use them without compensation to the country of origin. For example, the rosy or Madagascar periwinkle, a plant found only in the tropical rain forests of Madagascar, is used as a base for medication to treat Hodgkin's disease and childhood leukemia. Madagascar receives no compensation for use of the plant. The biotechnology treaty drafted in Rio called for compensation to be paid for the use of these genetic materials.

The United States did not sign the treaty at the time. The Bush administration, while agreeing with many provisions of the pact, believed the economic requirements for accomplishing these goals were unacceptable to U.S. businesses, because they would be forced to compensate for the use of these species. President Clinton signed the treaty in 1993. However, as of September 2007 the treaty had not been ratified by the U.S. Senate.

Invasive Species

An invasive species is one that is not native to a particular ecosystem and whose presence there causes environmental or economic harm or harm to human health. This includes species purposely introduced (such as the plant salt cedar, which was brought to the United States to control erosion) and unintentionally introduced (such as zebra mussels, which are thought to have arrived in the ballast water of ships). Invasive species often have high reproductive rates and lack predators in their new environments. They can choke out or outcompete native species.

Many scientists consider invasive species to be one of the most serious issues threatening the environment. In response to this threat, the National Invasive Species Council was established by the U.S. government in 1997. The council includes members from a variety of agencies including the EPA, the USDA, and the Department of the Interior. In 2001 the council issued its management plan for dealing with the invasive species problem in *Meeting the Invasive Species Challenge* (January 18, 2001, http://wric.ucdavis.edu/yst/legislation/national_management_plan.pdf).

The council states that invasive plants infest approximately one hundred million acres in the United States and cost around $137 billion annually for prevention and control. Zebra mussels are one invasive species that has spread rapidly. Figure 11.11 illustrates known occurrences of zebra mussels as of June 2005 and locations where the species has traveled overland on boat hulls. Originally limited to the Great Lakes area, invasive zebra mussels have now traveled all the way to the Gulf Coast. They are considered so permanently entrenched that wholesale eradication would be virtually impossible. Instead, authorities are concentrating on limiting the further spread of this pest, which clogs water intake pipes.

FIGURE 11.11

Distribution of zebra mussels, June 2005

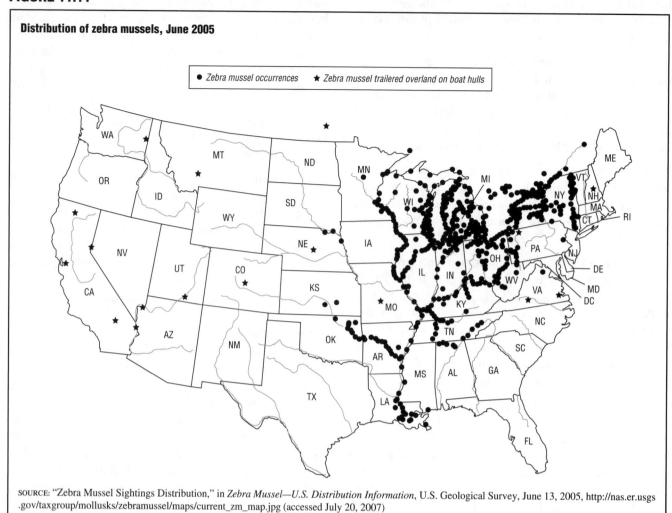

SOURCE: "Zebra Mussel Sightings Distribution," in *Zebra Mussel—U.S. Distribution Information*, U.S. Geological Survey, June 13, 2005, http://nas.er.usgs .gov/taxgroup/mollusks/zebramussel/maps/current_zm_map.jpg (accessed July 20, 2007)

In addition, authorities are increasingly concerned about the West Nile virus, an invasive pathogen that is thought to have originated in Africa. The virus was first detected in the United States in 1999 in New York. It infected animals and birds throughout the East and spread west quickly, carried by migratory birds. The virus can be transmitted to humans by mosquitoes that have bitten infected animals and birds.

In 1999 there were sixty-two human cases reported to the Centers for Disease Control and Prevention (CDC; September 11, 2007, http://www.cdc.gov/ncidod/dvbid/ westnile/), and seven people died from the virus. The number of cases and fatalities grew quickly until 2003, when 9,862 cases resulted in 264 deaths. Since then, case numbers have been down dramatically. In 2006 there were 4,269 cases reported to the CDC and 177 deaths. Figure 11.12 shows the distribution of cases by state as of July 2007.

Deep-Sea Harvesting

Worldwide, after centuries of steady growth, the total catch of wild fish peaked in the early 1990s and has declined ever since. In *State of World Fisheries and Aquaculture, 2006* (2007, ftp://ftp.fao.org/docrep/fao/009/a0699e/a0699e .pdf), the FAO reports that in 2005, 52% of all commercial fish stocks had been fully exploited. A further 25% of stocks were reported to be overexploited.

A result of the declining catches of fish in shallow fisheries is the recent scouring of the deep seas for other varieties of fish, such as the nine-inch-long royal red shrimp, rattails, skates, squid, red crabs, orange roughy, oreos, hoki, blue ling, southern blue whiting, and spiny dogfish. Even though limited commercial fishing of the deep has been practiced for decades, new sciences and technologies are making it more practical and efficient. As stocks of better-known fish shrink and international quotas tighten, experts say the deep ocean waters will increasingly be targeted as a source of seafood. Scientists worry that the rush for deep-sea food will upset the ecology of the ocean.

MINERALS AND OIL

Materials extracted from the Earth are needed to provide humans with food, clothing, and housing and to

FIGURE 11.12

Cases of West Nile Virus reported to CDC as of July 2007

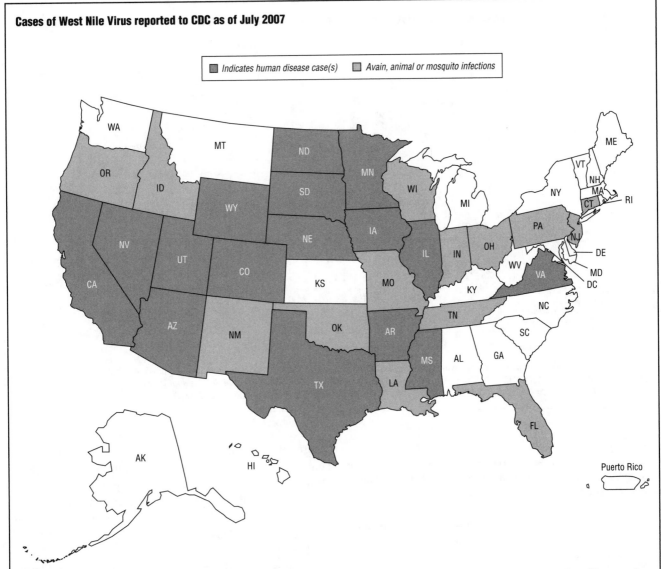

■ Indicates human disease case(s)   ■ Avain, animal or mosquito infections

SOURCE: "2007 West Nile Virus Activity in the United States (Reported to CDC as of July 17, 2007)," in *West Nile Virus: Statistics, Surveillance, and Control*, U.S. Department of Health and Human Services, Centers for Disease Control and Prevention, July 17, 2007, http://www.cdc.gov/ncidod/dvbid/ westnile/Mapsactivity/surv&control07Maps.htm (accessed July 20, 2007)

continually upgrade their standard of living. Some of the materials needed are renewable resources, such as agricultural and forestry products, whereas others are non-renewable, such as minerals and fossil fuels.

In "Mining Industry of the Future" (May 1, 2007, http://www1.eere.energy.gov/industry/mining/), the Industrial Technologies Program reports that nearly forty-seven thousand pounds of materials are mined each year for each person in the United States.

The Clean Air Act, the CWA, and the Resource Conservation and Recovery Act of 1976 regulate certain aspects of mining but, in general, the states are primarily responsible for regulation, which varies widely from state to state.

Oil in the Arctic

The search for oil has led to the exploration of the Alaskan wilderness. Because the oil supply from the existing North Slope Reserve will steadily decline and then eventually disappear, exploratory oil drillers are focusing their attention on the National Petroleum Reserve in Alaska (NPRA) in the Arctic wilderness. The USGS notes in *U.S. Geological Survey 2002 Petroleum Resource Assessment of the National Petroleum Reserve in Alaska (NPRA)* (2002, http://pubs.usgs.gov/ fs/2002/fs045-02/figure1.html) that the NPRA comprises twenty-three million acres in northwestern Alaska. (See Figure 11.13.) Geologists consider northern Alaska to be the last great untapped oil field in North America.

FIGURE 11.13

Northern Alaska, showing locations and relative sizes of the National Petroleum Reserve in Alaska (NPRA) and the Arctic National Wildlife Refuge (ANWR)

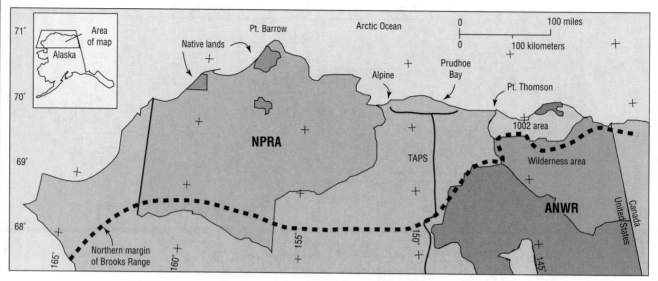

TAPS = Trans-Alaska Pipeline System

SOURCE: "Figure 1. Map of Northern Alaska Showing Locations and Relative Sizes of the National Petroleum Reserve in Alaska (NPRA) and the Arctic National Wildlife Refuge (ANWR)," in *U.S. Geological Survey 2002 Petroleum Resource Assessment of the National Petroleum Reserve in Alaska (NPRA)*, U.S. Department of the Interior, 2002, http://pubs.usgs.gov/fs/2002/fs045-02/figure1.html (accessed July 27, 2007)

TABLE 11.5

Public opinion on opening up the Arctic National Wildlife Refuge for oil exploration, selected years 2001–07

	Favor	Oppose	No opinion
	%	%	%
2007 Mar 11–14	41	57	2
2006 Mar 13–16	49	47	4
2003 Mar 3–5	41	55	4
2002 Mar 4–7	40	56	4
2001 Nov 8–11	44	51	5
2001 May 7–9	38	57	5
2001 Mar 5–7	40	56	4

SOURCE: "Next I am going to read some specific environmental proposals. For each one, please say whether you generally favor or oppose it. How about opening up the Arctic National Wildlife Refuge in Alaska for oil exploration?" in *Environment*, The Gallup Organization, 2007, http://www.galluppoll.com/content/?ci=1615&pg=1 (accessed June 19, 2007). Copyright © 2007 by The Gallup Organization. Reproduced by permission of The Gallup Organization.

Environmental experts fear that oil and gas development will seriously harm the area.

In 2002 the USGS assessed the NPRA and found a significantly greater supply of petroleum (5.9 billion to 13.2 billion barrels) than previously estimated. However, only up to 5.6 billion barrels of this petroleum are technically and economically recoverable at existing market prices. Furthermore, the USGS suspects that there may be as much as 83.2 trillion cubic feet of undiscovered natural gas in the same area. Transportation of this gas to markets would require a new pipeline. There is already a pipeline system in place for oil—the Trans-Alaska Pipeline System (TAPS), which lies between the NPRA and the Arctic National Wildlife Refuge (ANWR), as shown in Figure 11.13. The ANWR is a nineteen-million-acre area of pristine wilderness along the Alaskan-Canadian border. It, too, is being considered for oil exploration, a move strongly opposed by environmentalists.

The future of the refuge lies in the hands of the federal government. Under the Clinton administration, oil and mineral development was prohibited within the wildlife refuge. In 2002, following heated debate, the Senate killed a proposal by the Bush administration to allow oil companies to drill in ANWR. The proposal was raised again in subsequent years, particularly 2005, but defeated. As of September 2007, federal legislation had not been passed that would allow drilling in ANWR.

Public opinion on this issue has been gauged occasionally by the Gallup Organization. Table 11.5 illustrates that in the most recent poll conducted in March 2007 a majority (57%) of those asked were opposed to opening up ANWR for oil exploration, whereas 41% were in favor. These values have changed little since the question was first asked in 2001.

IMPORTANT NAMES
AND ADDRESSES

**American Association of Poison Control
Centers**
3201 New Mexico Ave., Ste. 330
Washington, DC 20016
(202) 362-7217
FAX: (202) 362-3240
E-mail: info@aapcc.org
URL: http://www.aapcc.org/

American Lung Association
61 Broadway, Sixth Fl.
New York, NY 10006
(212) 315-8700
1-800-LUNGUSA
URL: http://www.lungusa.org/

Bureau of Land Management
1849 C St., Rm. 406-LS
Washington, DC 20240
(202) 452-5125
FAX: (202) 452-5124
E-mail: woinfo@blm.gov
URL: http://www.blm.gov/

**Centers for Disease Control
and Prevention**
1600 Clifton Rd.
Atlanta, GA 30333
(404) 639-3311
1-800-311-3435
URL: http://www.cdc.gov/

Council on Environmental Quality
722 Jackson Place NW
Washington, DC 20503
(202) 395-5750
FAX: (202) 456-6546
URL: http://www.whitehouse.gov/ceq/

**Environmental Business
International Inc.**
4452 Park Blvd., Ste. 306
San Diego, CA 92116
(619) 295-7685
FAX: (619) 295-5743
URL: http://www.ebiusa.com/

Environmental Defense Fund
257 Park Ave. South
New York, NY 10010
(212) 505-2100
FAX: (212) 505-2375
E-mail: members@environmentaldefense.org
URL: http://www.environmentaldefense.org/
home.cfm

Environmental Industry Associations
4301 Connecticut Ave. NW, Ste. 300
Washington, DC 20008-2304
(202) 244-4700
FAX: (202) 966-4818
E-mail: membership@envasns.org
URL: http://www.envasns.org/

Greenpeace
702 H St. NW
Washington, DC 20001
(202) 462-1177
1-800-326-0959
E-mail: info@wdc.greenpeace.org
URL: http://www.greenpeaceusa.org/

**H. John Heinz III Center for
Science, Economics, and the
Environment**
900 Seventeenth St. NW, Ste. 700
Washington, DC 20006
(202) 737-6307
FAX: (202) 737-6410
URL: http://www.heinzctr.org/index.shtml

Idaho National Laboratory
2525 N. Fremont Ave.
Idaho Falls, ID 83415
(208) 526-0111
1-866-495-7440
URL: http://www.inl.gov/

**National Aeronautics and Space
Administration**
Goddard Space Flight Center
Office of Public Affairs, Mail Code 130
Greenbelt, MD 20771

(301) 286-2000
URL: http://www.gsfc.nasa.gov/

**National Atmospheric Deposition
Program, Illinois State Water Survey**
2204 Griffith Dr.
Champaign, IL 61820-7495
URL: http://nadp.sws.uiuc.edu/

National Audubon Society
700 Broadway
New York, NY 10003
(212) 979-3000
FAX: (212) 979-3188
URL: http://www.audubon.org/

**National Environmental Education
Foundation**
4301 Connecticut Ave. NW, Ste. 160
Washington, DC 20008
(202) 833-2933
FAX: (202) 261-6464
URL: http://www.neefusa.org/index.htm

National Interagency Fire Center
3833 S. Development Ave.
Boise, ID 83705
(208) 387-5512
URL: http://www.nifc.gov/

**National Oceanic and Atmospheric
Administration**
Fourteenth St. and Constitution Ave. NW,
Rm. 6217
Washington, DC 20230
(202) 482-6090
FAX: (202) 482-3154
E-mail: answers@noaa.gov
URL: http://www.noaa.gov/

National Safety Council
1121 Spring Lake Dr.
Itasca, IL 60143-3201
(630) 285-1121
FAX: (630) 285-1315

E-mail: info@nsc.org
URL: http://www.nsc.org/

National Weather Service Climate Prediction Center
5200 Auth Rd.
Camp Springs, MD 20746
(301) 763-8000
E-mail: Carmeyia.Gillis@noaa.gov
URL: http://www.cpc.noaa.gov/

National Wildlife Federation
11100 Wildlife Center Dr.
Reston, VA 20190
1-800-822-9919
URL: http://www.nwf.org/

Natural Resources Defense Council
40 W. Twentieth St.
New York, NY 10011
(212) 727-2700
FAX: (212) 727-1773
E-mail: nrdcinfo@nrdc.org
URL: http://www.nrdc.org/

Nature Conservancy
4245 N. Fairfax Dr., Ste. 100
Arlington, VA 22203-1606
(703) 841-5300
1-800-628-6860
URL: http://nature.org/

Sierra Club
85 Second St., Second Fl.
San Francisco, CA 94105
(415) 977-5500
FAX: (415) 977-5799
E-mail: information@sierraclub.org
URL: http://www.sierraclub.org/

Union of Concerned Scientists
Two Brattle Sq.
Cambridge, MA 02238-9105
(617) 547-5552
FAX: (617) 864-9405
URL: http://www.ucsusa.org/

United Nations Environment Program
PO Box 30552, 00100
Nairobi, Kenya
(254-20) 7621234

FAX: (254-20) 7624489/90
E-mail: unepweb@unep.org
URL: http://www.unep.org/

U.S. Bureau of Reclamation
1849 C St. NW
Washington, DC 20240-0001
(202) 513-0501
FAX: (202) 513-0309
URL: http://www.usbr.gov/

U.S. Climate Change Science Program
1717 Pennsylvania Ave. NW, Ste. 250
Washington, DC 20006
(202) 223-6262
FAX: (202) 223-3065
E-mail: information@climatescience.gov
URL: http://www.climatescience.gov/

USDA Forest Service
1400 Independence Ave. SW
Washington, DC 20250-0003
(202) 205-8333
E-mail: webmaster@fs.fed.us
URL: http://www.fs.fed.us/

U.S. Department of Agriculture
1400 Independence Ave. SW
Washington, DC 20250
URL: http://www.usda.gov/

U.S. Department of Energy
1000 Independence Ave. SW
Washington, DC 20585
(202) 586-5000
1-800-342-5363
FAX: (202) 586-4403
E-mail: the.secretary@hq.doe.gov
URL: http://www.energy.gov/

U.S. Environmental Protection Agency
Ariel Rios Bldg.
1200 Pennsylvania Ave. NW
Washington, DC 20460
(202) 272-0167
URL: http://www.epa.gov/

U.S. Fish and Wildlife Service
1849 C St. NW
Washington, DC 20242

1-800-344-9453
URL: http://www.fws.gov/

U.S. Food and Drug Administration
5600 Fishers Lane
Rockville, MD 20857-0001
1-888-463-6332
URL: http://www.fda.gov/

U.S. Geological Survey
12201 Sunrise Valley Dr.
Reston, VA 20192
(703) 648-4000
URL: http://www.usgs.gov/

U.S. Government Accountability Office
441 G St. NW
Washington, DC 20548
(202) 512-3000
E-mail: contact@gao.gov
URL: http://www.gao.gov/

U.S. Nuclear Regulatory Commission
Office of Public Affairs
Washington, DC 20555-0001
(301) 415-7000
1-800-368-5642
URL: http://www.nrc.gov/

Wilderness Society
1615 M St. NW
Washington, DC 20036
1-800-843-9453
URL: http://www.wilderness.org/

World Wildlife Fund
1250 Twenty-fourth St. NW
Washington, DC 20090-7180
(202) 293-4800
E-mail: membership@wwfus.org
URL: http://www.worldwildlife.org/

Worldwatch Institute
1776 Massachusetts Ave. NW
Washington, DC 20036-1904
(202) 452-1999
FAX: (202) 296-7365
E-mail: worldwatch@worldwatch.org
URL: http://www.worldwatch.org/

RESOURCES

The U.S. Environmental Protection Agency (EPA) monitors the status of the nation's environment and publishes a variety of materials on environmental issues. Publications consulted for this book include *Draft Report on the Environment: Science Report* (2007), *Air Quality and Emissions—Progress Continues in 2006* (June 2007), *Using Coal Ash in Highway Construction* (April 2005), *Protecting and Restoring America's Watersheds: Status, Trends, and Initiatives in Watershed Management* (June 2001), *Building Savings: Strategies for Waste Reduction of Construction and Demolition Debris from Buildings* (June 2000), "Green Vehicle Guide" (May 2007), *Pesticides Industry Sales and Usage* (May 2004), *Final Report: Superfund Subcommittee of the National Advisory Council for Environmental Policy and Technology* (April 2004), *About Superfund* (2005), *RCRA Orientation Manual* (January 2003), *Inventory of U.S. Greenhouse Gas Emissions and Sinks: 1990–2005* (April 2007), *Achievements in Stratospheric Ozone Protection: Progress Report* (April 2007), *Human Health Benefits of Stratospheric Ozone Protection* (April 2006), and *Acid Rain Program: 2005 Progress Report* (October 2006). The EPA Office of Inspector General published *Evaluation Report: Progress Made in Monitoring Ambient Air Toxics, but Further Improvements Can Increase Effectiveness* (March 2005).

Also useful from the EPA were *National Coastal Condition: Report II* (December 2004), *National Biennial RCRA Hazardous Waste Report* (December 2006), *EPA Assessment of Risks from Radon in Homes* (June 2003), *Guide for Industrial Waste Management* (June 1999), *A Plain English Guide to the EPA Part 503 Biosolids Rule* (September 1994), *Municipal Solid Waste in the United States: 2005 Facts and Figures* (October 2006), *Wadeable Streams Assessment: A Collaborative Survey of the Nation's Streams* (December 2006), *Light-Duty Automotive Technology and Fuel Economy Trends: 1975 through 2005* (July 2005), *National Estuary Program Coastal Condition Report* (June 2007), and *2005 EPA WIPP Recertification*

Fact Sheet No. 1 (June 2005). The EPA and the President's Task Force on Environmental Health Risks and Safety Risks to Children published *Eliminating Childhood Lead Poisoning: A Federal Strategy Targeting Lead Paint Hazards* (February 2000).

The EPA also provided *An Inventory of Sources and Environmental Releases of Dioxin-Like Compounds in the United States for the Years 1987, 1995, and 2000* (November 2006), *Redesign of the Pollution Abatement Costs and Expenditures (PACE) Survey: Findings and Recommendations from the Pretest and Follow-up Visits: Final Report* (December 2006), *EPA FY2006: Compliance & Enforcement Annual Results* (November 2006), *Environmental Education Grants Program: Grants Awarded 1992–2006* (2007), and the *2005 TRI Public Data Release: eReport* (March 2007).

U.S. Carbon Dioxide Emissions from Energy Sources: 2006 Flash Estimate (May 2007) by the U.S. Department of Energy's (DOE) Energy Information Administration (EIA) was a source of data on global warming. The EIA also published *International Energy Annual 2004* (July 2006), *International Energy Outlook 2007* (May 2007), *Annual Energy Outlook 2007* (February 2007), and *Annual Energy Review 2006* (June 2007). Also helpful from the DOE were *Transportation of Spent Nuclear Fuel and High-Level Radioactive Waste to Yucca Mountain* (January 2006) and "National Spent Nuclear Fuel Program" (July 2007). Oak Ridge National Laboratory produced *Transportation Energy Data Book: Edition 26* (May 2007).

Data from the Centers for Disease Control and Prevention's (CDC) *Morbidity and Mortality Weekly Report* were invaluable. The CDC also published the *Third National Report on Human Exposure to Environmental Chemicals* (2005).

The National Aeronautics and Space Administration (NASA) publishes a variety of materials on environmental and space issues. Useful in this book were *Biosphere, NASA Facts* (April 1998), *Ozone: What Is It, and Why Do We Care about It? NASA Facts* (May 1998), and *Looking at the Earth from Space* (1994). The U.S. Government Accountability Office publishes many useful reports on environmental issues, including acid rain, nuclear energy, air and water quality, solid and nuclear waste, wetlands, landfills, and pollution. The U.S. Climate Change Science Program and Subcommittee on Global Change Research published *The U.S. Climate Change Science Program: Vision for the Program and Highlights of the Scientific Strategic Plan* (July 2003) and *Strategic Plan for the U.S. Climate Change Science Program* (July 2003). The *Climate Action Report* (May 2002), prepared by the U.S. Global Change Research Information Office, was useful in explaining the scientific community's determinations about global warming.

Numerous other U.S. government publications were used in the preparation of this book. They included *Forest Resources of the United States, 2002* (W. Brad Smith et al., 2004), *National Report on Sustainable Forests—2003* (October 2003), *America's Forests: 2003 Health Update* (May 2003), and *Healthy Forests Report* (May 2007) from the Forest Service, an agency under the U.S. Department of Agriculture (USDA). The USDA also provided *Statistical Highlights of United States Agriculture, 2002/2003* (June 2003), *National Engineering Handbook Part 651: Agricultural Waste Management Field Handbook* (June 1999), *Pesticide Data Program: Annual Summary Calendar Year 2005* (November 2006), *Agricultural Resources and Environmental Indicators, 2006 Edition* (July 2006), *Major Uses of Land in the United States, 2002* (May 2006), and *National Resources Inventory: 2003 Annual NRI: Soil Erosion* (February 2007).

The U.S. Geological Survey (USGS) documents the use of the nation's waters every five years. *Estimated Use of Water in the United States in 2000* (Susan S. Hutson et al., April 2004) was used in the preparation of this book. The USGS also produced *The Quality of Our Nation's Waters: National Water-Quality Assessment Program Pesticides in the Nation's Streams and Ground Water, 1992–2001*

(Robert J. Gilliom et al., February 2007), *U.S. Geological Survey 2002 Petroleum Resource Assessment of the National Petroleum Reserve in Alaska (NPRA)* (2002), and *Obsolete Computers, "Gold Mine," or High-Tech Trash? Resource Recovery from Recycling* (July 2001). The U.S. Census Bureau published *Pollution Abatement Costs and Expenditures: 1999* (November 2002). The U.S. Commission on Civil Rights published *Not in My Backyard: Executive Order 12,898 and Title VI as Tools for Achieving Environmental Justice* (October 2003). Also useful were *Status and Trends of Wetlands in the Conterminous United States: 1998 to 2004* (Thomas E. Dahl, December 2005) from the U.S. Fish and Wildlife Service and *Total Diet Study: Market Baskets 1991–3 through 2003–4* (2006) from the U.S. Food and Drug Administration.

Material from the Gallup Organization's public opinion surveys was extremely useful. The National Environmental Education Foundation provided valuable information in *Environmental Literacy in America* (Kevin Coyle, September 2005). Also helpful was *Scrap Tire Markets in the United States* (November 2006) by the Rubber Manufacturers Association. The American Lung Association published *State of the Air: 2007* (May 2007). The American Cancer Society provided data on skin cancer through its Cancer Reference Information. The Environmental Investigation Agency, a private organization based in London that investigates international environmental crimes, provided information on the illegal trade in ozone depleting substances.

The J. G. Press provided its important biennial study, "The State of Garbage" (Phil Simmons et al., April 2006). *Clinical Toxicology* (2006) published toxin exposure data from the American Association of Poison Control Centers. The Environmental Defense Fund discussed the leading environmental concerns of Americans and also published *Evaluation of Erosion Hazards* (April 2000). The H. John Heinz III Center for Science, Economics, and the Environment provided the important report *The State of the Nation's Ecosystems: Measuring the Lands, Waters, and Living Resources of the United States* (2002).

INDEX